# CURRICULUM
# EVALUATION

# CURRICULUM EVALUATION

commentaries on purpose, process, product

edited by **DAVID A. PAYNE**
University of Georgia

**D. C. HEATH AND COMPANY**
Lexington, Massachusetts   Toronto   London

# PREFACE

The plea for improved *communication* in education has never been so plaintive or widespread as in recent years. Nowhere does this need have greater relevance than in the area of curriculum development and educational evaluation. Representatives of these two professional disciplines rarely attend each others' conventions or read each others' journals. How many members of the National Council On Measurement in Education, for example, read *Educational Leadership,* the house organ of the Association for Supervision and Curriculum Development? Conversely, how many ASCD members regularly read NCME's *Journal of Educational Measurement?* The massive growth of curriculum program and instructional materials development in both the public and private sectors is creating a great demand for the exchange of ideas, concepts, methodologies, data, designs, and concerns between these two groups. For whatever reason— a late report, poor advice, an impractical design, ivory-towerism, or unnecessarily complicated statistical results—the evaluator has not been completely accepted by the curriculum worker. A rapprochement is needed. One of the major purposes of this collection of articles, then, is to facilitate the exchange of information. This compilation is intended to appeal to both curriculum personnel and educational evaluators. It is particularly hoped that curriculum workers will gain knowledge that will (1) help them use the skills of evaluators more effectively, and (2) focus their attention on asking the most meaningful kinds of evaluation questions of themselves, their programs, and their data. In turn, it is hoped that evaluators will gain from these readings a better understanding of the evaluation problems and data requirements of curriculum developers. A second major purpose of collecting these papers is to facilitate the teaching of the growing number of graduate-level courses in curriculum evaluation, instructional evaluation, and related fields.

A volume such as this, which draws upon a variety of sources, fields, and authors, encounters a language problem. The terminology of evaluation is not standardized, and new terms are constantly being coined. The editor has attempted to make the terms *measurement* and *testing* interchangeable, and to treat the terms *evaluation, evaluative research,* and *assessment* as almost synonymous. The emphasis here is on the "evaluation" of curriculum evaluation. It is assumed that the reader will have had at least one formal course in curriculum, or equivalent work experience.

A book of this sort is probably used most frequently as an adjunct text. However, it could very well be used as a basic text, especially if supplemented by appropriate materials and experience in "real-life" evaluation.

A majority of the articles included in this book have been edited and abridged. Extensive reviews of the literature have been condensed (unless that was the primary reason for the inclusion of a particular paper), statistical data summarized, and all but major references to other works deleted. The remaining references are listed alphabetically at the back of the volume. An attempt was made to provide a variety of readings touching on the major aspects of curriculum evaluation. Both theoretical and practical issues are considered. Rather than attempting to present all sides of all issues, it was decided to select papers representing a cross-section of prevailing thought and practice. If biases exist, they perhaps reflect the character of the articles and reports currently being published.

The articles are grouped into five parts. Each part is introduced by a foreword highlighting its general significance and the contributions of the individual papers it includes. In addition, each paper is preceded by a brief introduction intended to orient the reader, point out parallel and interrelated themes that recur in the various articles, and provide leads to additional relevant literature. The first section is a general overview of the process of curriculum evaluation. The purposes and, to some extent, the products of this process are discussed in the second section. Next come two methodological sections, the first dealing with design and the second with specific measurement techniques. The final section contains descriptions of a variety of curriculum evaluation projects and activities.

Sincere heartfelt acknowledgements and thanks are extended to the authors and publishers who have so graciously consented to have their papers reproduced. They have been most generous and tolerant. To Ms. June McClain and the Curriculum and Supervision secretarial staff goes a special acknowledgement for their superlative typing efforts.

# CONTENTS

# PROLOGUE
## Toward a Characterization
## of Curriculum Evaluation

Revitalized interest in the teaching–learning process in American education during the past twenty-five years or so has resulted in, among other things, a plethora of new curricula. The impetus given curriculum development has come from both subject-matter scholars and educational researchers: from the former as a result of new knowledge and new insights into how their disciplines are structured; from the latter because of new insights into the learning process as it relates to the organization and presentation of knowledge.

The development of any "new" curriculum involves related problems of evaluation. See the writings of Caro (1971), Taylor and Cowley (1972), and Weiss (1972) for an overview of these problems. The evaluation of overall effectiveness, variables influencing effectiveness, and educational cost and relevance are a few areas in need of assessment (Westbury, 1970). Due to the mass of knowledge that must be transmitted and processed, the problems associated with evaluation are probably of greater concern today than at any time in history. Evaluation techniques previously considered adequate for assessing the effectiveness of small units of material are significantly less applicable to larger packages of information, the learning of which is highly complex and involves prerequisite learnings, sequential behaviors, and, perhaps, other programs of study.

The traditional dichotomy between experimental and control groups as examined by contrasting gross mean achievement scores in a pre/post-treatment design study, although generally useful, tends not to provide sufficiently detailed information upon which to base intelligent decisions about questions of curriculum effectiveness, validity, efficiency, and so on. Along this line, Guba (1969a) has lamented the failure of the evaluation designs for a group of government research proposals to meet even minimal requirements. Either the desire or the need to compromise results in far too many "no significant differences." Guba notes, for example, the problem that the practitioner who is seeking information regarding the success of his program has "invited interference." This condition is the opposite of control. If control is lacking, experimental design and methods of data analysis are considerably less applicable. Most applied studies are done in natural settings, and natural educational settings are anything but controlled. But it is in these relatively unstructured and uncontrolled situations that evaluation and decisions must be made. The field of curriculum evaluation is developing in response to the requirements of decision-making.

It is the purpose of this prologue to survey the origins of curriculum evaluation,

1

and to describe changes that have occurred over the years due to changes in society and education.

## THE CHANGING FACE OF EVALUATION

An excellent overview of some recent changes in the concepts and techniques of evaluation has recently been published by Merwin (1969). Let us briefly note some of these changes.

**Evaluative Standards**   Educational evaluators, responding to the task of evaluation and to the development of appropriate methodology, have moved to an absolute standard in assessing the effectiveness of learning experiences. Such an approach would seem more responsive to the true meaning of the concept of individual differences in education. Emphasis is now on intra-individual, rather than inter-individual, comparisons. This change in the standard of reference from normative to absolute has influenced the type of evaluation devices being developed. Greater attention is now given to criterion-referenced measures (Popham and Husek, 1969). Such measures derive their structure and meaning from a specified set of objectives, rather than from the performances of groups of individuals.

Criterion-referenced measures are intended to measure *what*, not *how much*, the student has or has not learned. Although originally used only with relatively simple learning outcomes, criterion-referenced measures are now beginning to be applied to complex objectives.

There is a minor controversy surrounding the use of criterion-referenced measures. Ebel (1971), for example, has argued that criterion-referenced measures have limited application in the day-to-day classroom setting because (1) such measures do not tell us all we need to know or, perhaps, the most important things we need to know about student learning; (2) it is difficult to base criterion-referenced measurement on meaningful criteria of achievement; and (3) the mastery learning to which criterion-referenced measures are geared represents only one classroom methodology, and one that is used a small percentage of the total class time.

In response to these allegations, Block (1971) has suggested that (1) although they do not tell "all," the results of criterion-referenced measures do provide information relevant to the excellence or deficiency of an individual's performance; (2) the development cost in terms of teacher time and effort is not as great as Ebel supposes, particularly in regard to the generation of the necessary objectives; and (3) the time spent on developing skills in the schools is greater than Ebel assumes and criterion-referenced measures are particularly well-suited to assessment in these areas.

**The Nature of the Objectives Evaluated**   The "what" of educational evaluation is also changing, in two dramatic ways. There is a movement away from preoccupation with subject matter or content toward a more process-oriented assessment. Educators are not merely concerned with what the product looks like, but also with how it got that way. As new curricula emphasize change in process, so too must the attendant evaluations.

While many believe that the explicit formulation of behavioral objectives is a useful technique, that position is not universally accepted. Scholars such as Atkin

(1968), Eisner (1967), Macdonald and Walfron (1970), and Broudy (1970) have voiced serious reservations about the extensive use of behavioral objectives in instruction, evaluation, and curriculum development. A majority of the objections involve what the critics perceive as a lock-step instructional setting and a concomitant lack of provision for dealing with spontaneity and creativity. The possibility of a mechanical approach to instruction admittedly exists. However, the advantages inherent in the use of explicit and specific statements of goals that aid in the clarification of intent, the selection of content and instructional material, and the identification of behavior to be changed probably outweigh the disadvantages.

It is imperative that instructional intent and expected behavior change be communicated. The following anecdote, told by Yelon and Scott (1970), illustrates a possible result of failure to do so.

> At a parent-teacher conference the teacher complained to Mr. Bird about the foul language of his children. Mr. Bird decided to correct this behavior. At breakfast he asked his oldest son, "What will you have for breakfast?" The boy replied, "Gimme some of those damn cornflakes." Immediately Mr. Bird smashed the boy on the mouth. The boy's chair tumbled over and the boy rolled up against the wall. The father then turned to his second son and politely inquired, "What would you like for breakfast?" The boy hesitated, then said "I don't know but I sure as hell don't want any of those damn cornflakes!" (p. 5)

Moral: If you want someone to change his behavior, tell him your goals.

Popham (1969), in a monograph treating the place of behavioral instructional objectives in curriculum evaluation, has summarized eleven major objections to the use of behavioral objectives. He goes on to respond to each of these points. The following parallel lists serve to outline the pros and cons of the controversy.

| Objection to Behavioral Objectives | Rebuttal to Objection |
|---|---|
| 1. Trivial behaviors are easiest to operationalize. Really important outcomes will be underemphasized. | 1. Explicit objectives more readily focus attention on important goals. |
| 2. Prespecification prevents teacher capitalization on unexpected instructional opportunities. | 2. Ends do not necessarily specify means. Serendipity is always welcome. |
| 3. There are other types of educational outcomes that are also important, e.g., for parents, staff, community. | 3. Schools can't do everything. Primary responsibility is to pupils. |
| 4. Objectively, mechanistically measured behaviors are dehumanizing. | 4. Broadened concept of evaluation includes "human" elements. |
| 5. Precise, preplanned behavior is undemocratic. | 5. Society knows what it wants. Instruction is naturally undemocratic. |
| 6. Behaviorally described teaching is not natural, makes unrealistic demands on teachers. | 6. Identifying the status quo is different than applauding it. |
| 7. In certain areas, e.g., fine arts and humanities, it is more difficult to measure behaviors. | 7. Sure it's tough; but still a responsibility. |

| Objection to Behavioral Objectives | Rebuttal to Objection |
|---|---|
| 8. General statements appear more worthwhile to outsiders. Precise goals appear innocuous. | 8. We must abandon the ploy of "obfuscation by generality." |
| 9. Measurability implies accountability. Teachers might be judged on their ability to produce particular results rather than being judged on many bases. | 9. Teachers should be held accountable for producing changes. |
| 10. It is more difficult to generate precise objectives than to talk of them in vague terms. | 10. We should allocate the necessary resources to accomplish the task. |
| 11. Unanticipated results are often most important. Prespecification may cause inattentiveness. | 11. Dramatic unanticipated outcomes cannot be overlooked. Keep your eyes open! |

The second change with regard to the nature of the objectives being evaluated is toward a greater concern with affective educational outcomes and more humanistic types of schooling. Educators and students are more aware of the importance of values, attitudes, beliefs, and interests as they influence the teaching learning process. The Krathwohl *et al.* (1964) handbook dealing with affective educational objectives did much to provide an impetus for the movement.

**Change in the Sampling Unit** Historically, evaluation has focused on the individual student and his learning. If we are to understand the complex process of instruction, we must also analyze the learning environment, the nature of the learner, and the subsequent interaction of these factors. This necessitates the development of new data-gathering techniques or the modification of old methods. New analytic procedures, compatible with the complex interaction of many variables, need to be applied. In general, we are moving from individual to group to program and to system-wide assessment. Evaluation is becoming more macro and less micro in its orientation. Also of growing significance is the application of anthropological methodologies (Sindell, 1969).

**The Nature of the Decisions to be Made** Evaluation has traditionally been aimed at making decisions about individual student learning. In recent years, however, there has developed a need for amassing data instrumental in making other kinds of judgments. We are now faced with critical decisions about the choice of curriculum, operating costs, selection of personnel, modification of programs, the adequacy of available resources, acceptance of programs by the community, and many other issues. Such determinations are different not only in kind but also in magnitude from those that previously confronted the professional educator.

**The Time of Evaluation** Evaluative data should be gathered when they are most germane to the decision-making process. But when is that time? It may be before the learning program is implemented, during its development, or at the end of the experience. In general, there is more emphasis today on measures of change than on status. Considerable attention is being paid to long-term and longitudinal methodologies in curriculum evaluation. Data-gathering during curriculum development and tryout, or during a student's progress through a set of learning experiences (formative evaluation), is equally if not more valuable than that which takes place at the termination of an experience (summative evaluation).

Definitions of curriculum are as divergent as are the writings of authorities in the field. At one extreme is the broad, all-encompassing definition, such as that of Saylor and Alexander (1954). They define curriculum as ". . . the sum total of the school's efforts to influence learning, whether in the classroom, on the playground, or out of school" (p. 5). A wide-ranging definition is probably desirable, because it emphasizes the relevance of many experiences for both the individual and society. It also allows for great flexibility in specifying the exact experiences which are adaptive and responsive to the thousands of different kinds of local educational needs. For example, the requirements of a program for the disadvantaged will vary from city to city, state to state, and region to region. Decisions on the allocation of community resources, combined with the definition of student needs, constitute a few of the factors influencing curriculum design.

A somewhat different definition is proposed by Smith, Stanley, and Shores (1957). They consider the curriculum ". . . a sequence of potential experiences set up in schools for the purpose of disciplining children and youth in group ways of thinking and acting" (p. 3). This somewhat narrower conception perhaps allows for clear explications of the exact scope and sequence of educational experiences. It has the advantage of being more responsive to the requirements of teaching-learning situations in the "Age of Behavioral Objectives."

Taba (1962), another recognized authority in the field, posits an effective definition somewhere between these two conceptualizations. For her, the key characteristic is a planned and systematic approach to curriculum design. Drawing upon information about (1) the needs and demands of culture and society, (2) the nature of learners and the learning process, and (3) the nature of knowledge and of the unique and specific subject-matter contributions, a dynamic process is brought into play. Basically it involves seven steps (p. 12):

1. Diagnosis of needs.
2. Formulation of objectives.
3. Selection of content.
4. Organization of content.
5. Selection of learning experiences.
6. Organization of learning experiences.
7. Determining the "what" and "how" of evaluation.

The result of applying this model should be a curriculum that allows the student to learn. Taba's systematic approach to curriculum development correlates well with the systematic approach taken by today's educational evaluators.

In the final analysis, we are talking about situations in which kids learn in class-out of class, formally-informally, planned-unplanned, individually-in groups, and self-directed-teacher-directed. However one ultimately defines curriculum, one must accept that it includes everything that directs and stimulates student experience and learning. For the most part, primary focus is on the educators' systematic and intentional efforts. Yet significant unplanned results do occur. See, for example, the thoughts expressed by Sawin and Loree (1959). This book, *Curriculum Evaluation*, could have been titled *The Evaluation of Educational Programs* or *Evaluating Instructional Systems*. The emphasis, nevertheless, is on evaluating the total curriculum, rather than individual student learnings.

## CHARACTERISTICS OF EVALUATION

The changing face of evaluation implies the changing roles it must assume. Educational evaluation is much more than the assessment of student performance, as was suggested by Tyler (1942). In addition to contributing to the assessment of underlying assumptions and of the overall effectiveness of the total educational program, evaluation data can be employed effectively to improve the teaching-learning process. The intimate relationship between the teaching-learning process and evaluation has been admirably described by Dressel (1954). He discusses five points at which the instructional process parallels that of evaluation. The following parallel lists are a brief comparison of the two processes.

| *Instruction* | *Evaluation* |
|---|---|
| 1. Instruction is effective as it leads to desired changes in students. | 1. Evaluation is effective as it provides evidence of the extent of the changes in students. |
| 2. New behavior patterns are best learned by students when the inadequacy of present behavior is understood and the significance of the new behavior patterns thereby made clear. | 2. Evaluation is most conducive to learning when it provides for and encourages self-evaluation. |
| 3. New behavior patterns can be more efficiently developed by teachers who know the existing behavior patterns of individual students and the reasons for them. | 3. Evaluation is conducive to good instruction when it reveals major types of inadequate behavior and the contributory causes. |
| 4. Learning is encouraged by problems and activities which require thought and/or action by each individual student. | 4. Evaluation is most significant in learning when it permits and encourages the exercise of individual initiative. |
| 5. Activities which provide the basis for the teaching and learning of specified behavior are also the most suitable activities for evoking and evaluating the adequacy of that behavior. | 5. Activities or exercises developed for the purposes of evaluating specified behavior are also useful for the teaching and learning of that behavior. |

**Summative and Formative Evaluation**  The focus on the relationship between instruction and evaluation, and on the potential contribution of evaluation to the improvement of quality and quantity in education, has been underscored by Scriven's recent (1967) distinction between "summative" and "formative" evaluation. He notes that the goal of evaluation is always the same, that is, to determine the worth and value of something. That "something" may be a microscope, a unit in biology, a science curriculum, or an entire educational system. Depending upon the role the value judgments are to play, evaluation data may be used developmentally or in a summary way. In the case of an overall decision, the role of evaluation is summative. An end-of-course assessment would be considered summative. Summative evaluation may employ absolute or comparative standards and judgments; however, it is more likely to utilize the latter.

Formative evaluation, on the other hand, is almost exclusively aimed at improving the educational experience or product during its developmental phases. A key element in the formative technique is feedback. Information is gathered during the developmental phase with an eye to improving the total product. The evaluation activities associated with the development of *Science—A Process Approach,* the elementary science curriculum supported by the National Science Foundation and managed by the American Association for the Advancement of Science, are illustrative. During the several years of the program's development, sample materials were used in centers throughout the country. Summer writing sessions were then held at which tryout data were fed back to the developers. A superior product resulted. The summative-formative distinction among kinds of evaluation reflects differences in intent, rather than different methodologies.

The use of evaluation in this formative way almost implies that evaluation may be viewed as a research effort. As a matter of fact, Suchman (1967) has formalized this idea. But there are dangers in treating the two processes alike.

**The Differences Between Research and Evaluation**  Many experts view evaluation as the mere application of the scientific method to assessment tasks. In this sense, which parallels Suchman's use of the term, "evaluative" becomes an adjective specifying a type of research. The emphasis is still on the noun "research," and on the procedures for collecting and analyzing data which increase the possibility of proving, rather than asserting, the worth of some social activity. It is perhaps best not to equate the two activities of research and evaluation because of differences in intent and applicability of certain methodologies. Hemphill (1969) has provided a very enlightening distinction between evaluation and research. The following parallel lists are a brief comparison of these two activities.

| Activity | Research | Evaluation |
|---|---|---|
| 1. Problem selection and definition. | Responsibility of investigator. | Determined by situation and constituents. |
| 2. Hypothesis testing. | Formal statistical testing. | Generally not done. |
| 3. Value judgments. | Limited to selection of problem. | Present in all phases of project. |
| 4. Replication of results. | High likelihood. | Low likelihood. |

| Activity | Research | Evaluation |
|---|---|---|
| 5. Data collection. | Dictated by problem. | Heavily influenced by feasibility. |
| 6. Control of relevant variables. | High. | Low. |
| 7. Generalizability of results. | Can be high. | Usually low. |

Some important differences between research and evaluation are evident in these contrasting emphases. Many further differences are implied.

It is argued by some scientists that the primary concern of research should be the production of new knowledge through the application of the "scientific method." Such information would be added to a general body of knowledge about a particular phenomenon or theory. A high proportion of the research in the physical, biological, and behavioral sciences is aimed at contributing to a particular theory or, at the very least, is derived from theory. Evaluation activities are generally not tied to theory except, perhaps, to the extent that any curriculum project is founded on a particular theoretical position. Curriculum evaluation studies are generally undertaken to solve some specific practical problems, usually at a local level. There is little interest in undertaking a project that will have implications for large widely-dispersed constituencies. Control of influential variables is generally quite restricted. It is for this reason that routine application of experimental designs—as described, for example, by Campbell and Stanley (1963)—may be inappropriate. Research in the behavioral sciences is, in a restricted sense, concerned with the systematic gathering of data aimed at testing specific hypotheses and contributing to a homogeneous body of knowledge.

**The Place of Judgments in Evaluation** Values play an important role in curriculum evaluation from at least two standpoints. The first point at which values are asserted, or should be asserted, is the identification of those objectives and goals that have evaluative priority. A decision about which objectives are most important should be made (Stake, 1970). Secondly, judgments are continually being made as performance data are contrasted with objectives. An excellent example of the molding of this idea into an evaluation model can be found in the writings of Provus (1971).

Judgments are involved at many different points during the completion of an evaluation study. In fact, the decision to do a study is itself a value judgment. In addition, several other judgments must be made. The role of judgment will depend on the amount of objective data available for decision making. The following list suggested by Brownell (1965) highlights some points on which judgments must be made.

1. Determination of appropriate grade level for evaluative study.
2. Selection of appropriate subjects.
3. Length of study.
4. Identification of objectives in common and those specific to curricula involved.
5. Determination of type of study to be undertaken (cross-sectional, longitudinal, comparative, and so on).
6. Decisions about nature of data to be collected.
7. Selection of data-gathering instruments available or decision to develop original devices.

8. Selection of appropriate control mechanisms aimed at uniformity of treatment.
9. Selection of appropriate analytic procedures.
10. Interpretation of findings.

When the teachers have taught, the students have studied, the administrators have administered, the supervisors have supervised, and the consultants have consulted, the practical limitations of the climate for evaluation and common sense will, despite recent extraordinary technological developments, play the most influential roles in the design and implementation of an evaluation program.

**The Role of the Evaluator**   Obviously, the evaluator will play many different roles, depending upon the specific requirements of the evaluative task at hand. A great variety of competencies and skills need to be developed, and vast quantities of knowledge are digested and entered on memory drums. An insight into the varieties of evaluators one might encounter is suggested by the following brief survey reported by Niehaus (1968). After declaring that evaluators range from the "knee-jerk conservatives" to the "wild-eyed liberals," he describes the different kinds he has observed (p. 333).

> There is the myopic nit picker who seems to have an anxiety compulsion to try to measure the differences between the tickle and itch. There is the cautious creeper who is terrified at the thought of any type of innovation. There is the free swinger who arrives at his evaluation through some weird mixture of ESP and dianoetics and whose ignorance is bolstered by emotion. There is the anxiety evaluator: the worrier, who lives under a perpetual state of existential threat and who feels that if what he evaluates does not coincide with his preconceived and doctrinaire attitudes, all is lost. There is the belaborer of the obvious who after a sizable expenditure of time and effort comes up with a ponderous announcement of something which has been obvious all along—something like the man who suggested, upon first viewing the Grand Canyon, "Something must have happened here." There is also the circumstantial evaluator who uses a hundred words to do the work of one. He gets his observations wound up into such a cocoon that no one can figure out just what he is trying to communicate.

In a more serious vein, it must be accepted that a well-trained, sensitive, effective, and competent evaluator must be both a scientist and a human relations expert. There are certain technical skills and knowledge to be mastered. In addition, a great part of the evaluator's time will be given over to working with individuals and groups to plan, implement, and communicate the results of his evaluative effort. The role of the evaluator, if viewed objectively and honestly, is an enormous one. To describe its dimensions is an almost impossible task. It is, therefore, not without some trepidation that the following list of behavioral objectives is suggested. These competencies represent a distillation of a variety of sources (Grobman, 1968; Sorenson, 1968; Worthington, undated; Owens, 1968).

The competent curriculum evaluator should be able to:

1. Specify information needs from program planning for evaluation.
2. Develop a plan for evaluating a specified curriculum.
3. Locate, read, and integrate relevant research, measurement, and evaluation literature.

4. Specify evaluation objectives and data base requirements in appropriate form(s).
5. Critically evaluate a given evaluative research design.
6. Relate theoretical evaluation models and "real-life" requirements.
7. Relate input, transaction, and outcome variables.
8. Demonstrate appropriate interpersonal relationship skills in working with evaluation team and program staff.
9. Differentiate advantages and disadvantages of cross-sectional and longitudinal studies.
10. Conduct systems, functions, and task analyses.
11. Design an effective measurement-management process.
12. Compile a master evaluation system from several systems.
13. Describe evaluation design and analysis requirements in computer programmer or data processing terms.
14. Specify criteria for selection or development of evaluation instruments.
15. Apply appropriate data-gathering procedures.
16. Apply appropriate data-analysis procedures.
17. Make a cost benefit analysis of a given curriculum.
18. Use evaluation information to make decisions about curricula.
19. Design a Program Planning Budgeting System.
20. Administer the activities of an evaluation unit.
21. Design a system of data presentation that describes format, responsibility, procedures, recipients, and schedule.
22. Redesign and refine evaluation system based on data implications of previous cycle.

This list is obviously not exhaustive. It does reflect, however, certain emphases dictated by real time and experience factors, and it is intended to suggest how and what the curriculum evaluator must actually do in a real-life situation to function effectively.

One dimension of the evaluator's role that is difficult to resolve is that associated with decision making. Scriven (1967) contends that it is in fact the responsibility of the evaluator to make final judgments about such things as the merits of Textbook A versus Textbook B, Curriculum C versus Curriculum D and so forth. True, the evaluator is deeply immersed in the entire problem definition-data collection-analysis process, so he may be in the best position to judge. On the other hand, educators are already threatened by evaluation, and this kind of final value judgment may just be enough to close off communication between evaluator and client. It is probably safe to say that the ground rules for decision making should be spelled out in detail, and the mechanism criteria and responsibilities described and assigned, prior to data collection.

## CHARACTERISTICS OF CURRICULUM EVALUATION

Curriculum evaluation could be defined as the sum total of the topics thus far discussed. Such a statement sounds almost platitudinous; but in a very real and meaningful sense the statement is true. Curriculum evaluation will play many roles contingent on the demands and constraints placed upon it. Heath (1969), for example, suggests three broad functions performed by curriculum evaluation:

1. Improvement of curriculum during the development phase. Again, the importance of formative evaluation is emphasized. Strengths and weaknesses of the program or unit can be identified and capitalized on or strengthened. As Heath notes, the process is replete with continuous tryout-evaluation-redesign cycles.
2. Facilitation of rational comparison among competing programs. Although there is the large problem of differing objectives, description and judgment of alternative programs can lead to rational decision making.
3. Contribution to the general body of knowledge about effective curriculum design. Freed from the constraints of formal hypothesis testing, curriculum evaluators are at liberty to search out basic principles relating to the interaction of learner, learning, and environment.

One is still left with the question of what ways curriculum evaluation is different from either pure research efforts or the straightforward evaluation of learning. The following list of variables reflects a differential emphasis within curriculum evaluation.

1. Content of goals. The objectives of curriculum evaluation tend to be more concerned with process and behavior than with subject-matter content.
2. Breadth of objectives. Not only are the objectives different in content, but a greater range of phenomena are involved.
3. Complexity of outcomes. Changes in the requirements for living and education, and the increased knowledge we now possess about the teaching-learning process, make for objectives that are quite complex from the standpoint of cognitive and performance criteria. The interrelation of cognitive, affective, and psychomotor variables further challenges our ability to see what must be evaluated.
4. Focus of total evaluation effort. There is a definite shift in focus from the individual learner to the total program.
5. Context of evaluation. As much as possible, curriculum evaluation should take place in a naturalistic setting. It is in the real-life setting, with all its unpredictable contingencies and uncontrolled variables, that education takes place. If we teach in that setting we must evaluate in that setting, and this is where decisions are made.

The following statement (Taylor and Maguire, 1966) probably best summarizes what contemporary curriculum evaluation is all about.

Curriculum evaluation can be viewed as a process of collecting and processing data pertaining to an educational program, on the basis of which decision can be made about that program. The data are of two kinds: (1) objective description of goals, environments, personnel, methods and content, and immediate and long range outcomes; and (2) recorded personal judgments of the quality and appropriateness of goals, inputs and outcomes. The data—in both raw and analyzed form—can be used either to delineate and resolve problems in educational programs being developed or to answer absolute and comparative questions about established programs.

This broad general description allows the form of a final curriculum evaluation plan to take on any shape dictated by its requirements. Some general plans or models have been proposed. Let us look at some illustrative models.

**Models for Curriculum Evaluation** It is frequently helpful to formalize a complex process, such as curriculum evaluation, into a model. The model will frequently take the form of a conceptual paradigm, flow chart, or other type of schematic representation. Several authorities have developed formal models. The value of such representations is open to question; nevertheless, they do assist in examining relationships among components and defining activities, and point the way toward possible new applications or research problems. In general, a model will aid in the planning and implementation of curriculum evaluation (Forehand, 1971). One major danger of too heavy reliance on a model is the distinct possibility of routinizing what should be an ever-changing process. Such a danger is particularly acute if the evaluation has been institutionalized.

Table 1 compares a representative group of curriculum evaluation models and briefly describes the major emphasis of each. Many educators have made significant contributions to these and related issues but have failed to make available a systematic design for curriculum evaluation with detailed descriptions or outlines of specific activities. The developers included in Table 1 have presented verbally or schematically detailed outlines of the elements of their models and descriptions of the sequence of activities.

Table 1 is presented merely to suggest the flavor of the models available. The overlap in terms of approach, content, and methodology is considerable among these models. The specification of instructional objectives plays a central role in nearly all

**TABLE 1**
**Key Emphases of Selected Curriculum Evaluation Models**[a]

| Model Developer | Key Emphasis |
| --- | --- |
| Tyler (1942) | Curriculum objectives and evaluation of student progress |
| Provus (1969) | Assessment of discrepancy between program performance and standards |
| Taylor & Maguire (1966), and Metfessel & Michael (1967) | Objectives and involvement of variety of personnel (laymen, professional educators, students, philosophers, psychologists) |
| NSSSE (1960) | Staff self-study with overview of content, facilities, and procedures |
| Stake (1967) | Gathering and processing of description and judgment data |
| Crane & Abt (1969) | Estimation of cost-effectiveness of alternative curriculum materials |
| Welch & Walberg (1968) | Improvement of college physics curriculum using change data |
| Stufflebeam (1968), and Klein et al. (1970) | Rational decision making among alternatives by administrator |
| Light & Smith (1970) | Evaluation of national intervention programs through post hoc survey |

[a] Based on an idea suggested by a chart developed by Dr. Robert E. Stake of the Center for Instructional Research and Curriculum Evaluation, University of Illinois, 1969.

models. All emphasize feedback and recycling phases, and all share the assumption that an assessment of needs has been carried out prior to program development. Models for the evaluation of a single curriculum differ from those that are comparative in nature. And finally, all models emphasize decision making and reflect the biases and individual intents of their developers.

Comments on some of the models are in order. Tyler's evaluation model is probably the best-known prototype, at least from a historical perspective. His thinking has significantly influenced both evaluation and curriculum for many years. The individual learner is his focal point. The Provus "discrepancy model" is probably the most detailed; it embodies a highly complex set of criterion questions. Taylor and Maguire, and Metfessel and Michael, are somewhat novel by virtue of their large sample of people concerned with the educational process. They point out five important groups whose opinions should be elicited at various stages of evaluation—spokesmen for society at large, subject-matter experts, teachers, parents, and students. The counsel of these groups is particularly important during the specification of objectives. This was the approach used by National Assessment in establishing their objectives. (See Article 42 in Section V). Too many opinions can have the adverse effect of diluting the product. The model proposed by Stake, with its emphasis on observation and judgment data, is potentially one of the most valuable yet conceived. The school accreditation model of NSSSE frequently leaves the staff exhausted and generally does not yield meaningful results. Finally, an example of the thoughts expressed by Light and Smith

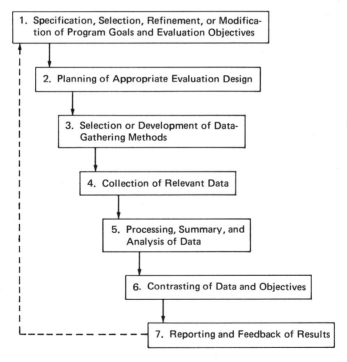

**Figure 1**
**Overview of Usual Steps in Curriculum Evaluation Process**

is reflected in the evaluations undertaken on behalf of Head Start. The CIPP (Context-Input-Process-Product) model developed by Stufflebeam has achieved considerable acceptance among theoreticians and working evaluators.

Figure 1 illustrates the usual steps in the evaluative process. The activities are in approximate order in terms both of logic and of temporal sequence. Application of PERT (Program Evaluation and Review Technique, Cook, 1966) and other management techniques can be extremely valuable when implementing an evaluation program such as that suggested by the activities listed in Figure 1. Only the major activities are identified there. The assumption is made that decision making is taking place both within and between blocks. Decisions may be of the go—no-go variety or relate to the appropriateness of criteria or to information, processing, reporting, and feedback. The development of a climate supportive of evaluation is an important dimension of the entire process. The importance to the evaluator of interpersonal skills, therefore, cannot be underestimated. The sequence of activities in Figure 1 may be followed exactly if summative evaluation is the role being played, or it may be repeated if formative evaluation is the primary focus.

If applied logically, intelligently, and realistically, the process of curriculum evaluation can lead to decisions that can serve as a powerful force to improve the conditions in our schools. In addition, in this day of "accountability" curriculum evaluation systems can make available a means for judging educational effectiveness.

Part I is an overview of evaluation, especially as it is applied to curriculum development. These papers serve as a general framework within which to view—as the title of this volume proclaims—the purposes, processes, and products of curriculum evaluation.

The first paper, a survey prepared by C. M. Lindvall, contains a description of his experience in a large-scale development and demonstration project. He describes the evolution of an evaluation design that includes a reasonable blend of traditional methods and custom-made data-gathering procedures and devices. By focusing in turn on (1) the nature of the program, (2) context, (3) objectives, (4) criteria, and (5) alternatives, Lindvall draws a vivid and fairly complete picture of a complex evaluation activity.

The second essay deals with the difficulties and challenges of curriculum evaluation. Clifford Bebell cautions against an excessive reliance on fallible evaluation data. He also urges improvement in the techniques and measurement application skills of educators. The plea for in-service training is particularly important because it highlights a deficiency of many teacher-training programs. Most beginning teachers are ill-prepared to evaluate student progress. This situation has prompted some critics to suggest that it would be more useful for prospective teachers to devote time to preparing for this important task than to sit through numerous hours of "methods courses." An alternative approach might be to expand the treatment of evaluation in methods courses, in an attempt to gain a better integration of teaching and evaluating.

Jack R. Frymier chides educational evaluators for not asking the right kinds of questions about how well we are educating our children. In curriculum evaluation, we frequently give the right answers

# Overview of Purposes and Problems of Evaluating Curricula

part

to wrong questions. Relevant questions and feedback are the keys to effective evaluation. There are few agencies whose sole function is to systematically gather data and feed it back for purposes of aiding revision and modification of programs. Again, National Assessment can have an impact. (See Article 42 in Part V.)

J. Thomas Hastings describes two major and extremely important roles of curriculum evaluation. These relate to (1) the feedback of data to stimulate program development or revision, and (2) the decisions to be made about the acceptance, rejection, or adoption of course-content–improvement packages. The peculiar kinds of data requirements for these two evaluation roles are discussed in light of new research strategies and illustrative projects.

Accountability is a vital issue today. At the insistence of the taxpayer, the educational establishment is undertaking a massive effort toward self-improvement. A recent Gallup poll indicated that 67 per cent of 1592 adults surveyed favored a system that would hold teachers and administrators more accountable for the progress of their students. In addition, 75 per cent would like the students in local schools to be given national tests so that their educational achievement could be compared with that of students in other communities. This statistic is interesting in light of the development and impact of National Assessment. To be effective, accountability must operate at all levels—national as well as local. Although the concept of accountability has been around for a long time, it is now really becoming operational. Stephen Barro tells us how an accountability system can be implemented. The process of accounting has an interesting and frequently overlooked side effect. When we are evaluating, we are not only forcing ourselves to look critically at what we are doing but also describing what we have done, so that we have a reasonable information base on which to judge why and how changes were implemented.

Joseph S. Renzulli shares with us some of the frustrations of the "in-the-field-doing-the-real-thing" evaluator and comments on some philosophical and methodological issues that need to be resolved before effective and meaningful evaluation can take place.

# 1. The Task of Evaluation in Curriculum Development Projects: A Rationale and Case Study

## C. MAURITZ LINDVALL

Lindvall begins by posing the evaluator's primary question: "Does this innovation, in this situation, accomplish what is desired better than do the alternatives?" He then provides us with an informative overview and analysis of the entire curriculum evaluation process. The emphasis in the project described is basically comparative. It is argued by some that curriculum evaluation can justifiably and more satisfactorily be focused on the absolute changes produced by a single curriculum package. The use of both traditional and tailor-made data-gathering procedures illustrates well the feedback-formative role that can be played by evaluation. The development and evaluation tasks described here are fairly typical. The interested reader is referred to Grobman (1968) for a similar narrative.

A problem of major concern to many educators is that of how the effectiveness of new curricula and other innovations can best be determined. The purpose of this paper is to describe a basic rationale for such evaluation procedures and to discuss certain steps associated with this rationale, as these have evolved as part of a large-scale curriculum development project.

### THE CURRICULUM CONTINUITY DEMONSTRATION

The Curriculum Continuity Demonstration (CCD), a joint project of the Pittsburgh Schools and the University of Pittsburgh (Lindvall *et al.,* 1964), has had as its goal the development and demonstration of an educational program which will be so co-ordinated from grade to grade as to constitute a true continuum for the student as he progresses from kindergarten

Reprinted with permission of the University of Chicago Press and C. Mauritz Lindvall from the *School Review,* **74** (Summer 1966), pp. 159–167.

to college. As a result of the CCD work, over twenty secondary level courses and an essentially complete elementary curriculum are now being given a careful trial in selected Pittsburgh schools. A key aspect of this program has been an attempt to provide a continuing evaluation of the materials and courses produced.

**The Initial Evaluation Program** The initial steps in evaluating CCD courses were employed with a limited number of high-school courses, the first ones to be given an actual trial in the classroom. These steps involved the use of some rather conventional instruments and procedures and had some obvious limitations, but also provided much worthwhile information in the early stages of the course development work. Although these steps were largely superseded as the evaluation program progressed, they are described here to provide necessary background for the rationale and procedures that eventually evolved.

1. Use of standardized tests. Students

in each of these classes were given a carefully selected standardized test as an end-of-course exam. One reason for this step was the feeling that some of the evidence concerning pupil achievement should be obtained through the use of an instrument that was largely independent of the judgments of the project staff. The use of these tests also made provision, in the norm group for the test, for a type of comparison group. In addition, by examining pupil performance on subscores and on individual items, it was possible to determine certain strengths and weaknesses produced by a course. This was of particular value at a stage when a course was being studied for purposes of revision.

2. Use of locally developed tests. In view of the recognized limitations in the validity of the standardized tests for use with these new and unique courses, the original evaluation plans of the CCD also involved the construction of local tests. Typically, these tests were developed by the teacher of the course working with selected members of the curriculum development committee. Results from these tests were also used in analyzing strengths and weaknesses of the new courses.

3. Use of "comparison" or "control" groups. The original evaluation plan also called for comparing achievement of pupils in CCD classes with that of pupils in "conventional" classes. One simple aspect of this involved an examination of the performance of the CCD pupils with respect to the norms on the standardized tests. In some cases it also involved a more direct comparison of the test scores, both on published and locally developed tests, of pupils in the experimental class with scores of pupils taking the same course in a non-CCD class. Here the rather predictable results occurred in that CCD pupils scored significantly higher on the specially developed tests while the comparison pupils scored significantly higher on the published tests. That is, the courses were designed to achieve different immediate goals and the pupils in each group performed at a higher level on the test which

covered the goals of their particular course.

4. Use of expert observers. The final aspect of the evaluation effort involved the selection of qualified persons to provide subjective assessments of the various courses. From one to three persons were selected to examine each course. Each person studied the course outline and related materials, visited the class to see it in action, and interviewed teachers and pupils. Each expert or team of experts then prepared a written report discussing the strong and weak points of the course and making suggestions for changes in content or procedure. Suggestions obtained in this way have proved to be of great value to the project.

It will be recognized that in employing the above steps the evaluation staff of the CCD was using some rather typical procedures. While these steps provided worthwhile information, a reassessment of the evaluation program at the end of the first two years of the project convinced the staff that new directions were indicated. This reassessment started with some rather elementary thinking concerning what is involved in the evaluation of any type of educational innovation. This led to the development of a simple and basic rationale which, in turn, provided the basis for revised evaluation efforts. The following sections describe the results of this re-thinking.

## A RATIONALE FOR PLANNING AN EVALUATION PROGRAM

Any evaluation effort is an attempt to provide answers to some question or questions. Unfortunately, in too many such efforts data are obtained and presented and comparisons made before the questions to be answered are clearly specified. From a re-examination of our CCD evaluation program and from contacts with persons attempting similar assessments in other projects, the staff became convinced that the starting point for new plans had to be a consideration of the basic question involved in any evaluation effort.

**The Evaluator's Question** Phrased in general terms, which would permit its application to a variety of types of innovations and situations, the comprehensive question to which an evaluator would ultimately be seeking an answer can be posed as follows:

The Question: Does *this innovation,* in the *situation* with which we are concerned, do *what* is desired *better* than *alternatives?*

In any specific case the evaluator might well be concerned with only a part of this question. He might, for example, be seeking an answer to the question, "Does this innovation do what is desired?" That is, can a given teaching procedure produce certain results? In such situations the broad question, including the concern for comparisons with possible alternatives, may ultimately be of concern, but before this step is appropriate good answers must be obtained concerning smaller parts of the total question.

The implications of the evaluator's question can probably best be seen if it is analyzed in terms of the following component parts:

1. Does *this innovation*—
2. in the *situation* with which we are concerned—
3. do *what* is desired—
4. *better*—
5. than *alternatives?*

The following sections examine each of these parts.

1. Does *this innovation*—. A first focus of attention must be on determining exactly what it is that is being evaluated. Just what does the innovation include? This may be a particular problem in situations where new instructional materials are being tried out and where the use of them requires major changes in method of presentation. If these accompanying changes in method are not included in a description of the innovation, any results may be erroneously ascribed solely to the new materials. Another illustration of this problem is found in many recent assessments of programmed instruction where, in ascribing either positive or negative results to programmed instruction per se, the evaluator overlooks the fact that the program may deal with somewhat different content, or differ from the comparison materials in many ways in addition to the fact that it is programmed.

2. in the *situation*—. All too frequently, efforts in evaluation tend to ignore the limitations placed on the generalizations that can be made from a study by the restricted nature of the tryout situation. In the development of an innovation, it is frequently essential that the first trial be carried out in a very limited situation. The person developing a teaching-machine program typically conducts his first trial of a sequence of frames with only one student. In the CCD work the first tryout of any course was with one class. The essential point is that, whether the trial being assessed is this type of preliminary effort or a later one involving broad-scale sampling, the evaluator should describe the situation quite clearly and not tempt readers to draw implications for situations that are quite different.

3. do *what is desired*—. Both parts 3 and 4 in our breakdown of the evaluator's question deal with aspects of the criterion used. The first of these, considered here under "what is desired," may be thought of as centering on the time at which criterion data are to be gathered. Frequently, or even typically, we concern ourselves with immediate criteria. We specify the abilities a pupil should have when he has completed a course and then use an end-of-course examination to assess these. This may be the ideal type of criterion in some cases. However, with many innovations, the real changes they are designed to produce are expected to manifest themselves at a much later time. A new high-school math curriculum may have as its main purpose the better preparation of pupils to do the type of thinking required

in college math. If an innovation is primarily intended to produce more ultimate changes of this type, then the evaluator should attempt to obtain information on these more ultimate criteria. Still another alternative is the use of intervening criteria. For example, in assessing a new curriculum it may be important to obtain data concerning teacher performance and pupil behavior while the new materials are being used in the classroom. For one thing, such evidence may serve as an important basis for any needed revisions. Determining the time when it is most meaningful to obtain criterion data is a key step in spelling out what an innovation is expected to produce.

4. *better*—. The second aspect of the question of the criterion to be employed concerns the type of data to be used. Probably the most common type of data is the level of achievement attained. However, it must be recognized that the real purpose of many innovations is to enable pupils to attain a standard level of achievement in a more efficient manner. In this case the real criterion may be the time needed to reach this level. Other innovations may have as their goal that of making the teacher's task somewhat simpler. If this is so, it is essential that the criterion involve some assessment of change in what the teacher must do. Too frequently, evaluation efforts are centered on measures of achievement, when the real purpose of the innovation is something quite different.

5. *than alternatives*—. As suggested previously, an evaluator may not be concerned with comparing an innovation with alternatives. This may be true because no true alternatives are available. In our CCD effort, it was decided that it was meaningless to compare the achievement of pupils in most of the new courses with that of pupils in "conventional" classes because, although the courses had the same names, the real objectives of instruction were quite different. In other cases, the true concern of the innovator may be to concentrate on the improvement of his in-

novation. For example, many persons doing basic work with programmed instruction feel that so much remains to be done in investigating the most effective procedures for programming that it is entirely premature to compare this method of instruction with more standard procedures.

When it is decided that meaningful comparative studies can be made, the evaluator is faced with the need for a careful identification of the alternatives so that the data obtained can be interpreted in terms of exactly what it is that is being compared. He must also take into consideration the various possible sources of error that must be of concern in any experimental or quasi-experimental design (Campbell and Stanley, 1963).

## THE REVISED CCD EVALUATION PROGRAM

The re-examination of the evaluation program of the CCD in the light of the rationale described in the preceding section served to make obvious some of the weaknesses associated with the steps that had been followed. As a result it was decided that, for the immediate future, evaluation efforts would be most fruitful if they were centered on only a part of the evaluator's total question, that of "Does this innovation do what is desired?" Phrased in terms specific to our project, the question was, "Does each CCD course as taught in the demonstration schools produce end-of-course pupil achievement in line with specified objectives?" We wished to be able to say something quite specific about the type and extent of pupil achievement produced by a given course. As has been suggested, this decision was based partly on the realization that there were no true alternatives against which the CCD courses could be compared. It was also a result of the feeling that the innovations, the new courses, needed further definition and further refinement. It was felt that a concentration on the above question would contribute to meeting both of these needs.

In line with the centering of attention on this question, the first step in the new evaluation effort involved a more careful and detailed specification of the objectives of each of the CCD courses. Although the original development of each course had included considerable attention to the defining of objectives in behavioral terms, it was felt that such lists of objectives did not involve sufficient detail or specificity. To develop the needed lists of objectives, a small committee of two or three members was assigned to each course. Each such list was to be so comprehensive that it could be said that the person who could exhibit all of the abilities listed would have command of all that the course was intended to teach. Also, each objective was to be so specific that there could be no disagreement between competent persons as to how a student would exhibit the ability involved. The resulting lists of objectives run from about ten to forty typewritten pages. These lists not only serve now as a basis for the development of evaluation instruments, but also serve as supplements to course outlines in providing a more specific definition of a course.

The second step in the revised evaluation effort was to develop new tests and evaluation devices. Each small committee assigned to this task was instructed to produce a device that would assess a representative sample of the objectives for a course. The resulting devices involved objective-type tests, essay questions, and certain project-type assignments.

The obvious next step was to administer these tests to the students and to analyze the results. For the most part, these de-

vices were used as end-of-course examinations. The results obtained were, in each case, given a detailed analysis by the person teaching the course. This analysis included a determination of the percentage of students passing each item as well as information on discriminating capacity. A major purpose of the analysis was to alert the teacher and the project staff to certain strengths and weaknesses of each course.

The final, formal step in the revised evaluation program was to make use of the information yielded by the foregoing steps. The reports prepared from the analysis of test results were used as a basis for course revision and changes in teaching tactics as well as for the development of improved evaluation devices.

## CONCLUSION

Certainly these evaluation steps that were developed for the CCD should not be considered as a final answer as to what steps will be most effective in the assessment of a curriculum innovation. These were found to be useful for the present needs of the CCD program. Other programs will probably require different steps. However, it is suggested that the rationale presented here, or some modification of it which can serve to center attention on the exact question being asked, should be useful in guiding the thinking of persons responsible for any of a number of types of evaluation efforts. Such efforts, together with efforts to attack most educational problems, can best be undertaken, not by jumping to employ whatever devices, techniques, and procedures seem to be in vogue, but by a careful and painstaking analysis of the task involved.

## 2. Evaluation and Curriculum Development
### CLIFFORD BEBELL

Despite all the good that has resulted from the "testing movement," a number of problems have also arisen. These problems, particularly troublesome in curriculum evaluation, might be characterized as (1) emphasis on ease of measurement, (2) assumed authoritativeness, (3) national orientation, and (4) inhibited communication between test developer and user. Bebell believes that in order to overcome these problems we need to (1) measure all important educational outcomes, not just those that lend themselves more easily to quantification; (2) improve the measurement and evaluative skills of in-service teachers; and (3) strongly consider the increased use of teacher-made tests to increase the relevance of our measurements.

The interaction between evaluation and curriculum development is intimate and total. Changes can legitimately be made in an instructional program only when careful evaluation demonstrates the strengths and weaknesses of such adjustments. Conversely, no curricular proposal can claim widespread support until and unless it has justified itself through carefully collected data. Evaluation may be called the other side of the coin of curriculum development.

Tests constitute the principal tool of those who evaluate, and indeed of all who would contribute to educational improvement. The testing movement represents a major breakthrough in the advance of education toward the status of a science: without accurate measures there can be no science. The achievements of test makers in quantifying elements of the human mind and personality have done much to multiply and extend the effectiveness of the teacher.

Reprinted with permission of the Association for Supervision and Curriculum Development and Clifford Bebell from *Educational Leadership*, **17** (October 1962), pp. 4–6, 79–80. Copyright 1962 by the Association for Supervision and Curriculum Development.

Consider a school without access to information about intelligence, aptitudes, interests, and achievement. Grouping would be done on a catch-as-catch-can basis, counseling would be largely guesswork, individualization of instruction would be based upon doubtful evidence.

However, the testing movement can constitute just as much a barricade to educational advance as it can provide a breakthrough, mainly because the act of evaluation is so charged with emotionality. During examinations and at report times nervous tensions may pervade a classroom like a fog. And teachers, facing evaluation in their own turn, whether from supervisors or college professors, usually view the process with anxiety. All the while the person who evaluates stands alone, filled with self-doubt, as he realizes his decisions present a picture of omniscience which is more apparent than real.

It is paradoxical that testing and evaluation present a simultaneous picture of objectivity and subjectivity. In no area is the goal of scientific preciseness sought with greater intensity than in that of educational measurement; test technicians struggle to increase the validity and reliability of their tools, using elaborate statistical analyses to this end. And yet the fear and insecurity with which educators approach the task of measurement go far to frustrate these efforts and to block educational progress.

## THE DIFFICULTIES

There are at least four problems which have resulted from the measurement movement, and especially from the development of standardized tests.

1. *There is greater emphasis upon that which is easy to measure than upon that which is important to measure.* The first successes in any comparatively new field usually take place in those aspects which are most amenable to attack. In educational testing this has meant an early emphasis upon measuring acquisition of facts and basic subject-matter skills. Today, in spite of the many efforts to move beyond such areas, a review of most tests, whether teacher-made or standardized, reveals a continuation of this emphasis.

Concurrently, there is neglect of more elusive and vital learnings such as critical thinking, problem solving, creativity, cultural appreciations, work habits, and the like. Because it has been easy to develop and use measuring devices associated with the simpler learnings, there has been a dangerous tendency to over-concentrate upon such learnings and ignore more complex ones. Or, perhaps it would be more accurate to say that the emotional hazards of venturing among these controversial and difficult areas have discouraged many persons from making such explorations.

2. *A spurious sense of certainty has come into widespread existence because of uncritical use of standardized instruments.* The drive for certainty characterizes all human beings. Paradoxically, this drive motivates both adventurers and stay-at-homes. It stimulates many to seek new learnings, among them those persons who have secured for all mankind the vast achievements of research. The same emotion epitomizes those who cling to the security of the past. This dualism partly explains the similar paradox in educational evaluation. One way in which educational stay-at-homes reveal themselves is through their uncritical use of standardized tests.

The trappings of science adorn most test manuals. This remark is not intended to imply hypocrisy or ineptness on the part of test makers, since there is nothing spurious about the efforts of those who create and standardize educational instruments. Indeed, their writings abound with cautions and provisos. Nevertheless, in spite of their careful efforts, or perhaps even because of these efforts, many persons are inclined to place greater reliance upon test results than the instruments warrant. The exactness with which scores are reported, and even the preciseness of the measures of error, delude many people into thinking that a test provides more certainty than it actually does. Further, the question is too rarely raised as to the degree of relevance which seemingly exact measures bear to the trait or learning they ostensibly describe.

Just because a test uses the words "Arithmetic Achievement" or "Critical Thinking" in its title does not mean that the definition of these terms is the same in the minds of the test makers as it is in the minds of the test users. Indeed, there is often a question as to whether or not an instrument even reflects the intention of its creators accurately.

3. *There is a de-emphasis on locally constructed measures.* Educational evaluation is in danger of becoming a spectator sport. The elaborate and costly preparation considered essential to the commercial production of tests has caused many local educators to lose faith in their own devices and skills. While it is true that such persons are generally not highly skilled in techniques of test construction, they do know boys and girls and they do know education. It is important not to discourage these educators from using their own insights in educational evalu-

ation; on the contrary, every effort should be made to encourage and assist their creative endeavors to assess students' learnings.

4. *There has been a notable lack of communication between teachers and test technicians.* Even as the medical specialist sometimes seems to patronize the general practitioner, so the test specialist often appears convinced that he has been vouchsafed a revelation not granted to lesser beings. Conversely, teachers sometimes act as though they possess an insight into the art of education totally beyond the grasp of those who would capture it in charts and graphs and statistics.

Too often teachers are unduly resistant to the complexities of standardized testing, in spite of its possible benefits. Too often, too, tests are selected and administered with little regard to the reality of the classroom and in a manner actively discouraging teacher experimentation and creativity. Apparently the emotional nature of evaluation creates barriers to communication.

## THE CHALLENGE

The challenge is to take full advantage of our existent measuring devices and to do so in a way which will encourage rather than retard further educational progress. We must strive to resolve the various areas of emotionality. Following are a few guidelines we might consider.

1. *"Teach for the test," but test all important educational outcomes.* We have heard many criticisms of the tendency of teachers to "teach for the test." However, such activity is surely defensible *if* the test (or tests) validly measures all significant student learnings, and *if* individual needs are recognized. Moreover, it is human nature to place emphasis upon that which will be used to evaluate one's efforts.

Consider, for instance, the difference in a student's study of a book if he is engaged only in self-improvement or if he is preparing for an examination. Teachers will very likely always teach for the test. This fact can be used as an important means of influencing the curriculum. Our job is to be certain of a wide range of valid measuring devices covering all important learnings.

2. *Improve the measurement skills of teachers and the educational skills of test specialists.* Through joint conferences and in-service education activities, teachers and test specialists must come to know each other's needs, concerns and insights. Both should possess a veto power over test selection in the individual school, since neither group alone is qualified to choose wisely. If the two cannot agree, it is probably best to avoid choosing any standardized instrument within the area of disagreement but to use locally developed devices instead. Further, such lack of agreement indicates a possible focus for in-service education.

3. *Make teacher-made tests an integral part of the total evaluation program.* It is a travesty to call a program "The Testing Program" of a school when this program contains only a minor fraction of the tests used. The bulk of educational measurement and evaluation is done in the classroom by the teacher, and must be harmonized with findings of "The Testing Program." An important part of this effort should be the continuous provision of specialized assistance to teachers in developing and improving their own instruments.

Planning an evaluation program and creating measurement devices are as much an exercise in educational philosophy as they are a task for the statistician. The validation of instruments and procedures requires coordinated efforts of everyone, since the task involves educational goals, classroom practices, conditions of learning, characteristics of children, as well as criteria of test construction. For too long a period, we have acted as though all this could be done without the participation of those who know curriculum and instruction best. It is clearly evident that this is not the case, and that the improvement of testing and evaluation in schools is interlocked with the improvement of instruction. Perhaps it might be said that the basic job is one of finding ways to quantify and communicate the observations, judgments and experiences of teachers.

## 3. Curriculum Assessment: Problems and Possibilities

### JACK R. FRYMIER

The intimate relationship between curriculum development and evaluation is again stressed in this article. It makes simple sense that if you do not ask the appropriate questions you will get the wrong answers or, at the very least, the right answers to the wrong questions. Perhaps, and unfortunately, American educators and evaluators are prone to ask questions related to efficiency rather than effectiveness.

Surely the quality of a curriculum package should not be judged on the basis of the frequency of its use. The most widely used package is not necessarily the best. Many factors in addition to adoption statistics and cost need to be considered, the most important being the nature of local educational objectives and the characteristics of teachers and student body.

Frymier's analogy between planning, doing, and assessing in government and in education—both social activities—is well drawn.

Every model for curriculum development includes the concept of assessment or evaluation. From the theoretical point of view, evaluation plays an important part in improving program in several ways. Purposes can be selected, for example, on the basis of good data about the nature of society or the nature of the learner. Or, content, experiences, organization, and methodology can be set forth in testable form.

For instance, rather than assuming that any particular selection of content or sequence of experiences or methodological approaches or organizational stratagems is

Reprinted with permission of the Association for Supervision and Curriculum Development and Jack R. Frymier from *Educational Leadership,* 21, (November 1966), pp. 124–128. Copyright 1966 by the Association for Supervision and Curriculum Development.

effective, responsible leaders in curriculum development can hypothesize about these things, then put their hypotheses to empirical test. Over a period of time such evaluative and assessment techniques should enable curriculum workers to make steady progress in terms of improving program.

Two major developments have forced the concepts of assessment and evaluation into special prominence. Talk of national assessment in education, on the one hand, and the requirement for evaluation built into the Elementary and Secondary Education Act program, on the other, are forcing curriculum workers to reexamine these notions as they apply to curriculum development today.

Any view of the educational scene suggests that programs are changing dramatically. At no time in the history of American schools have curricular changes been so widespread or so intensive as in the past decade. Modifications of course content, organizational structures, methodological approaches, evaluation procedures, and even purposes themselves have been instituted. Unless one is willing to accept change for its own sake, however, he is forced to ask: "Are the curriculum changes really significant?" Or to ask in another way, "Do children learn better in the new programs than they did in the old?"

This, of course, may be the wrong question. Some persons maintain that since the old purposes were not themselves appropriate, it is unreasonable to compare the new efforts today in terms of objectives which are actually obsolete. On the other hand, it may very well be that some kind of accumulated curriculum wisdom has been reflected in the decades of activity which have gone into what we generally describe as "conventional program." If this is true, comparisons of new efforts with previously existing programs may be perfectly legitimate.

## NEW QUESTIONS NEEDED

The fact is, these questions are academic. Even though changes in curriculum have been extensive, and many of these changes have been positive, few people are satisfied with the state of affairs in American curriculum today. The inadequacies are so obvious that thoughtful curriculum workers are continuously struggling to find new and more powerful ways to improve the program.

This dissatisfaction arises in part because of a kind of gnawing professional perspective which says: "No program is perfect. We must improve." Part of the dissatisfaction, however, stems from the very real fact that inappropriate and ineffective curricula can be found in almost any district or any building without difficulty at all. Too many children hate the very thought of having to learn in school. Too many find school a boring, unexciting place to be. Too many are unsuccessful in

acquiring those ways of behaving which seem desirable to those in charge.

Why is this so? Many factors probably account for such a state of affairs today. I would like to suggest two. In my opinion, we have tended to ask the wrong questions in curriculum, and secondly, assessment has been ineffectively utilized as part of the total educational scheme.

If we ask the wrong questions we always get the wrong answers. In curriculum development we often ask the *frequency* question or the *efficiency* question, for example, rather than the *effectiveness* question. We say, "How many schools are using language laboratories?" or "How many schools have PSSC physics this year?" "How many classrooms are nongraded?" "How many teachers utilize generative grammar or structural linguistics in their language arts programs?"

The assumption underlying these questions is that if more schools are using a particular program, it must be better. Obviously that is the wrong assumption. Frequency is not an appropriate criterion at all.

This fall, for instance, more than half of the youngsters who study physics in our secondary schools will be studying the PSSC physics program, but the proportional enrollment of high school students taking physics has steadily decreased during the same period of time that the new program has come into being. If we assume that the number of programs in use is important, we pose for ourselves the absurd possibility that the time might come when all of the schools would teach a particular course and none of the children would take it, that we would then be doing a perfect job.

Consider another example. Curriculum workers frequently make judgments about program in terms of money. "How much will it cost?" "How efficient will it be?" "Can we afford such an innovation?" These questions presuppose that the basic purpose of education is to save money. No one is willing to agree with that aloud, of course, but the fact remains that if we ask an economic question, we can only get an economic answer. But that is the wrong question.

If schools exist to save money, there are many ways in which expenditures can be reduced. We can lower teachers' salaries, we can increase class size, or we can eliminate expenditures for instructional materials, for instance. These will all save money. The purpose of education is not to save money, though. It is to help children learn.

Curriculum workers must always focus upon the effectiveness question. Does the new program, do the new materials, will the new techniques enable students to learn more, better, faster, than some other approach? Does it make a significant difference in the lives and minds of those we teach? If it does, the program is effective. If it does not, the program is ineffective. Whether it costs more money or less or whether it is widespread or is not evident in any other school at all is immaterial. Frequency questions or economic questions simply get in the way. We must learn to ask the effectiveness question every time.

## A CONCEPTUAL FLAW

A deeper, more elusive problem affecting program development, however, stems from the fact that education is a social system with a conceptual flaw. Every social system represents a human undertaking designed to fulfill human needs. Government, science, industry, education —these are all illustrations of different kinds of social systems in evidence today. Looked at in terms of systems theory, every effective social system reflects three phases of operation which accomplish separate functions, and these functions enable the system to maintain itself in an ongoing, dynamic, improving way.

Phase one includes the intellectual activities, the planning, policy making, hypothesizing function. Phase two involves the doing, accomplishing, effecting function. Phase three is the evaluating, assessing, reflecting, judgmental function. Taken together, they represent various aspects of social undertakings which are designed to allow the system to accomplish the objectives toward which it is aimed, and at the same time keep changing for the better.

These three phases of any social system are most clearly illustrated in our concept of government. The planning phase is represented by the legislative branch. The doing phase is represented by the executive branch. The evaluating or assessing phase is represented by the judicial branch. In industry, however, the model still holds. Somebody plans, somebody produces, and somebody judges the effectiveness of those activities in a realistic way.

Any careful study of social systems other than education suggests that these three functions have been made relatively discrete and that they are accomplished by different groups, each one of which has power. That is, the Congress is different than the President, and the Supreme Court is different still. The same notion holds at the state and local level, too. From the functional standpoint, our system of government has been conceptualized in such a way that these different functions are accomplished by separate groups.

Another point, however, rests on the fact that social systems in an open society actually depend upon the third phase of the operation to assure improvement and intelligent change. That is, when the courts decide that a particular law is constitutional or unconstitutional or that a particular action by the President either is or is not appropriate, they feed back into the system new data which guarantee that the enterprise will be able to change itself and to improve. In industry the same thing is also true.

Planning and producing a new product or service represent the first and second phases of that social system in operation. Once the product goes on sale, however, evaluation must occur. Judgments are made by those who buy. If the general public buys the product or service, what they really do is feed back into the system new data which tell those responsible for planning and production that they have done the job well. Or, if the product or service becomes available and the public refuses to buy, this too, constitutes corrective feedback. It tells those responsible that something about their operation is not satisfactory and it must be changed. In either event, evaluation plays the critical role of providing corrective feedback to the other parts of the system so that the entire operation can be improved.

## ROLE OF FEEDBACK

Two things are important about our discussion thus far. One is that the concept of corrective feedback, which is performed during the evaluation phase of the social systems operation, represents the precise point at which improvement can be assured. Second, in these illustrations it is also evident that the assessment or evaluation effort is best accomplished by a separate group which has appropriate influence of its own. Congress is not allowed to pass judgment on the constitutionality of its own laws, for example, nor are manufacturing companies permitted to have the ultimate say in the worthwhileness or value of the products they produce. These decisions are reserved for other groups.

In other words, feedback is imperative if the system is to operate at the highest possible level of effectiveness; yet, at the same time, it is probably not possible to assume that those who plan or those who implement can also accomplish the evaluation role. The power of evaluation rests in part upon the nature of the feedback information which is generated by the process, but in part upon the fact that the evaluation group has an authority of its own. Said still another way, our system of government and our system of economics, at least, presume that when the evaluation group makes its decision known, the rest of the system will have to pay attention to the feedback. The rest of the system is

not free to ignore the data, whether they are positive or negative in form.

Looked at in terms of such a social systems model, education obviously has a conceptual flaw. School boards accomplish the policy making role. Professional persons undertake the effecting, implementing, doing role. But there is no special group whose responsibilities encompass the assessment function in any meaningful way. The general public passes judgment on the effectiveness of schools, of course, but seldom do they have a way of communicating their concerns with precision to assure improvement in schools. They may vote down a bond issue, for instance, but often as not no one really knows what the negative vote means.

On the other hand, advisory councils or curriculum councils often attempt to perform the evaluation role. In the first instance the fact that their activities are advisory—no one has to pay attention to the feedback—illustrates the fact that the system is not assured of information in such a way that it has to improve. Likewise, curriculum councils may very well study a particular problem in program carefully and creatively, only to find that their recommendations go completely ignored. That such recommendations may be accepted and used only serves to reinforce the fact that they may also be ignored. There is no rigor in the system which insists that we utilize the best that we know.

Theoretically, education has this conceptual flaw. There is no aspect of the system which regularly generates evaluative data, nor is there anything in the concept which requires that the system pay attention to the feedback if it should appear.

Do we need curriculum evaluation? Is assessment important? On these questions everyone agrees. Of course! Where should evaluation occur? Who should accomplish the assessment role? How should these persons be selected? How can we assure ourselves that the system will be able to use and profit by the feedback data which are obtained? These are difficult problems.

Several alternatives seem to be available, but what is needed most now is a thoughtful consideration of analyses such as the one presented here, then extensive discussion of both the problems and possibilities which are involved. We may be on the verge of a genuine breakthrough in education, if we can muster the creative genius to explore the implications inherent in a consideration of the real power of assessing carefully everything we do.

## 4. Curriculum Evaluation: The Why of the Outcomes

### J. THOMAS HASTINGS

The purposes of evaluation are again addressed in this article. Two major aims of evaluation are identified by Hastings: (1) to determine adoption-rejection of curriculum and course-content-improvement packages, and (2) to determine the need for revision or further development of curriculum materials. These two purposes might be viewed as akin to what Scriven (1967) called summative and formative evaluation. The article concludes with a description of a series of evaluation and research activities that could significantly influence the development of teaching-learning materials and techniques.

For many years the expression "curriculum evaluation" has tended to mean to most people some sort of use and interpretation of achievement tests. Most assuredly, this is a very real part of the total concept of evaluation; but the thesis of this paper is that the concept must be broadened to include other sorts of ventures besides those of collecting and summarizing the test scores of students who have undergone a particular curricular treatment. The most commonly held idea of the sequence of evaluation endeavors starts with the act of stating the objectives of a set of materials—a full course, a unit of some sort, or a group of several units. This is followed by definition of these objectives in behavioral terms. Next comes the development of items, that is, situations which call for the behavior defined. These items are combined into scorable units, scores are obtained on appropriate samples of youngsters. Then, finally, the sequence ends in attempts to interpret these scores in terms of the extent to which the new materials have developed the behaviors which satisfy the purposes which the innovators had in mind.

A bit of experience in this area on a real job of evaluation will convince anyone that the steps of this total procedure—as simple as they are to state—are laden with problems of several kinds. We have the usual measurement problems of any test construction together with certain special problems of sampling and of the treatment of gain scores. Furthermore, all of this is imbedded in larger tactical problems of deriving the data from ongoing classroom settings. There is no denying the importance of solving these various problems if we are to move forward in evaluation of educational curricula.

Reprinted with permission of the publisher and J. Thomas Hastings from the *Journal of Educational Measurement*, **3** (Spring 1966), pp. 27–32.

## PURPOSES OF EVALUATION

At this point, however, it is important to raise the question of "What are the purposes of evaluation?" in order to lead into the theme that we need a considerably broader attack than is implied by the sequence described in the first paragraph. In curriculum innovation as a real ongoing venture there are *two* general purposes for evaluation. One of these concerns [is] collection of information to be used as feedback to the innovators for further revision of materials and methods. Without such feedback, either the decision to revise or the decision not to revise—and most certainly the decision of how to revise—must be based upon feeling tones and the arguments of personal preference. The second main purpose of evaluation of educational innovation is to provide information as input for decision-making by the schools about adoption of course-content–improvement packages. The extent to which the decision-making system of a school *does not have* empirical data concerning changes in the behavior of students who are undergoing particular curriculum treatments is the extent to which the decisions will be based upon such dimensions as glamor, public visibility, political expediency, and personal acquaintance with specific curriculum innovators.

## TWO KINDS OF DATA REQUIREMENTS

If the educational establishment is to move toward the point of basing decisions about revision and decisions about adoption on educational purpose and outcome, we need far more evaluation data of all kinds than we have had in any instance to date. We do need, however, somewhat different kinds of data for the two purposes I mentioned—revision and adoption.

First, here is a very sketchy description of a hypothetical instance of doing the evaluation job in a superior way using the usual model of test scores. To make the general model an example, the reader should think of the content and grade, or age level upon which he can focus most comfortably. This may be a full year's course—such as one of the Biological Sciences Curriculum Study versions or, as will be true if present plans hold, the new High School Geography Project; or the innovation of which you are thinking may consist of units of work which might be inserted at various places in the curriculum—as is true of the School Science Curriculum Project under Salinger's direction and, also, of some of the work in anthropology being carried on at the University of Chicago; or you may have in mind a program of innovation which will cover several years—like the Elementary School Science Project for grades five through eight, which is directed by Atkin, or the Social Science Curriculum Project for grades seven through twelve, which is directed by Leppert. Keep something such as one of these in mind while I give the following description of a *good* "test-centered evaluation." First, let us assume that there are eight definable objectives (we could play the game with three or with twenty-five). These objectives cover such things as knowledge of specific facts and assertions, attitudes toward operations or areas, the development of certain cognitive processes, and the ability to use knowledge in an interpretive fashion. Next, let us assume that we have put each of these objectives in behavioral terms, even to the extent of having two or more kinds of behaviors for each of the objectives. The next assumption is that we have been able to set up two comparable, reliable tests on each of the behaviorally defined objectives and these tests may consist of some paper-and-pencil material, some performance tests, or even some systematically summarized observational data. The two comparable tests are for the purpose of pretesting and post-testing in a design which calls for both immediate learning and for retention. The final assumption is that we now have results in the form of test scores from an appropriate sampling of relevant populations. This allows, if you want it that way, for us to have a sampling from treated groups and a sampling from untreated groups. The point is that there are sets of test scores from relevant samples of youngsters and these scores reflect reasonably well the kinds of behaviors which the curricular materials were intended to develop. These scores can be manipulated statistically in order to draw inferences concerning the extent to which the behaviors have been acquired at the time of use of the curricular materials.

Now let's take a look at what we have in terms of the two purposes mentioned earlier: (1) revision or development of new materials and (2) the adoption of the present materials. In making the adoption-decision we might very easily have sufficient data. The decision to adopt or reject would be based upon the relative values that school attached to this or that behavior and the extent to which those behaviors were developed.

Now let's look at the curriculum-revision-and-development decision. The data indicate that the new materials meet the criteria on the *average* at such and such a level or with such and such a probability. Shall the innovators try to revise the materials to do a better job? If so, what sorts of revision should they make? I contend that these decisions are of a different sort than those of adoption decision. The statistical summaries may give us hints that the material did work on this objective but did not work as well with that objective. In any real situation they certainly will tell us that the materials did not work perfectly on any of the objectives.

If we were the innovators, one of the first obvious next moves with the test data would be to pull away from the scores themselves and look more closely for interpretation in the test-item data. From the course-content–improvement standpoint this certainly might help us discover that, although we seem to have done fairly well with this particular attitude, we

missed rather dreadfully on that one. Test-item data might tell us that the students acquired certain ones of the concepts but missed other concepts further than we think should be necessary. The data still help us comparatively little with the question of *how to revise*. What we need are data which throw some light on the "why" of the test results.

This is the point then at which we need information in addition to any of the usual test-information which we might develop. Please understand that this is no assertion that the test-information has been useless. The information from a test-centered evaluation might be all we need for the adoption-rejection decision in the school —and the data would suggest clues to the curriculum builder. The point is that the course-content–improvement innovator needs, deserves, and can get more information than that which is encompassed in tests interpreted through scores or item data. The suggestion is that we should spend considerably more time than we have to date on what may be called instructional research. Perhaps you have a better name for it, but the general nature of the stuff may look a lot like the research on learning which has been going on for years in the psychology laboratories —as a matter of fact, at certain stages in the game it may be difficult to discriminate between standard learning research and instructional research except that in the long run the latter will collect data in an ongoing classroom. For purposes of explication, here are a few examples of the sorts of investigations which could be carried on and which, if carried on, should be of real use to the curriculum innovator in revising his materials.

## EVALUATION AND RESEARCH DESIGNS SUPPORTIVE OF CURRICULUM DEVELOPMENT

Easley (1964) and others connected with the University of Illinois Committee on School Mathematics, under the direction of Max Beberman (1963), have been taking a fresh look at the concept structure of the mathematics material presented to students. They are especially interested in the effects on concept formation and attainment of ordering or sequencing of mathematics exercises. Now, concept-formation research has been with us for a long time. Ordinarily the content is color, shape, or number—not real instructional material for the school. Richard C. Anderson (1964) points out, however, in a paper on stimulus sequence and concept learning, that the sequence of stimuli has been treated only incidentally, or at least very rarely, in concept-formation studies. We can be even more certain, however, that the notion of concept sequence has seldom been appropriately studied in the instructional setting of school classrooms using the new curriculum ventures. We certainly have the possibility, however, with the design techniques and the hardware we have at hand today to carry on fairly extensive studies both of sequence of stimuli and of sequence of concepts being developed in units of instructional work. The results of such studies would be important feedback information for decisions about whether or not to revise and in what way to revise new materials which are being tried out. Furthermore, within a given content domain and over some specified age or grade level (or perhaps conditioned by some readiness specification) we might be able to arrive at general rules for the development of new curricular material which would come closer to the target than would the guesses—reasoned as they are—of the subject-matter specialist or the experienced teacher.

Another example also comes from some work going on in connection with the University of Illinois Committee on School Mathematics. Hiroshi Ikeda (1965) studied the relationship between teacher-held objectives and student achievement. Far too simply stated, the work stems from observations that teachers trained specifically in institutes directed at helping them teach special new mathematics material seem to come out with quite different results. This kind of a fact could have been ascertained from a test-centered evaluation. The point of my argument is that we must go beyond ascertaining that there are differences and inquire into "Why does this difference exist?" Ikeda hypothesized that teachers hold, not necessarily explicitly, somewhat different objectives in their views of the classroom even though they may understand and appreciate the objectives set forth by the authors of the new curriculum materials— and that these "personal" objectives affect student attainment. Such studies could be helpful in locating points for revision of both student and teacher material.

A third example has to do with retention and could be adopted to transfer studies. Retention studies with straight test techniques demand a kind of retention which we think of as direct recall of assertions, principles, and perhaps processes. Another kind of retention, however —one which Cronbach (1963) has mentioned—is the type related to savings in learning. The idea is not new—but its application to course-content improvement is. For purposes of this kind of retention we need instructional research which would call for attempts to teach students (or reteach students) material which is based upon material which had been learned previously. By appropriate treatment-nontreatment design and by varying the length of time between the original learning situation and the savings investigation, it should be possible to collect a considerable amount of evidence which would be of real use to the curriculum innovator in revising old materials and developing new. This same general pattern could be used for investigating the savings which would occur in transferring from one domain to another after treatment with different curriculum materials in the same area.

One final type of investigation which would help immeasurably with the development of curriculum materials—and in this case would add valuable information for the adoption-rejection decision in the school—is exemplified by some studies by R. E. Stake and D. D. Sjogren (1964). Without going into detail about their studies, the general import is that they were investigating the relative advantages—for individuals with varying characteristics—of different modes of studying the same materials. If we apply this type of investigation to some of the new curriculum ventures, much more definite statements can be made in answer to the question "For whom are various activity levels effective and what treatments will be most useful for which students?"

Experience says it is important at this point to defend the proposition that such instructional research is a real part of evaluation. Defense may not be necessary for some readers; but others will say, "Why don't you separate the actual curriculum evaluation (the test-centered activities) from what you are calling instructional research, which is a type of investigation educational psychology has been carrying on for years?" First, any investigation that works in the direction of letting us know *why* students learn from this activity better than they do from that activity is by definition part of the input for evaluation decisions of either type. Secondly, the sort of research just described has not been carried on—at least very plentifully—in educational-psy-

chology investigations. Usually such investigations have not been concerned with a particular set of curricular materials. They have been concerned more generally with the concepts of retention, transfer, and concept formation. Such investigations should be centered upon specific curriculum materials. One can visualize the time in the future when a sufficient number of such investigations has been completed across various content areas and with various age levels so that broad principles or generalizations can be made about new materials without having to carry on additional investigations. The effective variables are so plentiful that the day when we can generalize in that fashion is certainly far in the future.

Test-item data and relationships among test scores and subscores would be much more useful, especially to the curriculum innovator, if we were to use techniques of instructional research to attempt to discover answers to the question "Why do we obtain these outcomes and for whom?" To do the job properly it will be necessary to carry on investigations in a replicative fashion with many different contents and at many different levels. The plea of this paper is simply that all of those involved in curriculum evaluation should attend much more wholeheartedly than they have in the past to instructional research as an important aspect of evaluation.

# 5. Accountability: Rationale and a Methodology
## STEPHEN M. BARRO

If any general characteristic of the public's attitude toward its schools has grown in intensity during the last several decades, it is *concern*. This concern is manifested in both the public and professional sectors by the call for accountability. Basically, accountability is instructional and fiscal responsibility. Educational personnel, both instructional and administrative, are facing the prospect of having to demonstrate their effectiveness in a systematic and continuous manner. Such procedures as performance contracting, external educational data auditing, performance incentives, and the like (Lessinger, 1970) are being used to help improve the quality of education in our schools. Barro, after providing an excellent rationale for the concept of accountability, leads us step-by-step through a methodology that will make it possible to estimate the contributions to pupil performance of individual agents in the educational process.

## THE CONCEPT OF ACCOUNTABILITY

Although the term "accountability" is too new in the educational vocabulary to have acquired a standard usage, there is little doubt about its general meaning and import for the schools. The basic idea it conveys is that school systems and schools, or, more precisely, the professional educators who operate them, should be held responsible for educational outcomes— for what children learn. If this can be done, it is maintained, favorable changes in professional performance will occur, and these will be reflected in higher academic achievement, improvement in pupil attitudes, and generally better educational results. This proposition—that higher quality education can be obtained by making

Reprinted with permission of the publisher and Stephen M. Barro from an article entitled "An Approach to Developing Accountability Measures for the Public Schools", which appeared in the *Phi Delta Kappan,* **52** (December 1970), pp. 196–205.

the professionals responsible for their product—is what makes accountability an attractive idea and provides the starting point for all discussion of specific accountability systems and their uses in the schools.

The unusual rapidity with which the accountability concept has been assimilated in educational circles and by critics of the schools seems less attributable to its novelty than to its serviceability as a unifying theme. Among its antecedents, one can identify at least four major strands of current thought and action in education: (1) the new, federally stimulated emphasis on evaluation of school systems and their programs; (2) the growing tendency to look at educational enterprises in terms of cost effectiveness; (3) increasing concentration on education for the disadvantaged as a priority area of responsibility for the schools; and (4) the movement to make school systems more directly responsive to their clientele and communities, either by establishing decentralized community control or by introducing consumer choice through a voucher scheme. Under the accountability banner, these diverse programs for educational reform coalesce and reinforce one another, each gaining strength and all, in turn, strengthening already powerful pressures for educational change.

## HOW THE SCHOOLS CAN BE MADE ACCOUNTABLE

Accountability in the abstract is a concept to which few would take exception. The doctrine that those employed by the public to provide a service—especially those vested with decision-making power—should be answerable for their product is one that is accepted readily in other spheres and that many would be willing to extend, in principle, to public education. The problems arise in making the concept operational. Then it becomes necessary to deal with a number of sticky questions:

> To what extent should each participant in the educational process—teacher, principal, and administrator—be held responsible for results?
> To whom should they be responsible?
> How are "results" to be defined and measured?
> How will each participant's contribution be determined?
> What will be the consequences for professional educators of being held responsible?

These are the substantive issues that need to be treated in a discussion of approaches to implementing the accountability concept.

Various proposals for making the schools accountable differ greatly in the degree to which they would require existing structures and practices to be modified. In fact, it is fair to say they range from moderate reform to revolution of the educational system. The follow paragraphs summarize the major current ideas

that, singly or in combination, have been put forth as approaches to higher quality education through accountability:

**Use of Improved, Output-Oriented Management Methods** What is rapidly becoming a new "establishment" position —though it would have been considered quite revolutionary only a few years ago —is that school district management needs to be transformed if the schools are to become accountable and produce a better product. The focus here is on accountability for effective use of resources. Specific proposals include articulation of goals, introduction of output-oriented management methods (planning-programming-budgeting, systems analysis, etc.), and—most important—regular, comprehensive evaluation of new and ongoing programs. Mainly internal workings of the school system rather than relations between school and community would be affected, except that better information on resource use and educational outcomes would presumably be produced and disseminated.

**Institutionalization of External Evaluations or Educational Audits** Proposals along this line aim at assuring that assessments of educational quality will be objective and comparable among schools and school districts and that appropriate information will be compiled and disseminated to concerned parties. They embody the element of comparative evaluation of school performance and the "carrot" or "stick" associated with public disclosure of relative effectiveness. A prototype for this function may be found in the "external educational audit" now to be required for certain federal programs. However, the need for consistency in examining and comparing school districts suggests that a state or even a federal agency would have to be the evaluator. This would constitute a significant change in the structure of American public education in that it would impose a centralized quality-control or "inspectorate" function upon the existing structure of autonomous local school systems.

**Performance Incentives for School Personnel** Perhaps the most direct way to use an accountability system to stimulate improved performance is to relate rewards for educators to measures of effectiveness in advancing learning. One way to do this is to develop pay schedules based on measured performance to replace the customary schedules based on teaching experience and academic training. An alternative approach would be to use differentiated staffing as the framework for determining both pay and promotion. The latter is a more fundamental reform in that it involves changes in school district management and organization as well as changes in the method of rewarding teachers. Professional organizations have tended to oppose such schemes, partly out of fear that performance criteria might be applied subjectively, arbitrarily, or inequitably. Although this may not be the only objection, if a measurement system could be developed that would be widely recognized as "objective" and "fair," the obstacles to acceptance of a system of performance incentives might be substantially reduced.

**Performance or Incentive Contracting** Performance contracting rests on the same philosophy as the proposals for incentives, but applies to organizations outside the school system rather than individual professionals within it. A school district contracts with an outside agency—a private firm or, conceivably, a nonprofit organization—to conduct specified instructional activities leading to specified, measurable educational results. The amount paid to the contractor varies according to how well the agreed-upon objectives are accomplished, thereby providing a very direct incentive for effective instruction. At present, there is too little experience with performance contracting to support conclusions about its potential. However, a large number of experiments

and several evaluation efforts are underway. Should they prove successful, and should this very direct method of making the purveyor of educational services responsible for his product become widely used, there would undoubtedly be substantial and lasting effects on both the technology and organization of American public education.

**Decentralization and Community Control** These are two conceptually distinct approaches to accountability that we lump together under one heading only because they have been so closely linked in recent events. Administrative decentralization, in which decision-making authority is shifted from central administrators to local area administrators or individual school principals, can itself contribute to accountability. The shift of authority should, for example, favor greater professional responsiveness to local conditions and facilitate the exercise of local initiative. Also, it allows responsibility for results to be decentralized and, in so doing, provides the framework within which various performance incentives can be introduced.

The movement for community control of the highly bureaucratized, big-city school systems aims at accountability in the sense of making the system more representative of and responsive to its clientele and community. In the context of community control, accountability can be defined very broadly to include not only responsibility for performance in achieving goals, but also for selecting appropriate or "relevant" goals in the first place. Most important, community control provides the means of enforcing accountability by placing decision-making and sanctioning powers over the schools in the hands of those whose lives they affect.

**Alternative Educational Systems** Probably the most radical proposal for achieving better education through improved accountability is this one, which would allow competing publicly financed school systems to coexist and would permit parents to choose schools for their children. Usually this is coupled with a proposal for financing by means of "educational vouchers," although this is not the only possible mechanism. The rationale for this "consumer-choice" solution is that there would be direct accountability by the school to the parent. Furthermore, there would be an automatic enforcement mechanism: A dissatisfied parent would move his child—and funds—to another school. Of course, the burden of becoming informed and evaluating the school would be on the individual parent. At present, there is very little experience with a system of this kind and little basis for judging how well it would operate or what effect it would have on the quality of education.

## THE NEED FOR ACCOUNTABILITY MEASURES

These proposals, though not mutually exclusive, are quite diverse both with respect to the kinds of restructuring they would imply and the prospective educational consequences. However, they are alike in one important respect: Each can be carried out only with adequate information on the individual and the collective effectiveness of participants in the educational process. At present, such information does not exist in school systems. Therefore, a major consideration in moving toward accountability must be development of information systems, including the data-gathering and analytical activities needed to support them. This aspect of accountability—the nature of the required effectiveness indicators and the means of obtaining them—will be the principal subject of the remainder of this paper.

Progress in establishing accountability for results within school systems is likely to depend directly on success in developing two specific kinds of effectiveness information: (1) improved, more comprehensive pupil performance measurements; and (2) estimates of contributions to measured pupil performance by individual teachers, administrators, schools, and districts. As will be seen, the two have very different implications. The first calls primarily for expansion and refinement of what is now done in the measurement area. The second requires a kind of analysis that is both highly technical and new to school systems and poses a much greater challenge.

The need for more extensive pupil performance measurement is evident. If teachers, for example, are to be held responsible for what is learned by their pupils, then pupil performance must be measured at least yearly so that gains associated with each teacher can be identified. Also, if the overall effectiveness of educators and schools is to be assessed, measurement will have to be extended to many more dimensions of pupil performance than are covered by instruments in common use. This implies more comprehensive, more frequent testing than is standard practice in most school systems. In the longer run, it will probably require substantial efforts to develop and validate more powerful measurement instruments.

But no program of performance measurement alone, no matter how comprehensive or sophisticated, is sufficient to establish accountability. To do that, we must also be able to attribute results (performance gains) to sources. Only by knowing the contributions of individual professionals or schools would it be possible, for example, for a district to operate an incentive pay or promotion system; for community boards in a decentralized system to evaluate local schools and their staffs; or for parents, under a voucher system, to make informed decisions about schools for their children. To emphasize this point, from now on the term "accountability measures" will be used specifically to refer to estimates of contributions to pupil performance by individual agents in the educational process. These are described as "estimates" advisedly, because, unlike performance, which can be measured directly, *contributions* to performance cannot be measured directly but must be *inferred* from comparative analysis of different classrooms, schools, and districts. The analytical methods for determining individual contributions to pupil performance are the heart of the proposed accountability measurement system.

## A PROPOSED APPROACH

In the following pages we describe a specific approach that could be followed by a school system interested in deriving accountability measures, as they have just been defined. First, a general rationale for the proposed approach is presented. Then the analytical methodology to be used is discussed in more detail.

**For What Results Should Educators Be Held Responsible?** Ideally, a school system and its constituent parts, as appropriate, should be held responsible for performance in three areas: (1) selecting "correct" objectives and assigning them appropriate priorities, (2) achieving all the stated (or implicit) objectives, and (3) avoiding unintentional adverse effects on pupils. Realistically, much less can even be attempted. The first of the three areas falls entirely outside the realm of objective measurement and analysis, assessment of objectives being an intrinsically subjective, value-laden, and often highly political process. The other two areas can be dealt with in part, subject to the sometimes severe limitations to the current state of the art of educational measurement. The answer to the question posed above must inevitably be a compromise, and not necessarily a favorable one, between what is desirable and what can actually be done.

Any school system aims at affecting many dimensions of pupil peformance. In principle, we would like to consider all of them—appropriately weighted—when we assess teacher, school, or district effectiveness. In practice, it is feasible to work with only a subset of educational outcomes, namely, those for which (a) objectives are well defined and (b) we have

some ability to measure output. The dimensions of performance that meet these qualifications tend to fall into two groups: first, certain categories of cognitive skills, including reading and mathematics, for which standardized, validated tests are available; second, certain affective dimensions—socialization, attitudes toward the community, self-concept, and the like—for which we have such indicators or proxies as rates of absenteeism, dropout rates, and incidence of vandalism and delinquency. For practical purposes, these are the kinds of educational outcome measures that would be immediately available to a school system setting out today to develop an accountability system.

Because of the limited development of educational measurement, it seems more feasible to pursue this approach to accountability in the elementary grades than at higher levels, at least in the short run. Adequate instruments are available for the basic skill areas—especially reading—which are the targets of most efforts to improve educational quality at the elementary level. They are not generally available—and certainly not as widely used or accepted—for the subject areas taught in the secondary schools. Presumably, this is partly because measurement in those areas is inherently more difficult; it is partly, also, because there is much less agreement about the objectives of secondary education. Whatever the reason, establishing accountability for results at the secondary level is likely to be more difficult. Pending further progress in specifying objectives and measuring output, experiments with accountability measurement systems would probably be more fruitfully carried on in the elementary schools.

Fortunately, existing shortcomings in the measurement area can be overcome in time. Serious efforts to make accountability a reality should, themselves, spur progress in the measurement field. However, for the benefits of progress to be realized, the system must be "open"—not restricted to certain dimensions of performance. For this reason, the methodology described here has been designed to be in no way limiting with respect to the kinds of outcome measures that can be handled or the number of dimensions that can ultimately be included.

**Who Should Be Accountable for What?**
Once we have determined what kinds of pupil progress to measure, we can turn to the more difficult problem of determining how much teachers, principals, administrators, and others have contributed to the measured results. This is the key element in a methodology for accountability measurement.

The method proposed here rests on the following general principle: *Each participant in the educational process should be held responsible only for those educational outcomes that he can affect by his actions or decisions and only to the extent that he can affect them.* Teachers, for example, should not be deemed "ineffective" because of shortcomings in the curriculum or the way in which instruction is organized, assuming that those matters are determined at the school and district level and not by the individual teacher. The appropriate question is, "How well does the teacher perform, given the environment (possibly adverse) in which she must work and the constraints (possibly overly restrictive) imposed upon her?" Similarly, school principals and other administrators at the school level should be evaluated according to how well they perform within constraints established by the central administration.

The question then arises of how we know the extent to which teachers or administrators can affect outcomes by actions within their own spheres of responsibility. The answer is that we do not know *a priori*; we must find out from the performance data. This leads to a second principle: *The range over which a teacher, a school principal, or an administrator may be expected to affect outcomes is to be determined empirically from analysis of results obtained by all personnel working in comparable circumstances.* Several implications follow from this statement. First, it clearly establishes that the accountability measures will be relative, involving comparisons among educators at each level of the system. Second, it restricts the applicability of the methodology to systems large enough to have a wide range of professional competence at each level and enough observations to permit reliable estimation of the range of potential teacher and school effects. Third, it foreshadows several characteristics of the statistical models needed to infer contributions to results. To bring out the meaning of these principles in more detail, we will explore them from the points of view of teachers, school administrators, and district administrators, respectively.

*Classroom Teachers.* We know that the educational results obtained in a particular classroom (e.g., pupils' scores on a standard reading test) are determined by many other things besides the skill and effort of the teacher. The analyses in [and of] the Coleman report (1966) and other statistical studies of the determinants of pupil achievement show that a large fraction of variation in performance levels is accounted for by out-of-school variables, such as the pupils' socioeconomic status and home environment. Another large fraction is attributable to a so-called "peer group" effect; that is, it depends on characteristics of a pupil's classmates rather than on what takes place in the school. Of the fraction of the variation that *is* explained by school variables, only part can be attributed to teachers. Some portion must also be assigned to differences in resource availability at the classroom and school level and differences among schools in the quality of their management and support. Thus, the problem is to separate out the teacher effect from all the others.

To illustrate the implications for the design of an accountability system, consider the problem of comparing teachers who teach very different groups of children. For simplicity, suppose that there are two groups of pupils in a school system, each internally homogeneous, which we may call "middle-class white" and "poor minority." Assume that all non-teacher inputs associated with the schools are identical for the two groups. Then, based on general experience, we would probably expect the whole distribution of results to be higher for the former group than for the latter. In measuring gain in reading performance, we might well find, for example, that even the poorest teacher of middle-class white children obtains higher average gains in her class than the majority of teachers of poor minority children. Moreover, the ranges over which results vary in the two groups might be unequal.

If we have reason to believe that the teachers associated with the poor minority children are about as good, on the average, as those associated with the middle-class white children—that is, if they are drawn from the same manpower pool and assigned to schools and classrooms without bias—then it is apparent that both the difference in average performance of the two groups of pupils and the difference in the range of performance must be taken into account in assessing each teacher's contribution. A teacher whose class registers gains, say, in the upper 10 per cent of all poor minority classes should be considered as effective as one whose middle-class white group scores in the upper 10 per cent for that category, even though the absolute performance gain in the latter case will probably be much greater.

This illustrates that accountability measures are relative in two senses. First, they are relative in that each teacher's contribution is evaluated by comparing it with the contributions made by other teachers in similar circumstances. In a large city or state school system, it can safely be assumed that the range of teacher capabilities covers the spectrum from poor to excellent. Therefore, the range of observed outcomes, after differences in circumstances have been allowed for, is likely to

be representative of the range over which teacher quality can be expected to influence results, given the existing institutional framework. It may be objected that the range of outcomes presently observed understates the potential range of accomplishment because present classroom methods, curricula, teacher training programs, etc., are not optimal. This may be true and important, but it is not relevant in establishing teacher accountability because the authority to change those aspects of the system does not rest with the teacher.

Second, accountability measures are relative in that pupil characteristics and other nonteacher influences on pupil performance must be taken fully into account in measuring each teacher's contribution. Operationally, this means that statistical analyses will have to be conducted of the effects of such variables as ethnicity, socio-economic status, and prior educational experience on a pupil's progress in a given classroom. Also, the effects of classroom or school variables other than teacher capabilities will have to be taken into account. Performance levels of the pupils assigned to different teachers can be compared only after measured performance has been adjusted for all of these variables. The statistical model for computing these adjustments is, therefore, the most important element in the accountability measurement system.

*School Administrators.* Parallel reasoning suggests that school administrators can be held accountable for relative levels of pupil performance in their schools to the extent that the outcomes are not attributable to pupil, teacher, or classroom characteristics or to school variables that they cannot control. The question is, having adjusted for differences in pupil and teacher inputs and having taken account of other characteristics of the schools, are there unexplained differences among schools that can be attributed to differences in the quality of school leadership and administration? Just as for teachers, accountability measures for school administrators are measures of relative pupil performance in a school after adjusting the data for differences in variables outside the administrators' control.

Consideration of the accountability problem at the school level draws attention to one difficulty with the concept of accountability measurement that may also, in some cases, be present at the classroom level. The difficulty is that although we would like to establish accountability for individual professionals, when two or more persons work together to perform an educational task there is no statistical way of separating their effects. This is easy to see at the school level. If a principal and two assistant principals administer a school, we may be able to evaluate their relative proficiency as a team, but since it is not likely that their respective administrative tasks would relate to different pupil performance measures there is no way of judging their individual contributions by analyzing educational outcomes. Similarly, if a classroom teacher works with a teaching assistant, there is no way, strictly speaking, to separate the contributions of the two. It is conventional in these situations to say that the senior person, who has supervisory authority, bears the responsibility for results. However, while this is administratively and perhaps even legally valid, it provides no solution to the problem of assessing the effort and skills of individuals. Therefore, there are definite limits, which must be kept in mind, to the capacity of a statistically based accountability system to aid in assessing individual proficiency.

*District Administrators.* Although the same approach applies, in principle, to comparisons among districts (or decentralized components of larger districts), there are problems that may limit its usefulness in establishing accountability at the district level. One, of course, is the problem that has just been alluded to. Even if it were possible to establish the existence of overall district effects, it would be impossible to isolate the contributions of the local district board, the district superintendent, and other members of the district staff. A second problem is that comparisons among districts can easily fail to take account of intangible community characteristics that may affect school performance. For example, such factors as community cohesion, political attitudes, and the existence of racial or other intergroup tensions could strongly influence the whole tone of education. It would be very difficult to separate effects of these factors from effects of direct, district-related variables in trying to assess overall district performance. Third, the concept of responsibility at the district level needs clarifying. In comparing schools, for example, it seems reasonable to adjust for differences in teacher characteristics on the grounds that school administrators should be evaluated according to how well they do, given the personnel assigned to them. However, at the district level, personnel selection itself is one of the functions for which administrators must be held accountable, as are resource allocation, program design, choice of curriculum, and other factors that appear as "givens" to the schools. In other words, in assessing comparative district performance, very little about districts can properly be considered as externally determined except, perhaps, the total level of available resources. The appropriate policy, then, seems to be to include district identity as a variable in comparing schools and teachers so that net district effects, if any, will be taken into account. Districts themselves should be compared on a different basis, allowing only for differences in pupil characteristics, community variables, and overall constraints that are truly outside district control.

## A PROPOSED METHODOLOGY

The basic analytical problem in accountability measurement is to develop a technique for estimating the contributions to pupil performance of individual agents in the educational process. A statistical method that may be suitable for that purpose is described here. The basic technique is multiple regression analysis of the relationship between pupil performance and an array of pupil, teacher, and school characteristics. However, the proposed method calls for two or three separate stages of analysis. The strategy is first to estimate the amount of performance variation that exists among classrooms after pupil characteristics have been taken into account; then, in subsequent stages, to attempt to attribute the interclassroom differences to teachers, other classroom variables, and school characteristics. This methodology applies both to large school districts, within which it is suitable for estimating the relative effectiveness of individual teachers and schools in advancing pupil performance, and to state school systems, where it can be used, in addition, to obtain estimates of the relative effectiveness of districts. However, as noted above, there are problems that may limit its utility at the interdistrict level.

**Pupil Performance Data**   Since we are interested in estimating the contributions of individual teachers and schools, it is appropriate to use a "value-added" concept of output. That is, the appropriate pupil performance magnitudes to associate with a particular teacher are the *gains* in performance made by pupils while in her class. Ideally, the output data would be generated by a program of annual (or more frequent) performance measurement, which would automatically provide before and after measures for pupils at each grade level.

It is assumed that a number of dimensions of pupil performance will be measured, some by standardized tests and some by other indicators or proxy variables. Specific measurement instruments to be used and dimensions of performance to be measured would have to be determined by individual school sytems in accordance with their educational objectives. No attempt will be made here to specify what items should be included. The methodology is intended to apply to any dimension of performance that can be quantified at least on an ordinal scale. Therefore, within a very broad range, it is not affected by the choice of output measures by a potential user.

**Data on Pupils, Teachers, Classrooms, and Schools**   To conform with the model to be described below, the variables entering into the analysis are classified according to the following taxonomy:

1. Individual pupil characterisics (ethnicity; socioeconomic status; home, family, and neighborhood characteristics; age; prior performance, etc.).
2. Teacher and classroom characteristics.
   a. Group characteristics of the pupils (ethnic and socioeconomic composition, distribution of prior performance levels, etc., within the classroom).
   b. Teacher characteristics (age, training, experience, ability and personality measures if available, ethnic and socioeconomic background, etc.).
   c. Other classroom characteristics (measures of resource availability: class size, amount of instructional support, amount of materials, condition of physical facilities, etc.).
3. School characteristics.
   a. Group characteristics of the pupils (same as 2a, but based on the pupil population of the whole school).
   b. Staff characteristics (averages of characteristics in 2b for the school as a whole, turnover and transfer rates; characteristics of administrators—same as 2b).
   c. Other school characteristics (measures of resource availability: age and condition of building, availability of facilities, amount of administrative and support staff, etc.).

No attempt will be made to specify precisely what items should be collected under each of the above headings. Determination of the actual set of variables to be used in a school system would have to follow preliminary experimentation, examination of existing data, and an investigation of the feasibility, difficulty, and cost of obtaining various kinds of information.

**Steps in the Analysis** The first step is to determine how different pupil performance in each classroom at a given grade level is from mean performance in all classrooms, *after* differences in individual pupil characteristics have been allowed for. The procedure consists of performing a multiple regression analysis with gain in pupil performance as the dependent variable. The independent variables would include (a) the individual pupil characteristics (category 1 of the taxonomy), and (b) a set of "dummy" variables, or identifiers, one for each classroom in the sample. The latter would permit direct estimation of the degree to which pupil performance in each classroom differs from pupil performance in the average classroom. Thus, the product of the first stage of the analysis would be a set of estimates of individual classroom effects, each of which represents the combined effect on pupil performance in a classroom of all the classroom and school variables included in categories 2 and 3 of the taxonomy. At the same time, the procedure would automatically provide measures of the accuracy with which each classroom effect has been estimated. Therefore, it would be possible to say whether average performance gains in a particular classroom are significantly higher or lower than would be expected in a "typical" classroom or not significantly different from the mean.

Heuristically, this procedure compares performance gains by pupils in a classroom with gains that comparable pupils would be likely to achieve in a hypothetical "average" classroom of the system. This can be thought of as comparison of class performance gains against a norm, except that there is, in effect, a particular norm for each classroom based on its unique set of pupil characteristics. It may also be feasible to carry out the same analysis for specific subgroups of pupils in each class so as to determine, for example, whether there are different classroom effects for children from different ethnic or socioeconomic groups.

*Estimation of Teacher Contributions.* The second stage of the analysis has two purposes: (1) to separate the effects of the teacher from effects of nonteacher factors that vary among classrooms; and (2) to determine the extent to which pupil performance can be related to specific, measurable teacher attributes. Again, the method to be used is regression analysis, but in this case with a sample of classroom observations rather than individual pupil observations. The dependent variable is now the classroom effect estimated in stage one. The independent variables are the teacher-classroom characteristics and "dummy" variables distinguishing the individual schools.

Two kinds of information can be obtained from the resulting equations. First, it is possible to find out what fraction of the variation in performance gains among classrooms is accounted for by nonteacher characteristics, including group characteristics of the pupils and measures of resource availability in the classroom. The remaining interclassroom differences provide upper-bound estimates of the effects that can be attributed to teachers. If there is sufficient confidence that the important nonteacher variables have been taken into account, then these estimates provide the best teacher accountability measures. They encompass the effects of both measured and unmeasured teacher characteristics on teacher performance. However, there is some danger that such measures also include effects of group and classroom characteristics that were inadvertently neglected in the analysis and that are not properly attributable to teachers. This problem is referred to again below.

Second, we can find out the extent to

which differences among classrooms are explained by measured teacher characteristics. Ideally, of course, we would like to be able to attribute the whole "teacher portion" of performance variation to specific teacher attributes and, having done so, we would be much more confident about our overall estimates of teacher effectiveness. But experience to date with achievement determinant studies has shown that the more readily available teacher characteristics—age, training, experience, and the like—account for only a small fraction of the observed variance. It has been shown that more of the variation can be accounted for when a measure of teacher verbal ability is included. Still more, presumably, could be accounted for if a greater variety of teacher ability and personality measurements were available. At present, however, knowledge of what teacher characteristics influence pupil performance is incomplete and satisfactory instruments exist for measuring only a limited range of teacher-related variables. This means that with an accountability information system based on current knowledge, the excluded teacher characteristics could be at least as important as those included in determining teacher effectiveness. For the time being, then, the interclassroom variation in results that remains after nonteacher effects have been allowed for probably provides the most useful accountability measures, though the danger of bias due to failure to include all relevant nonteacher characteristics must be recognized.

The principal use of these estimates would be in assessing the relative effectiveness of individual teachers in contributing to gains in pupil performance. More precisely, it would be possible to determine whether each teacher's estimated contribution is significantly greater or significantly smaller than that of the average teacher. At least initially, until there is strong confirmation of the validity of the procedure, a rather stringent significance criterion should be used in making these judgments and no attempt should be made to use the results to develop finer gradations of teacher proficiency.

The analysis will also make it possible to determine the extent to which measured teacher characteristics are significantly correlated with teacher effectiveness. Potentially, such information could have important policy implications and impacts on school management, resource allocation, and personnel practices. A number of these potential applications are noted at the end of the paper.

*Estimation of Contributions by School Administrators.* The same analytical techniques can be used in estimating the relative effectiveness of different schools in promoting pupil performance. Conceptually, a school accountability index should measure the difference between pupil performance in an individual school and average pupil performance in all schools after all pupil, teacher, and classroom variables have been accounted for. Such measures can be obtained directly if school dummy variables are included in the regression equation, as described earlier. Of course, the results measure *total* school effects, without distinguishing among effects due to school administration, effects of physical attributes of the school, and effects of characteristics of the pupil population. It may be feasible to perform a third-stage analysis in which the results are systematically adjusted for differences in the latter two categories of variables, leaving residual effects that can be attributed to the school administrators. These would constitute the accountability measures to be used in assessing the effectiveness of the principal and his staff. The results may have policy implications with respect to differential allocation of funds or resources among the different schools and, of course, implications with respect to personnel. Also, as would be done for teachers, an attempt could be made to relate measured characteristics of the school administrators to the estimated school effects. By so doing, it might be possible to learn whether administrator training and experience and other attributes are reflected in measured school output. Even negative results could provide important guidance to research on administrator selection and assignment.

*Comparisons Among Districts.* For reasons that have already been stated, it would probably be desirable to treat comparisons among districts separately from comparisons among classrooms and schools. This could be done by means of yet another regression analysis, with individual pupil performance gain as the dependent variable and with independent variables consisting of pupil and community characteristics, measures of resource availability, and a dummy variable or identifier for each district being compared. The purpose would be to determine whether there are significant differences in results among districts once the other factors have been allowed for. If there are, the findings could be interpreted as reflections of differences in the quality of district policy making and management. But as pointed out earlier, there would be uncertainty as to the causes of either shortcomings or superior performance. Nevertheless, the results could have some important, policy-related uses, as will be noted shortly.

## THE NEED FOR EXPERIMENTAL VERIFICATION OF THE APPROACH

The methodology described here carries no guarantee. Its success in relating outcomes to sources may depend both on features of the school systems to which it is applied and on the adequacy of the statistical models in mirroring the underlying (and unknown) input-output relationships in education. The validity and usefulness of the results must be determined empirically from field testing in actual school systems. Experimental verification, possibly requiring several cycles of refinement and testing, must precede implementation of a "working" accountability system.

**Potential Problems** Three kinds of technical problems can threaten the validity of the system: intercorrelation, omission of variables, and structural limitations of the models. None of these can be discussed in detail without mathematics. However, a brief explanation of each is offered so that the outlook for the proposed approach can be realistically assessed.

*Intercorrelation.* This is a problem that may arise where there are processes in a school system that create associations (correlations) between supposedly independent variables in the model. An important example is the process—said to exist in many systems—whereby more experienced, better trained, or simply "better" teachers tend to be assigned or transferred to schools with higher socioeconomic status (SES) pupils. Where this occurs, pupil SES will be positively correlated with those teacher characteristics. On the average, high SES children would be taught by one kind of teacher, low SES children by another. This would make it difficult to say whether the higher performance gains likely to be observed for high SES pupils are due to their more advantaged backgrounds or to the superior characteristics of their instructors. There would be ambiguity as to the magnitude of the teacher contribution and a corresponding reduction in the reliability of estimates of individual teacher effectiveness. Thus, the quality of accountability information would be impaired.

This problem can take many forms. There may be strong correlations between characteristics of pupils and characteristics of school staffs, between teacher characteristics and nonteacher attributes of the schools, between classroom-level and district-level variables, and so on. The general effect is the same in each instance: ambiguity resulting in diminished ability to attribute results to sources.

There are several things that can be done to mitigate the effects of intercorrelation. One is to stratify the data. For example, if teacher characteristics were linked to pupil SES, it would be possible to stratify the classrooms by pupil SES and to perform separate analyses for each stratum. This would eliminate some of the ambiguity *within* strata. On the other hand, comparisons of teachers *across* strata would be precluded. Another possible solution would be to take account of interdependence explicitly in the statistical models. Some attempts along this line have been made in studies of determinants of school performance. However, this solution is likely to raise a whole new array of technical problems as well as questions about the feasibility of routine use of methodology within school systems.

*The Problem of Omitted Variables.* The validity and fairness of the proposed approach would depend very strongly on inclusion of all major relevant variables that could plausibly be cited by teachers or administrators to "explain" lower-than-average estimated contributions. This means that all variables would have to be included that (a) have significant, independent effects on performance and (b) are likely to be nonuniformly distributed among classrooms and schools.

It will never be possible to demonstrate in a positive sense that all relevant variables have been included. Many intangible, difficult-to-measure variables, such as pupil attitudes, morale, "classroom climate," etc., can always be suggested. What can be done is to determine as well as possible that none of the additional suggested variables is systematically related to the estimated teacher and school contributions. In an experimental setting, administrators could be interviewed for the purpose of identifying alleged special circumstances, and tests could be carried out to see whether they are systematically related to performance differences.

*Structural Limitations of the Models.* The models described here may be too simple to take account of some of the important relationships among school inputs and outputs. One such shortcoming has already been noted: The models do not allow for possible interdependencies among the various pupil and school characteristics. Another, which may prove to be more troubling, is that interactions among the various output or performance variables have also not been taken into account.

Researchers have pointed to two distinct kinds of relationships. First, there may be trade-offs between performance areas. A teacher or school may do well in one area partly at the expense of another by allocating resources or time disproportionately between the two. Second, there may be complementary relationships. Increased performance in one area (reading, for example) may contribute directly to increased performance in others (social studies or mathematics). Therefore, treatment of one dimension of output at a time, without taking the interactions into account, could produce misleading results.

Econometricians have developed "simultaneous" models, consisting of whole sets of equations, specifically to take account of complex, multiple relationships among variables. Some attempts have been made to apply these models to studies of determinants of educational outcomes. It may prove necessary or desirable to use them in an accountability measurement system, despite the complexity they would add, to eliminate biases inherent in simpler models.

**Validity** Another important reason for thoroughly testing the accountability measurement system is that its validity needs to be assessed. Some of the procedures mentioned above contribute to this end, but more general demonstration would also be desirable. Two procedures that may be feasible in an experimental situation are as follows:

*Replication.* A strong test of whether the method really gets at differences in effectiveness instead of differences in circumstances would be to apply it to the same teachers and schools during two or more years. Consistency in results from year to year would strongly support the methodology. Lack of consistency would show that major influences on performance remained unmeasured or neglected. Certainly, if the results were to be used in any way in connection with personnel assignment, reward, or promotion, the use of several years' estimates would be an important guarantee of both consistency and fairness.

*An External Test of Validity.* The most direct way to test the validity of the statistical approach is to compare the results with alternative measures of teacher and school effectiveness. The only measures that are likely to be obtainable are subjective assessments by informed and interested parties. Though such evaluations have many shortcomings, it could be valuable in an experimental situation to see how well they agreed with the statistical results. Two important questions that would have to be answered in making such a comparison are: (1) Who are the appropriate raters—peers, administrators, parents, or even pupils? and (2) What evaluation instruments could be used to assure that subjective assessments apply to the same dimensions of performance as were taken into account in the statistical analysis? It may not be possible to provide satisfactory answers. Nevertheless, the feasibility of a comparison with direct assessments should be considered in connection with any effort to test the proposed accountability measurement system.

## POTENTIAL USES OF ACCOUNTABILITY MEASURES

Space does not permit a full review of the potential uses of an accountability measurement system. However, an idea of the range of applications and their utility can be conveyed by listing some of the main possibilities.

**Identification of Effective Schools** The most rudimentary use of the proposed accountability measures is as an identification device. Once relative school effectiveness is known, a variety of actions can follow, even if there is ambiguity about causes. As examples, less formal evaluation efforts can be more precisely targeted once school effectiveness with different kinds of children is known and campaigns can be initiated to discover, disseminate, and emulate good practices of high-performing schools.

**Personnel Assignment and Selection** Accountability measures may help to improve both staff utilization and selection of new personnel. Personnel utilization could be improved by using information on teacher effectiveness in different spheres and with different types of students for guidance in staff assignment. Selection and recruitment could be aided by using information from the models as a guide to performance-related characteristics of applicants and as a basis for revising selection procedures and criteria.

**Personnel Incentives and Compensation** An accountability measurement system can be used to establish a connection between personnel compensation and performance. One use would be in providing evidence to support inclusion of more relevant variables in pay scales than the universally used and widely criticized training and experience factors. Another possibility would be to use accountability measures as inputs in operating incentive pay or promotion systems. The latter, of course, is a controversial proposal, long resisted by professional organizations. Nevertheless, putting aside other arguments pro and con, the availability of objective measures of individual contributions would eliminate a major objection to economic incentives and help to make the idea more acceptable to all concerned.

**Improved Resource Allocation**  An accountability measurement system could also contribute to other aspects of resource allocation in school systems. Analytical results from the models could be of value, for example, in setting policies on class size, supporting services, and similar resource variables. More directly, school accountability measures could provide guidance to district administrators in allocating resources differentially among schools according to educational need. Similarly, state-level results could be used in determining appropriate allocations of state aid funds to districts.

**Program Evaluation and Research**  Models developed for accountability could prove to be valuable tools for program evaluation and research. They could be readily adapted for comparing alternative ongoing programs simply by including "program" as one of the classroom variables. Also, "norms" provided by the models for specific types of pupils could be used as reference standards in evaluating experimental programs. This would be preferable, in some cases, to using experimental control groups. Viewed as research tools, the models could help to shed light on one of the most basic, policy-related problems in education, the relationship between school inputs and educational output. The process of developing the models could itself be very instructive. The results could add substantially to our knowledge of how teachers and schools make a difference to their pupils.

In sum, there are many potential uses of the proposed measures and models, some going well beyond what is generally understood by "accountability." If the development of a system is undertaken and carried through to completion, the by-products alone may well prove to be worth the effort.

# 6. The Confessions of a Frustrated Evaluator
## JOSEPH S. RENZULLI

The educational evaluator is called upon to play many roles. Due to the influence of many forces, a number of which are beyond his control, the evaluator is frequently caught between opposing sides in a controversy. Among the conflicts enumerated by Renzulli are (1) the evaluator's status as both an employee and an independent agent relative to the project, (2) the seemingly incompatible philosophies of the behavioral objectives approach and the humanistic education movement, (3) the desirability of research rigor as contrasted with the practical objectives of evaluation, and (4) the efficiency but frequent lack of relevance of standardized tests as evaluative tools. These and many other factors make the evaluator's task a difficult and, as Renzulli notes, a frustrating one.

Anyone planning to deal with a theoretical or practical problem in educational evaluation these days cannot help but be overwhelmed by the massive and often conflicting body of literature that has grown up around this topic. With the possible exception of . . . segregation, sex education, and student power it is difficult to find an educational issue that has generated more rhetoric and greater controversy than the current concern for *evaluation* and the related issue of *accountability*.

As educators with dollar signs in their eyes busily scrambled to scoop up their fair share of the federal windfall that began with the enactment of the National Defense Education Act (NDEA), only the very foolish were not haunted by the inescapable realization that sooner or later they would be held accountable for the brave but often vague promises and grandiose schemes that were unblushingly written into thousands of proposals by well-intentioned but often starry-eyed ed-

ucators who gave little or no serious attention to the problems of evaluation. Thus, the schemes that promised to provide solutions to schoolmen's prayers turned out, in most cases, to have little or no significant impact on the education system in general; and although the trimmings in today's schools may be a little fancier, the main course that is served to most youngsters is not very different from the educational menu of two or three decades ago. The main question is, of course, why is this so? Why in the face of unprecedented financial support for educational programs and projects have we been unable to demonstrate in any definitive fashion the effectiveness of proposed innovations in the system? The challenge of answering this question must be laid squarely at the feet of the educational evaluator. Although great strides have been made in the science of evaluation in recent years, our inability to master certain basic problems still prevents us from bringing about the often discussed but still illusive transformation of the schools.

The early chaos and misapplication of many federally financed programs have undoubtedly contributed to our height-

Reprinted with permission of the publisher and Joseph S. Renzulli from *Measurement and Evaluation in Guidance*, **5** (1972), pp. 298–305.

ened concern for evaluation and account-ability, and this concern has given rise to a new methodology or second generation of educational evaluation. Unlike the first generation that seemed to be hung up on psychometrics and problems related to the measurement of individual differences, the second generation is concerned with system or program evaluation, and its main purpose is simply to find out how specific modifications in system inputs will bring about specific changes in system outputs. Although this methodology has focused so far mainly on special projects and externally financed programs, it does not take a great deal of imagination to envision the day when this rapidly expanding technology is refined to the point where it can be brought to bear on virtually every activity that parades under the banner of education.

But before we can reach the seemingly impossible dream of isolating cause-effect relationships in education, certain basic and essentially unresolved problems in evaluation must be mastered. This article attempts to provide a structural overview of some of the major problems and issues that continue to plague educational program evaluation. By isolating and pointing out the main dimensions of these problems, we hope to provide some direction for future efforts and to bring the problems into sharper focus so that the second generation of evaluators will be better able to resolve them.

## POLITICS OF EDUCATIONAL EVALUATION

The first problem is concerned with the relationship that exists between the evaluator and the program being evaluated —that is, the politics of educational evaluation. Educational enterprises, and especially those that involve large amounts of funds from external sources, are managed by people and institutions that stand to gain certain benefits if their projects prove successful.

Although the main criteria for the suc-cess of any educational program should be in terms of benefits realized by students, we cannot deny that institutions stand to gain such benefits as continued funding and prominence from a successful program, and that the persons operating these programs stand to gain job security, prestige, and power in the form of decision-making authority. With these stakes consciously or unconsciously in mind, the administrators of programs and projects seek personnel who are euphemistically dubbed "independent external evaluators." In most cases the project managers have complete freedom in selecting the evaluator, and it is from their budget that the costs of evaluation are paid.

Notwithstanding the fact that project administrators are genuinely interested in finding ways in which their programs can be improved, we would be deluding ourselves if we believed that they are not primarily interested in getting a good overall evaluation, or at least avoiding an evaluation that might conclude with such statements as: "This project is a complete waste of time and money, and shows no noticeable benefits for the students" or "The project director is incompetent and should be fired immediately." Please remember that this is the same project director that hired the evaluator, squired him through several three-martini lunches, and suggested that he publish the results of his evaluation in a professional journal.

If project administrators' motives, so far as evaluation is concerned, appear to be somewhat less than virtuous, we should keep in mind that they have been forced into a situation over which they have had little control. In most cases, program evaluation is mandated by higher-level administration or funding agencies, and as such is usually considered a necessary evil by project administrators and staff members who are asked to avail themselves of the evaluator's instruments of oppression so that their competence can be judged.

A few years ago I was involved in the evaluation of a large compensatory education program for inner-city youngsters. On one occasion a large group of teachers and administrators were called together for a briefing on evaluation and the distribution of evaluative materials. As the group began to leave the auditorium, a quiet chant began to reverberate throughout the room—"Two, four, six, eight—we don't wanna evaluate!" That was among some of the kinder things that were said throughout the course of this particular evaluation.

It is difficult to understand how the need for evaluation is almost universally accepted at the cognitive level, and yet the efforts of the evaluator are likely to be greeted with all the warmth and understanding of a husband who finds his wife in bed with his best friend. Where have we gone wrong? Must practitioners feel threatened by evaluators and ambivalent about taking part in an evaluation? Must the role of the evaluator bring him into conflict with the role of the practitioner? If the answers to these questions are anything less than a resounding "No," what can we do to gain the understanding and support of persons on whom we must eventually pass judgment? A closer look at the evaluator may help us isolate a few more problems.

First, the evaluator usually stands to make a financial gain from his involvement with a funded project. While there is nothing inherently evil about turning a reasonable profit from one's labors, there are a few inherent subtleties that all of us who have played the evaluation game are aware of. If we come up with a generally favorable evaluation we are likely to be rehired, and under these circumstances it is difficult to dismiss from our minds the great temptation on the part of the evaluator to report some needed improvement in minor areas while at the same time pointing out the general value and effectiveness of the bulk of a program.

A second problem is somewhat less embarrassing to talk about; however, it certainly must be considered as a source of evaluative bias. Good evaluation theory

tells us that the evaluator should be involved in a project from the outset. He should work closely with the administrators and staff from the proposal-writing stage to the preparation of the final report. He is a full-fledged member of the team and, as such, he is quite likely to develop both a close personal relationship with project personnel and a strong emotional tie with the project itself. He starts to talk about *our* students, and *our* control group, and how much money we have left in *our* budget. Under these circumstances, we must raise the question: Is the independent external evaluator sufficiently detached from the project to take an objective look at it, or is he likely to approach evaluation with some of the same positive biases as a person who sets out to evaluate his own program?

We have somewhat of a dilemma here. If we were able to create a completely independent cadre of external evaluators —political untouchables with all the consumer concerns of a group like Nader's Raiders, would we not also widen the gap between the evaluator and the people whose honesty, trust, and cooperation are needed to mount an effective evaluation? In one situation where this kind of independence existed, teachers prepared students for a post-test by teaching lessons directly from the test booklet.

As long as factors such as funding, prestige, and power are involved, the political relationship between the evaluator and those being evaluated will not be an easy problem to solve.

## ONE IRRESISTIBLE FORCE MEETS ANOTHER

Two irresistible forces in education seem hell-bent on a collision course, and I am afraid that our friend the evaluator is going to be caught squarely at the point of impact. The first irresistible force is the *behavioral objectives movement*. Although there is some growing controversy about the role of behavioral objectives in curriculum planning and evaluation, one cannot deny the value that it has had in helping to build evaluation and accountability models and to advance the science of education beyond the vagueness and lack of specificity that seems to have made us the stepchild of the sciences. Further, some of the new experiments in education such as performance contracting and the voucher plan, and systems analysis approaches such as the planning, programming, and budgeting systems (PPBS) could not have been implemented had we not been able to specify in precise behavioral terms the objectives toward which our efforts are directed. Some educators, however, may be carrying their concern for behavioral objectives a bit too far. Nevertheless, this movement has been nothing less than a blessing to the evaluator who must know what is *supposed* to happen before he can begin figuring out how to measure it.

There is still another irresistible force growing in education today—a renewed concern for the total development of the individual as a human being, dealing with such difficult-to-measure objectives as self-actualization, Consciousness III, and sociability. This force is somewhat more obscure than the behavioral objectives movement, but is nevertheless growing in force and magnitude.

As youngsters on college campuses across the country began to revolt against curricular irrelevance and lack of concern for the affective domain, educators from primary grades through graduate school began to give serious attention to the benefits that might be realized from a much more informal and humanistic education—one that replaces punch-card relationships with primary-group experiences, classroom activities and didacticism with experiences in the real world, and punitive testing and grading practices with concerns that focus on individual satisfaction. Supporters of this humanistic point of view remind us that a large proportion of man's behavioral repertoire is *not* acquired in formal learning situations, and

that although the school can claim credit for giving youngsters the three R's and other skills and information, they have done so at the expense of other equally important objectives. Another argument is that this lack of humanistic concern for individuals has made schools essentially oppressive places and learning essentially coercive. Education, the humanists say, has degenerated to a process of conformity-oriented hurdle-jumping, and they point accusingly [at] the behavioral objectivists for making the process even more mechanistic.

Those with a humanistic orientation are also concerned with the objectives of education, but they do not agree with the behaviorally-oriented about the precision with which the objectives can be measured. How can we determine in an objective and scientific manner, argue the behaviorists, when an educational experience has contributed to the development of a fully functioning, self-actualized, socially conscientious human being?

Herein lies the problem for the evaluator. Some truly relevant experiments are taking place in education today—experiments such as open classrooms modeled after the British primary system, alternate learning centers that do not have a formal curriculum, and experiences in group dynamics that are designed to improve race relations and to narrow the generation gap. Recently I read a very exciting Title III proposal designed to advance innovation and creativity in education. The guidelines for evaluating this proposal had a strong behavioral-objectives orientation, and, using these criteria, I was forced to give the evaluation design of this particular project a very low rating. Although objective tests were written into the evaluation design of the proposal, what was clearly written *between* the lines was a ritualistic compliance with state department of education regulations, a compliance that I believe would yield little useful information about the true objectives of the proposed program. Further, if this proposal should be funded, determining its effectiveness will be nothing less than an evaluator's nightmare.

I wish that I could offer some concrete suggestions for softening the impact of the collision between the two forces. The usual impassioned plea for research into the measurement of affective processes can only be reiterated, but perhaps we should also make a plea to funding agencies that will result in some relaxation of the rigid behavioral-objectives model that governs so much of the thinking so far as evaluation is concerned.

## WHAT IS WAGGING WHAT?

Another major problem with which the front-line evaluator is concerned is the distinction between *evaluation* and *research*. How much of the rigor and control that one finds in traditional research design is necessary in order to carry out a "respectable" evaluation? Like the researcher, the evaluator does not want to be accused of employing an inappropriate or sloppy design, and since many second-generation evaluators have entered this field with a strong research background, they are constantly haunted by the fear that they will lose the respect of their more rigorous colleagues.

Unfortunately, the theorists and model builders in evaluation have shown us little consistent direction in this regard. For example:

One of the more obvious blots on the otherwise nearly-clean escutcheon of the educational research community stems from its ill-fated involvement with evaluation. In responding particularly to Federal mandates for better evidence of program success, educational practitioners have sought the assistance of educational researchers in designing and carrying out evaluative studies. The resulting effort has been a failure so conspicuous that I regard it as unnecessary to attempt to document it. That failure, I contend, has, as one of its chief (but not only) roots, the mistaken

assumption that the research paradigm is appropriate to evaluative inquiry. Nothing could be further from the truth. The unfortunate marriage produced by this error in judgment has left irremedial scars on both parties (Guba, 1969, p. 4).

Contrast this statement with the following comments in a recent issue of the *Urban Review* (1969) which was devoted solely to program evaluation:

Both [research and evaluation] should be serving the same function of supplying information to planners and policy makers about what does and does not work . . . but accurate information can stem only from rigorous experimental design and data collection techniques, whether in research or evaluation (Hawkridge and Chalupsky, 1969, p. 8).

There are no formal differences between "basic" and "applied" research or between "research as such" and "evaluation research." Research designs, statistical techniques, or data collection methods are the same whether applied to the study of the most basic principles of human behavior or to the most prosaic of social action programs (Rossi, 1969, p. 17).

From a technological viewpoint evaluation is a fundamental research activity. It can be conducted with as much precision as any other form of research, though it presents certain specialized problems such as controlling for the amount of attention given to the experimental group or that of executing a scientific design under naturalistic conditions (Mann, 1969, p. 12).

These last three statements are in sharp contrast to the first by Guba, and his divergence of opinion raises some significant problems for the evaluator. Should the evaluator insist on research that is rigorous in helping people to evaluate educational programs or should he evaluate the program in its naturalistic setting? Is the tail not wagging the dog when we change a program so that it will conform with an experimental design?

Some prominent researchers (Mackie

and Christensen, 1967; Ottinger, 1969) have told us that "a very small percentage of findings from leading research studies are useful, in any direct sense, for the improvement of training and educational practice" (Mackie and Christensen, 1967, p. 5) because conditions employed by the research bear no determinable relationship to conditions outside the research setting. Commenting in a similar fashion in a recent issue of the *Review of Educational Research*, Cohen has expressed the opinion that:

> Experiments with decentralization, tuition vouchers, doubling per-pupil expenditures, and radical changes in secondary education have two salient attributes in common: to have meaning they would have to be carried out in existing schools, and few schools would be likely to oblige (Cohen, 1970, p. 233).

Thus we are faced with another dilemma. If our evaluations do not respect some of the mandates of good educational research, then they are unlikely to hold any water and the evaluator may be accused of not *really* demonstrating the effectiveness of the program under consideration. This is especially true when the evaluator depends heavily on soft data such as interviews and observations, data that usually cannot be treated with sophisticated statistical techniques as easily as hard data. Although the soft-nosed evaluator does not completely negate the value of statistics, he argues with great vehemence that the sights, sounds, and smells of the real classroom are easily hidden by statistics. Further, if the evaluator imposes strict controls over the program he is evaluating, he may be accused of ignoring the real world in favor of a design that has scientific respectability. Not only may the tail be wagging the dog in this case, but we must also question the impact that three-decimal research has had in bringing about major changes in education to decide whether or not the evaluator with a research bent wants to play the same game. Change is often

governed by the heart as well as the head and, whether we like it or not, I think that much of the impact of a book like *Crisis in the Classroom* is the result of its heart-rending anecdotes rather than tables of means, standard deviations, and correlation coefficients.

## WHEN IN DOUBT— GIVE ANOTHER TEST

The last problem discussed here concerns the role of testing, and especially achievement testing, in the evaluative process. If we were fortunate enough to have at our disposal a series of standardized measures that accurately reflect the stated objectives of our program, the problem would be quickly solved. But because of the vast changes that are taking place in the curriculum these days this is seldom the case. Thus we are left with the choice of either using standardized tests that are inappropriate in varying degrees, or attempting to develop our own tests. The latter choice, however, presents us with another kind of problem. If we are going to build our own measuring instruments, we must also deal with the psychometric problems with which the first generation of educational evaluators were concerned. Without some assurances that our homegrown instruments possess reliability, validity, objectivity, and practicality, our results are likely to be viewed with suspicion. Building in these scientific requirements is of course within the realm of possibility; however, it is often a luxury that the evaluator of a relatively small project cannot afford.

The use of standardized tests in evaluation also poses another kind of problem. A growing body of research findings indicates a somewhat limited relationship between the typical achievement criteria for program success and the presumed adult consequences of education, such as better jobs and higher income. This nonrelationship is particularly apparent among black students. A study by Blau and Duncan

(1968) showed that once inherited status is controlled for, years of school completed is only moderately related to adult occupational status, and the relationship between education and occupation is much weaker for blacks than for whites.

It appears then that a word of caution is in order here for at least the evaluators of compensatory programs who use school achievement as a proxy for the long-range criteria of success in adult life. We might even raise the question of whether standardized achievement batteries have outlived their usefulness, a usefulness that a few brave souls in education have always questioned. With the trend moving away from grouping (one of the major uses of standardized achievement tests), the limited relationship between these tests and curricular experiences, and the dangers of self-fulfilling prophecies always hanging over our heads, perhaps the evaluator can take the lead in questioning the usefulness of those tests.

The first several decades of the twentieth century saw the emergence of a behavioristic orientation in education. Educational evaluation in particular was, depending upon one's philosophy, either tainted or enhanced by this development. Nevertheless, the movement laid the groundwork for a concern on the part of educators and evaluators for systematically stating and  evaluating expected outcomes. Not only should improved and more effective programs result from this increased concern, but valid evaluation should also be facilitated.

General

1. Broad objectives of education stated by national organizations.

2. Statements of aims and objectives by regional associations.

3. Statement of aims and objectives by state systems of education.

4. Statement of aims by local school systems.

5. Subject area aims and objectives.

6. Course aims and objectives.

7. Unit or block aims and objectives.

Specific

8. Daily lesson aims and objectives.

**Figure 1**
**Hierarchy of Educational Objectives**

Inasmuch as education takes place at a number of different levels and involves personnel and decision making at different echelons (Krathwohl and Payne, 1971), several levels of objectives need to be specified. One schema for examining multilevel objectives is summarized in Figure 1. It is based on a continuum that runs from general to specific. Degree of specificity is correlated with level of instruction: the lower the level, the higher the degree of specificity. The broad goals of education are at the top, the specific outcomes at the bottom.

Thanks to the impact of a book by

# Identifying and Specifying Relevant Educational Goals and Curriculum Objectives

part

Mager (1962), the behavioral approach to education has gained new impetus. Its relative advantages and disadvantages are discussed in several of the following articles. Many authors are now proselytizing for the gospel of objectives, judging by the rash of new books on educational objectives (Bernabei and Leles, 1970; Gronlund, 1970; Kapfer, 1971; Kibler, Barker, and Miles, 1970; McAshan, 1970; Popham and Baker, 1970). Strong arguments are also being made against the pure "behavioral" approach (Macdonald and Walfson, 1970). Whatever the ultimate result of the "objectives revolution," the fact that educators have stopped to look critically at what they are doing must be considered beneficial.

Statements of goals and objectives have many and valuable uses. They may be used to investigate priorities, as perceived by teachers and professors (Housedorff, 1965; Ohnmacht, 1965), or to investigate the congruence between the intent of a curriculum and actual outcomes (Charters, 1970). In a similar vein, Walker (1969) has described how statements of goals can be used in kind of a *post hoc* analysis of curricula.

An article by Henry Dyer sets the tone of Part 2. His perspective on both the technology of measurement and evaluation and the trials and tribulations of the whole educational enterprise helps us to reformulate the questions we should be asking about teaching and learning.

One of the most important points Ralph W. Tyler makes in the next article is that the process of specifying and working toward objectives allows one to discover additional objectives that were overlooked initially. In many instances, the subsequent objectives and effects are as important as the original ones. Tyler's criteria for selecting objectives make sense philosophically as well as pedagogically, although Kliebard (1970) has sounded a discordant note.

David R. Krathwohl, a co-author of the *Taxonomy of Educational Objectives* (TOEO), next presents an overview of this hierarchical noncontent classification of educational outcomes. In addition to the cognitive and affective domains, Krathwohl briefly describes Gagné's learning system. Preliminary attempts to order phenomena in the psychomotor domain have been made by Simpson (1966) and Harrow (1972).

A handy reference is presented by Metfessel, Michael, and Kirsner in the next article. The plea for a more "operational" taxonomy of educational objectives is at least partially heeded by these authors. By providing action words and verbs, they have approximated a behavioral translation of the *Taxonomy.*

The title of the article by the late Earl Kelley almost serves as its own introduction. After so many years we are truly beginning to realize the importance of attitudes, values, interests, and sentiments in the educational process. Their importance is due not only to their influence on the effectiveness of instruction, but also to their value as legitimate educational objectives in themselves.

As we have noted, the emphasis of objectives today is *behavioral.* Some of the advantages and many of the disadvantages of a wholesale subscription to this philosophy are highlighted by J. Myron Atkin. He considers such matters as the ease with which we can identify and behavioralize all relevant educational outcomes, the inhibitory effect on innovation of requiring behavioral statements of objectives, the possible lack of instructional responsiveness and flexibility, and the likelihood of overlooking unplanned but worthwhile outcomes.

In the final article, Thomas O. Maguire describes one of the few available empirical investigations of educational objectives. For some reason, this area has not received much attention from behavioral scientists. After presenting a brief history of curriculum evaluation, Maguire describes a cleverly designed and implemented study aimed at yielding information about how teachers value educational objectives and how they use this information in decision making.

## 7. The Discovery and Development of Educational Goals
### HENRY S. DYER

Statements of educational goals set the tone and direction of educational practice. From them, more clearly defined and specified objectives emerge or are derived. In the broadly based, almost philosophical article that follows, some reasons are presented for the lack of functionalism in traditional educational goals and the processes used to determine them. In addition, some of the potential and partially realized contributions of educational measurement and evaluation to the search for, and refinement of, educational goals are suggested. Approximations of the ideas suggested by Dyer relating to comprehensive listings of relevant educational objectives can be seen in the efforts of Popham and his colleagues in the Instructional Objectives Exchange at the U.C.L.A. Center for the Study of Evaluation, as well as in comprehensive sets of objectives developed in conjunction with National Assessment (see Article 42 by Merwin and Womer).

Professional philosophers in the last 30 or so years, with some notable exceptions, have backed away from rows over the goals of education and have stuck more or less consistently to analyzing the absurdities in all such forms of discourse. Before the philosophical silence set in, however, practically every major philosopher, from Confucius and Plato and Aristotle down to Whitehead and Russell and Dewey, had had a good deal to say about the aim of education and its functions in society. There has been an increasing volume of writing on the subject by eminent nonphilosophers

Reprinted and abridged with permission of the publisher and Henry S. Dyer from the *Proceedings of the 1966 Invitational Conference on Testing Problems* (Princeton, N.J.: Educational Testing Service, 1967), pp. 12–24. Copyright 1967 by Educational Testing Service. All rights reserved.

inside and outside the academic community.

One would think that the accumulation of so much high-level verbiage on the subject of goals over at least two and one-half millennia would have exhausted the subject if not the discussants. One would suppose that by now the question of educational goals would have been fairly well settled, and the problem of how to define them would have found some useful answers. But the question is still very much open. The problem of goals is today, more than ever, a top-priority, and largely unsolved, problem.

The trouble is that in spite of all the hard thinking and earnest talk about educational goals and how to define them, the goals produced have been essentially nonfunctional—and I mean even when they have come clothed in the so-called behavioral terms we so much admire. They have had little or no effect on the deals and deliberations that go on in faculties and school boards and boards of trustees and legislative chambers where the little and big decisions about education are being made. As you watch the educational enterprise going through its interminable routines, it is hard to avoid the impression that the whole affair is mostly a complicated ritual in which the vast majority of participants—pupils, teachers, administrators, policy makers— have never given a thought to the question *why,* in any fundamental sense, they are going through the motions they think of as education.

## REASONS FOR NONFUNCTIONAL GOALS

Why is it that the goals formulated in the past—even the recent past—have been largely nonfunctional? I think there are three principal reasons: too much reliance on the magic of words, too little public participation in formulating the goals, and too great a readiness to suppose that the goals are already given and require only to be achieved.

**Word Magic** In the 1947 report of the President's Commission on Higher Education there is the following paragraph:

> The first goal in education for democracy is the full, rounded, and continuing development of the person. The discovery, training, and utilization of individual talents is of fundamental importance in a free society. To liberate and perfect the intrinsic powers of every citizen is the central purpose of democracy, and its furtherance of individual self-realization is its greatest glory.

This is an example of word magic. It is an expression of an ideal to which presumably the great majority of Americans would enthusiastically give verbal assent, *without having the foggiest notion of what the words are saying.* And this failure is not to be chalked up as a flaw in

the thinking of the American people. For it is no mean task for anybody, however sophisticated in words and metaphoric expressions, [to understand such phrases] as "full, rounded, and continuing development of the person" or "liberate and perfect the intrinsic powers of every citizen." Phrases like these sing to our enthusiasms, but they don't tell us what to do about them. The difficulty is that the metaphors in which they are couched are extremely hard to translate in terms of what little we really know of human growth and functioning. How do you know, for instance, when you have liberated and perfected the intrinsic powers of a citizen? Or how do you calibrate the roundedness of his development?

To ask such questions is to suggest why the word magic has not worked and why such goal statements leave school people with barely a clue for determining what the lines of progress ought to be or whether the system is making any headway in the desired directions. And this failure has led to more than a little disillusionment about the practical utility of any kind of goal statements and to a considerable degree of offhand cynicism about pious platitudes that have no relevance for practical operations beyond that of providing useful window dressing to keep the public happy.

**Lack of Public Involvement** A second reason that the usual statements of goals fail to function is that there has not been enough genuine participation by the public in the goal-making process. The typical approach to working out education objectives for pupils or schools or school systems is for a group of educators or academicians or psychometricians or some mixture of these to hole up and bring their combined expertise to bear on working out what *they* think should happen to people as a consequence of going to school. In the presentation of their findings they have occasionally involved representatives of the citizenry at large, but this wider involvement has been usually little more than a series of gestures aimed at getting acceptance rather than participation.* The result, again, is usually assent without understanding, and the goals produced turn out to be a dead letter.

The approach of the experts is back-end-to. It should not be one of trying to convince the public of what it *ought* to want from its schools but of helping the public to discover what it *really* wants; and among the public I include those who will be in charge in the next 15 years or so—namely, the pupils themselves, as well as their teachers, their parents, their prospective employers, and behind all these, the school boards and legislators who make the ultimate decisions. This is partly what I mean by the discovery and development of educational goals. By its nature this process of discovery will be necessarily tedious and often frustrating and, most important, never-ending. So far as I know, it has never been given a serious trial on any broad or continuous basis to the point where the actual needs and desires of individuals and of society become the determiners of such subsidiary matters as whether school budgets are to be voted up or down, whether school districts will be consolidated, or kindergartens shall become mandatory, or whether a foreign language shall be taught to all children or some children or no children at all in the third grade.

It is easy to dismiss this idea, the idea of the public search for goals, as utopian. How can one possibly bring about genuine public involvement in the goal-making process or expect that anything really useful will come of it when everybody knows that 90 per cent of what happens in and to the schools is determined by the power blocs and pressure groups and influence agents whose prime interest is keeping taxes down, or getting bus contracts, or simply gathering in the symbols

* See Article 42 by Merwin and Womer for an example of how public involvement in goal setting can influence evaluation.

that add up to prestige and power for their own sake? Nevertheless, in an essay on "Who Controls the Schools?" Neal Gross (1965), who has looked these hard realities square in the eye, can still make the hopeful observation that: "The control is ultimately, of course, in the hands of the people. If they really want it, they can have it any time, since it is they, after all, who elect the school boards." The problem is to get them to take control and to know what they want their schools to deliver. The chances of a solution will be much improved when the experts stop talking exclusively to themselves and broaden their conversations to include the public.

**Goals Have Been Assumed as Given**  The third reason that educational goals have been nonfunctional is that too frequently they have been assumed as, in some sense, already given, and the only problem has been to figure out how to attain them.

The fact that "all men do not honor the same virtue" (Aristotle, *Politics*, Book vii, Paragraph i) is precisely what makes the structuring and conduct of education in a free society so complicated and frequently so frustrating. If schools are to keep at all, they must somehow accommodate themselves the the pluralism in the values of those whom they serve and from whom they derive their support. Any system that tries to operate on the assumption that there is one fixed set of goals to which all people must aspire is bound to be so far out of touch with the actualities of the human condition that such effects as the schools may have are likely to be altogether unrelated to the needs of the pupils in them or to the society they are expected to serve.

Each individual and each generation has to create its own truth by which to know the world of its own time and place, and, by the same token, it has to create its own goals for ordering its efforts to cope with its world. Thus, the discovery and development of educational goals has to be part of the educational process itself, starting with the child and continuing with the adult as he works his way through to the personal, social, and economic decisions that determine the shape of the free world he is to live in.

## THE ROLE OF EDUCATIONAL MEASUREMENT IN DEFINING GOALS

I think the way out is to hold the search for long-term goals in abeyance for awhile and concentrate on getting a clearer idea of what is happening in the schools right now and making up our minds about how much we like what we see.

Every morning, Monday through Friday, millions of children leave millions of homes and are funneled into thousands of schoolhouses where they have an uncountable number of experiences affecting their thoughts, feelings, aspirations, physical well-being, personal relations, and general conception of how the world is put together. The extraordinary fact is, however, that in spite of the mountains of data that have been piled up from teachers' reports, tests, questionnaires, and demographic records of all kinds, we still have only very hazy and superficial notions of what the effects of the school experience actually are.

There are some things we are beginning to suspect that leave us more or less comfortable—mostly less. For instance, all but a very few children learn to read, at least up to the point where most of them can and do enjoy comic strips. It has been estimated that by the time students reach college, half of them will admit to some form of academic dishonesty, but the grade norms for this form of academic achievement are not yet known. According to the Project Talent data, the career plans most students make in high school are unrealistic and unstable (Flanagan and Cooley, 1966), but nobody knows for sure whether this situation is good or bad or how far the schools can or should be held accountable for it. In elementary schools, according to the recent Educational Opportunities Survey by the Office of Education (Coleman et al., (1966), 10 per cent of white children and 18 per cent of Negro children have acquired an attitude that prompts them to agree with the proposition: "People like me don't have much of a chance to be successful in life"; and in high school 15 per cent of whites and 19 per cent of Negroes say they have reached the conclusion: "Every time I try to get ahead, something or somebody stops me." To what extent can attitudes like these be attributed to school experiences and how much to the education supplied by the city streets? Again, we don't know, but information of this sort seems indispensable to the process of arriving at educational goals and deciding on priorities among them.

The point I am trying to make is very simply this: People are more likely to get clear in their minds what the outcomes of education *ought* to be if they can first get clear in their minds what the outcomes actually *are*. To know that a considerable number of pupils are learning to cheat on examinations or learning that the cards are stacked against them should help to suggest, if only in a negative way, what educational outcomes are to be preferred.

It has been customary to take the view that before one can develop measures of educational outcomes, one must determine what the objectives of education are. What I am suggesting is that it is not possible to determine the objectives until one has measured the outcomes. This sounds more like a paradox than it really is. Evaluating the *side* effects of an educational program may be even more important than evaluating its intended effects. An up-to-date math teacher may be trying to teach set theory to fourth graders and may be doing a good job at it, but one wants to know whether he is also teaching some of the youngsters to despise mathematics.

The educational tester must provide instruments and procedures for displaying and accurately ordering as many of the behavioral outcomes of the educational process as he, with the help of everybody involved, can imagine, regardless of whether these outcomes are to be judged good or bad, helpful or harmful, desirable or undesirable. The educational tester must not allow his thinking to become trapped in the traditional categories of the curriculum such as English, mathematics, and science; he must be concerned with the whole spectrum of human behavior as possible ways of categorizing it and measuring it that will make sense to the general public that decides on what schools are for.

In the *Taxonomy of Educational Objectives, Handbook II: Affective Domain,* David Krathwohl and his collaborators have made an enormous contribution to this effort if for no other reason than that they insist one must attend to human functioning beyond the cognitive. Their focus, however, is on "classifying and ordering responses specified as *desired* outcomes of education" (Bloom *et al.,* 1956; Krathwohl *et al.,* 1964). What is now required, it seems to me, is a taxonomy of all possible educational outcomes without reference to whether they are desirable or undesirable, good or bad, hurtful or helpful. Only as this requirement is met are we likely to approximate testing programs that will begin to tell us all we need to know for evaluating educational programs.

Any achievement testing program that is limited to measuring performance in the basic skills and mastery of academic subject matter—and this, I suspect, is the pattern of most such programs—is almost certain to do more harm than good by not raising the question whether excellence in performance in such things as reading and mathematics and science and literature is not being bought at the expense of something left unmeasured, such as academic honesty and individual sense of self-worth. Granted the tremendous

importance of mastery of the basic intellectual tools for these times, it seems axiomatic that they hardly compare in importance with common honesty and mutual trust as the indispensable ingredients of a viable free society.

It is easy to argue that the present state of the art leaves much to be desired in the measurement of the affective and social outcomes of the educational system. It is easy to argue that such instruments as we have for these purposes are productive of soft data, full of superficialities and pitfalls that can lead people astray in assessing what the educational system is really doing to students. This is all too true, and anyone with a conscience rooted in sound measurement knows it only too well. But successful arguments only point to the need for firming up the soft data by going after the correlates of behavior that get beneath the semantic confusions inherent in self-report devices. They also point to the need for keeping a spotlight on the limitations of the data we have, when, for want of anything better, such data have to be consulted. Not to consult them at all is to keep our eyes shut to many of the products of schooling that most need attention.

Finally, educational measurement has its uses not only in the discovery, but also in the development, of the goals. In an ideal world, this developmental process is a continual series of approximations— an unending iterative process for constantly checking the validity of concept against the behavior of the measures derived from them, and checking the validity of the measures against the concepts from which they have been derived. This back-and-forth process begins in the vague concerns of the public for what it wants but has not defined—personal fulfillment, effective citizenship, the good life, the open society, and so on. All of which terms are still word magic. They are no good in themselves as goals. But as symbols of human hope, they cannot be neglected in the *search* for goals. They have an extremely high heuristic value in getting the search started. The first practical approximation in the search, however, is some combination of tests and other measures that can begin to delineate, for all to see, the dimensions along which we think we want to progress. This is to say that, in the last analysis, an educational goal is adequately defined only in terms of the agreed-upon procedures and instruments by which its attainment is to be measured. It is to say that the development of educational goals is practically identical with the process by which we develop educational tests. It is to imply what in some quarters might be regarded as the ultimate in educational heresy: *teaching should be pointed very specifically at the tests the students will take as measures of output;* otherwise, neither the students nor their teachers are ever likely to discover where they are going or whether they are getting anywhere at all.

A great problem—probably the greatest problem—in the development of meaningful goals is that of making sure that the tangible tests that come out of the process bear a determinable relationship to all the vague individual and collective concerns that go into it. The only way this relationship can be assured is through some sort of continuous dialogue among testers, students, educators, and the public bodies that control the educational enterprise.

# 8. Considerations in Selecting Objectives
## RALPH W. TYLER

Before settling down to the task of specifying or selecting objectives for curriculum development or evaluation, a reasonable set of criteria should be developed. Nobody is in a better position to help us define these criteria than Ralph W. Tyler, one of the prime movers in developing "curriculum evaluation" as a scientific activity. His contributions during the Eight Year Studies are as fresh and relevant today as they were in the 1930s and 1940s (Smith, Tyler et al., 1942). Basically, Tyler's suggested criteria could be generated by seeking answers to the following five questions: is the objective (1) something of value to society as a whole and to its individual members? (2) consonant with student knowledge and ability, and can it be mastered? (3) compatible with the current state of knowledge? (4) compatible with school educational philosophy? (5) teachable?

Realizing that there is so much to be taught, so much that it would be valuable for people to learn in a complex society such as ours, and so little time to learn,

Reprinted and abridged with permission of the publisher and Ralph W. Tyler from an article entitled "Some Persistent Questions on the Defining of Objectives," which appeared in *Defining Educational Objectives*, ed. C. M. Lindvall (Pittsburgh: University of Pittsburgh Press, Copyright 1964).

how do we decide what objectives are worth teaching? I have found it useful to keep in mind several different factors.

### CULTURAL NEEDS

One of these is an analysis of our culture. Other things being equal it is important to teach those kinds of behavior, those ways of thinking, feeling, and acting that have value in our society and that help the person to become an effective human being in it. As an example of this, the question of foreign language instruction might be used. Some schools have been quite successful in teaching a foreign language at a very early age so that we know that this is something that can be done if it is desirable. But the question that faces the curriculum planner is this: How significant is this foreign language as a means for the pupil's further development? It is more important for the Englishman to learn French that it is for the average American because the Englishman usually has many more opportunities to use it. For the same reason it is more important for the people in Texas to learn Spanish than it is for the people in Illinois to learn Spanish. Where a foreign language can be used it becomes an important tool of communication.

A related question in which the facts of the culture must be considered is one of the proper grade placements for given objectives or subjects. Where possible, instruction should be planned so that the initial stages of learning will be under the supervision of the school but so that continued learning and reinforcement can and will take place outside the school. For example, if a person is going to Venezuela as a member of the Peace Corps in September, it would be most effective if he were taught Spanish in the months prior to his leaving. This would mean that as soon as he has completed some of the initial stages in learning the language he will have the opportunity to use it outside the classroom and continue to learn under the reinforcing conditions provided by this practical application.

## STUDENT KNOWLEDGE AND ABILITY

A second factor in selecting appropriate objectives is the present status of the student. What has he already learned? What is he ready for? One of the problems here may be illustrated by developments in mathematics where many high schools are now offering advanced courses. For this reason, as reported to me by some of my college colleagues, some of the topics typically taught in college mathematics courses turn out to be "old stuff" for students coming from the better high schools. I encountered another example of this situation in a recent conversation with a friend whose daughter is a freshman at a leading eastern college. This girl has been greatly disappointed in her first college history course. In her high school history classes use was made of a variety of interesting source materials, but the college course is using only a textbook which is read and commented on, chapter by chapter. For this student, what had been exciting about the study of history is no longer there. So a key problem in selecting objectives is that of determining the "entering behavior" of the student, just where he is in his educational development and what abilities he brings to the given class or learning situation. Only when this is known can we answer the question of whether or not certain objectives are appropriate for his next stage of development. This requires a procedure for finding out about the students, where they are now, and what their capabilities are.

## STATE OF KNOWLEDGE

A third factor in selecting objectives is what we know enough about to teach. It might be nice, for example, to teach a person to employ extrasensory perception, but we don't know enough about this to teach it. On the other hand, we do know enough about the art of writing to have something to teach children. And, new knowledge in the various subjects is being obtained at a rapid rate. These new developments should be continually examined to see if they provide materials that can be of real value to youngsters. But these new ideas and understandings were not available to teachers at the time they were receiving their education so that we have a problem of keeping our objectives, and our ability to teach them, abreast of the most recent developments in a given field. This is a reason for the continuing effort to involve scientists and other scholars in working with teachers in the development of curricula. New subject resources are becoming available continually and these should be scrutinized by someone or some curriculum center as a basis for making decisions as to whether or not they should be incorporated into classroom content.

## SCHOOL PHILOSOPHY OF EDUCATION

A fourth basic consideration in the selection of objectives is their relevance to the school's philosophy of education. This philosophy outlines our conception of the "good person" we are trying to develop. It is certainly possible to teach a person as though he were an automaton, and some kinds of training programs in industry are operated pretty much in this way. We can teach him to do all the required things. He can run all of the machines without understanding them. But is this the kind of person we are trying to develop?

We have come to place an emphasis on such things as problem solving and open-endedness, that is, helping the learner to become conscious of the fact that he doesn't have the final answers in this area, that a continuing process of inquiry is involved. We also are putting an emphasis upon the values that come from esthetic experiences in such areas as art and music. But we also have problems of conflicting values and often need to clarify our guiding philosophy. We must continuously be asking the question of what kind of young person it is that is the responsibility of our schools and colleges to help develop. I have my own answer to the question and I suppose that each one of us does. But the clarification of our values is a basic step in curriculum planning and in the selection of objectives

because we can teach in such a way that values or ends are helped, or we can teach in such a way that they are denied.

## RELATION TO LEARNING THEORY

Finally, a fifth factor in selecting and stating our objectives is the consistency of these objectives with our theory of learning. As an illustration of this consideration, the question frequently arises of the possibility of meeting the demands made upon people today through the preparation provided by our present sixteen years of school. Surely, our people are required to meet problems of such range and complexity that they can't learn enough in their youth. This dilemma has resulted in a variety of suggestions for the school curriculum. One proposal is that we teach most youth to be a "garden-variety" of citizen who will not be expected to understand much but who can be taught the skills of a particular occupation and a respect for leadership. This is the view often expressed in the English elementary schools. This proposal includes the idea that the responsibility for more adequate understanding and competence to deal with the complexities of modern life will be in the hands of the more privileged group that goes on to secondary schools and colleges.

Another proposal is based on the view that the fields of knowledge are getting so large (as the scientific fields, for example) that we can only expect to cover them rather superficially with some kind of survey. This seems to be a rather common approach.

But a proposal which is currently gaining attention is to start the student from the beginning as an inquirer, as a person who is seeking to learn, giving him the skills and the incentives that lead him to dig deeper into some sample of a content area, and then encouraging him to go on independently while he is in school, and in later life. As one example of this, the new social studies material being developed [by Education Development Center] begins at the third-grade level with a study of the Eskimo and two other primitive cultures. This program says, in effect, that the culture of man is a developing thing and that its basic elements with the procedure for studying it can best be understood by starting with certain simple samples. The Eskimo is selected not for the usual romantic reasons that have led to his inclusion in elementary school courses, but because he represents a type of culture which can be studied through the methods of the anthropologist. Then the children study a tribe from central Africa and another from Oceana. These offer the third grader the opportunity to become familiar with primitive societies. And the students begin their study, not by reading a textbook, but by bringing together a variety of materials and resources that are pertinent to the understanding of the culture and appropriate for third graders so that, from the first, they employ the methods that are useful in beginning to understand what another culture is like. The effort is to develop persons who have the ability and the desire to be continuing inquirers.

Projects of this type are trying to attack the problem caused by the ever-increasing mass of material that should be learned by producing students who have the tools and the general ability to proceed on their own. This approach views education not merely as a process of giving answers, but as a process of producing persons who can find answers on their own, can discover additional questions that need to be answered, can come up with answers to these questions, and engage in an intelligent process of continual inquiry. This approach seeks to develop in students a conviction that the world is an interesting and exciting place where there is much to be seen and understood. The students are out to understand the kinds of problems that are found and the modes of inquiry that are used. They should develop an understanding of how one makes an inquiry if one were looking at a topic from the point of

view of the geographer, or from the point of view of the chemist, or from the point of view of the writer of a literary document. They learn to inquire into the behavior of people as well as the behavior of things, of plants and of animals. This approach seeks to develop the necessary skills and the mastery of many of the pertinent concepts. The school is not expected to present all of the details or all of the specific facts or examples. The important learning is for the pupil to understand the basic concepts such as that of social mobility, in sociology, of motivation, in psychology, or of energy transfer, in physics. Concepts of this type are basic to continued investigation in a given area. For example, the new high school physics course developed by the Physical Science Study Committee builds its work around 34 concepts. If the pupil masters these he has the foundation for further investigation of physical phenomena. He can learn how these concepts are related and can discover many important principles. As an example in the arts, the courses are built around concepts of form and of esthetic values such as that of unity in literature, of the illusion of reality, etc.

The hope is, with this approach, that students really become involved in a lifelong process of learning in which the school's role is to get them fairly well started. With such a view the problem of defining objectives becomes that of determining the behaviors, appropriate to the given grade level, that the pupil can carry out so that when he has done this he will have a feeling for the open-endedness of the situation, the new questions to be asked, the new knowledge to be gained and not feel that the learning is finished. For example, the fifth-grade pupil in such a program will not feel that now he knows all there is to know about Egypt but will begin to see how what he knows about Egypt relates to other countries, will see, for example, the relationships between rigid social structure and economic backwardness.

When formulating objectives, it is very

important that you have clearly in mind your concept of the learning process and the process of education. In this last illustrative approach, this conception included the notion that the learner is active, that he is looking at the world, and is trying to make something out of it. We are trying to guide him in his continued activity rather than trying to close the world for him by giving him all the answers. We don't want to tell him, "You have learned what there is in this course." The student must see his learning as a constantly continuing process. To achieve this you will have to think of objectives of the sort that lead from the third grade to the fourth grade to the fifth grade and so on. It might be that in studying science in the third grade the pupils are looking at rocks and trying to make sense out of them while in the fourth grade they are looking at plants and growing flowers. But in both cases they are concerned with the same general notion of the world and how it is to be interpreted. The types of science problems involved and the kinds of skills employed can be stepping stones for continued development.

In closing I would note something that was experienced by Bob Glaser in producing his individualized learning programs. This is that as you work with objectives and with your efforts to teach them you frequently have a basis for the redefinition of your objectives. As you see what really is possible, you may see more clearly the kinds of things the pupils need in addition to those that you thought of in your original planning. The process of clarifying goals, then working toward them, then appraising progress, then re-examining the goals, modifying them and clarifying them in the light of the experience and the data is a never-ending procedure.

# 9. Stating Appropriate Educational Objectives

## DAVID R. KRATHWOHL

Objectives at several levels of generality and specificity are needed to meet different institutional and individual requirements. At the most general level, gross statements are needed to guide program development. "Principles of education" and the abstract statements of government commissions and professional organizations are illustrative. At an intermediate level, where more specific objectives are needed for curriculum development, the *Taxonomy of Educational Objectives* could be used effectively. At a very specific level, highly refined behavioral objectives are necessary for instructional materials development and evaluation. At a possible fourth level, test items or performance tasks could be considered operational definitions of objectives. In addition to the *Taxonomy of Educational Objectives*, Krathwohl employs Gagné's "conditions of learning" as a framework for his presentation. Elaboration of many of the points raised here may be found in Krathwohl and Payne (1971).

The emphasis upon making educational objectives specific by defining the goals of an instructional course or program has gone through many cycles since Ralph Tyler gave the topic considerable prominence in the late thirties. For some educators, careful attention to spelling out in detail the objectives of a course has become a kind of religion. Others, interestingly enough, seem to have heard of the practice of delineating objectives but, somehow or other, have been early inoculated against the notion and have so become immune. Those of us who work as advisors to various fields of higher education, particularly with our colleagues in liberal arts, home economics, etc., are impressed with the power of this simple

Reprinted and abridged with permission of the publisher and David R. Krathwohl from an article entitled "Stating Objectives Appropriately for Program, for Curriculum, and for Instructional Materials Development," which appeared in the *Journal of Teacher Education*, **16** (March 1965) pp. 83–92.

tool to help people structure courses and view their own process of teaching with a renewed interest and from a new perspective.

Viewed both in retrospect and contemporaneously, specifying educational objectives as student behaviors seems to be a useful and powerful approach to the analysis of the instructional process. Granted it implies a particular view of the educational process. In it, "education" means changing the behavior of a student so that he is able, when encountering a particular problem or situation, to display a behavior which he did not previously exhibit. The task of the teacher is to help the student learn new or changed behaviors and determine where and when they are appropriate.

A major contribution of this approach to curriculum building is that it forces the instructor to spell out his instructional goals in terms of overt behavior. This gives new detail; indeed it yields an operational definition of many previously general and often fuzzy and ill-defined objectives. Such goals as "the student should become a good citizen" are spelled out in terms of the kinds of behaviors which a good citizen displays. There are then statements, such as, "the student shall be able to identify and appraise judgments and values involved in the choice of a course of political action"; "he shall display skill in identifying different appropriate roles in a democratic group"; or "he will be able to relate principles of civil liberties and civil rights to current events." Thus the instructor knows what kinds of behavior he is to try to develop in the classroom. In addition, the problem of assessing the extent to which he has achieved his goals becomes markedly simplified. He needs only to provide the student with a situation in which the kind of behavior he is seeking to instill should be evoked and then observe to see whether indeed it appears. Spelling out the behaviors involved in an objective such as the above frequently means specifying several pages of concrete behaviors. Such specification often gives teachers a fresh perspective on their courses and new insights into ways to teach and to evaluate their teaching. This kind of analysis of objectives is clearly a step forward.

This approach to instruction fits in very well with the behaviorist school of psychology, the well-spring from which came the recent emphasis on teaching machines and programmed instruction. It is not surprising, then, that a renewed emphasis on educational objectives resulted from the development of programmed learning. The careful specification of a step-by-step procedure for the learner calls for clearly understood objectives specified at a level of detail far beyond that usually attempted. In programmed learning, such objectives have come to bear the name of "terminal behaviors." As psychologists, physicists, systems development specialists, and others have attempted instructional programming, they have turned to education for a greater understanding of

how adequately to specify educational objectives so that they concretely describe a "terminal behavior."

## THE NEED OF OBJECTIVES AT SEVERAL LEVELS OF ANALYSIS

The renewed emphasis has given new insight into and perspective on the whole problem of the level of specificity needed in objectives. It is now clear that we need to analyze objectives to several levels of specificity depending upon how we tend to use them. At the first and most abstract level are the quite broad and general statements most helpful in the development of programs of instruction, for the laying out of types of courses and areas to be covered, and for the general goals toward which several years of education might be aimed or for which an entire unit such as an elementary, junior, or senior high school might strive.

At a second and more concrete level, a *behavioral* objectives orientation helps to analyze broad goals into more specfic ones which are useful as the building blocks for curricular instruction. These behaviorally stated objectives are helpful in specifying the goals of an instructional unit, a course, or a sequence of courses.

Third and finally, there is the level needed to create instructional materials —materials which are the operational embodiment of one particular route (rarely are multiple routes included) to the achievement of a curriculum planned at the second and more abstract level, the level of detailed analysis involved in the programmed instruction movement. Just as the second level of analysis brought into concrete, detailed form the ideas of goals and purposes that were in the mind of the good teacher as he planned at the first and more abstract level, so this kind of detailed analysis brings into focus the objectives of specific lesson plans, the sequence of goals in these plans, and the level of achievement required for each goal or objective if successful accomplishment of the next goal in this sequence is to be achieved.

In realization of this, we find Gagné (1963), Mager (1962) and Miller (1961) all writing about the analysis of objectives for programmed instruction with a plea that objectives be given a great deal more specificity so that they may be more easily turned into instructional materials. They call for a description of the situation which ought to initiate the behavior in question, a complete description of the behavior, the object or goal of the behavior, and a description of the level of performance of the behavior which permits us to recognize a successful performance.

We may note in passing that even this may not be enough specification for the development of instructional materials. There is no mention in this of the characteristics of the learner and his relation to the learning situation. Thus, not all objectives or terminal behaviors will be appropriate for all kinds and types of students. Neither will the same level of proficiency be appropriate for, nor expected of, different levels of ability. Thus a successful performance cannot have a single definition. Further, those planning instructional materials need to know where the student starts, what he brings to the situation (the "entry behaviors"). We may also need to know something about the motivation for learning (or lack of it if, for example, we are dealing with the culturally disadvantaged), and the pattern of problem solving available to us (for example, in teaching the social studies, one approach for those with rigid value patterns, another for those more flexible). While this is not a complete list, it clearly indicates that a great deal more specification is required in developing instructional materials than in laying out curricular goals.

But to return to our main theme, if we make our goals specific enough to prepare instructional materials, why use the other levels at all? Should we not, for example, discard at least the second level? Not at all! Four points need to be made.

First of all, curriculum construction requires a process of moving through descending abstractions from very general and global statements of desirable behaviors for a program, to intermediate level statements that indicate the blocks from which the program will be constructed, and finally to quite detailed statements which spell out the sub-goals, their relation to one another, and the level of achievement which results in the successful attainment of the intermediate-level behavioral descriptions. All levels of specification of objectives are needed to guide the planning of the educational process. Only as each level is completed can the next be begun. The first level guides the development of the second, the second guides the third.

To return to our example of the development of citizenship, we earlier noted three objectives at the intermediate level. Once these are specified, we can begin to think at the third level of very specific goals and their teaching sequence. For example, one would specify the different possible desirable roles in a democratic group, how these roles would build on one another, to what situations each was appropriate, and how successfully each should be displayed before passing on to the next. Each level thus permits and guides the development of the next level of specification.

Second, not all objectives lend themselves to the *complete* specification at the third level. In some instances, the universe of behaviors is completely circumscribed. For example, there are only 45 sums of the two numbers 0 through 9 which need be learned, and we can specify that these must be mastered with perfect accuracy. But in many instances we cannot specify all the instances of behavior. Gagné's contrasting terminology of "mastery" objective to apply to the former and "transfer" objectives to the latter helps to illumine this difference. We cannot predict all situations the student will encounter or all the situations to which he should be able to transfer the behaviors, but we can specify a currently known sample. Nearly all our complex ability and skill objectives—application, analysis, evaluation, etc.—are "transfer" objectives. Their specification will be inexact and confined to a known sample of relevant and typical kinds of behaviors. Transfer objectives seem to constitute the major *ultimate* goals for the bulk of the educational process. More exact specification of mastery goals may be possible in industrial or vocational training for specific occupations than in general education. Thus the level of detail with which educational goals can be usefully specified will depend somewhat on their nature. Again we see that several levels of specificity are needed to handle different kinds of objectives.

Third, we need to have objectives at several levels of abstraction so that we can continually examine their interrelation to one another. When developing a curriculum, we try to get those involved to agree at as detailed a level as possible. But complete agreement can probably be reached only at the more abstract levels. Thus we can get general agreement that students should be good citizens, but we may get some disagreement as to what this means operationally or in behavioral terms. For some teachers this may mean that all students are taught to engage in some political action—ringing doorbells at election time, writing congressmen, etc. To others this may be confined to voting and attempting to understand and to discuss issues with others. Further, such definitions will change as society and its pressures and fads change. It helps to have agreed-upon general and global objectives to which all curricula can relate. These objectives can then be redefined at the less abstract level in relation to the overall goals.

Fourth, and finally, there are many routes from the intermediate level objective to the specification of instructional materials. For example, take the objec-

tive: "The student shall be able to recognize form and pattern in literary works as a means to understanding their meaning." This is a useful objective at the intermediate or curricular-building level of abstraction, but how does the teacher translate this into a choice of instructional materials? Does he choose those literary forms and patterns which are likely to have maximum transfer to all kinds of literary materials and teach them, or does he choose those forms and patterns that will permit the deepest penetration of meaning and concentrate on them, assuming the other forms and patterns will be picked up in the course of reading? Both approaches might be acceptable. It helps to have the objective in its original abstract form to serve as a basis for judging the routes to its achievement. The routes might be thought of as sub-objectives needing evaluation to help in learning which route best achieves the intermediate-level objective.

We do not have enough psychological knowledge for the teacher and the developer of instructional materials to move with certainty from an intermediate-level objective to a single set of very detailed and concrete objectives. In the example given above, for instance, we have little theoretical basis for judging the language forms and patterns that will permit the most complete understanding of literary material. Both the instructional material specialist and the teacher precede the psychologists into an area of most-needed research. They must make choices while the psychologist is still developing the knowledge to help them.

Thus, there are at least four reasons why objectives at various levels of analysis are useful and needed in the instructional processes:

1. Each level of analysis permits the development of the next more specific level.
2. Mastery objectives can be analyzed to greater specificity than transfer objectives.

3. Curricula gain adoption by consensus that what is taught is of value. Consensus is more easily gained at the more abstract levels of analysis.
4. There are usually several alternative ways of analyzing objectives at the most specific level. Objectives at the more abstract level provide a referent for evaluating these alternatives.

It seems clear then that objectives at several levels of abstraction are useful and important in the educational process. Let us turn now to some of the structures that have been constructed to aid exploration at these levels.

## FRAMEWORKS TO FACILITATE THE STATEMENT OF OBJECTIVES

**1. The Taxonomy of Educational Objectives—A Framework for Curriculum Building** The need for objectives at various levels of abstraction has given rise to frameworks or structures that assist in the analysis and development of these objectives. One of these frameworks, the *Taxonomy of Educational Objectives* (Bloom et al., 1956; Krathwohl et al., 1964), appears to have proven useful in the analysis of objectives at the intermediate curriculum-building level.

Basically the taxonomy grew out of an attempt to resolve some of the confusion in communication which resulted from the translation of such general terms as "to understand" into more specific behaviors. Thus the "understanding" of Boyle's law might mean that the student could recall the formula, tell what it meant, interpret the particular meaning of the law in an article about it, use the formula in a new problem situation he had never met, or think up new implications of its relationship.

The problem of precisely identifying what is meant by particular terms plagues the evaluator as well as the curriculum builder. For one thing, these two must communicate with each other, since the test constructor seeks accurately to translate the curriculum builders' objectives into situations where the student can display the behavior if he knows it. Accuracy in this translation is essential. Further, evaluators working at different institutions on similar curricula know they have something in common but frequently find it difficult to communicate accurately about it. Given precise communication, they could share and compare the effectiveness of learning devices, materials, and curricula organization. It was with this in mind that a group of college and university examiners, under the leadership of Dr. Benjamin S. Bloom of the University of Chicago, attempted to devise a framework or taxonomy that would help to hold terms in place, provide a structure which would relate one term to another, and thus provide additional meaning for a given term through this interrelationship.

The *Taxonomy of Educational Objectives* is basically a classification scheme, just as the biological taxonomy is a classification scheme for animals into class, order, family, genus, and species. In the educational objectives taxonomy, the kinds of behavior we seek to have students display as a result of the learning process are classified. Every behavioral objective is composed of two parts—the behavior the student is to display and the subject matter or content that is then used in the display. The taxonomy deals only with the behavioral part of the objectives; the content of subject-matter classification is left to the Library of Congress, the Dewey Decimal System, and such other similar classifications.

For purposes of convenience the taxonomy was divided into three domains, the cognitive, affective, and psychomotor. *Handbook I, The Cognitive Domain* (Bloom et al., 1956) has been available for about twelve years. It deals with objectives having to do with thinking, knowing, and problem solving. *Handbook II, The Affective Domain* was published in 1964. It includes objectives dealing with attitudes, values, interests, appreciations, and social-emotional adjustment. The psychomotor domain covers objectives having to do with manual and motor skills (Simpson, 1966). The feasibility of developing it is being studied by a group at the University of Illinois, under Dr. Elizabeth Simpson.

> Basically the taxonomy is an educational-logical-psychological classification system. The terms in this order reflect the emphasis given to the organizing principles upon which it is built. It makes educational distinctions in the sense that the boundaries between categories reflect the decisions that teachers make among student behaviors in their development of curriculums, and in choosing learning situations. It is a logical system in the sense that its terms are defined precisely and are used consistently. In addition, each category permits logical subdivisions which can be clearly defined and further subdivided as necessary and useful. Finally the taxonomy seems to be consistent with our present understanding of psychological phenomena, though it does not rest on any single theory.

> The scheme is intended to be purely descriptive so that every type of educational goal can be represented. It does not indicate the value or quality of one class as compared to another. It is impartial with respect to views of education. One of the tests of the taxonomy has been that of inclusiveness—could one classify all kinds of educational objectives (if stated as student behaviors) in the framework? In general, it seems to have met this test (Krathwohl, 1964).

*The Cognitive Domain of the Taxonomy.* Similar to the distinctions most teachers make, the cognitive domain is divided into the acquisition of knowledge and the development of those skills and abilities necessary to use knowledge. Under the heading "Knowledge", which is the first major category of the cognitive domain, one finds a series of subcategories, each describing the recall of a different category of knowledge. Each of the subheadings is accompanied by a definition of the

behavior classified there and by illustrative objectives taken from the educational literature. In addition, there is a summary of the kinds of test items that may be used to test for each category, a discussion of the problems which beset the individual attempting to evaluate behavior in the category, and a large number of examples of test items—mainly multiple choice but some essay type. These illustrate how items may be built to measure each of the categories.

The taxonomy is hierarchical in nature, that is, each category is assumed to involve behavior more complex and abstract than the previous category. Thus the categories are arranged from simple to complex behavior, and from concrete to abstract behavior.

Perhaps the idea of the continuum is most easily gained from looking at the major headings of the cognitive domain, which include knowledge (recall of facts, principles, etc.), comprehension (ability to restate knowledge in new words), application (understanding well enough to break it apart into its parts and make the relations among ideas explicit), synthesis (the ability to produce wholes from parts, to produce a plan of operation, to derive a set of abstract relations), and evaluation (the ability to judge the value of material for given purposes).

See Table 1 for a brief outline of the Cognitive Domain.

Since the cognitive domain has been available for some time, perhaps this brief summary will suffice to remind the reader of its nature or to intrigue him to look into it if it has not previously come to his attention. Since the affective domain is new, let us examine it in more detail.

*The Affective Domain of the Taxonomy.* Though there is confusion in communication with respect to terms in the cognitive domain, those who worked on the taxonomy found the confusion much greater when they began work on the affective domain. The state of communi-

**TABLE 1**
**Synopsis of the Taxonomy of Educational Objectives: Cognitive Domain**

Knowledge

1.00 *Knowledge.* Recall of information.

1.10 Knowledge of specifics. Emphasis is on symbols with concrete referents.
    1.11 Knowledge of terminology.
    1.12 Knowledge of specific facts.

1.20 Knowledge of ways and means of dealing with specifics. Includes methods of inquiry, chronological sequences, standards of judgment, patterns of organization within a field.
    1.21 Knowledge of conventions: accepted usage, correct style, etc.
    1.22 Knowledge of trends and sequences.
    1.23 Knowledge of classifications and categories.
    1.24 Knowledge of criteria.
    1.25 Knowledge of methodology for investigating particular problems.

1.30 Knowledge of the universals and abstractions in a field. Patterns and schemes by which phenomena and ideas are organized.
    1.31 Knowledge of principles and generalizations.
    1.32 Knowledge of theories and structures (as a connected body of principles, generalizations, and interrelations).

Intellectual Skills and Abilities

2.00 *Comprehension.* Understanding of material being communicated, without necessarily relating it to other material.
    2.10 Translation. From one set of symbols to another.
    2.20 Interpretation. Summarization or explanation of a communication.
    2.30 Extrapolation. Extension of trends beyond the given data.

3.00 *Application.* The use of abstractions in particular, concrete situations.

4.00 *Analysis.* Breaking a communication into its parts so that organization of ideas is clear.
    4.10 Analysis of elements. E.g., recognizing assumptions.
    4.20 Analysis of relationships. Content or mechanical factors.
    4.30 Analysis of organizational principles. What holds the communication together?

5.00 *Synthesis.* Putting elements into a whole.
    5.10 Production of a unique communication.
    5.20 Production of a plan for operations.
    5.30 Derivation of a set of abstract relations.

6.00 *Evaluation.* Judging the value of material for a given purpose.
    6.10 Judgments in terms of internal evidence. E.g., logical consistency.
    6.20 Judgments in terms of external evidence. E.g., consistency with facts developed elsewhere.

cation with respect to a term like "really understand" is nothing compared to the confusion that surrounds objectives dealing with attitudes, interests, and appreciation. When we say that we want a child to "appreciate" art, do we mean that he should be aware of art work? Should he be willing to give it some attention when it is around? Do we mean that he should seek it out—to go to the museum on his own, for instance? Do we mean that he should regard art work as having positive values? Should he experience an emotional kick or thrill when he sees art work? Should he be able to evaluate it and to know why and how it is effective? Should he be able to compare its esthetic impact with that of other art forms?

This list could be extended, but it is enough to suggest that the term "appreciation" covers a wide variety of meanings. And worse, not all of these are distinct from the terms "attitude" and "interest." Thus, if appreciation has the meaning that the student should like art work well enough to seek it out, how would we distinguish such behavior from an interest in art—or are interests and appreciations, as we use these words, the same thing? If the student *values* art, does he have a favorable *attitude* toward it? Are our appreciation objectives the same as, overlapping with, or in some respects distinct from our attitude objectives?

In addition to the greater confusion of terms, the affective domain presented some special problems. For example, the hierarchical structure was most difficult to find in the affective part of the taxonomy. The principles of simple to complex and concrete to abstract were not sufficient for developing the affective domain. Something additional was needed.

By seeking the unique characteristics of the affective domain, it was hoped that the additional principles needed to structure an affective continuum would be discovered. Analysis of affective objectives showed the following characteristics which the continuum should embody; the emotional quality which is an important distinguishing feature of an affective response at certain levels of the continuum, the increasing automaticity as one progresses up the continuum, the increasing willingness to attend to a specified stimulus or stimulus type as one ascends the continuum, and the developing integration of a value pattern at the upper levels of the continuum.

A structure was first attempted by attaching certain meanings to the terms "attitude," "value," "appreciation," and "interest." But the multitude of meanings

which these terms encompassed in educational objectives showed that this was impossible. After trying a number of schemes and organizing principles, the one which appeared best to account for the affective phenomena and which best described the process of learning and growth in the affective field was the process of internalization.

Internalization refers to the inner growth that occurs as the individual becomes aware of and then adopts attitudes, principles, codes, and sanctions which become inherent in forming value judgments and in guiding his conduct. It has many elements in common with the term socialization. Internalization may be best understood by looking at the categories in the taxonomy structure:

We begin with the individual's being aware of the stimuli which initiate the effective behavior and which form the context in which the affective behavior occurs. Thus, the lowest category is 1.0 *Receiving*. It is subdivided into three categories. At the 1.1 *Awareness* level, the individual merely has his attention attracted to the stimuli (e.g., he develops some consciousness of the use of shading to portray depth and lighting in a picture). The second sub-category, 1.2 *Willingness to Receive*, describes the state in which he has differentiated the stimuli from others and is willing to give it his attention (e.g., he develops a tolerance for bizarre uses of shading in modern art). At 1.3, *Controlled or Selected Attention*, the student looks for the stimuli (e.g., he is on the alert for instances where shading has been used both to create a sense of three-dimensional depth and to indicate the lighting of the picture; or he looks for picturesque words in reading).

At the next level, 2.0 *Responding*, the individual is perceived as responding regularly to the affective stimuli. At the lowest level of responding, 2.1 *Acquiescence in Responding*, he is merely complying with expectations (e.g., at the request of his teacher, he hangs reproductions of famous paintings in his dormitory room; he is obedient to traffic rules). At the next higher level, 2.2 *Willingness to Respond,* he responds increasingly to an inner compulsion (e.g., voluntarily looks for instances of good art where shading, perspective, color, and design have been well used, or has an interest in social problems broader than those of the local community). At 2.3 *Satisfaction in Response* he responds emotionally as well (e.g., works with clay, especially in making pottery for personal pleasure). Up to this point he has differentiated the affective stimuli; he has begun to seek them out and to attach emotional significance and value to them.

As the process unfolds, the next levels of 3.0 *Valuing* describe increasing internalization, as the person's behavior is sufficiently consistent that he comes to hold a value: 3.1 *Acceptance of a Value* (e.g., continuing desire to develop the ability to write effectively and hold it more strongly), 3.2 *Preference for a Value* (e.g., seeks out examples of good art for enjoyment of them to the level where he behaves so as to further this impression actively); and 3.3 *Commitment* (e.g., faith in the power of reason and the method of experimentation).

As the learner successively internalizes values, he encounters situations for which more than one value is relevant. This necessitates organizing the values into a system, 4.0 *Organization.* And since a prerequisite to interrelating values is their conceptualization in a form which permits organization, this level is divided in two; 4.1 *Conceptualization of a Value* (e.g., desires to evaluate works of art which are appreciated, or to find out and crystallize the basic assumptions which underlie codes of ethics) and 4.2 *Organization of a Value System* (e.g., acceptance of the place of art in one's life as one of dominant value, or weighs alternative social policies and practices against the standards of public welfare).

Finally, the internalization and the organization processes reach a point where the individual responds very consistently to value-laden situations with an interrelated set of values, a structure, a view of the world. The taxonomy category that describes this behavior is 5.0 *Characterization by a Value or Value Complex* and it includes the categories 5.1 *Generalized Set* (e.g., views all problems in terms of their aesthetic aspects,

or readiness to revise judgments and to change behavior in the light if evidence) and 5.2 *Characterization* (e.g., develops a consistent philosophy of life).

Stripped of their definitions, the category and sub-category titles appear in sequence as follows:

1.0 Receiving (attending)
    1.1 Awareness
    1.2 Willingness to receive
    1.3 Controlled or selected attention

2.0 Responding
    2.1 Acquiescence in responding
    2.2 Willingness to respond
    2.3 Satisfaction in response

3.0 Valuing
    3.1 Acceptance of a value
    3.2 Preference for a value
    3.3 Commitment (conviction)

4.0 Organization
    4.1 Conceptualization of a value
    4.2 Organization of a value system

5.0 Characterization by a value or a value complex
    5.1 Generalized set
    5.2 Characterization (Krathwohl et al., 1964)

*Uses of Taxonomy.* The nature of the taxonomy should now be clear. What, however, are its uses? We have indicated that a prime use is the analysis and classification of objectives.

No longer should a teacher be faced with an objective like "the student should understand the taxonomy of educational objectives," or "he should appreciate the value of taxonomic frameworks." Rather the teacher can now specify whether the first of these objectives would be at the lowest level of comprehension where he would at least expect the student to be able to translate the term "taxonomy" into something like "a classification system of educational goals," or perhaps at a deeper level of understanding, classified as interpretation, where the student could restate the ideas of the taxonomy in his own words. In short, the taxonomy is a relatively concise model for the analysis of educational objectives.

The taxonomy, like the periodic table of elements or a check-off shopping list, provides the panorama of objectives. Comparing the range of the present curriculum with the range of possible outcomes may suggest additional goals that might be included. Further, the illustrative objectives may suggest wordings that might be adapted to the area being explored.

Frequently, when searching for ideas in building a curriculum, the work of others is most helpful. Where one's own work and that of others are built in terms of the taxonomy categories, comparison is markedly facilitated. Translation of objectives into the taxonomy framework can provide a basis for precise comparison. Further, where similarities exist, it becomes possible to trade experiences regarding the values of certain learning experiences with confidence that there is a firm basis for comparison and that the other person's experience will be truly relevant.

It is perhaps also important to note the implication of the hierarchical nature of the taxonomy for curriculum building. If the analysis of the cognitive and affective areas is correct, then a hierarchy of objectives dealing with the same subject matter concepts suggests a readiness relationship that exists between those objectives lower in the hierarchy and those higher.

The development of the affective domain has pointed up the problems of achieving objectives in this domain. For instance, a study of the relation of the cognitive and affective domains made it apparent that achievement in the affective domain is markedly underemphasized. Thus, the garden variety of objectives concentrates on specifying behavior in only one domain at a time. No doubt this results from the typical analytic approaches to building curricula. Only occasionally do we find a statement like "the student should learn to analyze a good argument with pleasure." Such a statement suggests not only the cognitive behavior but also the affective aspect that accompanies it.

In spite of the lack of explicit formulation, however, nearly all cognitive objectives have an affective component if we search for it. Most instructors hope that their students will develop a continuing interest in the subject matter taught. They hope they will have learned certain attitudes toward the phenomena dealt with or toward the way in which problems are approached. But they leave these goals unspecified. This means that many of the objectives which are classified in the cognitive domain have an implicit but unspecified affective component that could be concurrently classified in the affective domain. Where such an attitude or interest objective refers, as it most often does, to the content of the course as a whole or at least to a sizeable segment of it, it may be most convenient to specify it as a separate objective. Many such affective objectives—the interest objectives, for example—become the affective components of all or most of the cognitive objectives in the course.

The affective domain is useful in emphasizing the fact that affective components exist and in analyzing their nature. Perhaps by its very existence it will encourage greater development of affective components of cognitive objectives.

Further, in the cognitive domain, we are concerned that the student shall be able to do a task when requested. In the affective domain, we are more concerned that he *does do* it when it is appropriate after he has learned that he *can do* it. Even though the whole school system rewards the student more on a *can do* than on a *does do* basis, it is the latter which every instructor seeks. By emphasizing this aspect of the affective components, the affective domain brings to light an extremely important and often missing element in cognitive objectives.

Another aspect which came to light was the extremely slow growth of some of the affective behaviors. We saw this as having implications for both the cognitive and affective domains. Thus, every teacher attempts to evaluate the changes that he has made in his students, and it is clear that it is entirely possible for him to do so successfully at the lower levels of the taxonomy. But a teacher will rarely have the same students over a sufficient period of time to make measurable changes in certain affective behaviors. Some objectives, particularly the complex ones at the top of the affective continuum, are probably attained as the product of all or at least a major portion of a student's years in school. Thus measures of a semester's or year's growth would reveal little change. This suggests that an evaluation plan covering at least several grades and involving the coordinated efforts of several teachers is probably a necessity. A plan involving all the grades in a system is likely to be even more effective. Such efforts would permit gathering longitudinal data on the same students so that gains in complex objectives would be measurable. Patterns of growth in relation to various school efforts would be revealed. Planned evaluation efforts to measure certain cognitive objectives on a longitudinal basis are to be found in some school systems, particularly where they use achievement test batteries designed to facilitate this. Similar efforts with respect to affective objectives are quite rare. If we are serious about attaining complex affective objectives, we shall have to build coordinated evaluation programs that trace the successes and failures of our efforts to achieve them.

In particular, we noted that there was a great deal of "erosion" with respect to the affective domain objectives. When a curriculum is first conceived, affective objectives play an important part in the conceptual structure of the courses. But as time goes on, they cease to have influence on the direction of the courses or in the choice of instructional activities. In part, this results from the fact that rarely are affective objectives reflected in the grading process. Students tend to concentrate on what counts, and affective objectives rarely appear to do so. Since a part of this lack of emphasis on affective objectives in grading is due to the inadequacy of measures and ways of relating measures to objectives, it is possible that the sections of the taxonomy dealing with measurement in the affective domain may help to make these objectives more realistic parts of those courses in which affective objectives are important.

**2. A Framework to Facilitate Construction of Instructional Materials** Perhaps this is enough to indicate the existence and potential usefulness of the taxonomy structure as a means of working with objectives at the curriculum-building level. What about the specification of objectives at the instructional-material–building level? Gagné writes:

Is it in fact possible to divide objectives into categories which differ in their implications for learning? To do this, one has to put together a selected set of learning conditions on the one hand, and an abstracted set of characteristics of human tasks on the other. This is the kind of effort which has been called *task analysis*. Its objective is to distinguish, not the tasks themselves (which are infinitely variable), but the inferred behaviors which presumably require different conditions of learning. Such behavior categories can be distinguished by means of several different kinds of criteria, which in an ultimate sense should be completely compatible with each other. What I should like to try to do here, however, is to use one particular set of criteria, which pertain to the question of "What is learned?" (Gagné, 1964, 1965)

Gagné's structure, which was used in the American Association for the Advancement of Science and National Science Foundation sponsored curriculum— *Science—A Process Approach*—is a blending of behavioristic and cognitive psychology. It is intended to distinguish those types of behaviors from one another which are learned under different conditions. Since it is also a hierarchical scheme, each capability depends on having learned the next simpler one. Gagné's categories in order are:

*Signal Learning*—This refers to the general diffuse and emotional reaction which involuntarily results as a learned reaction to certain stimuli. Fear of water or of heights, or the pleasurable feeling on entering an art gallery, would be examples of this kind of learning.

*Stimulus-Response Learning*—This learning involves a precise skeletal muscle response to a particular complex of stimulation. This form of learning, for example, appears to govern the acquisition of a new vocalization habit by a young child.

*Chaining*—Chaining results from connecting in sequence two previously learned stimulus-response behaviors. Our language is filled with chains of verbal sequences (e.g., horse and buggy). Motor acts such as starting a car or properly putting a specimen under a microscope are also chains.

*Verbal Association*—This type of learning is a sub-variety of chaining which depends on a code or clue which provides the link between the learned responses in the chain. Gagné uses the example of the French student who uses the word "illuminate" as his code or clue. As the student visualizes the illumination of the flame of a match, it provides the code or clue to "alumette," the French word for match.

*Multiple Discrimination*—This type of learning occurs when a number of learned chains interfere with one another so that retention of certain individual chains is shortened and forgetting occurs. Multiple discrimination learning occurs when the teacher is learning to call each of his pupils by his right name.

*Concept Learning*—Concept learning requires response to stimuli in terms of abstract properties such as "shape," "color," "position," or "number." Examples of such concepts are up and down, near and far, and right and left.

*Principle Learning*—Learning a principle requires the chaining of two or more concepts. It is exemplified by the acquisition of the "idea" contained in such propositions as "gases expand when heated."

*Problem Solving*—The chaining of principles into new combinations to fit particular circumstances is the heart of problem solving. Examples would include the solution of simple problems such as the reorganization of an office staff to fit the space available in a new building or the abstract manipulation of physics principles to derive a new theory.

## IMPORTANT NEEDED RESEARCH— HOW TO RELATE FRAMEWORKS

One may question whether either or both of these frameworks are adequate to the tasks that they have set for themselves. If nothing else, however, perhaps they have heuristic value. In fact, by their very existence, they immediately raise the question, How are the two frameworks related? and its derivative question, What instructional methods are of most value in achieving certain categories in either framework? For example, how does Gagné's strategy development relate to the skills of the cognitive domain in applying, analyzing, synthesizing, evaluating? What instructional methods most efficiently and effectively permit achievement of these goals? These are questions that should be the focus of considerable educational research.

# 10. Instrumentation of the Taxonomy of Educational Objectives in Behavioral Terms

## NEWTON S. METFESSEL, WILLIAM B. MICHAEL, and DONALD KIRSNER

One criticism sometimes leveled at the *Taxonomy of Educational Objectives* (see Article 9 by David R. Krathwohl), particularly by evaluators, is that it is not couched in behavioral terms. The latitude deliberately allowed in interpreting the various categories of the *Taxonomy* frequently makes the task of curriculum evaluation and test construction difficult. Metfessel, Michael, and Kirsner have made a very practical contribution by identifying infinitives and direct objects useful in operationalizing levels in both the cognitive and affective domains.

An educational objective consists of a description of the behaviors of an individual (the learner or examinee) in relation to his processing information embodied in subject matter—that is, what the learner must be capable of doing with certain characteristics or properties of subject matter. The behavioral component, which may be described as a process involved at an appropriate level of the taxonomic classification, is usually expressed in the form of a noun "ability" or a verb of being "able" followed by an infinitive such as the "ability to do" or "able to do." The second component of the objective, which consists of the specific content often found in the formal learning experience (e.g., in the curricular or instructional unit), constitutes a direct object of the verb or infinitive form. The terms "subject matter" or "content" are used in a fairly broad sense, as their level of specificity is highly variable, depending upon the characteristics of the curriculum unit.

Reprinted and abridged with permission of the publisher and Newton S. Metfessel from an article entitled "Instrumentation of Bloom's and Krathwohl's Taxonomies for the Writing of Educational Objectives," which appeared in *Psychology in the Schools,* **6** (1969), pp. 227–231.

## INSTRUMENTATION: COGNITIVE DOMAIN

To facilitate the formulation of statements of specific behavioral objectives within the framework of Bloom's taxonomy, the writers have included a table (see Table 1) made up of three columns. The first column contains the taxonomic classification identified by both code number and terminology employed in Bloom's (1956) taxonomy. The entries in the second column consist of appropriate infinitives which the teacher or curriculum worker may consult to achieve a precise or preferred wording of the behavior or activity desired. In the third column somewhat general terms relative to subject matter properties are stated. These direct objects, which may be expanded upon to furnish specificity at a desired level, may be permuted with one or more of the infinitive forms to yield the basic structure of an educational objective—activity (process) followed by content (subject matter property). At the discretion of the reader the words "ability" or "able" can be inserted in front of each of the infinitives.

Although within a given major process level or sublevel of the taxonomy each infinitive cannot in all instances be mean-

**TABLE 1**
**Instrumentation of the Taxonomy of Educational Objectives: Cognitive Domain**

| Taxonomy Classification | Key Words | |
| --- | --- | --- |
| | Examples of Infinitives | Examples of Direct Objects |
| 1.00 Knowledge | | |
| 1.10 Knowledge of Specifics | | |
| 1.11 Knowledge of Terminology | to define, to distinguish, to acquire, to identify, to recall, to recognize | vocabulary, terms, terminology, meaning(s), definitions, referents, elements |
| 1.12 Knowledge of Specific Facts | to recall, to recognize, to acquire, to identify | facts, factual information, (sources), (names), (dates), (events), (persons), (places), (time periods), properties, examples, phenomena |
| 1.20 Knowledge of Ways and Means of Dealing with Specifics | | |
| 1.21 Knowledge of Conventions | to recall, to identify, to recognize, to acquire | form(s), conventions, uses, usage, rules, ways, devices, symbols, representations, style(s), format(s) |
| 1.22 Knowledge of Trends and Sequences | to recall, to recognize, to acquire, to identify | action(s), processes, movement(s), continuity, development(s), trend(s), sequence(s), causes, relationship(s), forces, influences |
| 1.23 Knowledge of Classification and Categories | to recall, to recognize | area(s), type(s), feature(s), class(es), set(s), division(s), arrangement(s), classification(s), category/categories |
| 1.24 Knowledge of Criteria | to recall, to recognize, to acquire, to identify | criteria, basics, elements |
| 1.25 Knowledge of Methodology | to recall, to recognize, to acquire, to identify | methods, techniques, approaches, uses, procedures, treatments |
| 1.30 Knowledge of the Universals and Abstractions in a Field | | |
| 1.31 Knowledge of Principles and Generalizations | to recall, to recognize, to acquire, to identify | principle(s), generalization(s), proposition(s), fundamentals, laws, principal elements, implication(s) |

**TABLE 1** (continued)

| | Taxonomy Classification | Key Words | |
|---|---|---|---|
| | | Examples of Infinitives | Examples of Direct Objects |
| 1.32 | Knowledge of Theories and Structures | to recall, to recognize, to acquire, to identify | theories, bases, interrelations, structure(s), organization(s), formulation(s) |
| 2.00 | Comprehension | | |
| 2.10 | Translation | to translate, to transform, to give in own words, to illustrate, to prepare, to read, to represent, to change, to rephrase, to restate | meanings(s), sample(s), definitions, abstractions, representations, words, phrases |
| 2.20 | Interpretation | to interpret, to reorder, to rearrange, to differentiate, to distinguish, to make, to draw, to explain, to demonstrate | relevancies, relationships, essentials, aspects, new view(s), qualifications, conclusions, methods, theories, abstractions |
| 2.30 | Extrapolation | to estimate, to infer, to conclude, to predict, to differentiate, to determine, to extend, to interpolate | consequences, implications, conclusions, factors, ramifications, meanings, corollaries, effects, probabilities |
| 3.00 | Application | to apply, to generalize, to relate, to choose, to develop, to organize, to use, to employ, to transfer, to restructure, to classify | principles, laws, conclusions, effects, methods, theories, abstractions, situations, generalizations, processes, phenomena, procedures |
| 4.00 | Analysis | | |
| 4.10 | Analysis of Elements | to distinguish, to detect, to identify, to classify, to discriminate, to recognize, to categorize, to deduce | elements, hypothesis/ hypotheses, conclusions, assumptions, statements (of fact), statements (of intent), arguments, particulars |
| 4.20 | Analysis of Relationships | to analyze, to contrast, to compare, to distinguish, to deduce | relationships, interrelations, relevance, relevancies, themes, evidence, fallacies, arguments, cause-effect(s), consistency, consistencies, parts, ideas, assumptions |
| 4.30 | Analysis of Organizational Principles | to analyze, to distinguish, to detect, to deduce | form(s), pattern(s), purpose(s), point(s) of view(s), techniques, bias(es), structure(s), theme(s), arrangement(s), organization(s) |

**TABLE 1** (continued)

| Taxonomy Classification | Key Words | |
| --- | --- | --- |
| | Examples of Infinitives | Examples of Direct Objects |
| 5.00 Synthesis | | |
| 5.10 Production of a Unique Communication | to write, to tell, to relate, to produce, to constitute, to transmit, to originate, to modify, to document | structure(s), pattern(s), product(s), performance(s), design(s), work(s), communications, effort(s), specifics, composition(s) |
| 5.20 Production of a Plan, or Proposed Set of Operations | to propose, to plan, to produce, to design, to modify, to specify | plan(s), objectives, specification(s), schematic(s), operations, way(s), solution(s), means |
| 5.30 Derivation of a Set of Abstract Relations | to produce, to derive, to develop, to combine, to organize, to synthesize, to classify, to deduce, to develop, to formulate, to modify | phenomena, taxonomies, concept(s), scheme(s), theories, relationships, abstractions, generalizations, hypothesis/hypotheses, perceptions, ways, discoveries |
| 6.00 Evaluation | | |
| 6.10 Judgments in Terms of Internal Evidence | to judge, to argue, to validate, to assess, to decide | accuracy/accuracies, consistency/consistencies, fallacies, reliability, flaws, errors, precision, exactness |
| 6.20 Judgments in Terms of External Criteria | to judge, to argue, to consider, to compare, to contrast, to standardize, to appraise | ends, means, efficiency, economy/economies, utility alternatives, courses of action, standards, theories, generalizations |

ingfully or idiomatically paired with every direct object listed, many useful permutations of infinitives and direct objects that furnish entirely readable statements are possible. Certainly use of these tables should lead to a substantial gain in the clarity and speed with which teachers and curriculum specialists, as well as those involved in construction of achievement tests, may state curriculum objectives. The writers have found that these tables have been of considerable help to their students, as well as to personnel in public schools who are concerned with writing objectives prior to curriculum development, constructing test items, or to carrying out evaluation studies. Slight modifi-cations can be made with the entries to meet the requirements of specific learning situations.

## INSTRUMENTATION: AFFECTIVE DOMAIN

The instrumentation of the Affective Domain is the same as that of the Cognitive Domain, to wit, the selection of behaviorally oriented infinitives combined with selected direct objects (see Table 2). As in the case of the Cognitive Domain, these are to be conceptualized as examples for the stimulation of other infinitives and objects and, more important, meaningful objectives in a total framework.

**TABLE 2**
**Instrumentation of the Taxonomy of Educational Objectives: Affective Domain**

| Taxonomy Classification | Key Words | |
| --- | --- | --- |
| | Examples of Infinitives | Examples of Direct Objects |
| 1.0 Receiving | | |
| 1.1 Awareness | to differentiate, to separate, to set apart, to share | sights, sounds, events, designs, arrangements |
| 1.2 Willingness to Receive | to accumulate, to select, to combine, to accept | models, examples, shapes, sizes, meters, cadences |
| 1.3 Controlled or Selected Attention | to select, to posturally respond to, to listen (for), to control | alternatives, answers, rhythms, nuances |
| 2.0 Responding | | |
| 2.1 Acquiescence in Responding | to comply (with), to follow, to commend, to approve | directions, instructions, laws, policies, demonstrations |
| 2.2 Willingness to Respond | to volunteer, to discuss, to practice, to play | instruments, games, dramatic works, charades, burlesque |
| 2.3 Satisfaction in Response | to applaud, to acclaim, to spend leisure time in, to augment | speeches, plays, presentations, writings |
| 3.0 Valuing | | |
| 3.1 Acceptance of a Value | to increase measured proficiency in, to increase numbers of, to relinquish, to specify | group membership(s), artistic production(s), musical productions, personal friendships |
| 3.2 Preference for a Value | to assist, to subsidize, to help, to support | artists, projects, viewpoints, arguments |
| 3.3 Commitment | to deny, to protest, to debate, to argue | deceptions, irrelevancies, abdications, irrationalities |
| 4.0 Organization | | |
| 4.1 Conceptualization of a Value | to discuss, to theorize (on), to abstract, to compare | parameters, codes, standards, goals |
| 4.2 Organization of a Value System | to balance, to organize, to define, to formulate | systems, approaches, criteria, limits |
| 5.0 Characterization by Value of Value Complex | | |
| 5.1 Generalized Set | to revise, to change, to complete, to require | plans, behavior, methods, effort(s) |
| 5.2 Characterization | to be rated high by peers in, to be rated high by superiors in, and to be rated high by subordinates in | humanitarianism, ethics, integrity, maturity |
| | and | |
| | to avoid, to manage, to resolve, to resist | extravagance(s), excesses, conflicts, exorbitancy/ exorbitancies |

# 11. The Importance of Affective Learning Outcomes
## EARL C. KELLEY

A theme previously touched on in Articles 7, 9, and 10 is here expanded and forcefully articulated by Earl C. Kelley. This strong statement reflects a movement pervading all of education to get back to the total human being, a kind of refocusing on humanistic concerns. Educational evaluators must be particularly conscious of this movement because (1) these goals are often left unspecified by their constituents and (2) great effort needs to be made in developing affective evaluation instruments. Those who can implement affectively sensitive evalution programs are in a state of readiness, and many of the needed techniques and devices have been developed. Now is the time to move.

Kelley's comments as they apply to the educationally and economically disadvantaged are particularly relevant today.

Also see Article 29, by Donald R. Chipley, on a related subject.

It has now become abundantly clear, from research and from reason, that *how a person feels is more important than what he knows.* This seems true because how one feels controls behavior, while what one knows does not. What one knows is used in behavior, to be sure, but the way it is used depends upon positive or negative feelings. It is possible to be a saint or a demon with similar knowledge. History furnishes ample illustrations of knowledge being put to evil uses.

We in education are slowly waking up to the fact that feelings are really important. This can be seen in educational literature. There is much discussion of the self-concept, the self-image, and of the fact that if one thinks too little of himself he becomes immobile and unable to learn.

Reprinted and abridged with permission of the Association for Supervision and Curriculum Development and Earl C. Kelley from an article entitled "The Place of Affective Learning," which appeared in *Educational Leadership,* **22** (1965), pp. 455–457. Copyright, 1965 by the Association for Supervision and Curriculum Development.

In fact, the person who has come to hate himself and others does not take in much subject matter.

All of this causes us to take another look at subject matter and its uses. None of the above is to imply that what one knows is not important. One's proper subject matter is the universe around him, and without some comprehension of that universe and his relation to it, he could not know how to deal with it, no matter how he felt.

Subject matter and feeling are so closely intertwined that they can no longer be considered a duality. Everyone who learns something has some feeling about it, and so, as in so many other areas, they are inseparable. No matter what we do, affective learning goes on anyway. When this affective learning is positive, the learner becomes constructive in his behavior.

We need to reconsider our ideas and attitudes toward subject matter itself. It has long been considered an end in itself. If the learner came through in possession of a large store of subject matter, we have said he is "good." If the subject matter was something the learner could not or would not store, and be able to prove that he had stored it, he has been considered "bad," or at least a failure.

We ought to be able to reconsider the role of subject matter in the education of our young without being accused of not valuing subject matter. It is not a question of reducing the importance of what is learned, but of seeing the relationship between accumulated information and the unique learner. Humanistic scholars have on occasion been charged with not wanting learners to learn anything, but only to feel good. This is not true. One basic criticism of the traditional school is that those in attendance do not learn nearly enough. We have reared a generation of people who have been schooled but not educated.

The main reason for this outcome is that with our rigorous subject matter approach we have closed personalities when we should have been opening them. We have used fear and anxiety as motivating devices, and this has repelled the learner when we should have been attracting him. When the learner has not, because of these destructive feelings, learned what we adults purpose him to learn, we have had to resort to coercion of one form or another. Coercion sets in motion a whole cycle of negative affects, often resulting in open hostility and rejection on the part of both learner and teacher. Many such learners are then headed toward the human scrap-heap—the rejects known as dropouts, the educationally disinherited, who in most cases will be unable to cope with the society of the future. It is from this human scrap-heap that most of our delinquent and mentally ill are drawn.

The basic error in most of our curriculum work is that we start with the materials, which are the tools of education, not the product. We choose our tools first, and then look around to see what we are going to do with them. These materials are usually chosen without regard to the individual differences among the learners, often without regard to the culture of the community where the school is located. Curriculum building is the only operation I know about where the tool is chosen before what is to be built is known or decided upon.

We have for so long chosen the curriculum with little regard for the feelings of the learner that we are of course unskilled in planning curriculum with affect in mind. When new understandings show us that how a person feels is more important than what he knows, our old assumptions and procedures will no longer suffice. We are faced with a requirement to learn new methods of using materials. If we had spent as much time in considering the feelings of the learner as we have in choosing and presenting information, we would by now know how to go about it.

## 12. Behavioral Objectives in Curriculum Design: A Cautionary Note

### J. MYRON ATKIN

To say that the "behavioral objectives philosophy" is not subscribed to by all educators and evaluators is a gross understatement. There are certainly many dangers in wholehearted but undisciplined subscription to this approach to planning and assessment. Some of these dangers are discussed by J. Myron Atkin in the following well-reasoned article. A related argument has been presented by Eisner (1967). The implicit plea for a rapprochement between the behaviorist and the discipline scholar is, in particular, in need of consideration.

In certain influential circles, anyone who confesses to reservations about the use of behaviorally stated objectives for curriculum planning runs the risk of being labeled as the type of individual who would attack the virtues of motherhood. Bumper stickers have appeared at my own institution, and probably at yours, reading, *STAMP OUT NON-BEHAVIORAL OBJECTIVES.* I trust that the person who prepared the stickers had humor as his primary aim; nevertheless the crusade for specificity of educational outcome has become intense and evangelical. The worthiness of this particular approach has come to be accepted as self-evident by ardent proponents, proponents who sometimes sound like the true believers who cluster about a new social or religious movement.

Behavioral objectives enthusiasts are warmly endorsed and embraced by the systems and operations analysis advocates, most educational technologists, the cost-benefit economists, the planning-programing budgeting system stylists, and many others. In fact, the behavioral objectives people are now near the center of curriculum decision making. Make no mistake; they have replaced the academicians and the general curriculum theorists—especially in the new electronically based education industries and in governmental planning agencies. The engineering model for educational research and development represents a forceful tide today. Those who have a few doubts about the effects of the tide had better be prepared to be considered uninitiated and naive, if not slightly addlepated and antiquarian.

To utilize the techniques for long-term planning and rational decision making that have been developed with such apparent success in the Department of Defense, and that are now being applied to a range of domestic and civilian problems, it is essential that hard data be secured. Otherwise these modes for developmental work and planning are severely limited. Fuzzy and tentative statements of possible achievement and questions of conflict with respect to underlying values are not compatible with the new instructional systems management approaches—at least not with the present state of the art. In fact, delineating instructional objectives in terms of identifiable pupil behaviors or performances seems essential in 1968 for assessing the output of the educational system. Currently accepted wisdom does not seem to admit an alternative.

There are overwhelmingly useful purposes served by attempting to identify

Reprinted with permission of the publisher and J. Myron Atkin from *The Science Teacher,* **35** (1968), pp. 27–30.

educational goals in non-ambiguous terms. To plan rationally for a growing educational system, and to continue to justify relatively high public expenditures for education, it seems that we do need a firmer basis for making assessments and decisions than now exists. Current attention to specification of curriculum objectives in terms of pupil performance represents an attempt to provide direction for collection of data that will result in more informed choice among competing alternatives.

Efforts to identify educational outcomes in behavioral terms also provide a fertile ground for coping with interesting research problems and challenging technical puzzles. A world of educational research opens to the investigator when he has reliable measures of educational output (even when their validity for educational purposes is low). Pressures from researchers are difficult to resist since they do carry influence in the educational community, particularly in academic settings and in educational development laboratories.

Hence I am not unmindful of some of the possible benefits to be derived from attempts to rationalize our decision-making processes through the use of behaviorally stated objectives. Schools need a basis for informed choice. And the care and feeding of educational researchers is a central part of my job at Illinois. However, many of the enthusiasts have given insufficient attention to underlying assumptions and broad questions of educational policy. I intend in this brief paper to highlight a few of these issues in the hope that the exercise might be productive of further and deeper discussion.

Several reservations about the use of behaviorally stated objectives for curriculum design will be catalogued here. But perhaps the fundamental problem, as I see it, lies in the easy assumption that we either know or can readily identify the educational objectives for which we strive, and thereafter the educational outcomes that result from our programs. One contention basic to my argument is that we presently are making progress toward thousands of goals in any existing educational program, progress of which we are perhaps dimly aware, can articulate only with great difficulty, and that contribute toward goals which are incompletely stated (or unrecognized), but which are often worthy.

For example, a child who is learning about mealworm behavior by blowing against the animal through a straw is probably learning much more than how this insect responds to a gentle stream of warm air. Let's assume for the moment that we can specify "behaviorally" all that he might learn about mealworm *behavior* (an arduous and never-ending task). In addition, in this "simple" activity, he is probably finding out something about interaction of objects, forces, humane treatment of animals, his own ability to manipulate the environment, structural characteristics of the larval form of certain insects, equilibrium, the results of doing an experiment at the suggestion of the teacher, the rewards of independent experimentation, the judgment of the curriculum developers in suggesting that children engage in such an exercise, possible uses of a plastic straw, and the length of time for which one individual might be engaged in a learning activity and still display a high degree of interest. I am sure there are many additional learnings, literally too numerous to mention in fewer than eight or ten pages. When any piece of curriculum is used with real people, there are important learning outcomes that cannot have been anticipated when the objectives were formulated. And of the relatively few outcomes that can be identified at all, a smaller number still are translatable readily in terms of student behavior. There is a possibility the cumulative side effects are at least as important as the intended main effects.

Multiply learning outcomes from the mealworm activity by all the various curriculum elements we attempt to build into a school day. Then multiply this by the number of days in a school year, and you have some indication of the oversimplification that *always* occurs when curriculum intents or outcomes are articulated in any form that is considered manageable.

If my argument has validity to this point, the possible implications are potentially dangerous. If identification of all worthwhile outcomes in behavorial terms comes to be commonly accepted and expected, then it is inevitable that, over time, the curriculum will tend to emphasize those elements which have been thus identified. Important outcomes which are detected only with great difficulty and which are translated only rarely into behavioral terms tend to atrophy. They disappear from the curriculum because we spend all the time allotted to us in teaching explicitly for the more readily specifiable learnings to which we have been directed.

We have a rough analogy in the use of tests. Prestigious examinations that are widely accepted and broadly used, such as the New York State Regents examinations, tend over time to determine the curriculum. Whether or not these examinations indeed measure all outcomes that are worth achieving, the curriculum regresses toward the objectives reflected by the test items. Delineation of lists of behavioral objectives, like broadly used testing programs, may admirably serve the educational researcher because it gives him indices of gross achievement as well as details of particular achievement; it may also provide input for cost-benefit analysts and governmental planners at all levels because it gives them hard data with which to work; but the program in the schools may be affected detrimentally by the gradual disappearance of worthwhile learning activities for which we have not succeeded in establishing a one-to-one correspondence between curriculum elements and rather difficult-to-measure educational results.

Among the learning activities most readily lost are those that are long term and private in effect and those for which a single course provides only a small increment. If even that increment cannot be identified, it tends to lose out in the teacher's priority scheme, because it is competing with other objectives which have been elaborately stated and to which he has been alerted. But I will get to the question of priority of objectives a bit later.

The second point I would like to develop relates to the effect of demands for behavioral specification on innovation. My claim here is that certain types of innovation, highly desirable ones, are hampered and frustrated by early demands for behavioral statements of objectives.

Let's focus on the curriculum reform movement of the past 15 years, the movement initiated by Max Beberman in 1952 when he began to design a mathematics program in order that the high school curriculum would reflect concepts central to modern mathematics. We have now seen curriculum development efforts, with this basic flavor, in many science fields, the social sciences, English, esthetics, etc. When one talks with the initiators of such projects, particularly at the beginning of their efforts, one finds that they do not begin by talking about the manner in which they would like to change pupils' behavior. Rather they are dissatisfied with existing curricula in their respective subject fields, and they want to build something new. If pressed, they might indicate that existing programs stress concepts considered trivial by those who practice the discipline. They might also say that the curriculum poorly reflects styles of intellectual inquiry in the various fields. Press them further, and they might say that they want to build a new program that more accurately displays the "essence" of history, or physics, or economics, or whatever. Or a program that better transmits a comprehension of the elaborate and elegant interconnections among various concepts within the discipline.

If they are asked at an early stage just how they want pupils to behave differently, they are likely to look quite blank. Academicians in the various cognate fields do not speak the language of short-term or long-term behavioral change, as do many psychologists. In fact, if a hard-driving behaviorist attempts to force the issue and succeeds, one finds that the disciplinarians can come up with a list of behavioral goals that looks like a caricature of the subject field in question. (Witness the AAAS elementary-school science program directed toward teaching "process.")

Further, early articulation of behavioral objectives by the curriculum developer inevitably tends to limit the range of his exploration. He becomes committed to designing programs that achieve these goals. Thus if specific objectives in behavioral terms are identified early, there tends to be a limiting element built into the new curriculum. The innovator is less alert to potentially productive tangents.

The effective curriculum developer typically begins with *general* objectives. He then refines the program through a series of successive approximations. He doesn't start with a blueprint, and he isn't in much of a hurry to get his ideas represented by a blueprint.

A situation is created in the newer curriculum design procedures based on behaviorally stated objectives in which scholars who do not talk a behavioral-change language are expected to describe their goals at a time when the intricate intellectual subtleties of their work may not be clear, even in the disciplinary language with which they are familiar. At the other end, the educational evaluator, the behavioral specifier, typically has very little understanding of the curriculum that is being designed—understanding with respect to the new view of the subject field that it affords. It is too much to expect that the behavioral analyst, or anyone else, recognize the shadings of meaning in various evolving economic theories, the complex applications of the intricacies of wave motion, or the richness of nuance reflected in a Stravinsky composition.

Yet despite this two-culture problem—finding a match between the behavioral analysts and the disciplinary scholars—we still find that an expectation is being created for early behavioral identification of essential outcomes.

(Individuals who are concerned with producing hard data reflecting educational outputs would run less risk of dampening innovation if they were to enter the curriculum development scene in a more unobstrusive fashion—and later—than is sometimes the case. The curriculum developer goes into the classroom with only a poorly articulated view of the changes he wants to make. Then he begins working with children to see what he can do. He revises. He develops new ideas. He continually modifies as he develops. *After* he has produced a program that seems pleasing, it might then be a productive exercise for the behavioral analyst to attempt with the curriculum developer to identify *some* of the ways in which children seem to be behaving differently. If this approach is taken, I would caution, however, that observers be alert for long-term as well as short-term effects, subtle as well as obvious inputs.)

A third basic point to be emphasized relates to the question of instructional priorities, mentioned earlier. I think I have indicated that there is a vast library of goals that represent possible outcomes for any instructional program. A key educational task, and a task that is well handled by the effective teacher, is that of relating educational goals to the situation at hand —as well as relating the situation at hand to educational goals. It is impractical to pursue all goals thoroughly. And it does make a difference *when* you try to teach something. Considerable educational potential is lost when certain concepts are taught didactically. Let's assume that some third-grade teacher considers it important to develop concepts related to sportsmanship. It would be a rather naive teacher who decided that she would undertake this task at 1:40 PM on Friday of next week. The experienced teacher has always realized that learnings related to such an area must be stressed in an appropriate context, and the context often cannot be planned.

Perhaps there is no problem in accepting this view with respect to a concept like sportsmanship, but I submit that a similar case can be made for a range of crucial cognitive outcomes that are basic to various subject-matter fields. I use science for my examples because I know more about this field than about others. But equilibrium, successive approximation, symmetry, entropy, and conservation are pervasive ideas with a broad range of application. These ideas are taught with the richest meaning only when they are emphasized repeatedly in appropriate and varied contexts. Many of these contexts arise in classroom situations that are unplanned, but that have powerful potential. It is detrimental to learning not to capitalize on the opportune moments for effectively teaching one idea or another. Riveting the teacher's attention to a few behavioral goals provides him with blinders that may limit his range. Directing him to hundreds of goals leads to confusing, mechanical pedagogic style and loss of spontaneity.

A final point to be made in this paper relates to values, and it deals with a primary flaw in the consumption of much educational research. It is difficult to resist the assumption that those attributes which we can measure are the elements which we consider most important. This point relates to my first, but I feel that it is essential to emphasize the problem. The behavioral analyst seems to assume that for an objective to be worthwhile, we must have methods of observing progress.

But worthwhile goals come first, not our methods for assessing progress toward these goals. Goals are derived from our needs and from our philosophies. They are not and should not be derived primarily from our measures. It borders on the irresponsible for those who exhort us to state objectives in behavioral terms to avoid the issue of determining worth. Inevitably there is an implication of worth behind any act of measurement. What the educational community poorly realizes at the moment is that behavioral goals may or may not be worthwhile. They are articulated from among the vast library of goals because they are stated relatively easily. Again, let's not assume that what we can presently measure necessarily represents our most important activity.

I hope that in this paper I have increased rather than decreased the possibilities for constructive discourse about the use of behavioral objectives for curriculum design. The issues here represent a few of the basic questions that seem crucial enough to be examined in an open forum that admits the possibility of fresh perspectives. Too much of the debate related to the use of behavioral objectives has been conducted in an argumentative style that characterizes discussions of fundamental religious views among adherents who are poorly informed. A constructive effort might be centered on identification of those issues which seem to be amenable to resolution by empirical means and those which do not. At any rate, I feel confident that efforts of the next few years will better inform us about the positive as well as negative potential inherent in a view of curriculum design that places the identification of behavioral objectives at the core.

# 13. Value Components of Teacher's Judgments of Educational Objectives

## THOMAS O. MAGUIRE

There is a paucity of research on objectives or, at least of research in the sense of empirical investigation. The investigation reported by Maguire describes value components of teachers' judgments of educational objectives. Such an outcome is valuable in and of itself. But a potentially more important outcome is the attempt to tie teacher decision making and teacher characteristics to the value components. Because of the relatively small sample of teachers involved, the results should probably be accepted with some caution. Perhaps the chief value of this article lies in the design of the research project, which may serve as a prototype of the kinds of research that should be undertaken on educational objectives.

Within the past few years, the isolated practices of curriculum evaluators have been merged into a formal technology. Concurrent with this merger, an expansion in the legitimate domain of the evaluator has occurred. One aspect of this broadened domain has been the acknowledgment by evaluators that curricular objectives are deserving of the same precise scrutiny that was formerly lavished only on the measurement of their attainment. This acknowledgment has been a gradual process, and it is interesting to trace its emergence.

Perhaps the forerunner of all modern curriculum evaluation was the work carried out by the evaluation staff of the Commission on the Relation of School and College (the eight-year study). Tyler and his staff (Smith et al., 1942) devised and implemented a philosophy of evaluation that formed the basis of almost all subsequent evaluation thought. Five major purposes of evaluation were seen by them:

1. To make a periodic check on the effectiveness of an educational program.
2. To validate the hypotheses upon which the school operates.
3. To provide information basic to the effective guidance of individual students.
4. To provide a certain psychological security to school, staff, students, and parents by furnishing evidence as to whether or not the school was achieving the goals it had set for itself.
5. To provide a sound basis for public relations by indicating the value of the school program.

In accordance with their responsibility for advising participating schools in devising and improving their evaluation programs, the evaluation committee formulated seven steps for setting up an effective educational evaluation program.

1. Formulating objectives.
2. Classifying objectives.
3. Defining objectives in terms of behavior.

Reprinted and abridged with permission of the publisher and Thomas O. Maguire from *Audio-Visual Communication Review,* **16** (Spring 1968), pp. 63–86.

4. Suggesting situations in which achievement of objectives would be shown.
5. Selecting and trying promising evaluation methods.
6. Developing and improving appraisal methods.
7. Interpreting results.

These seven steps provided the now familiar framework upon which many evaluation programs are hung. Of most interest to the present study was the first step. The evaluation committee stated that to carry out an evaluation, it was necessary to know the objectives of the program. However, the evaluation of the objectives themselves was not considered to be a concern of an external evaluator. This is not to imply that Tyler and his committee did not recognize the importance of justifying objectives, but merely that such a task was not perceived as being in their domain.

During the mid-1950's, a second large evaluation study was carried out by the American Council on Education. The description of the Cooperative Study of Evaluation in General Education provided by Dressel and Mayhew (1954) indicated that there were six possible purposes of evaluation in general education.

1. Clarification and possible redefinition of the objectives of general education.
2. Development of more adequate and reliable means of measurement.
3. Appraisal of the development of students.
4. Adaptation of the courses and programs to the individual students.
5. Motivation of student learning through continued self-evaluation.
6. Improvement of instruction.

From the reports of each of the subcommittees which dealt with a particular broad objective, it is apparent that considerable effort was devoted to classifying broad objectives and developing more adequate and reliable means of measurement. This may have been more indicative of the state of measurement in the field of general education than a reflection on the utilities of the subcommittees. It appeared that members of each subcommittee considered the broad aim they had been assigned and attempted to redefine it in terms of more specific objectives. These more specific aims or areas of interest were then treated differentially in the remainder of the committee's consideration. No report was made as to how such decisions were made. It seems obvious, however, that while priorities were implicit in decisions to study certain objectives, the assessment of the value of the objectives was not explicitly undertaken.

Thus, important evaluation thought up to the late 1950's was characterized by its stress on the behavioral statement of objectives. Since very few competing curricula had completely common objectives, the assessments of curricula generally were made in terms of how well they met their stated objectives rather than how well they fared when matched against each other. At the time such ideas were being advocated, there was a legitimate need for their forceful presentation, but a point of sophistication has been reached in contemporary curriculum evaluation where attention can now be directed to additional problems.

With the coming of the large federally endowed curriculum projects, scholars from many disciplines have become interested in the problems of curriculum development and in the concomitant problems of evaluation. Thus, recent curriculum evaluation thought can be characterized by an expansion in the range of evaluation activities brought about in part by the demands of the funding agencies for proof of results; in part by the demands of the noneducationist curriculum developers for more knowledge about the educational process; and in part by pressures from educationists like Cronbach, who saw the need for evaluation in course improvement. A further characteristic of the new era of evaluation has been the attempt by several writers to formulate a conceptual framework of curriculum evaluation. Notable among these has been Scriven's "Methodology of Evaluation" (1967).

Following the theme of the Scriven pronouncements, Taylor and Maguire (1966) attempted to formulate a theoretical model of curriculum evaluation. Their model was based on a rational-sequential approach to curriculum development. The needs of society were conceived of as being interpreted by various social agents (newspapers, professional organizations, government, industry, parents, etc.) into broad objectives. These broad objectives were said to be translated into behavioral objectives by curriculum developers. In turn, the behavioral statements became translated into strategies for the classroom. The student interaction with these strategies was described as resulting in observable behaviors.

The model was not a strong model, subject to empirical verification, but rather was a representation of curriculum development geared to curriculum evaluation which was intended to suggest variables to be measured, judgments to be obtained, and contingencies to be determined. Its validity as a mode of representation lies in whether an evaluator, aware of the model, attends to variables, judgments, and contingencies that he would not have attended to otherwise.

The authors noted that evaluation activities have two components, a measurement component and a value-assessment component. In the context of the model, the measurement component consisted of establishing the degree of fidelity of each of the translations, i.e., how accurately broad objectives are represented by behavioral statements, how completely behavioral objectives are manifested in strategies, and how congruent outcomes are with objectives. The judgmental role of evaluation with respect to the broad objectives was seen as being concerned with the worth of the broad objectives to society as a whole. It was suggested that the worth of the behavioral objectives be judged in terms of their priority to the entire educational program; that the value of the strategies be judged in terms of the efficiency and adequacy of the set of strategies for bringing about student outcomes; and that judgments of the student outcomes also be made to determine how well they fit with the objectives.

## USES OF EDUCATIONAL OBJECTIVES

That educational objectives serve a variety of purposes has been [frequently] pointed out. Some of the purposes are to direct the ongoing classroom instruction, to guide in the selection of content, to aid in the evaluation of student progress, to direct course evaluation activities, and to aid in the development of new programs. Because of their many purposes, it is useful to conceive of objectives as existing at several levels of abstraction as, for example, Krathwohl's (1965) three-level classification. The most abstract level (level one) consists of broad general statements which are useful for laying out extended educational programs. In many respects this level is similar to Taylor and Maguire's broad objectives although the latter imply a vagueness of statement as well as a generality of aim. At Krathwohl's second level, objectives are stated behaviorally but are still broad in the sense that they cover an instructional unit. At the most concrete level are the objectives of specific lesson plans. These are the behavioral objectives of Mager (1962), for example. It is at this specific behavioral level that much of the attention of an important segment of the programed instruction philosophy has been focused.

It has been noted earlier that the assessment of objectives at all levels of abstraction has become as important an activity in a complete evaluation as the measurement of student outcomes. A potentially fruitful method of evaluating objectives is to delineate frames of reference within which judgments of worth should be made and then to suggest groups of judges who are qualified to make judgments within each framework. Thus, if as Taylor and Maguire suggested, one wished to determine the significance of an objective in terms of the public good, social philosophers would appear to be an appropriate group of judges. If one were concerned with assessing several sequential objectives in terms of the appropriateness to a particular age level, one might elicit judgments from developmental psychologists. As an illustration of how one could use special groups to make assessments about objectives in terms of a particular framework of value, Taylor (1966), as one part of a larger study, asked groups of biological scientists, curriculum writers, and teachers to judge several high school biology objectives in terms of their importance to biological sciences' curriculum development. The results of this portion of Taylor's study indicated that if one asks pertinent questions of appropriate judges, a replicable assessment of an objective within a particular value-framework is possible.

In the Taylor-Maguire model, as in the Krathwohl classification, objectives were conceived of as being expressible at more than one level of abstraction. Taylor and Maguire suggested that judgments regarding the broadest objectives are most properly in the domain of those most concerned with the relationship between education and the broad directions of society. At more concrete levels, experts in pedagogy and subject-matter areas would seem to be an appropriate pool from which to draw judges.

The present study was directed particularly toward the judgments of the group of experts who are most immediately concerned with the implementation of the curriculum at its point of contact with the student—the teacher. It is contended that teachers' assessments of curricular objectives can control the impact that a curriculum has on a student. It is important to consider the level of objectives at which the teacher operates in order to understand the mechanism of this control.

At the instructional level, some behaviorists would insist that teachers should make a prior statement of objectives at Krathwohl's level three. Such an insistence may be defensible when applied to the writers of programed materials and perhaps also textbook writers, although Atkin (1963) and Eisner (1966) would argue otherwise, but it is unrealistic to expect it of the classroom teacher. To create the detailed list of objectives necessary for five 45-minute classroom discussions would require exceedingly large amounts of nonclassroom time. Secondly, and more importantly, if there is any advantage to the teacher over other methods of presentation, it likely lies in the flexibility of the teacher which allows him to take advantage of the unpredictable occurrences in a classroom discussion and turn them into useful learning experiences. Although it does not necessarily follow that the expression of specific objectives preempts the taking advantage of momentary occurrences, what is known about cognitive set makes such preemption seem very likely.

It is more realistic to suppose that the kinds of objectives that the teacher makes use of in his classroom activities are the objectives of Krathwohl's second level. (This is not to say that all teachers explicitly state their objectives in this form, but it does suggest that the implicit objectives are of this level.) Although there is no absolute line of demarcation between the objectives of level three and level two, the latter tend to be expressed in terms of conglomerations of behaviors or in terms of behavioral constructs such as understanding, appreciating, enjoying, etc., whereas level-three objectives must be stated in terms of observable behaviors.

For classroom use, level-two objectives

are useful for determining the content to be covered in a unit, for selecting experiences to be arranged for the students, and for guiding in the construction of evaluation instruments. The source of these objectives is usually traceable to curriculum guides or to textbooks, although, occasionally, a creative group of teachers may develop their own. In any case, the teacher has a profound influence on whether or not the objectives of a unit are achieved. This influence may be formal as in the case of curriculum committees made up of teachers of a subject-matter department who decide which are the important aspects of a proposed curriculum. Or, at the classroom level, the teacher may choose to ignore one section of a text and its concomitant objectives. Although the formal influence is significant, the more important influence may be the informal one that the teacher exerts in his treatment of various aspects of a course. For example, if a psychology teacher is required to teach a unit on drug addition and its effects on the individual and society, with the objective of dissuading students from using harmful drugs, and if the teacher feels that this objective, though worthy, is of tertiary importance to his course, then the likelihood of successful achievement of the objective would appear to be small. Certain studies concerning teacher attitudes would lead us to believe that these attitudes can be conveyed to the students along with the primary message of the instruction (Runkel, 1956).

## VALUE AND OBJECTIVES

Thus, for a curriculum developer to implement his curriculum successfully, it is essential that he know what teachers' assessments of program objectives are. In the context of the Taylor-Maguire model, this suggests that one of the judgmental groups that must be consulted in order to determine the value of objectives is the teacher group.

Few empirical studies have been undertaken to determine how objects in general and objectives in particular possess value. Most value reference systems have arisen from logical analyses of the phenomena of interest. In this vein, Butler (1957) developed a scheme for evaluating activities. Based on Parsons' (1951) classification of evaluative action orientations, the scheme consisted of four frames of value reference: *instrumental, ethical, aesthetic,* and *hedonistic.* With some modification, it was felt that objectives could be evaluated in these terms as well. Morris (1964) reported the results of a study designed to abstract evaluational frames of reference from individuals' ratings of several statements of ways to live. Closer scrutiny revealed that the results of Morris' study provided empirical validation for Butler's frames of reference.

In the more specific consideration of value in educational objectives, a study by Downey and associates (1960) proved valuable. After reviewing a considerable number of reports, studies, and opinions, Downey suggested that there were 16 broad objectives or "tasks" of public education. By asking several groups of individuals to rate these tasks according to their indispensability, they found that the tasks were evaluated according to their contribution to each of four kinds of development: *intellectual, social, personal,* and *productive.*

Ohnmacht (1965) analyzed ranked educational objectives as an approach to determining the value orientations of a group of college professors. The rankings were correlated over people, and an obverse factor analysis was carried out. The description of individuals classified as a result of the analysis indicated that they had value orientations subsumable under previously mentioned classifications.

From these studies and other more philosophical works, a core of evaluational frames of reference which seemed pertinent to educational objectives was obtained, which formed the basis of the present study.

**The Procedure** Specifically, the study had four purposes:

1. To suggest a set of verbal labels which describe the value attributed to educational objectives by teachers; and to group these labels into more parsimonious clusters, or value aspects.
2. To suggest a model of decision-making behavior which relates teachers' assessments of the value of an objective to a set of hypothetical decisions about the objective.
3. To group teachers into homogeneous decision-making groups.
4. To search for biographical characteristics which differentiate the groups found in item 3.

Two sets of instructional objectives were selected at random from a pool of objectives which had been set up to represent objectives from all subject-matter areas and to represent objectives derived from all of the broad tasks of public education defined by Downey. These objectives are shown in Tables 13.1 and 13.2. Thirty bipolar adjectival scales, each of which appeared to be descriptive of some component of value, were assembled from two sources. The first source was the group of studies reviewed earlier. The second was a pilot group of teachers who were

**TABLE 1**
**List of Objectives**

1. The student will be able to read literary classics in their original language. *(Foreign Languages) (Communication of Knowledge)*
2. The student will be able to differentiate authentic antiques from fraudulent ones. *(Fine Arts) (Consumer Preparation)*
3. The student will be able to add two digit octal (base eight) numbers. *(Mathematics) (Possession of Knowledge)*
4. The student will become physically fit by dancing. *(Fine Arts) (Physical Development)*
5. The student will be able to discriminate between literal and implied meaning in advertising. *(Language Arts) (Consumer Preparation)*
6. The student will be able to distinguish between facts and false notions in matters relating to sex. *(Biology) (Preparation for Home and Family)*
7. The student will be able to gain emotional relaxation by listening to classical music. *(Fine Arts) (Aesthetic Development)*
8. The student will be able to list the services provided by the government for the treatment of mental disorders. *(Social Studies) (Emotional Development)*
9. The student will know enough modern math to be able to tutor his (or her) future children. *(Mathematics) (Preparation for Home and Family)*
10. The student will become sufficiently interested in a particular vocation to voluntarily seek out a vocational counselor. *(Vocational Education) (Desire for Knowledge)*
11. The student will be able to discuss the social responsibilities involved in applying scientific discoveries. *(Physical Sciences) (Ethical Development)*
12. The student will be able to read and understand the significance of "lay" translations of medical reports. *(Health) (Communication of Knowledge)*
13. The student will be motivated to read a daily newspaper to keep abreast of world affairs. *(Social Studies) (Desire for Knowledge)*
14. The student will be able to break an English sentence into components. *(Language Arts) (Possession of Knowledge)*
15. The student will be able to list the qualifications necessary for employment in various fields of recreation. *(Physical Education) (Vocation Selection)*

**TABLE 2**
**List of Objectives**

1. The student will be able to add, subtract, multiply, and divide three digit numbers with speed and accuracy. *(Mathematics) (Possession of Knowledge)*
2. The student will be able to recite the definitive characteristics of the animal classes. *(Biology) (Possession of Knowledge)*
3. The student will be able to describe the relationships of the various components of the automobile. *(Vocational Education) (Communication of Knowledge)*
4. The student will be able to speak in a grammatically correct fashion in an employment interview situation. *(Language Arts) (Vocation Preparation)*
5. The student will be able to name the general requirements of city ordinances regarding home improvements. *(Industrial Arts and Home Economics) (Preparation for Home and Family)*
6. The student will be able to read foreign language newspapers to determine foreign opinion of American policies. *(Foreign Languages) (Man's Relationship to Man)*
7. The student will be able to discuss the role played by the Olympic games in the furtherance of world peace. *(Physical Education) (Man's Relationship to World)*
8. The student will be able to describe the struggles, sacrifices, and achievements of the people who built this nation. *(Social Studies) (Man's Relationship to Country)*
9. The student will be able to read a road map. *(Social Studies) (Preparation for Home and Family)*
10. The student will be able to interpret graphical representations of defense commitments in terms of subjective probabilities for world peace. *(Mathematics) (Man's Relationship to World)*
11. The student will be able to understand semipopular scientific journals such as *Scientific American*. *(Science) (Communication of Knowledge)*
12. The student will be able to give the names of the common household objects in one language other than English. *(Foreign Languages) (Consumer Preparation)*
13. The student will be able to describe the relationship of job satisfaction to mental health. *(Vocational Education) (Emotional Development)*
14. The student will be able to overcome his emotional problems by painting. *(Fine Arts) (Emotional Development)*
15. The student will be motivated to pursue a program of physical fitness as a patriotic duty *(Social Studies) (Physical Development)*

asked to consider each of several objectives and to write down several terms which indicated how the objectives possessed value. In all, over 200 adjective phrases were considered. Because the incidence of near synonymity was high, 30 scales were selected as being representative of the value space of educational objectives. These scales are shown in Table 13.3.

Four hypothetical decisions were created to simulate different kinds of judgments that teachers are called upon to make. In the first, subjects were asked to estimate the number of classroom hours that should be devoted to the pursuit of each objective. Secondly, they were asked to indicate on a seven-point scale their subjective feeling as to the amount of commitment that they would personally feel toward pursuit of the objective. Thirdly, they were asked to indicate the amount of commitment that the high school system in general should have in pursuing the objective. The subjects were also asked to rank the objectives from

**TABLE 3**
**Thirty Bipolar Descriptions of Value**

1. morally valuable—morally worthless
2. value oriented—knowledge oriented
3. authoritarian—democratic
4. society oriented—individual oriented
5. traditional—progressive
6. topical—out of date
7. practical—theoretical
8. enjoyable—boring
9. socially valuable—socially worthless
10. concrete—abstract
11. transmission of culture—life adjustment
12. not economically feasible—economically feasible
13. not motivating—motivating
14. broad—specific
15. divergent—convergent
16. complex—simple
17. nonhumanitarian—humanitarian
18. interesting to all—interesting to only a few
19. appropriate for all—appropriate for only a few
20. not transferable—highly transferable
21. precise—vague
22. easy to teach—difficult to teach
23. difficult to learn—easy to learn
24. difficult to evaluate—easy to evaluate
25. requires reasoning—requires rote memory
26. peripheral to the subject—basic to the subject
27. vocationally worthless—vocationally valuable
28. academically valuable—academically worthless
29. objective—subjective
30. isolated—integrative

most important in the school program to least important.

Three hundred teachers were asked to participate in the study. Of these, 98 actually completed the tasks. These teachers were randomly assigned into two groups of 50 (Sample I) and 48 (Sample II) teachers. Biographical data such as sex, age, years of teaching experience, years of college, population of school where now teaching, location of school, type of school, and subject matter area taught were gathered.

The analysis was carried out independently for each sample to determine whether or not any conclusions would generalize across different samples of teachers and objectives.

Intercorrelations among scales across people and objectives were calculated, and the resulting matrices were resolved into their principal components. Components corresponding to roots greater than one were rotated to the varimax criterion. The rotated components . . . were termed "value-aspects." . . . For Sample I, the value aspects were labeled: Motivational Qualities and Moral Value, Subject-Matter Value, Ease of Implementation, Statement Properties, Individual versus Social Value, and Subjective versus Objective. For Sample II, they were labeled: Motivational Qualities, Statement Properties, Ease of Implementation, Moral Value, Subject-Matter Value, and Individual versus Socio-Cultural. . . . The results [also] indicated that four of the aspects appeared to have counterparts in both samples. These four were Subject-Matter Value, Motivational Qualities, Ease of Implementation, and Statement Properties. The Subject-Matter aspect referred to an estimation of how the students would react to an objective, the Statement Properties aspect referred to the phrasing of the objective itself as distinct from its content, and Ease of Implementation aspect referred to how easily the object could be taught, learned, evaluated, etc.

A model of decision making was proposed, in which the decision made was considered to be dependent upon a linear combination of the value aspect scores of the objectives as perceived by the teachers. The use of this model was supported by the literature on clinical decisions (for example, Hoffman [1960]) and by the literature on interpersonal perception (for example, Rodwan and Hake [1964]). It was suggested that for a given teacher, the dependency of a given decision on a particular value aspect was proportional to the validity coefficient existing between the decision and the aspect for that teacher. For each teacher, six such validity coefficients were calculated over the 15 objectives between the aspect scores and the decision scores. As an indication of the upper limit of the accuracy of the model, multiple correlations were calculated between each decision and the aspect scores.

## CONCLUSIONS

Because different samples of teachers and objectives were used, the study is really one study and a replication. Only those conclusions which occurred in both samples were considered to be worthy of serious consideration. Briefly, the conclusions were as follows:

1. Six value aspects were isolated for each sample. Of these, four were found to be stable across different sets of teachers and different sets of objectives. These four were described as Subject-Matter Value, Motivational Qualities, Ease of Implementation, and Statement Properties.
2. It was found that the output of a judgmental decision concerning an educational objective could be accurately described using a linear model in which value aspect scores for objectives were combined to predict the decision. Further, it was found that apparent judgmental policies of the teachers were very consistent over different decisions.
3. The only relationship which occurred for both samples was the tendency for older teachers to be less Subject-Matter Value oriented than their younger colleagues.

**Some Thoughts on Value Aspects of Educational Objectives** The resolution of the 30 bipolar scales into six value aspects resulted in a loss of approximately

40 percent of the variance that was present in the original scales. Nonetheless, almost all of the scales had a substantial loading on at least one of the aspects. The major exception to this was scale twelve, Economically Feasible vs. Not Economically Feasible. This scale apparently was not sufficiently related to any of the other scales to show on one of the common aspects—a finding which occurred in both samples. It suggests that the economic value of an objective (or better, the cost of implementing it) is quite distinct from other types of value. It also suggests that teachers may not be practiced in conceptualizing objectives in such terms. A similar study conducted with administrators might reveal quite a different structure.

A comparison of the value structures for the two samples has been made. The structures are reexamined here to put them into the context of the literature cited earlier. In both samples, using different objectives, a Motivational Qualities aspect appeared. The common theme of this aspect for both samples was a prediction of what the students' reaction would be to an objective. In terms of Butler's (1957) scheme, it seems to be a prediction of the hedonistic value that the objective would have for the student.

The aspects which were called Statement Properties and Ease of Implementation also occurred in both samples. The Statement Properties aspect is an aesthetic evaluation of the objective in that it refers to the precision of statement of the objectives rather than to the meaning of the objective. The Ease of Implementation aspect could be conceived of as being somewhat hedonistic from the teachers' viewpoint. Its meaning appears to refer to the amount of trouble that the teacher would have in implementing the objective.

The Subject-Matter Value aspect appears in both samples as well. It has more than one counterpart in the dimensions of value mentioned earlier, being a combination of instrumental value (by inclusion of scales like Vocationally Valuable), transfer value (from scales such as Integrative), and intrinsic academic value.

For Sample I, the anticipated Moral Value aspect did not occur, but, instead, scales which might have composed this aspect were clustered with the Motivational Qualities aspect. In Sample II, these scales fell out as a separate aspect. This irregularity may have arisen from the differences between the samples of objectives. The correlation which apparently existed between the Motivational Quality scales and the Moral Value scales may exist only for certain sets of objectives. An alternative explanation might be that the current moral revolution is construed by the teachers as a substantial force in the lives of their students and therefore of interest to them.

Two other dimensions of value were anticipated, "Importance to the Individual" and "Importance to Society." The structure of scale four (Society Oriented vs. Individual Oriented) tended to force the two suggested dimensions into a single bipolar aspect. In Sample I, aspect five was labeled Individual vs. Social Value. The scales of which it is composed seem to differentiate between man, the master of his own fate, and man, dependent on society. This aspect corresponds to valuing objectives in terms of their importance to the individual.

Aspect six of Sample I was not foreseen in the literature review; its structure is defined mainly by the Life Adjustment-Transmission of Culture, and Subjective-Objective scales. If the study had been conducted 20 years ago, one would have expected the Progressive-Traditional scale to make a contribution to this aspect since at that time progressive education and life adjustment education elicited the same connotations.

**Some Implications** The most immediate extension that must be made is to expand the range of decisions to which the findings apply. Recent developments in video-taping teaching episodes would allow us to put teachers in common classroom situations where decisions about objectives have to be made, to observe their reactions to these situations, and to determine the value components that went into their decisions. Such techniques would allow us to look at objectives which are more specific—for example, the objectives of Krathwohl's (1965) level three.

A second extension is to expand the study to include other groups who have an effect on the selection and promulgation of objectives. Such groups would include administrators, school board members, parents, local pressure groups, etc. Are the combinational policies of these groups any different from those of the teachers? If so, how do they differ and how are the differences resolved in practice? One can see that we soon begin to impinge on the area of the social psychologists, and there will be a need to incorporate the experimental and observational techniques of social psychology with the "inference from model" technique illustrated by the present study.

It was seen in the analysis of the biographical data that more information descriptive of the teachers' personalities was needed. Succeeding investigations might focus on studying individuals in greater depth, even if it calls for using fewer individuals.

The preeminent concern in initiating this study has been to further the development of a methodology of evaluation. What has been found suggests that there are several dimensions of value which must be considered when objectives are assessed. One of the dimensions, Subject-Matter Value, has long been acknowledged as an important component of value to be investigated in a thorough evaluation. Other of our aspects of value, such as the Motivational Qualities of an objective, are attended to less often.

The technique which has been developed can be applied to other groups from which judgments of value are elicited.

The biographical data analysis suggests that there may be subtle differences in the value structures of various educator groups; consequently, the successful implementation of a program may be determined in part by the agreement among these value structures. It is hoped that future studies will be concerned with investigating this relationship between program success and value congruence among the principal agents of curriculum development and implementation.

After noting several clinical signs of a general malaise, such as (1) avoidance of involvement in evaluation, (2) fear of being evaluated, (3) misadvice offered by evaluators, (4) lack of meaningful guidelines for evaluation, and (5) unresponsiveness to the concept of evaluation or even to available data, Guba (1969) could only conclude that educational evaluation, as it is practiced today, is a failure and requires reshaping and revitalization. He goes on to cite a number of deficiencies in the concepts and goals of evaluation, deficiencies that must be remedied if progress is to be made. These deficiencies are related to the lack of adequate (1) definitions of evaluation, (2) evaluation models and theory, (3) knowledge about decision processes, (4) criteria for judging value, (5) multilevel technology, (6) mechanisms for organizing, processing and reporting information, and (7) training of personnel.

Guba has painted a rather dismal picture of the state of the art and science of evaluation, and one might question why we begin this part on such a negative note. The editor's intent is to show that things are not as bad as they might appear. Only by identifying the shortcomings of current conceptualizations and methodologies can we hope to search out new solutions to new and old evaluation problems.

With his tongue securely in his cheek, Richard Wolf begins this part by describing the "5-C" model of curriculum evaluation. Each of the five methods (cosmetic, cardiac, colloquial, curricular, and computational) has been used more frequently than we would like to admit. By holding these methods up to ridicule, Wolf enables us to see better what not to do.

Next, G.A. Forehand considers some general problems faced by the evaluator, such as design adequacy, use of control groups, and the nature of objectives.

# Planning for the Design and Analysis of Evaluation Studies

part

There follows a group of three papers presenting different kinds of evaluation models. Each model has its own distinctive flavor and intent, though there are both similarities and differences among the models. Many apparent differences are merely a function of emphasis. The first of the models, by Lee J. Cronbach, focuses primarily on the improvement of the classroom teaching-learning process through the application of evaluative techniques. Cronbach proposes a more-or-less "absolute" framework of standards and criteria for evaluating curricula. A somewhat more abstract model, presented by Robert E. Stake, emphasizes the collecting and processing of descriptive and judgmental data, and examination of the congruence between intents and observations, on the one hand, and contingencies between antecedents, transactions, and both logical and empirical outcomes on the other. One outstanding characteristic of this model is its responsiveness to the expectations of those concerned with the evaluation project. Stake's plea for greater attention to judgment data should be heeded. The third model would fit well into a school or school system. Metfessel and Michael suggest an eight-step procedural outline of the evaluation process. One interesting dimension of their model is the specification of roles for lay individuals, professional personnel, and students.

The next article, by Richard C. Anderson, should be contrasted with Cronbach's, for we see espoused two relatively different evaluation strategies. Here the comparative study is suggested as generally the most relevant in curriculum research, particularly if the ultimate intent is to differentiate among competing programs.

Traditionally, curriculum development has been approached on the basis of content. Recent trends are toward more process-, concept-, or behaviorally-based programs. Henry H. Walbesser illustrates the influence of the behavioral approach on the design and implementation of an evaluation project. Using the AAAS-NSF elementary science curriculum *Science—A Process Approach* as a starting point, Walbesser describes the evolution of an evaluation plan.

The final article, by J. Alan Thomas, concerns cost-benefit analysis, or cost-effectiveness. Basically, the question is "How much valuable output do I get per unit of input?" The main problem in implementing such studies is the specification of units of measurement involved or to the attempt to translate educational and personological variables into monitary units. His hoped that economists and educators can iron out the methodological problems, for it would be a useful source of information bearing on the effectiveness of our schools. For further information on this topic, the reader is referred to Hemphill, 1969; Crane and Abt, 1969; and Alkin, 1970.

# 14. A Model for Curriculum Evaluation

## RICHARD WOLF

> The following pointedly satiric article by Richard Wolf describes some of the responses too frequently made at the state and local level to federal requirements for project evaluation. This paper might well be subtitled "What Not To Do While Waiting for the Educational Auditor." The strategies described illustrate some of the evaluation ills discussed by Guba (1969) and Stufflebeam (1970) as needing medication, treatment, and therapy.

The cornucopia of federal programs for elementary and secondary schools was initially enthusiastically received by educators. On closer examination, however, it was found that each plum contained a pit. This was the requirement that a systematic evaluation be carried out for all programs financed by federal funds. The difficulties encountered in meeting this requirement of the federal legislation have led a number of school personnel to seek out methods, procedures and techniques for systematically evaluating their federally financed programs. The purpose of this paper is to present a model for the evaluation of such programs. It is hoped that this model will be of assistance when evaluation time comes around each year.

The main task in curriculum evaluation is to determine whether a particular program has attained its objectives. While a number of curriculum and evaluation specialists have devoted considerable attention to the problems of formulating and specifying objectives for educational programs, the use of the model presented in this paper does not require that any attention be accorded this matter. This should result in a considerable saving of

time and effort for school personnel. The determination of the effectiveness of a particular educational program may be carried out in one of five ways according to the "5-C" model. The five C's of curriculum evaluation are: cosmetic, cardiac, colloquial, curricular, and computational. The remainder of this paper will describe each of these methods of evaluating educational programs.

## COSMETIC METHOD

This method is easily applied. Essentially, it involves taking a cursory look at a program and deciding if it looks good. Some of the things worth noting about a program when using this method include whether: students look busy and involved, student projects emanating from the program can be easily and attractively displayed on bulletin boards, and one can easily develop an assembly or PTA presentation based on activities of the program. When using the cosmetic method, one need not be concerned about objectives or gathering evidence about student learning. All such questions can be easily dealt with by showing an inquiring person the program in action and saying, "Look at all the wonderful things that are happening here. Who needs any more evidence to know we're doing a good job!"

Reprinted with permission of the publisher and Richard Wolf from *Psychology in the Schools,* **6** (1969), pp. 107–108.

# CARDIAC METHOD

The cardiac method is often used in conjunction with a systematic empirical approach. The use of planned evaluation procedures often results in showing that students enrolled in a new program learn no more than students in a conventional program, or that the new program did not attain its objectives. This can often present a dilemma since one always wants to claim beneficial results for a new program. The cardiac method resolves this dilemma. All one must do is dismiss the data and believe in his heart that the new program is indeed a good one. This method is quite similar to the use of "subclinical findings" in medical research.

# COLLOQUIAL METHOD

This method is somewhat easier to apply than the cardiac method. Social psychological research has demonstrated that decisions arrived at by a group will achieve greater acceptance than decisions arrived at by an individual. This finding is the basis of the colloquial method. In applying this method, one need merely assemble a group of people who have been associated with a particular program to discuss its effectiveness. After a brief discussion, the group will usually conclude that the program has been indeed successful. This conclusion can then be transmitted to funding agencies and other school personnel. It is unlikely that such evaluations will be challenged since they have been arrived at by a group.

# CURRICULAR METHOD

The curricular method is an indirect way of evaluating programs. Instituting a new program can often present problems. For example, a new program may require special facilities, staff or materials. In some extreme cases, a new program may even require changes in the school sched-ule or pupil placement practices. The extent to which such changes and modifications are required in order to institute a new program can be an indicator of the soundness (or lack of soundness) of the program. Thus, a program which can be installed without disturbing any existing programs, arrangements or schedules is judged to be sounder than a program which requires adjustments in other parts of the school program. Just as individuals are often judged by how well they fit in with a group, the curricular method judges new programs on how well they fit in with the rest of the school's programs. Programs which are truly different are to be eschewed at all costs under the curricular method.

# COMPUTATIONAL METHOD

Occasionally, it is considered desirable to actually gather some evidence about student performance in a particular program. Once collected, such data have to be subjected to some form of analysis. In the computational method, one takes as evidence of the success of the program not whether the data show that objectives were attained, but rather that two or more clerks analyzing the data came up with the same results. A useful way of presenting the results of such analyses is to show the correlation between two sets of computations. If the correlation is high, this will likely impress those charged with reading the report of the program. One, of course, must be careful *not* to say what the high correlation is between.

The five methods presented above should go a long way toward providing educational workers with a set of procedures for evaluating any educational program. In any given situation, one should select the method or methods which are most suited to the program being evaluated. Thus, if a new program is intended to be truly innovative and different, one should probably use the cosmetic method rather than, say, the curricular method. On the other hand, if preservation of the status quo is considered to be an important factor, the curricular method should be used. It may be possible to utilize all of the above methods in the evaluation of a single program, but this remarkable achievement has not yet taken place to this writer's knowledge. With true dedication, perhaps the day will soon arrive when it will.

# 15. Problem Areas in Designing and Implementing Curriculum Evaluation Research

## GARLIE A. FOREHAND

> For many reasons, both theoretical and practical, curriculum evaluation studies should not be considered formal, tightly-controlled psychological experiments. Some of the reasons for this conclusion are spelled out in the Prologue. If the techniques associated with experimental studies cannot be applied wholesale to curriculum evaluation projects, what methodologies are available? Some useful suggestions are made by Garlie A. Forehand in the following article. The reader's attention is directed particularly to the discussion of the use of control groups in evaluative research. Another important aspect of design considered by Forehand is the use of comparative or noncomparative hypotheses. It would be instructive to compare this discussion with the comments of Cronbach in Article 16 and Stake in Article 17.

In almost every formal curriculum development project there is a person responsible for the measurement and evaluation of the curriculum's effect upon student performance. Both the responsibilities and the professional backgrounds of these "evaluators," as they have come to be called, vary from project to project, and common themes and principles are only beginning to become apparent. This paper discusses problems related to three issues that arise consistently in a variety of curriculum evaluation projects: the nature of curriculum as a research variable, the behavioral definition of educational objectives, and professional responsibilities of evaluators.

Reprinted with permission of the publisher and Garlie A. Forehand from an article entitled "The Role of the Evaluator in Curriculum Research," which appeared in the *Journal of Educational Measurement*, **3** (1966), pp. 199–204.

## CURRICULUM AS AN INDEPENDENT VARIABLE

Evaluation studies are often built on the model of a psychological experiment. The curriculum defines the independent variable, one level of which is the "experimental group," embodying the methods and philosophy of curriculum innovation, and the other the control or traditionally-taught group. This paradigm has been tried and found wanting by a number of evaluators. One difficulty is the impossibility of controlling or isolating the effective features of an experimental curriculum. Another lies in the attempt to define a control group that differs with respect—and only with respect—to the central innovative idea of the experimental program.

Though often treated as if it were unitary, a curriculum actually involves many elements, not all of which covary systematically: reading materials, sequences of instruction, training and indoctrination of teachers, teaching methods, teaching manuals, and teaching aids, to name a few. Each of these elements is in fact a variable, and does in fact take on different values in curriculum variation. Complexity of an independent variable does not necessarily preclude treating it as unitary in an experiment. However, such treatment can provide a result that might meaningfully be termed an evaluation of a curriculum only if (a) all of the relevant elements adhere in a unified whole and converge in their effects on student performance, or (b) any two instances of a particular curriculum (e.g., any two experimental classes) share only the relevant features while the others occur randomly. The first, the holistic assumption, appears to be dear to the hearts of many curriculum developers. A number of evaluators report resistance to any attempt to vary curriculum features independently, on the grounds that they are all conceptually interrelated to define the essence of the new curriculum. Both sets of assumptions appear to be unrealistic in current curriculum study, in view of the apparent interaction of curriculum elements.

**Alternatives to the "Experimental Design" Approach to Curriculum Evaluation** If we set aside—temporarily or permanently—the experimental psychology paradigm of curriculum evaluation, what strategies are available to us? Several suggestions have been made by evaluators, some of which are being explored in current studies.

1. An attempt might be made to isolate characteristics of a curriculum, and to vary them independently. For example, it is frequently observed that teachers in a tryout vary widely in their degree of endorsement of curriculum methods and objectives. Teacher attitudes are under the control of neither evaluators nor developers of curricula, but they might be measured, and their effects on performance studied. This might be an especially interesting variable to examine in interaction when a "new course" is being contrasted with an "old course." Other suggested studies would contrast use of new innovative materials with and without special teacher training, and different systems for determining the sequence of materials.

2. Greater use might be made of descriptive statistics to suggest the process of learning as related to curriculum elements. For example, a facet of behavior relevant to a curriculum emphasis might be assessed at several times during the school year, and plotted graphically against points representing introduction of curriculum elements. The investigation could look for trends, plateaus, or changes of slope. Such information could be accumulated over a number of course tryouts, and differences between years, teachers, schools and similar variables explored. Such analyses might lead both to more formal hypothesis testing and to quick feedback to course designers.

3. The investigator might concentrate upon intensive "clinical" studies of a small number of students. Such studies might have as their aim the development of a developmental psychology that relates cognitive growth to educational experience. Both precedent and techniques are provided by the work of Piaget and of the numerous psychologists who have been influenced by him.

4. Rather than seek either to decompose or to by-pass curriculum as a variable, one might try to redefine it at the point of its effect, that is, at the point of interaction between the teacher and students. The materials, lesson plans, and other accoutrements of course development are relevant only as they are reflected in the behavior of teachers. This strategy calls for intensive classroom observation and the development of ways to classify teacher-student interaction (Medley and Mitzel, 1963), and could result in new and useful concepts of curriculum. Few current projects have the resources

to carry out this plan in detail, but several are using procedures to learn more about this behavior. Some projects involve classroom visitation on a sampling basis, to determine if teachers are pursuing the program outlined by course developers. Others are using systematic diaries kept by cooperating teachers and intensive interviews with teachers. Finally the assessment of teachers' attitudes is an economical way to tap a variable related to the teachers' behavior.

**Arguments Against the Use of Control Groups** A second facet of the ambiguity of curriculum as a variable is the "control group issue." Many evaluation studies began with the premise that the experimental program should be paralleled by a matched control treatment using a "traditional method," although some reservations about how such controls might be defined were voiced (Forehand, 1963; McKeachie, 1963). The present trend is for evaluators to eschew control groups (Cronbach, 1963). Among the arguments against using control groups are: (a) In many instances there are no meaningful comparisons between new courses and traditional courses. There are no traditional high school programs, for example, that teach structural linguistics, economics, or population biology, as do some of the new curricula. (b) Control group studies cast the evaluator in the role of an academic Consumer's Union; they assume that the two treatments are constant and final, and thus do not contribute to their development. (c) The assumption that new and traditional programs are comparable may lead to emphasis on traditional rather than modern objectives. (d) While the experimental curriculum is difficult to define, as we have seen, the control group is completely *terra incognita*. Traditional courses have no consistency in method or material, and the evaluator is seldom able to discover—much less to generalize—their points of variance with experimental courses. (e) Neither experimental nor traditional

courses stand still. Many teachers have long employed some of the "innovations" of the new curricula, and the overlap will increase as the influence of curriculum development spreads. Moreover the experimental program evaluated today may well be revised tomorrow. (f) The use of control groups is highly expensive relative to the information about curriculum effects that they yield. And (g) many of the points for comparative evaluation are matters of value judgment.

These arguments speak convincingly against the mechanical use of the pretest-posttest control group design. One wonders, however, if the pendulum has not swung too far. In particular, one may question whether the dethronement of the control group provides remedy for the real problems that control groups were intended to guard against. The proposed purpose of the control group is to prevent attribution of behavior changes to the curriculum when they are in fact attributable to other variables. Despite all of the above-cited deficiencies of control groups, the problem remains, and must be faced, if not eliminated, in evaluation research.

**Comparative Versus Absolute Evaluations** A distinction can be drawn between comparison hypotheses and non-comparison hypotheses, and some meaningful evaluation hypotheses imply comparisons. A language program built upon structural linguistics might lead to the expectation that students will learn to recognize certain functional relationships among syntactic structures. There is not a prior reason to believe that such skills will not be attained through increased experience with language and through study of "traditional" grammar. If the reasoning is extended to include related skills in composition, a comparison between programs is even more clearly called for. Similar points could be made with regard to attitudes toward public issues and experimental reasoning about scientific questions. In these instances the objectives are *extrinsic* to the particular content of the course, as contrasted with intrinsic objectives such as the mastery of particular subject matter. In such situations statistical comparisons of groups may be appropriate. One way of making such comparisons that would avoid many control-group pitfalls would be to set up the study one year before introduction of the new curriculum and use the pre-experimental year as a comparison course for the experimental year.

The testing of non-comparison hypotheses, in which the objective is unique to a particular treatment, must also take into account the dangers of falsely attributing effects to the curriculum. The perils of the single group pre- and post-test design are too familiar to permit its uncritical adoption (McKeachie, 1963). A resolution of this dilemma may accrue from recognizing curriculum as a process, a succession of events changing systematically over time. It is possible, in such a conception, to consider *variation* in curriculum and covariation of curriculum and performance. Demonstration of such covariation would be convincing evidence of program effects. It should be noted that this conception does not imply any particular technique, such as correlation or covariance, for assessing such covariation. More complicated non-linear models would probably need to be worked out. The descriptive analyses discussed above could provide an elementary approach.

## BEHAVIORAL DEFINITION OF EDUCATIONAL OBJECTIVES

The translation from educational objectives to evaluation instruments is always a point of contact, and sometimes a point of friction, between evaluators and course designers. The friction is especially pronounced when evaluators insist that course designers state their objectives in behavioral terms, and accept such statements as defining their aims. Most evaluators are willing to accept more vaguely defined objectives on the part of the course designers, and see as the evaluator's role to internalize the educational objectives and construct behavioral items on the basis of inference concerning manifestations of desired cognitive changes. Yet most evaluators report difficulty in communicating with "subject-matter people" on these topics. In many cases the designer's reaction to the evaluator's behavioral statements is, "That's something like it, but it's still not *quite* what we're looking for."

Part of the difficulty in communication stems from the evaluator's tendency to equate *behavior* with *items*. The objectives stated by course developers refer to cognitive *processes*, to changes in state over time. Test items, in general, try to capture behavior at a given *point* in time. Processes implied by objectives like understanding, appreciation, sensitivity, or critical evaluation sound mentalistic, because we have been unable to construct test items that seem adequate to define them. But it would be premature to conclude that they cannot be operationally defined. Several approaches suggest that workable measures of process can be developed. "Tab tests" (Glaser, Damrin, and Gardner, 1954) in which the subject makes a sequence of decisions, receiving feedback at each step, provide a means of studying problem solving process, and have recently been applied to educational evaluation (McGuire, 1963). Heath's work on cognitive preferences (Heath, 1964) approaches a facet of process, in its focus upon stylistic preferences at choice points. Other potentially useful approaches include in-basket tests (Frederiksen, 1962) and various kinds of games and simulations (Guetzkow, 1962).

Many evaluators agree that tests of achievement are not sufficient to assess the objectives of curriculum developers. Several proposals include plans to study such "typical performance" variables as attitudes, styles, and preferences, and the development of instruments for measuring such variables is one of the major technical problems of evaluation studies.

The relevance of such variables is particularly evident in English, where appreciation in literature and style in composition are emphasized, but representatives of other fields also cite typical-performance objectives, including attitudes toward public issues, interest in new scientific developments, and desire to continue study in a particular field. Heath's work on cognitive preferences in physics provides a model for measurement of some typical performance measures. Theoretical orientations like those of Gardner (1962), also suggest approaches.

Some evaluators go so far as to minimize the importance of "can do" measures relative to "will do" measures. Even when skill or knowledge is an aim of an educational program, it is sometimes argued that the skill or knowledge must be applied in voluntary situations for the objectives to be met.

## THE PROFESSIONAL RESPONSIBILITY OF THE EVALUATOR

The new curricula are, for the most part, oriented toward subject matter, and developed by subject-matter specialists. Project directors often reject the contributions of "educationists," and distrust the behavioral concepts of curriculum that evaluators seek to inject. Evaluators thus confront a dilemma. Their training in psychological and educational research leads them to want to dissect and understand their independent variables; yet a curriculum is constructed on principles foreign to them, and its parts are interrelated in a way that makes them inaccessible to partitioning. How can the evaluator play an active role in curriculum construction under such conditions?

A requisite for impact of behavioral ideas is a behavioral theory of curriculum. It is clear that present theories of laboratory learning and cognition do not provide this requirement (Bruner, 1960). If curriculum studies suffer from the lack of a theory of instruction, they enjoy a unique opportunity to participate in its development. The activities subsumed under the rubric evaluation can provide an empirical basis for theoretical development.

The shape of a behavioral theory of curriculum can only be guessed at, but some of the recurrent problems encountered by evaluators suggest questions to be put to the theory, and, as a consequence, directions for its development. We have noted that both a curriculum and its behavioral objectives are in fact processes. Process has been a much used concept in educational thought, but one that has resisted operational specification. Newell and Simon (1961) point out that the physical sciences deal successfully with processes, using difference equations as a model for computing subsequent states from prior states of a process. In present cognitive research, they suggest computer models as an analog to difference equations. Such a model specifies the rules of going from one state to another, and strives to stimulate the behavioral processes being modeled. Over the long range, such models offer potential ways of stating theories of both curriculum and outcome in disciplined ways without sacrifice of their complexity. More immediately they can serve as a valuable paradigm for conceptualizing process.

Current curriculum studies offer an unprecedented configuration of resources for developing a behavioral theory of curriculum: cooperating school systems, an atmosphere expectant of innovation, subject-matter specialists dedicated to examining their disciplines in relation to the learning of them, and behavioral scientists, in the guise of "evaluators," who are concerned with the problems of education. Each participant in these studies bears the responsibility for contributing not only to the improvement of teaching of a particular subject in particular circumstances, but also to the understanding of the process of education.

# 16. Course Improvement Through Evaluation

### LEE J. CRONBACH

The focus of this article is on the ways in which evaluation may be brought into play in answering three basic questions: (1) how can we improve courses, (2) how well is an individual learning, and (3) how effective is the entire educational system? The nature of the answers to these questions will dictate the kind of data collected, and to some extent the way in which they are gathered. It should again be emphasized that, although difficult to assess, attitudes and other so called "affective" outcomes need to be evaluated (see Articles 9 and 11). Cronbach's comments apply equally well to a traditional or a recently instituted or newly developed curriculum or course of study. The ongoing and feedback nature of an effective evaluation system cannot be overemphasized. It is probably true that the most useful evaluation information is that which allows for adjustments and modifications during the developmental stages of course or curriculum development, rather than examining the end product only. See an article by Forehand (1971) for description of such a system.

The national interest in improving education has generated several highly important projects to improve curricula, particularly at the secondary-school level. In conferences of directors of "course content improvement" programs . . . questions about evaluation are frequently raised. Those who inquire about evaluation have various motives, ranging from sheer scientific curiosity about classroom events to a desire to assure a sponsor that money has been well spent. While the curriculum developers sincerely wish to use the skills of evaluation specialists, I am not certain that they have a clear picture of what evaluation can do and should try to do. And, on the other hand, I am becoming convinced that some techniques and habits of thought of the evaluation specialist are ill suited to current curriculum studies. To serve these studies, what philosophy and methods of evaluation are required? And particularly, how must we depart from the familiar doctrines and rituals of the testing game?

## DECISIONS SERVED BY EVALUATION

To draw attention to its full range of functions, we may define "evaluation" broadly as the *collection and use of information to make decisions about an educational program*. The program may be a set of instructional materials distributed nationally, the instructional activities of a single school, or the educational experiences of a single pupil. Many types of decisions are to be made, and many varieties of information are useful. It becomes immediately apparent that evaluation is a diversified activity and that no one set of principles will suffice for all situations. But measurement specialists have so concentrated upon one process—the prep-

Reprinted with permission of the publisher and Lee J. Cronbach from the *Teachers College Record*, **64** (May 1963), pp. 672–683. This version of the original paper is based on changes incorporated in an earlier version published in *New Curricula*, ed. Robert Heath (New York: Harper & Row, 1964), pp. 231–248.

aration of pencil-and-paper achievement tests for assigning scores to individual pupils—that the principles pertinent to that process have somehow become enshrined as *the* principles of evaluation. "Tests," we are told, "should fit the content of the curriculum." Also, "only those evaluation procedures should be used that yield reliable scores." These and other hallowed principles are not entirely appropriate to evaluation for course improvement. Before proceeding to support this contention, I wish to distinguish among purposes of evaluation and to relate them to historical developments in testing and curriculum making.

We may separate three types of decisions for which evaluation is used:

1. Course improvement: deciding what instructional materials and methods are satisfactory and where change is needed.
2. Decisions about individuals: identifying the needs of the pupil for the sake of planning his instruction, judging pupil merit for purposes of selection and grouping, acquainting the pupil with his own progress and deficiencies.
3. Administrative regulation: judging how good the school system is, how good individual teachers are, etc.

Course improvement is set apart by its broad temporal and geographical reference; it involves the modification of recurrently used materials and methods. Developing a standard exercise to overcome a misunderstanding would be course improvement, but deciding whether a certain pupil should work through that exercise would be an individual decision. Administrative regulation likewise is local in effect, whereas an improvement in a course is likely to be pertinent wherever the course is offered.

It was for the sake of course improvement that systematic evaluation was first introduced. When that famous muckraker Joseph Rice gave the same spelling test in a number of American schools, and so gave the first impetus to the educational testing movement, he was interested in evaluating a curriculum. Crusading against the extended spelling drills that then loomed large in the school schedule— "the spelling grind"—Rice collected evidence of their worthlessness so as to provoke curriculum revision. As the testing movement developed, however, it took on a different function. . . .

The greatest expansion of systematic achievement testing occurred in the 1920s. At that time, the content of any course was taken pretty much as established and beyond criticism save for small shifts of topical emphasis. At the administrator's direction, standard tests covering the curriculum were given to assess the efficiency of the teacher or the school system. Such administrative testing fell into disfavor when used injudiciously and heavyhandedly in the 1920s and 1930s. Administrators and accrediting agencies fell back upon descriptive features of the school program in judging adequacy. Instead of collecting direct evidence of educational impact, they judged schools in terms of size of budget, student-staff ratio, square feet of laboratory space, and the number of advanced credits accumulated by the teacher. This tide, it appears, is about to turn. On many university campuses, administrators wanting to know more about their product are installing "operations research offices." Testing directed toward quality control seems likely to increase in the lower schools as well. . . .

After 1930 or thereabouts, tests were given almost exclusively for judgments about individuals—to select students for advanced training, to assign marks within a class, and to diagnose individual competences and deficiencies. For any such decisions, one wants precise and valid comparisons of one individual with other individuals or with a standard. Much of test theory and test technology has been concerned with making measurements precise. Important though precision is for most decisions about individuals, I shall argue that in evaluating courses we need not struggle to obtain precise scores for individuals.

While measurers have been well content with the devices used to make scores precise, they have been less complacent about validity. Prior to 1935, the pupil was examined mostly on factual knowledge and mastery of fundamental skills. Tyler's research and writings of that period developed awareness that higher mental processes are not evoked by simple factual tests, and that instruction that promotes factual knowledge may not promote—indeed, may interfere with—other more important educational outcomes. Tyler, Lindquist, and their students demonstrated that tests can be designed to measure such general educational outcomes as ability to comprehend scientific method. Whereas a student can prepare for a factual test only through a course of study that includes the facts tested, many different courses of study may promote the same *general* understandings and attitudes. In evaluating today's new curricula, it will clearly be important to appraise the student's general educational growth, which curriculum developers say is more important than mastery of the specific lessons presented. Note, for example, that the Biological Sciences Curriculum Study offers three courses with substantially different "subject matter" as alternative routes to much the same educational ends.

Although some instruments capable of measuring general outcomes were prepared during the 1930s, they were never very widely employed. The prevailing philosophy of the curriculum, particularly among "progressives," called for developing a program to fit local requirements, capitalizing on the capacities and experiences of local pupils. The faith of the 1920s in a "standard" curriculum was replaced by a faith that the best learning experience would result from teacher-pupil planning in each classroom. Since each teacher or each class could choose different content and even different objectives, this philosophy left little place for standard testing. . . .

Many evaluation specialists came to see test development as a strategy for training the teacher in service, so that the process of test making came to be valued more than the test—or the test data—that resulted. The following remarks by Bloom (1961) are representative of a whole school of thought [Also see Tyler, 1951]:

> The criterion for determining the quality of a school and its educational functions would be the extent to which it achieves the objectives it has set for itself. . . . Our experiences suggest that unless the school has translated the objectives into specific and operational definitions, little is likely to be done about the objectives. They remain pious hopes and platitudes. . . . Participation of the teaching staff in selecting as well as constructing evaluation instruments has resulted in improved instruments on one hand and, on the other hand, it has resulted in clarifying the objectives of instruction and in making them real and meaningful to teachers. . . . When teachers have actively participated in defining objectives and in selecting or constructing evaluation instruments, they return to the learning problems with great vigor and remarkable creativity. . . . Teachers who have become committed to a set of educational objectives which they thoroughly understand respond by developing a variety of learning experiences which are as diverse and as complex as the situation requires.

Thus, "evaluation" becomes a local and beneficial teacher-training activity. The benefit is attributed to thinking about what data to collect. Little is said about the actual use of test results; one has the impression that when test-making ends, the test itself is forgotten. Certainly, there is little enthusiasm for refining tests so that they can be used in other schools, for to do so would be to rob those teachers of the benefits of working out their own objectives and instruments.

Bloom and Tyler describe both curriculum making and evaluation as integral parts of classroom instruction, which is necessarily decentralized. This outlook is far from that of "course improvement." The current national curriculum studies assume that curriculum making can be centralized. They prepare materials to be used in much the same way by teachers everywhere. It is assumed that having experts draft materials, and revising these after tryout, produces better instructional activities than the local teacher would be likely to devise. In this context, it seems wholly appropriate to have most tests prepared by a central staff and to have results returned to that staff to guide further course improvement.

*When evaluation is carried out in the service of course improvement, the chief aim is to ascertain what effects the course has—that is, what changes it produces in pupils* [editor's italics]. This is not to inquire merely whether the course is effective or ineffective. Outcomes of instruction are multidimensional, and a satisfactory investigation will map out the effects of the course along these dimensions separately. To agglomerate many types of post-course performance into a single score is a mistake, because failure to achieve one objective is masked by success in another direction. Moreover, since a composite score embodies (and usually conceals) judgments about the importance of the various outcomes, only a report that treats the outcomes separately can be useful to educators who have different value hierarchies.

*The greatest service evaluation can perform is to identify aspects of the course where revision is desirable* [editor's italics]. Those responsible for developing a course would like to present evidence that their course is effective. They are intrigued by the idea of having an "independent testing agency" render a judgment on their product. But to call in the evaluator only upon the completion of course development, to confirm what has been done, is to offer him a menial role and to make meager use of his services. To be influential in course improvement, evidence must become available midway in curriculum development, not in the home stretch, when the developer is naturally reluctant to tear open a supposedly finished body of materials and techniques. Evaluation, used to improve the course while it is still fluid, contributes more to improvement of education than evaluation used to appraise a product already placed on the market. . . .

Insofar as possible, evaluation should be used to understand how the course produces its effects and what parameters influence its effectiveness. It is important to learn, for example, that the outcome of programmed instruction depends very much upon the attitude of the teacher; indeed, this may be more important than to learn that on the average such instruction produces slightly better or worse results than conventional instruction.

Hopefully, evaluation studies will go beyond reporting on this or that course and help us to understand educational learning. Such insight will, in the end, contribute to the development of all courses rather than just the course under test. In certain of the new curricula, there are data to suggest that aptitude measures correlate much less with end-of-course achievement than they do with achievement on early units (Ferris, 1962). This finding is not well confirmed, but it is highly significant if true. If it is true for the new curricula and only for them, it has one implication; if the same effect appears in traditional courses, it means something else. Either way, it provides food for thought for teachers, counselors, and theorists. Evaluation studies should generate knowledge about the nature of the abilities that constitute educational goals. Twenty years after the Eight-Year Study of the Progressive Education Association, its testing techniques are in good repute, but we still know very little about what these instruments measure. Consider "Application of Principles in Science." Is this in any sense a unitary ability? Or has the able student only mastered certain principles one by one? Is the ability demonstrated on a test of this sort more prognostic of any later achievement than is factual knowledge? Such questions ought to receive substantial attention, although to the makers of any one course they are of only peripheral interest.

*The aim to compare one course with another should not dominate plans for evaluation* [editor's italics]. To be sure, decision makers have to choose between courses, and any evaluation report will be interpreted in part comparatively. But formally designed experiments, pitting one course against another, are rarely definitive enough to justify their cost. Differences between average test scores resulting from different courses are usually small relative to the wide differences among and within classes taking the same course. At best, an experiment never does more than compare the present version of one course with the present version of another. A major effort to bring the losing contender nearer to perfection would be very likely to reverse the verdict of the experiment.

Any failure to equate the classes taking the competing courses will jeopardize the interpretation of an experiment—and such failures are almost inevitable. In testing a drug, we know that valid results cannot be obtained without a double-blind control in which the doses for half the subjects are inert placebos; the placebo and the drug look alike, so that neither doctor nor patient knows who is receiving medication. Without this control, the results are useless even when the state of the patient is checked by completely objective indices. In an educational experiment, it is difficult to keep pupils unaware that they are an experimental group. And it is quite impossible to neutralize the biases of the teacher as those of the doctor are neutralized in the double-blind design. It is thus never certain whether any observed advantage is attributable to the educational innova-

tion as such, or to the greater energy that teachers and students put forth when a method is fresh and "experimental." Some have contended that any course, even the most excellent, loses much of its potency as soon as success enthrones it as "the traditional method." . . .

Since group comparisons give equivocal results, I believe that a formal study should be designed primarily to determine the post-course performance of a well described group with respect to many important objectives and side effects. Ours is a problem like that of the engineer examining a new automobile. He can set himself the task of defining its performance characteristics and its dependability. It would be merely distracting to put his question in the form, "Is this car better or worse than the competing brand?" Moreover, in an experiment where the treatments compared differ in a dozen respects, no understanding is gained from the fact that the experiment shows a numerical advantage in favor of the new course. No one knows which of the ingredients is responsible for the advantage. More analytic experiments are much more useful than field trials applying markedly dissimilar treatments to different groups. Small-scale, well controlled studies can profitably be used to compare alternative versions of the same course; in such a study, the differences between treatments are few enough and well enough defined that the results have explanatory value.

The three purposes—course improvement, decisions about individuals, and administrative regulation—call for measurement procedures having somewhat different qualities. When a test will be used to make an administrative judgment on the individual teacher, it is necessary to measure thoroughly and with conspicuous fairness; such testing, if it is to cover more than one outcome, becomes extremely time consuming. In judging a course, however, one can make satisfactory interpretations from data collected on a sampling basis, with no pretense of measuring thoroughly the accomplishments of any one class. A similar point is to be made about testing for decisions about individuals. A test of individuals must be conspicuously fair and extensive enough to provide a dependable score for each person. But if the performance will not influence the fate of the individual, we can ask him to perform tasks for which the course has not directly prepared him, and we can use techniques that would be prohibitively expensive if applied in a manner thorough enough to measure each person reliably.

## METHODS OF EVALUATION

**Range of Methods** Evaluation is too often visualized as the administration of a formal test, an hour or so in duration, at the close of a course. But there are many other methods for examining pupil performance, and pupil attainment is not the only basis for appraising a course.

It is quite appropriate to ask scholars whether the statements made in the course are consistent with the best contemporary knowledge. This is a sound and even a necessary procedure. One may go on to evaluate the pedagogy of the new course by soliciting opinions, but here there is considerable hazard. If the opinions are based on some preconception about teaching method, the findings will be controversial and very probably misleading. There are no theories of pedagogy so well established that one can say, without tryout, what will prove educative. . . .

One can accept the need for a pragmatic test of the curriculum and still employ opinions as a source of evidence. During the tryout stages of curriculum making, one relies heavily on the teachers' reports of pupil accomplishment—"Here they had trouble"; "This they found dull"; "Here they needed only half as many exercises as were provided," etc. This is behavior observation

even though unsystematic, and it is of great value. The reason for shifting to systematic observation is that this is more impartial, more public, and sometimes more penetrating. While I bow to the historian or mathematician as a judge of the technical soundness of course content, I do not agree that the experienced history or mathematics teacher who tries out a course gives the best possible judgment on its effectiveness. Scholars have too often deluded themselves about their effectiveness as teachers—particularly, have they too often accepted parroting of words as evidence of insight—for their unaided judgment to be trusted. Systematic observation is costly, and introduces some delay between the moment of teaching and the feedback of results. Hence, systematic observation will never be the curriculum developer's sole source of evidence. Systematic data collection becomes profitable in the intermediate stages of curriculum development, after the more obvious bugs in early drafts have been dealt with.

The approaches to evaluation include process studies, proficiency measures, attitude measures, and follow-up studies. A process study is concerned with events taking place in the classroom, proficiency and attitude measures with changes observed in pupils, and follow-up studies with the later careers of those who participated in the course.

The follow-up study comes closest to observing ultimate educational contributions, but the completion of such a study is so far removed in time from the initial instruction that it is of minor value in improving the course or explaining its effects. The follow-up study differs strikingly from the other types of evaluation study in one respect. I have already expressed the view that evaluation should be primarily concerned with the effects of the course under study rather than with comparisons of courses. That is to say, I would emphasize departures of attained results from the ideal, differences in apparent effectiveness of different parts of the course, and differences from item to item; all these suggest places where the course could be strengthened. But this view cannot be applied to the follow-up study, which appraises effects of the course as a whole and which has very little meaning unless outcomes can be compared with some sort of base rate. Suppose we find that 65 per cent of the boys graduating from an experimental curriculum enroll as scientific and technical majors in college. We cannot judge whether this is a high or low figure save by comparing it with the rate among boys who have not had the course. In a follow-up study, it is necessary to obtain data on a control group equated at least crudely to the experimental cases on the obvious demographic variables.

Despite the fact that such groups are hard to equate and that follow-up data do not tell much about how to improve the course, such studies should have a place in research on the new curricula, whose national samples provide unusual opportunity for follow-up that can shed light on important questions. One obvious type of follow-up study traces the student's success in a college course founded upon the high-school course. One may examine the student's grades or ask him what topics in the college course he found himself poorly prepared for. It is hoped that some of the new science and mathematics courses will arouse greater interest than usual among girls; whether this hope is well founded can be checked by finding out what majors and what electives these ex-students pursue in college. Career choices likewise merit attention. Some proponents of the new curricula would like to see a greater flow of talent into basic science as distinct from technology, whereas others would regard this as potentially disastrous; but no one would regard facts about this flow as lacking significance. . . .

Attitudes are prominent among the outcomes with which course developers are concerned. Attitudes are meanings or beliefs, not mere expressions of approval or disapproval. One's attitude toward science includes ideas about the matters on which a scientist can be an authority, about the benefits to be obtained from moon shots and studies of monkey mothers, and about depletion of natural resources. Equally important is the match between self-concept and concept of the field: What roles does science offer a person like me? Would I want to marry a scientist? And so on. Each learning activity also contributes to attitudes that reach far beyond any one subject, such as the pupil's sense of his own competence and desire to learn.

Attitudes can be measured in many ways; the choices revealed in follow-up studies, for example, are pertinent evidence. But measurement usually takes the form of direct or indirect questioning. Interviews, questionnaires, and the like are quite valuable when not trusted blindly. Certainly, we should take seriously any *un*desirable opinion expressed by a substantial proportion of the graduates of a course (e.g., the belief that the scientist speaks with peculiar authority on political and ethical questions, or the belief that mathematics is a finished subject rather than a field for current investigation).

Attitude questionnaires have been much criticized because they are subject to distortion, especially where the student hopes to gain by being less than frank. Particularly if the questions are asked in a context far removed from the experimental course, the returns are likely to be trustworthy. Thus, a general questionnaire administered through homerooms (or required English courses) may include questions about liking for various subjects and activities; these same questions administered by the mathematics teacher would give much less trustworthy data on attitude toward mathematics. While students may give reports more favorable than their true beliefs, this distortion is not likely to be greater one year than another, or greater among students who take an experimental course than among those who do not. In group averages, many distortions balance out. But questionnaires insufficiently valid for individual testing can be used in evaluating curricula, both because the student has little motive to distort and because the evaluator is comparing averages rather than individuals. . . .

For measuring proficiency, techniques are likewise varied. Standardized tests are useful. But for course evaluation it makes sense to assign *different* questions to different students. Giving each student in a population of 500 the same test of 50 questions will provide far less information to the course developer than drawing for each student 50 questions from a pool of, say, 700. The latter plan determines the mean success of about 75 representative students on every one of the 700 items; the former reports on only 50 items (Lord, 1962). Essay tests and open-ended questions, generally too expensive to use for routine evaluation, can profitably be employed to appraise certain abilities. One can go further and observe individuals or groups as they attack a research problem in the laboratory or work through some other complex problem. Since it is necessary to test only a representative sample of pupils, costs are not as serious a consideration as in routine testing. Additional aspects of proficiency testing will be considered below.

Process measures have special value in showing how a course can be improved because they examine what happens during instruction. In the development of programmed instructional materials, for example, records are collected showing how many pupils miss each item presented; any piling up of errors implies a need for better explanation or a more gradual approach to a difficult topic. Immediately after showing a teaching film, one can interview students, perhaps asking them to describe a still photograph taken from the film. Misleading presentations, ideas given insufficient emphasis, and matters left unclear will be identified

by such methods. Similar interviews can disclose what pupils take away from a laboratory activity or a discussion. A process study may turn attention to what the teacher does in the classroom. In those curricula that allow choice of topics, for example, it is worthwhile to find out which topics are chosen and how much time is allotted to each. A log of class activities (preferably recorded by a pupil rather than the teacher) will show which of the techniques suggested in a summer institute are actually adopted and which form "part of the new course" only in the developer's fantasies.

**Measurement of Proficiency** I have indicated that I consider item data to be more important than test scores. The total score may give confidence in a curriculum or give rise to discouragement, but it tells very little about how to produce further improvement. And, as Ferris (1962) has noted, such scores are quite likely to be mis- or overinterpreted. The score on a single item, or on a problem that demands several responses in succession, is more likely than the test score to suggest how to alter the presentation. When we accept item scores as useful, we need no longer think of evaluation as a one-shot, end-of-year operation. Proficiency can be measured at any moment, with particular interest attaching to those items most related to the recent lessons. Other items calling for general abilities can profitably be administered repeatedly during the course (perhaps to different random samples of pupils) so that we can begin to learn when and from what experiences change in these abilities comes.

In course evaluation, we need not be much concerned about making measuring instruments fit the curriculum. However startling this declaration may seem, and however contrary to the principles of evaluation for other purposes, this must be our position if we want to know what changes a course produces in the pupil. An ideal evaluation would include measures of all the types of proficiency that might reasonably be desired in the area in question, not just the selected outcomes to which this curriculum directs substantial attention. If you wish only to know how well a curriculum is achieving *its* objectives, you fit the test to the curriculum; but if you wish to know how well the curriculum is serving the national interest, you measure all outcomes that might be worth striving for. One of the new mathematics courses may disavow any attempt to teach numerical trigonometry, and indeed, might discard nearly all computational work. It is still perfectly reasonable to ask how well graduates of the course can compute and can solve right triangles. Even if the course developers went so far as to contend that computational skill is no proper objective of secondary instruction, they will encounter educators and laymen who do not share their view. If it can be shown that students who come through the new course are fairly proficient in computation despite the lack of direct teaching, the doubters will be reassured. If not, the evidence makes clear how much is being sacrificed. Similarly, when the biologists offer alternative courses emphasizing microbiology and ecology, it is fair to ask how well the graduate of one course can understand issues treated in the other. Ideal evaluation in mathematics will collect evidence on all the abilities toward which a mathematics course might reasonably aim; likewise in biology, English, or any other subject.

Ferris states that the ACS Chemistry Test, however well constructed, is inadequate for evaluating the new CBA and CHEM programs because it does not cover their objectives. One can agree with this without regarding the ACS test as inappropriate to use with these courses. It is important that this test not stand *alone,* as the sole evaluation device. It will tell us something worth knowing, namely, just how much "conventional" knowledge the new curriculum does or does not provide. The curriculum developers deliberately planned to sacrifice some

of the conventional attainments and have nothing to fear from this measurement, competently interpreted (particularly if data are examined item by item). . . .

The demand that tests be closely matched to the aims of a course reflects awareness that examinations of the usual sort "determine what is taught." If questions are known in advance, students give more attention to learning their answers than to learning other aspects of the course. This is not necessarily detrimental. Wherever it is critically important to master certain content, the knowledge that it will be tested produces a desirable concentration of effort. On the other hand, learning the answer to a set question is by no means the same as acquiring understanding of whatever topic that question represents. There is, therefore, a possible advantage in using "secure" tests for course evaluation. Security is achieved only at a price: One must prepare new tests each year and consequently cannot make before-and-after comparisons with the same items. One would hope that the use of different items with different students, and the fact that there is less incentive to coach when no judgment is to be passed on the pupils and the teachers, would make security a less critical problem.

The distinction between factual tests and tests of higher mental processes, as elaborated for example in the *Taxonomy of Educational Objectives* (Bloom et al., 1956), is of some value in planning tests, although classifying items as measures of knowledge, application, original problem solving, etc., is difficult and often impossible. Whether a given response represents rote recall or reasoning depends upon how the pupil has been taught, not solely upon the question asked. One may, for example, describe a biological environment and ask for predictions regarding the effect of a certain intervention. Students who have never dealt with ecological data will succeed or fail according to their general ability to reason about complex events; those who have studied ecological biology will be more likely to succeed, reasoning from specific principles; and those who have lived in such an ecology or read about it may answer successfully on the basis of memory. We rarely, therefore, will want to test whether a student "knows" or "does not know" certain material. Knowledge is a matter of degree. Two persons may be acquainted with the same facts or principles, but one will be more expert in his understanding, better able to cope with inconsistent data, irrelevant sources of confusion, and apparent exceptions to the principle. To measure intellectual competence is to measure depth, connectedness, and applicability of knowledge.

Too often, test questions are course-specific, stated in such a way that only the person who has been specifically taught to understand what is being asked for can answer the question. Such questions can usually be identified by their use of conventions. Some conventions are commonplace, and we can assume that all the pupils we test will know them. But a biology test that describes a metabolic process with the aid of the $\rightleftharpoons$ symbol presents difficulties for students who can think through the scientific question about equilibrium but are unfamiliar with the symbol. A trigonometry problem that requires use of a trigonometric table is unreasonable, unless we want to test familiarity with the conventional names of functions. The same problem in numerical trigonometry can be cast in a form clear to the average pupil *entering* high school; if necessary, the tables of functions can be presented along with a comprehensible explanation. So stated, the problem becomes course-independent. It is fair to ask whether graduates of the experimental course can solve such problems, not previously encountered, whereas it is pointless to ask whether they can answer questions whose language is strange to them. To be sure,

knowledge of certain terminology is a significant objective of instruction, but for course evaluation, testing of terminology should very likely be separated from testing of other understandings. To appraise understanding of processes and relations, the fair question is one comprehensible to a pupil who has not taken the course. This is not to say that he should know the answer or the procedure to follow in attaining the answer, but he should understand what he is being asked. Such course-independent questions can be used as standard instruments to investigate any instructional program.

Pupils who have not studied a topic will usually be less facile than those who have studied it. Graduates of my hypothetical mathematics course will take longer to solve trigonometry problems than will those who have studied trig. But speed and power should not be confused; in intellectual studies, power is almost always of greater importance. If the course equips the pupil to deal correctly, even though haltingly, with a topic not studied, we can expect him to develop facility later when that topic comes before him frequently. . . .

The chief objective in many of the new curricula seems to be to develop aptitude for mastering new materials in the field. A biology course cannot cover all valuable biological content, but it may reasonably aspire to equip the pupil to understand descriptions of unfamiliar organisms, to comprehend a new theory and the reasoning behind it, and to plan an experiment to test a new hypothesis. This is transfer of learning. It has been insufficiently recognized that there are two types of transfer. The two types shade into one another, being arranged on a continuum of immediacy of effect. We can label the more immediate pole *applicational transfer,* and speak of slower-acting effects as *gains in aptitude* (Ferguson, 1954).

Nearly all educational research on transfer has tested immediate performance on a partly new task. We teach pupils to solve equations in $x$, and include in the test equations stated in $a$ or $z$. We teach the principles of ecological balance by referring to forests, and as a transfer test, ask what effect pollution will have on the population of a lake. We describe an experiment not presented in the text, and ask the student to discuss possible interpretations and needed controls. Any of these tests can be administered in a short time. But the more significant type of transfer may be the increased ability to learn in a particular field. There is very likely a considerable difference between the ability to draw conclusions from a neatly finished experiment, and the ability to tease insight out of the disorderly and inconsistent observations that come with continuous laboratory work on a problem. The student who masters a good biology course may become better able to comprehend certain types of theory and data, so that he gains more from a subsequent year of study in ethnology; we do not measure this gain by testing his understanding of short passages in ethnology. There has rarely been an appraisal of ability to work through a problem situation or a complex body of knowledge over a period of days or months. Despite the practical difficulties that attend an attempt to measure the effect of a course on a person's subsequent learning, such "learning to learn" is so important that a serious effort should be made to detect such effects and to understand how they may be fostered.

The techniques of programmed instruction may be adapted to appraise learning ability. One may, for example, test the student's rate of mastery of a self-contained, programmed unit on the physics of heat or some other topic not studied. If the program is truly self-contained, every student can master it, but the one with greater scientific comprehension will hopefully make fewer errors and progress faster. The program can be prepared in several logically complete versions, rang-

ing from one with very small "steps" to one with minimal internal redundancy, on the hypothesis that the better educated student could cope with the less redundant program. Moreover, he might prefer its greater elegance.

## CONCLUSION

Old habits of thought and long established techniques are poor guides to the evaluation required for course improvement. Traditionally, educational measurement has been chiefly concerned with producing fair and precise scores for comparing individuals. Educational experimentation has been concerned with comparing score averages of competing courses. But course evaluation calls for description of outcomes. This description should be made on the broadest possible scale, even at the sacrifice of superficial fairness and precision.

Course evaluation should ascertain what changes a course produces and should identify aspects of the course that need revision. The outcomes observed should include general outcomes ranging far beyond the content of the curriculum itself—attitudes, career choices, general understandings and intellectual powers, and aptitude for further learning in the field. Analysis of performance or single items or types of problems is more informative than analysis of composite scores. It is not necessary or desirable to give the same test to all pupils; rather, as many questions as possible should be given, each to a different, moderate sized sample of pupils. Costly techniques, such as interviews and essay tests, can profitably be applied to samples of pupils, whereas testing everyone would be out of the question.

Asking the right questions about educational outcomes can do much to improve educational effectiveness. Even if the right data are collected, however, evaluation will have contributed too little if it only places a seal of approval on certain courses and casts others into disfavor. Evaluation is a fundamental part of curriculum development, not an appendage. Its job is to collect facts the course developer can and will use to do a better job, and facts from which a deeper understanding of the educational process will emerge.

# 17. Language, Rationality, and Assessment
## ROBERT E. STAKE

There is much of value in this article. Stake alerts us to questions that should be asked prior to designing an evaluation study. He then gives us a matrix that will help to organize the elements of both the design and the evaluative decision-making process itself, and to plan for the organization of data. Stake is concerned about monitoring what goes in, what goes on, and what comes out of the program. He concludes that four major types of evaluation can be differentiated in terms of the generalizability of the findings. The ever-present problem of educational objectives is then treated in detail. Language is the key —it can be barrier or facilitator. Finally, Stake asks us to give rationality a chance to serve as a reasonable complement to empiricism in the search for "truth."

It is my belief that we are not very effective in assessment because we are not very effective at formal communication. If I make such a claim and then support it (in *my* communication with you) with fastidious reasoning; if I cite just the right number of illustrations and speak with clarity and persuasion—then I weaken the claim. To support my claim that language is our shortcoming I will commit certain ambiguities of expression, I will violate some conventional definitions of terms, and I will read these unending passages in a mesmerizing drone. If I am successful, you will be unable to recall a single confrontation with Truth. You will be convinced . . . that "Words

Forever Fail Us"; which, of course, is my point.

Several years ago I was dismayed by the consternation shown by some experts in our field about the distinction between measurement and evaluation. As far as I was concerned the differentiation was an instance of "nit-picking." I said, "Measurement implies evaluation. Testing just is not testing unless there is test interpretation. No 'assessment' occurs without an underlying intent to generalize." I have joined the "nit-pickers." Now I rally to the distinction. I want us to think of "something more" when we think of evaluation. I want us to think about the desirability of a student's response as well as the quality of a student's response.

And there is a second distinction. Most of my colleagues think of evaluation as measurement of individual student progress, but I want to focus some evaluation on individual school progress, and some on individual nation progress. I think it

Reprinted with permission of the Association for Supervision and Curriculum Development and Robert E. Stake from a paper which appeared in *Improving Educational Assessment and an Inventory of Affective Behavior,* ed. W. H. Beatty (Washington: ASCD, 1969), pp. 14–40. Copyright 1969 by the Association for Supervision and Curriculum Development.

is important to define evaluation differently than would most measurement specialists. My hortatory working definition goes like this:

*As evaluators we should make a record of all of the following: what the author or teacher or school board intends to do, what is provided in the way of an environment, the transactions between teacher and learner, the student progress, the side effects, and last and most important, the merit and shortcoming seen by persons from divergent viewpoints.*

I see a useful distinction between measurement and evaluation. Am I able to make a useful distinction between measurement and assessment? I like to think of assessment as one form of measurement. Going along with Jum Nunnally (1959), I say that assessment is direct measurement, in contrast to psychometric testing, which almost always is indirect measurement. Assessment, as represented by the National Assessment Project (Tyler, 1965), pertains to direct measurement of performance on important reference tasks. Both psychometric testing and assessment are useful techniques for gathering information.

## CURRICULUM EVALUATION

Here I am going to talk about something broader. I will discuss inquiries into the worth of any instructional program. Such inquiries depend on direct assessment, on objective testing, and on subjective judgments. I will call such an inquiry: evaluation. If what I call "evaluation" is much different from what you call "assessment" then perhaps I should retitle this paper: "Language, Rationality, and What I Call Evaluation."

Ralph Tyler has done a magnificent job of describing the multiplicity of evaluation roles. One of the distinctions most helpful for understanding a theory of evaluation, I believe, is the distinction Mike Scriven (1967) makes between the *roles* and the *goal* of evaluation. The goal of evaluation is always the same: to determine the worth of something. The roles depend on *what* that something is and on *whose* standards of value will apply. A student's performance can be evaluated by those considering his admissibility to advanced training. That is one role for evaluation. A million student performances can be evaluated by persons concerned about a nation's academic curricula. Competing textbooks can be evaluated—that is, their relative merits can be examined. Environments can be evaluated. Educational goals can be evaluated. By mentioning these I illustrate the roles that evaluation can play.

By this definition it is inappropriate to claim that all evaluation should focus on student performance. It is inappropriate to claim that all educational evaluation should focus on goals specified by the curriculum designer. There are other important roles for evaluation than to determine the extent to which teaching objectives have been attained. People who set objectives—programmers, teachers, experimenters—may be particularly interested in attainment of the goals *they* specified; but others have other goals. A group of taxpayers, philosophers, or students will choose to look at different criteria of merit, and will have different standards against which to make value judgments. As people have different uses for evaluation information, the roles of evaluation will differ.

Most people will use evaluation information, directly or indirectly, for making decisions. Curriculum developers make decisions; teachers make other decisions; counselors make still other decisions. If we can anticipate the choices, we will have some of the guidelines for an evaluation plan. Daniel Stufflebeam (1966) discusses evaluation for decision making, so I will not; but I do want to talk about the generalizability of evaluation information. Let me summarize what I have said about evaluation so far by suggesting three questions that should be asked prior to drawing up an evaluation plan:

1. What is the entity that is to be evaluated?
2. Whose standards will be used as reference marks?
3. What subsequent decisions can be anticipated?

Answers to these three questions should be sought prior to planning the evaluation.

Now let us inventory the data I believe the evaluation plan should call for. In my paper, "The Countenance of Educational Evaluation" (1967a), I suggested use of a huge matrix of evaluation information. A representation of this matrix is included in Table 1. You will see there an array of *row entries* that help identify the many characteristics of the instructional program to be evaluated. The evaluator must choose the variables to be described and judged.

The column entries in this matrix identify separate *sources* of information: teachers, administrators, counselors professors, parents, and so on. My matrix does not say which sources and which variables are important. It just reminds the evaluator that he has to pick and choose among a potential deluge of information. Ob-

**TABLE 1**
**Illustration of Data Possibly Representative of the Contents of Four Cells of the Matrices for a Given Educational Program**[a]

| Program Rationale | Data for the Evaluation of an Educational Program | | | |
|---|---|---|---|---|
| | Intents Sources | Observations Sources | Standards Sources | Judgments Sources |
| *Antecedents*<br>Student Characteristics<br>Teacher Characteristics<br>Curricular Content<br>Curricular Context<br>Instructional Materials<br>Physical Plant<br>School Organization<br>Community Context | **A** | | | |
| *Transactions*<br>Communication Flow<br>Time Allocation<br>Sequence of Events<br>Reinforcement Schedule<br>Social Climate | | | | **D** |
| *Outcomes*<br>Student Achievement<br>Student Attitudes<br>Student Motor Skills<br>Effects on Teachers<br>Institutional Effects | | **B** | **C** | |

*Example A:* Manufacturer Specification of an Instructional Materials Kit
*Example B:* Teacher Description of Student Understanding
*Example C:* Expert Opinion on Cognitive Skill Needed for a Class of Problems
*Example D:* Administrator Judgment of Feasibility of a Field Trip Arrangement

[a] Adapted from Robert E. Stake, "The Countenance of Educational Evaluation," *Teachers College Record* **68**, No. 7 (April 1967), p. 529. Used by permission.

viously, information to fill the thousands of sub-cells of this matrix could not be obtained in any one evaluation study. A principal task of the evaluator is to concentrate attention on variables that are related to the goals of his audience, variables leading to decisions, and variables that are available—within his budget—from appropriate sources. (I might add that evaluators will have different degrees of interest and talent for measuring different variables. I think the sponsor of an evaluation study should pay considerable attention to what it is that the evaluator *likes* to measure.)

If a set of instructional materials is to be evaluated, the variables might be organized as shown in Table 2. Here, great attention is paid to the "conditions of use" for the textbook or science kit or whatever entity is being evaluated (Stake, 1967b).

Back in the grid in Table 1 we have 12 major cells—plus a thirteenth in which to represent the rationale. We find out what different goals people have; I call these *intents*. We note our perceptions of what actually happens; I call these *observations*. We list statements by certain experts as to what should happen in a situation like ours; these are *standards*. And we gather data on how people feel about aspects of our situation; and these are our *judgments*.

In any curriculum—even in the briefest lesson—different people have different intents. And there are many relevant observations that we can schedule. There are many standards that could be useful to the audience that will receive our report, and there are many judgments that will be made. These are the classes of descriptive and judgmental data that I believe are needed in curriculum evaluation.

**Congruence and Contingency** I perceive two principal ways of processing the descriptive evaluation data: finding the contingencies among antecedents, transactions, and outcomes and finding the congruence between Intents and Observations. The processing of judgmental data follows a different model. The first two main columns of the data matrix in Table 1 contain the descriptive data. The format for processing these data is represented in Table 2 (Stake, 1967a).

Intents and Observations are *congruent* if what was intended actually happens. To be fully congruent the intended antecedents, transactions, and outcomes must be identical with the observed antecedents, transactions, and outcomes. (This seldom happens and often should not.)

Some evaluation studies concentrate only on the congruence between intended and observed outcomes. If our purpose is to continue a good curriculum or revise a poor one we should know about congruence of antecedents and transactions as well. Working horizontally in the data matrix, the evaluator will compare the information labeled Intents with the information labeled Observations—he will note the discrepancies and describe the amount of congruence for that row. Congruence does not indicate that outcomes are reliable or valid, but that what was intended did in fact occur.

It should be obvious that congruence and lack of congruence are more easily discovered when the same language is used to describe the goals and the actual operations. One way to synchronize language is to focus on teacher, administrator, and student behaviors.

So much for the moment for congruence. How about contingency? Contingencies are relationships among the variables. An evaluator's search for contingency is in effect the search for causal relationships. These are what Hastings (1966) called the "whys of the outcomes." Knowledge of what causes what obviously facilitates the improvement of instruction. One of the evaluator's tasks is identifying outcomes that are contingent upon particular antecedent conditions and particular instructional transactions.

For as long as there has been schooling, curriculum planning has rested upon

**TABLE 2**
**Subdivisions of Information Classes for Evaluating Educational Products**[a]

| Subdivision | Examples of variables in the subdivision |
|---|---|
| *Conditions of Use* | |
| Local Circumstances | |
| Student types | (background, aptitude, aspiration . . .) |
| Teacher type· | (experience, style, personality . . .) |
| Type of school | (physical plant, intellectual climate . . .) |
| Type of community | (support of schools, attitudes, controversy . . .) |
| Curricular Context | |
| Subject matter— coverage | (concepts, structure, methods of inquiry . . .) |
| Instructional aids— available | (library, models, maps, equipment . . .) |
| Concurrent— course work | sequence and time allotment, projects . . .) |
| Classroom Transactions | |
| Teaching strategies | (discourse, inquiry, assignments . . .) |
| Student-teacher— interaction | (information, flow, counseling . . .) |
| Student-student— interaction | (social climate, reaction to authority . . .) |
| Incentives,— grades, etc. | (motivation, goal orientation testing . . .) |
| *Results of Use* | |
| Gain in Student Competence | |
| Knowledge | (data, understanding, application . . .) |
| Skill | (problem solving, communication . . .) |
| Incidental learning | (synthesis, learning sets, side effects . . .) |
| Change in Student Attitude | |
| Interest | (opinion, avocation, exploration . . .) |
| Commitments | (prejudice, aspiration, advocacy . . .) |
| Effects on Staff | |
| Teacher changes | (insights, revision, grievances . . .) |
| Administrative— changes | (organizational rearrangements permitted . . .) |
| Other Effects | |
| Institutional effects | (prestige, solidarity . . .) |
| Community effects | (controversy, dedication, esprit . . .) |

[a] From Robert E. Stake, "A Research Rationale for EPIE," *The EPIE Forum* 1 (September 1967), pp. 7–15. Used by permission.

faith in certain contingencies. Day to day, every teacher arranges his presentation and the learning environment in a way that—according to his logic—leads to the attainment of his instructional goals. His contingencies, in the main, are logical, intuitive, supported by a history of satisfactions and endorsements. To various degrees teachers test out these contingencies. (Some of us would have them use more deliberate, more standardized, confirmation techniques.) Even the master teacher and certainly less experienced teachers need to examine the logical and empirical bases for their "believed-in"

contingencies. Do colleagues agree that their plans are logical? Have experts found such arrangements and teaching methods to "pay off" in that way?

One first step in evaluation is to record the potential contingency. A film on floodwaters may be scheduled (intended transaction) to expose students to background for understanding conservation legislation (intended outcome). Of those who know both subject matter and pedagogy, we ask, "Is there a logical connection between this event and this purpose?" If so, a logical contingency exists between these two Intents.

Descriptive data

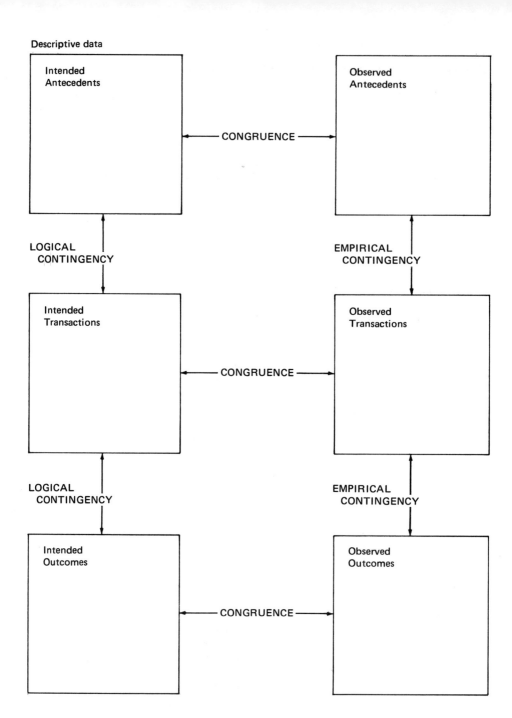

**Figure 1**
**A Representation of the Processing of Descriptive Data**

*Source:* Robert E. Stake, "The Countenance of Educational Evaluation," *Teachers College Record* **68** (April 1967):533. Used by permission.

Whenever Intents are evaluated, the contingency criterion is one of logic. To test the logic of an educational contingency, evaluators rely on previous experience, perhaps on research experience, with similar observables. No immediate observation of these variables, however, is necessary to test the strength of the contingencies among Intents.

Evaluation of Observation contingencies depends on empirical evidence. To say, "This arithmetic class progressed rapidly because the teacher was somewhat but not too sophisticated in mathematics" demands empirical data, either from within the evaluation or from the research literature. The usual evaluation of a single program will not alone provide the data necessary for contingency statements. Relationships require variation in the independent variables. What happens with various teaching treatments? Here, too, as Ausubel has contended (1966), previous experience with this content and with these teaching methods is a basic qualification of the evaluator.

The contingencies and congruences identified by evaluators should be judged as to importance by experts and interested parties just as the descriptive data are. The importance of non-congruence will vary with different viewpoints. The school superintendent and the school counselor may disagree as to the importance of cancellation of the scheduled lessons on sex hygiene in the health class. Here is an example of judging contingencies: the degree to which teacher morale is contingent on the length of the school day may be deemed cause enough to abandon an early morning class by one judge and not by another. *Perceptions* of the importance of congruence and contingency deserve the careful study of the evaluator.

We could now shift over to the right-hand side of the grid and consider the processing of standards and judgments for evaluation purposes. I am not going to do that here, for several reasons, one of which is that I really do not know much about processing judgments. I discussed this briefly in my "Countenance" paper (Stake, 1967a), but I am sure I gave the reader little guidance for that important step between reading the evaluation report and making the educational decision.

**Generalizability of Findings** Looking back at the emphasis I have given so far to rationality and to specification and to contingencies, the reader may be thinking that I cannot see the distinction between instructional research and evaluation. I do have difficulty drawing a line separating them. In fact, I am now going to draw a line connecting them. I see inquiry about instruction placed on a continuum. At one end, the findings are quite generalizable. At the other end, the findings are less generalizable. The line is a continuum of generalizability. I will put four important points on this continuum, one for instructional research, one for formative evaluation, the other two for summative evaluation and institutional evaluation.

| Instructional Research | Formative Evaluation | Summative Evaluation | Institutional Evaluation |
|---|---|---|---|
| [High] | Generalizability of Findings | | [Low] |

All four of these kinds of studies can be called applied research. All of them seek important information for the conduct of education. No one of them is necessarily more abstract than the other —they all deal with the concrete, the practical, the everyday components of education. They do differ with regard to generalizability. Findings from *instructional research* are more generalizable than findings from the others. Classroom studies of problem solving, modeling behavior, achievement need, content sequencing, and reinforcement are usually instructional research studies. These studies are expected to generalize—extensively if not completely—over subject matters, over school settings, over student types, over teacher types, and over time.

*Formative evaluation* leads to findings less generalizable than instructional research, but more generalizable than summative evaluation. Formative evaluation seeks information for the development of a curriculum or instructional device. The developer wants to find out what arrangement or what amount of something to use. Western Electric does formative evaluation when it tries out various plastics to determine which will make the more durable casing for a particular telephone. The Educational Testing Service does formative evaluation when it researches the effect of item vocabulary-difficulty on the discriminability of the National Teachers Examination. The BSCS Biology Project does formative evaluation when it studies the number of positive and negative instances of "genetic mutation" needed to get the concept across to an anticipated student body. The developer assumes that for subsequent revisions of that device the findings will hold. He assumes—sometimes incorrectly—that the findings are not specific to student types and teacher types; certainly he is comfortable in the belief that a separate finding is not necessary for each teacher and each student. Findings from the formative evaluation study are generalized over school setting, teacher and student types, and within the various versions of the particular instructional device, but are not generalized across subject matters and curricula.

Now, what about *summative evaluation?* I see summative evaluation aimed at giving answers to an educator about the merits and shortcomings of a particular curriculum or a specific set of instructional materials. This decision maker has little opportunity to modify or revise those packages. Particularly in the future, as computers, audio-visual equipment,

laboratory kits, and other distantly-developed units are increasingly used, the local consumer will be in no position to modify or revise them. He must learn about them as they are.

The monthly *Consumer Reports* does a good job of summatively evaluating refrigerators and various kinds of cameras. It expects these products to be used in a variety of ways, but each product will be accepted as a unit. Little rearrangement of its components is to be expected. Buros' *Mental Measurements Yearbook* (1965) does a good job of summative evaluation of standardized achievement tests. The findings are expected to be generalizable across large numbers of schools, teachers, and students. A large responsibility for the local educator remains in determining how similar are his uses, how similar are his teachers and students, to those described in the summative evaluation report. Particularly in this matter of deciding the appropriate bounds of generalization, words have often failed us.

*Institutional evaluation,* like summative evaluation, is aimed at a specific curriculum or instructional device but, in addition, is oriented to a specific setting—with its distinctive goals, classrooms, teaching staff, and student body. . . . The evaluation of the Tampa, Florida, First Grade Reading Program would be an example of institutional evaluation. So would the evaluation of the Peace Corps. For any institutional evaluation the curriculum, setting, staff, and students are specified. They may not all be examined but they are fixed. External norms are not of highest importance. The reader of the institutional evaluation report has relatively little need to know how his educational setting and personnel compare to others. He is little concerned about generalization to other settings or to other curricula. He is concerned about congruences and contingencies for inputs and outcomes for a specified teaching situation.

All four of these kinds of studies can

be based in the curriculum project or in the local school. What I have in mind is not so much the classification of different evaluation efforts but the importance of generalizability. A primary consideration in organizing an evaluation study is deciding on the degree to which the findings should be generalizable across curricula, school settings, teachers, and students. Different limits, of course, call for different data-gathering plans.

One of the reasons that many teachers and administrators pay little attention to research and evaluation studies is that they do not believe the findings will be generalizable to their situations. There is a common belief among educators that ideal programs can only be those tailored to the local community, to a particular teaching style, and sometimes, to each and every child separately. If this belief is well founded, all methods of educational evaluation are going to be very expensive. If instructional devices and situational features do yield an interaction effect, our studies become much more complex. If there is little generalizability —if, for example, the worth of a curriculum is highly dependent upon the value commitments of the teacher—then the value commitments of the individual teachers must be studied.

Educators do expect interactions such as these; yet apparently there is very little research evidence to substantiate them. Of course teachers are different. There is evidence that each should be paced individually. Different step sizes are appropriate for different teachers and different students. Yet this is not to say there is a disordinal (cross-over) interaction between program and personnel. This does not say that one version of the new mathematics program will be better with one population and another program better with a second population. At the present time there is little evidence that age, race, or sex and little evidence that cognitive style or temperament are keys to selecting better instructional treatments. We need

to know more about these bases for individualization of instruction before we will know how customized evaluation plans will have to be.

## RATIONALISM AND EMPIRICISM

Now let us look at some similarities and differences between research and evaluation methods. Scientists are observers. Evaluators are observers.[1] Both are seeking generalizations. A majority of scientists are manipulators. Developers of educational devices are manipulators. Evaluators are not. They are only free to manipulate themselves into better positions for observation. Even so, their presence may affect the outcomes. Scientists and evaluators alike must worry about such reactive effects.

Scientists, at least basic scientists, are not burdened by the demands of social utility. Their responsibility is revelation. A major scientific contribution reveals things in a different light, from a different perspective, in a different language—almost always in a way more parsimonious than the last. The evaluator need little concern himself with parsimony—in fact, he should err on the side of complexity and redundancy and detail. The educational evaluator's obligation is not to discover the essence of human learning, but to discover the diversity of viewpoints and explanations of what is going on in the school. His obligation is not to find the simplest explanations but the ones most amenable to control. The evaluator does shoulder the burden of utility. He must anticipate the uses of the evaluation.

Both the scientist and the evaluator hold "rationality" in high esteem. The inquiry methods of both the scientist and the evaluator are orderly, constrained, deliberate, based on reason. The more respectable designs—among scientists and

[1] Of course this does not say that the same man cannot be both scientist and evaluator. Even in the same study, each of us may choose to play both roles.

evaluators—are those that proceed from theory to hypothesis testing, from general rule to specific instance, and from program rationale to specific practice. It is said that an evaluation plan should be rational.

Now the important contradistinction here is not between rationality and irrationality. (To most people *that* distinction is parallel to the distinction between good and bad.) The important distinction is between rationalism and empiricism. Here are two systems for seeking generalizations. According to the rationalist, we should think first, plan ahead, anticipate the generalization, draw a flow chart or map or blueprint—then act, then test out the idea, confirm the generalization. According to the empiricist, we should act first, observe, build up a backlog of experience—then abstract, then infer, the generalization. The rationalist would have us invest more in planning; the empiricist would have us invest more in experience.

The distinction I am making might be more familiar to the reader as the distinction between the hypothetico-deductive method of inquiry and the heuristic method of inquiry. I find it easier to use the terms rational and empirical.

For evaluation, as for science, these alternate methods can be compared as to usefulness. We can compare the results of inquiries based upon a more rational approach with results of inquiries based upon a more empirical approach. Which do we like better? It *is* reasonable to anticipate that one will be narrower in coverage than the other. Which one? It *is* reasonable to anticipate that one will have more internal consistency than the other. Which one? In both cases, choice (a). The rational study, with its greater focus, is always in danger of ignoring important accoutrements. The empirical study, with its greater scope, is always in danger of having relevancies obscured by the irrelevant. Both can be powerful methods of inquiry; both can be carried to unwarranted extremes.

Although it may not be possible to have too much experience, it is possible to emphasize "knowing the classroom" so much that no attention is given to putting experience into order. An evaluation plan may fail because it deals only with vague, personal impressions.

Although it may not be possible to be too reasonable, it is possible to emphasize rationality so much that encounters with reality are unduly delayed or narrowly conceived. An evaluation plan may fail because it squanders its resources on organization, on instrument development, and on delimitation of the problem.

The technologist, the measurement expert, the proponent of rationalism says, "You misunderstand us, sir. Give rationalism a chance to work before you conclude it will not." No true empiricist could refuse that plea. As for me, personally, I do not want to be counted among those who are sure the worst will happen, who expect the misuse of technology to outrank the gain. Let us think about what rationality may do for us, good and bad. Maybe we should give it a "real" try. Like the empiricist says, "The making of something better depends on trying out things that we don't know much about." What does the contemporary rationalist want us to try out first?

The cornerstone of contemporary rationalism in education is the statement of objectives. Most plans call for the formulation of objectives prior to the operationalization of them. Most plans involving students call for the statement of objectives in behavioral language.[2] The argument is made that teachers do not analyze their teaching; that they are not aware of many of the goals that they really are

---

2 Behavior is associated with overt personal experience, so behaviorism traditionally has been associated with empiricism. Goal statements of behavior, however, are often outside the language repertoire of the educators involved, thus little associated with personal experience. An emphasis on any abstraction, e.g., a statement, is more characteristic of the rational than the empirical point of view. Thus, working with behavioral objectives is for most educators consorting with rationalism, not empiricism.

teaching for. It is claimed that teachers should commit themselves to "modification of specific behaviors." Unfortunately, it is not at all a demonstrated fact that teachers teach better when they state their objectives behaviorally and when they critically analyze their own teaching behavior.

When I look at teachers who seem to be doing a superb job of teaching my advisees and my children, I seldom find evidence that they are conceptualizing their task in behavior-modification language. Many seem little disposed to analysis of the teaching act. I do not know of any studies of preservice or in-service teacher education that suggest that teaching effectiveness is increased by allocating more of the teacher's time to planning and analytical evaluation. There is a lack of congruence between the expectation of the behaviorists and my observation of classroom teaching. It has prompted me to write an informal position statement. This statement summarizes a number of points I am attempting to make here.

## EDUCATIONAL OBJECTIVES:
## A POSITION STATEMENT

1. A great number of educational objectives are simultaneously pursued. The high-priority, immediate objectives should usually be apparent to teacher and learner alike. Occasionally, either will do better *without* being aware of them. High-quality education does often occur with educators having only an approximate realization of the objectives. Sometimes it will increase teaching-learning effectiveness to make participants more aware of objectives; sometimes it will not.

2. With all who share the responsibility of educating, there lies the responsibility for stating objectives, arranging environments, providing stimulation, evoking responses, and evaluating those responses. Yet each author and teacher does not share equally in those responsibilities. Time and talent are not available in limitless abundance to anyone. Each educator's assignment should capitalize on what he can do best. Few classroom teachers are skilled in stating objectives. Most are more highly skilled in adapting teaching to immediate circumstances, motivating students, and appraising responses. In the interest of effectiveness, seldom should they be required to formulate or conform to behavioral specifications.

3. There are more objectives to pursue than we can follow. Time and resources restrict us. We assign priorities to our goals in a highly informal way. This priority list is not the only determinant of the daily lesson or the minute-by-minute dialogue. Some moments are ripe for teaching toward an unplanned objective. A sound educational system is one which provides for occasional reassignment of immediate objectives to take advantage of the special opportunities that occur.

4. The development of a new curricular program or set of instructional materials often proceeds better by successive approximations than by linear programming. With successive approximations, major attention is given to getting an enterprise in operation, even though the initial runs are crude and faulty, so that corrections can be based on experience. With linear programming, major attention is given to planning, precise specification, and symbolic representation so that corrections can be based on logical analysis. Advice on curriculum planning should be oriented to the experiential and logical skills already developed in the developers or that can be readily obtained by them.

5. For creating lists of objectives, the technology of education should

have some methods that rely on behavioral specification and symbolic delimitation and other methods that rely on illustrative examples and inferable definitions. We need methods by which educators and others can endorse, reject, or revise statements of objectives. Two colossal problems lie before us: how to *translate* global objectives into specific behavioral objectives and how to *derive* appropriate teaching tactics.

6. Our curriculum development projects and our evaluation studies seldom reach a satisfactory specification by asking educators to state their objectives. Educators' global objectives give little guidance to teaching and evaluation. Their specific objectives ignore vast concerns that they have. In our present state the derivation of the specific from the general is some form of intuitive magic. Luckily this process often works pretty well. We need to understand it, to simulate it, not necessarily to replace it.

## A SECOND TEST

Let us go back to what the contemporary rationalist wants tried out in the classroom. He says teachers should stick to the lesson plan. Should a teacher be denounced because he does not stick to the syllabus? Departure from prescribed goals would be a sin indeed if we could just barely accomplish all our goals in the time available. The fact is, of course, that we cannot accomplish nearly all our goals. Furthermore, there are many important goals which can be pursued only when the situation is right, and for which it is difficult to create that situation. It is difficult to program many objectives, especially in the affective domain. Yet there are times when the classroom situation seems just right for teaching them.

Consider a teacher in an advanced biology class. A dialogue approximately

like this occurred recently at the University of Illinois University High School. Miss Betty K. was teaching a small group of students about metabolism.

". . . DNA (coded instructions) received from the previous generation are transcribed into RNA (again coded instructions) which ultimately are translated into specific molecules. What is unique about this whole system is that the fact that each individual gets a unique set of coded instructions and ultimately ends up again with a unique set of proteins. Okay? Now with this understood, we can look at the details of metabolism, how we get . . ."

"Uh, wait a minute, I'd like to know how you can transplant, if each thing is unique, if each set of proteins is unique, how can you transplant an organ from one race to another. Like, for instance, in the recent heart transplants. They used a mulatto."

"Oh. Well . . . do you remember what they did as they reported this case in the paper, before they prepped the person for the transplant?"

"They lowered the antibodies, well, they lowered the resistance of the person to make antibodies."

"And what else?"

"So he couldn't reject the heart."

"Okay, but what other tests do they perform on the donor before they would . . ."

"They had to have the same blood type."

"They ran tissue tests to see if the tissues were similar and same type of proteins."

"They also had to have the same size heart, so they wouldn't die because it was inadequate to pump the blood."

"I heard they can even transplant the organs from monkeys or something like that to human beings."

"Is something like that right?"

"Uh, well, what do you mean by right?"

"Well, I don't know, is it legal or moral, I mean you might be half-human and half-monkey by the time you're finished."

"I think it's, I don't know, it seems to me that if you're on your deathbed, then you're going to grasp at anything. If you can live for a little longer with a monkey heart, then it's probably best for you to use it."

"Well, these are the kinds of questions that you can't answer yes or no. Maybe we should pause and consider this kind of question, because these are the kinds of . . ."

"Like do you think it's right to have a monkey heart?"

"Well, not that specific example, but this kind of thing. Who should make these kinds of decisions, and how should they go about making decisions like this. . . ."

The opening statements of this transaction are analyzed in Table 3.

I have guessed at what was going through the teacher's mind during that exchange. On the two sides of Table 2 are represented some of what is stored in the teacher's memory. Her objectives are of two kinds: she plans to stimulate her students in various ways (the s's) and she plans to work with certain responses that will occur (the r's). In some way she appears to compare the responses she encounters in the classroom to those she wants to occur. When an unusual re-

TABLE 3

**A Representation of Classroom Instructional Transaction Emphasizing Continuous Teacher Evaluation of the Situation and Potential for Revision of Immediate Objectives and Priorities**

Analysis of Opening Statements

| Curriculum Guide<br><br>Lesson Plans<br><br>Short-Range Objectives | Transaction<br><br>. . . DNA (coded instructions) received from the previous generation are transcribed into RNA (again coded instructions) which ultimately are translated into specific molecules. What is unique about this whole system is the fact that each individual gets a unique set of coded instructions and ultimately ends up again with a unique set of proteins. Okay? | Rationale<br><br>Long-Range Objectives |
|---|---|---|
| Content  Response | | Content  Response |
| . . s s s   r r r . . | *Here the teacher checks to see if anyone wants further clarification on the background.* | . . s s s   r r r . . |
| . . s s s   r r r . . | | . . s s s   r r r . . |
| . . s s s   r r r . . | Now with this understood, we can look at the | . . s s s   r r r . . |
| . . s s s   r r r . . | details of metabolism; how we get . . . | . . s s s   r r r . . |
| . . s s s   r r r . . | Wait a minute. I'd like to know how you can | . . s s s   r r r . . |
| . . s s s   r r r . . | transplant an organ from one race to another. Like, | . . s s s   r r r . . |
| . . s s s   r r r . . | for instance, in the recent heart transplants. They | . . s s s   r r r . . |
| . . s s s   r r r . . | used a mulatto. | . . s s s   r r r . . |
| . . s s s   r r r . . | Oh. Well . . . | . . s s s   r r r . . |
| . . s s s   r r r . . | | . . s s s   r r r . . |
| . . s s s   r r r . . | *Here the teacher considers whether this digres-* | . . s s s   r r r . . |
| . . s s s   r r r . . | *sion has any potential merit, whether or not this* | . . s s s   r r r . . |
| . . s s s   r r r . . | *might lead to goals difficult to "teach for" in other* | . . s s s   r r r . . |
| . . s s s   r r r . . | *contexts.* | . . s s s   r r r . . |
| . . s s s   r r r . . | | . . s s s   r r r . . |
| . . s s s   r r r . . | . . . Well, do you remember what they did (as | . . s s s   r r r . . |
| . . s s s   r r r . . | reported in the paper) before they prepped the | . . s s s   r r r . . |
| . . s s s   r r r . . | person for the transplant? | . . s s s   r r r . . |
| . . s s s   r r r . . | | . . s s s   r r r . . |
| . . s s s   r r r . . | *The teacher is stalling for time at the start, but* | . . s s s   r r r . . |
| . . s s s   r r r . . | *by the time she has completed the question she* | . . s s s   r r r . . |
| . . s s s   r r r . . | *has decided to pursue the topic, at least a little.* | . . s s s   r r r . . |

sponse occurs she examines its potential for leading to some long-range objectives, then seeks other ideas and responses which more nearly approximate that goal.

It seemed to me that this teacher tried to provide opportunity for reflection and reaction. Quite unlike the linear and branching programmed instruction we knew, hers was the operant conditioning paradigm. The teacher seemed prepared to identify, reinforce, and shape many kinds of responses. It was as if she had an inventory of immediate objectives and an inventory of long-range objectives. She set things up so that immediate objectives were attended to until there arose the occasional opportunity to work on a hard-to-program objective.

The operant conditioning paradigm begins with a desired response, voluntary on the part of the learner. Many educationally desirable responses can be elicited just by asking for them or by "fishing" for them; many cannot. While in Miss K.'s class, I encountered another example of these unusual, unexpected, pregnant responses. A student said, "Isn't that the sort of relationship you can show with a graph?" It is very difficult to teach graphing as language in contrast to graphing as a form of (shall I say) penmanship. *There* was an opportunity. A skilled teacher will seize the opportunity to reconsider objectives. She will reassign priorities to goals on the spot. She may do this without being aware of the old or the new priorities. She may do it because "that's just the way you teach." But there is no rule that the teacher must recognize the operant paradigm, or call it that, for it to be effective.

This conscious or unconscious review of objectives seems to me to be the important purchase we make in assigning curriculum control to the teacher. There are many advantages to external programming, e.g., writing lessons in advance as the programmed instruction people do or as the well-organized lecturer does, but these advantages should be weighed against the advantages of assigning control to teachers who are sensitive to conditions optimally suited for the pursuit of elusive, long-range goals.

I would like to make a point here that should have been made previously. Teachers and evaluators need not have the same commitment to rationalism. It is not undesirable for us to have a high majority of teachers whose style is intuitive, spontaneous, and empirical; and at the same time to have a high majority of evaluators who are programmatic, deliberate, and rational. The successful practice of evaluation should not depend on teachers' being able to anticipate their information needs or to formulate their goals behaviorally. It is one thing for us to advise our colleagues in evaluation to commit themselves to rationalism; it is quite another to contend that teachers and curriculum supervisors do likewise.

I have examined here some contrasts between being rational and being empirical, particularly as they affect evaluation and as they affect the giving of advice to fellow educators. I singled out two of the propositions of the rationalists in education and found objections to both. This is only a small sample, so we should not conclude that all rationalist advice is objectionable, or that empiricist advice is better. We need to examine carefully more advice of both kinds.[3] In the final section of this paper I want to talk about language.

## THE LANGUAGE BARRIER

Each evaluation has its audiences. We evaluate in order to tell those audiences

[3] One basis for evaluating rationalist advice against empiricist advice relates to Kuhn's (1962) classification of scientific behavior: prescience (discrete experience); natural history (organized experience); normal science (testing theories and application); and extraordinary science (the breakthrough in theory). If a branch of education is devoid of theory, it is in a natural–history state of science and its practitioners might best rely on orderly experience, empiricism. If it has a substantial formal theory, its practitioners might be unwise to rely heavily on personal though orderly experience, wiser to specify purpose and plan on rational grounds.

about an instructional program. The quality of the evaluation will not exceed the quality of its communication. It is my contention that the greatest constraint upon evaluation today is the low quality of the language of evaluation. Our concern for goals is adequate, but our ability to represent goals is inadequate. Our talent for measuring educational outcomes is admirable, but our ability to convey their meaning is disappointing. Our ability to select the variables that people want to know about is often satisfactory, but the concepts we use are misunderstood. We are capable of restricting the subjectivity of our observations, but we are less capable of translating those observations into a language the audience can share with us. Our audience seeks certain information but we often misinterpret the needs.

How can they tell us? How can we talk to them? How can we indicate, for example, that the students are now more ready to participate in a formal learning experience than they were at the outset? What words can we use when we think we see, for example, a resistance-to-change on the part of a teachers association? It *is* true that these are measurement questions, but better observation schedules, better attitude scales, alone will not suffice. We need to improve the language, to talk more coherently to people about education. Without losing what precision of measurement we have, without jargon but yet without stirring up all the connotation of our childhood vocabularies, we need to increase our capacity to share meaning with others.

It is not necessarily sensible to say that we will teach them *our* language, nor necessarily sensible for us to translate, to mold our ideas into their language. Both or perhaps neither. I do not know how languages are nurtured, but ours must grow.

Let me give some examples of what I think we need in the way of new or improved language. First of all, we need concepts. We have the concepts of achievement, verbal ability, grade equivalents, vocational training. I have mentioned the concepts of congruence and contingency. Contingency (the idea, not the label) is common to discourse on the quality of schools, but the concept of congruence is not so common. Illustrative of other concepts that may be worth developing are the concepts of colinearity of classroom proceedings and homework assignments, relevance of instances used in concept formation learning, student concern for the learning difficulties of other students, and community responsiveness to changes in extracurriculars.

Many of the concepts become better understood as we use indices or models to represent them. Second, then, we need indicators of many aspects of school function. The National Assessment Project proposed new indicator items of student competence. Norm Kurland of New York State proposed a number of scholastic indicators. Project YARDSTICK in Cleveland is looking for an index of school efficiency. The difference between indicators and test scores or measurements, of course, is their acceptability as standard representations of important concepts. The I.Q. is an indicator of intelligence, though no longer acceptable as such to some. The Achievement Quotient, purportedly an indicator of over- and under-achievement, has not proved to be useful in most situations. Average daily attendance has.

There are those who protest the use of such indicators because they are not error-free, because they oversimplify. But all language is an approximation of the thought process. Most words and descriptions are simpler than the phenomena they represent. The only total safeguard against miscommunication is no communication. I understand that there are economists who have been protesting 30 years against the Gross National Product as an indicator of national productivity. Yet that indicator is useful. If its meaning needs refining, additional indicators can be used. There will be times when there is a real danger that an indicator will be misused and the consequences will be costly, so the indicator should be abandoned before it has really been tried out. Usually not, however. The lay of the land is not better understood by decreasing the number of bench marks. We need more. How to develop indicators and other forms of evaluation language is a question I will postpone until the very conclusion of this paper.

As a third component of language, I think that we need a better way of delimiting objectives. As I have said, I feel that neither the behavioral specification of goals nor the global summary of goals represents what the schools are trying to do. Either may be a suitable point of departure for developing more accurate language. Neither is satisfactory now.

A truly representative list of educational goals will contain competing and even contradictory goals. Goals compete with each other. Each pursuit costs something and the total of our resources will always be less than the cost of pursuing all goals. We have to choose among our goals. We assign priorities to them. We may do this unconsciously but we do it.

Some goals will be contradictory. We seek incompatible outcomes. We try to teach faith and skepticism. We try to instill deep appreciation, and yet provoke aspiration for something better. We hope that any one teaching effort will aid persons with different aims. We seek to serve a pluralistic society. Contradictory goals are to be expected in a pluralistic society. We cannot hope to pursue only goals that are perfectly complementary and universally wanted.

Evaluators should be alert to the fact that goals are changing. Our world changes. Our needs change. Our values change. Some of our goals change even as a function of what happens during instruction. A program evaluation is incomplete if it goes no further than designating several specific goals at time zero. To understand what is happening in a training activity and to ascertain its value, we

are obligated to identify groups of goals, ascertain priorities, and reveal the dynamics of changing priorities. This is not to say that these things must happen before we do any training, nor is it to say that we must be as specific as a blueprint. But as part of the evaluation we must obtain some communicable representation of the different things different people want the training to accomplish.

**Signs of Priority** The grand weakness in our present representation of goals is that we reveal few priorities, little ground for deciding which goals to pursue most vigorously. Our instructional technologists have ignored the problem, claiming responsibility only for already chosen goals. To read their literature is to learn that a goal unreached is a goal unsuitably pursued. That is no help. We will continue to aspire for goals beyond our reach. A major responsibility of curriculum development is to assign priorities that indicate how much should be invested in the pursuit of each goal, and a major responsibility of curriculum evaluation is to point out less successful pursuits as a basis for reallocation of effort.

The notion of priorities is simple enough, but we have yet to represent them in operational language. To give real meaning to the term, we must choose among different implications for priority levels. My colleague, Tom Maquire, has acquainted me with several different implications of priority levels. I will mention two: priorities can imply either the initial assignment of resources or the rank order of guarantees of outcome. These two are surely correlated, but they do lead to different plans of action. The first definition says that greater effort will be allotted to higher priority goals. The second definition indicates that regardless of what initial emphasis is given to different goals, when formal or informal evaluation findings indicate that a high priority goal is not being satisfactorily pursued, other work will be dropped in favor of the high priority goal. One requires a careful plan, the other an effective monitoring device. Considerably more study needs to be given to operational definitions of the concept "priority among goals." We should be working toward the day when an outside evaluator could examine the goal specifications, priority lists, and progress reports and identify objectively the areas of under- and over-support.

A fourth advancement in language would be the development of more systematic rules for deriving teaching tactics from immediate goals and for deriving immediate goals from long-range goals. David Krathwohl (1965) has identified four levels of specificity of goals. Peter Taylor and Tom Maguire (1966) built a model to represent stages in the transformation of objectives, from societal press to terminal student behaviors. I would not claim that teaching tactics should be derived mechanically, but we should understand more about how appropriate tactics are selected and we should be in a position to compare tactics chosen intuitively with those obtained deductively.

Goals evolve over time; they should, of course. How can we distinguish between logical and capricious changes? In Table 4 are my representations of the principal goals of Public Law 89-10 Title III as they have changed during the past few years. As an evaluator I should be able to say whether this restatement of purpose is a major or minor change, whether or not this representation is valid, and whether or not the change is logical. I cannot. At least one of my weaknesses is language.

There is a popular movie showing in the neighborhood theaters called *Cool Hand Luke*. Inside or outside prison, Luke is at cross purposes with the Establishment. He seals his fate by throwing back the warden's words:

"What we've got here is a failure to communicate."

That is just the way it is with educational evaluators. Course grades, test scores, federal project reports, accreditation standings, and research findings usually are hollow words and thoughtless patter to the educational decision maker. How can we tell him what he wants to know?

We have borrowed some of our better quantitative language from experimental psychology and from psychometric testing, a little from the school survey movement. We have many concepts from philosophy and the subject matter areas, many from the study of educational curricula. We need to develop some more for the express purpose of *telling others* about the antecedents, transactions, and outcomes of schooling. How can we build up this language? What should we do, for example, when some new languages like those in the National Assessment Program come along?

If we ask the rationalist for advice he will tell us to think through our needs for new language, to choose our indicators carefully, and to define our terms explicitly. He will say to hold work conferences, to talk it over among ourselves. He will tell us to invite the curriculum developer, teacher, and taxpayer to study our glossary, to learn our new language, perhaps even to help us evaluate it.

If we ask the empiricist for advice he will tell us to *try out* some new language. He will say to try lots of things, to see how they work with the people we really want to talk to. Try to figure out what the curriculum developer, teacher, and taxpayer mean when they use the same language. Use examples. Use illustrations. Let everyone share in the experience.

I wonder.

**TABLE 4**
**Evolution of Priorities for Title III Education Programs**

| President's Task Force on Education: | FL 89-10 Title III Purpose: | Title III Advisory Committee. | Nolan Estes Associate Commissioner; Priority Funding (early 1967): | Revised Priorities (mid-1967): | Harold Howe, Commissioner; Primary Priority, FY 1968: | Secondary Priority, FY 1968: |
|---|---|---|---|---|---|---|
| To stimulate and expand experimentation and innovation in education | To provide supplementary centers and services not now available | Fostering innovation, exemplary programs | Equalizing educational opportunities | Aid to deprived children in city core | Aid to deprived children in city core | Better education in geographically isolated areas |
| | To create exemplary educational programs | Funding new uses of available facilities | Planning for metropolitan areas | Programs to advance "individualized instruction" | | |
| | | Multipurpose, high cost, visible projects | Meeting needs of rural communities | Exemplary programs of early childhood education | | |
| | | | Coordinating all community resources | Quality education for minority groups | | |
| | | | | Better education in geographically isolated areas | | |
| | | | | Build planning and evaluation competence | | |

# 18. A Multi-Criterion Evaluation Model

## NEWTON S. METFESSEL and WILLIAM B. MICHAEL

The evaluation model proposed in this article represents a composite of many different ideas. Metfessel and Michael have drawn upon the thinking of the most outstanding authorities in the field in generating this eight-phase paradigm. The model makes logical sense and could be implemented at varying degrees of complexity and sophistication. Perhaps the chief contribution of the article, however, is contained in the Appendix, which lists a large number of different kinds of criterion measures that could be used to evaluate the effectiveness of a school program.

Although much of what is to be presented has been said before, the writers believe that in the light of the recent emphasis upon evaluation of exemplary and innovative school programs receiving federal support it may be helpful to set forth a rationale to facilitate their evaluation. Despite the risk of redundancy with the previous efforts of Tyler (1942, 1964), Bloom et al. (1956), Krathwohl (1964), Krathwohl et al. (1964), Lindvall et al. (1964), and Michael and Metfessel (1967), both the paradigm to be presented and the list of suggested criterion measures that may be used in evaluation of the attainment of objectives in school programs may be of some help to teachers, administrators, counselors, consultants to public schools, and certain other professional personnel whose experience in evaluation may be somewhat limited.

## PURPOSE

Thus, the twofold purpose of this paper is (1) to present an eight-step procedural

Reprinted with permission of the publisher and Newton S. Metfessel from an article entitled "A Paradigm Involving Multiple Criterion Measures for the Evaluation of the Effectiveness of School Programs," which appeared in Educational and Psychological Measurement, 27 (1967), pp. 931–943.

outline of the evaluation process in the form of a paradigm (or flow chart) that maps out in a step-by-step sequence the key features of the evaluation process and (2) to furnish a detailed listing of multiple criterion measures that may be used in the evaluation of specific behavioral objectives. (For maximum clarity and usability these objectives are preferably stated as operational definitions involving measurable and observable changes in behaviors that have been judged to be significant and relevant to the broad goals and the philosophy of the educational institution under study.) The experience of the writers in working with school personnel has pointed to the need not only for a model which can be followed in evaluation of school programs but also for a listing of multiple criterion measures of potential utility in the instrumentation phase of the evaluation process.

## THE PARADIGM

Since the purposes and assumptions underlying the evaluation process as well as ways in which specific objectives in both the cognitive and affective domains can be stated have been explicitly formulated in the sources already indicated as well as in many textbooks in college courses in educational measurement and evaluation, no attention will be given at this point to these specific concerns. Instead, emphasis will be placed on a brief statement of the key steps of the evaluation process, the details of which are outlined in the paradigm portrayed in Figure 1. The multiple criterion measures that correspond to the fourth segment of the evaluation process as shown in Figure 1 are included in the self-explanatory appendix. The eight major steps in the evaluation process may be enumerated as follows:

1. Involve both directly and indirectly members of the total school community as participants, or facilitators, in the evaluation of programs—lay individuals and lay groups, professional personnel of the schools and their organizations, and students and student-body groups.
2. Construct a cohesive paradigm of broad goals and specific objectives (desired behavioral changes) arranged in a hierarchical order from general to specific outcomes (both cognitive and noncognitive) in a form, for example, that might resemble one or both of the taxonomies set forth by Bloom et al. (1956) and Krathwohl et al. (1964). Substeps involved in this second phase include (a) setting broad goals that embrace the philosophical, societal, and institutional expectations of the culture; (b) stating specific objectives in operational terms permitting relatively objective measurement whenever possible and/or empirical determination of current status or of changes in behaviors associated with these objectives; and (c) developing judgmental criteria that permit the definition of relevant and significant outcomes as well as the establishment of realistic priorities in terms of societal needs, of pupil readiness, of opportunities for pupil-teacher

feedback necessary in motivating and directing learning, and of the availability of staff and material resources.
3. Translate the specific behavioral objectives into a form that is both communicable and applicable to facilitating learning in the school's environment.
4. Develop the instrumentation necessary for furnishing criterion measures from which inferences can be formulated concerning program effectiveness in terms of the objectives set forth.
5. Carry out periodic observations through use of the tests, scales, and other indices of behavioral change that are considered valid with respect to the objectives sampled.
6. Analyze data furnished by the status and change measures through use of appropriate statistical methods.
7. Interpret the data in terms of certain judgmental standards and values concerning what are considered desirable levels of performance on the totality of collated measures—the drawing of conclusions which furnish information about the direction of growth, the progress of students, and the effectiveness of the total program.
8. Formulate recommendations that furnish a basis for further implementation, for modifications, and for revisions in the broad goals and specific objectives so that improvements can be realized—recommendations which for their effectiveness depend upon adequate feedback of information to all individuals involved in the school program and upon repeated cycles of the evaluation process.

In addition the paradigm points to the individuals having primary responsibility for evaluation at each of the successive stages of the process. These responsibilities in the form of facilitating roles are indicated by the insertion of the letter *L* for lay individuals and lay groups, the letter *P* for professional staff members and their professional groups, and the letter *S* for students and student-body groups. These letters are placed in the lower right-hand corner of each of the principal blocks of the paradigm. Each block corresponds to a given phase of the evaluation process. Whenever the individuals designated by *P*, *L*, or *S* serve as primary or major agents (facilitators or inhibitors) at a given stage of the evaluation process, the letter is *not* placed within a parenthesis; whenever the individuals serve as secondary or indirect agents, a parenthesis is placed around the corresponding letter. The arrows from one block to the next indicate the approximate temporal sequence in which the steps occur, although in practice the order may be quite varied.

**A Few Cautions**  It should also be emphasized that judgmental decisions are involved throughout all phases of the evaluation process, as the participants at each stage may be expected to make adjustments in their activities in terms of the amount and kinds of feedback received. The alert evaluator needs also to be aware that measures may yield indications of false gains or false losses that are correlated with (1) experiences in the school environment as well as outside the school environment that go beyond the intent of the specific behavioral objectives, (2) uncontrolled differences in the facilitating effects of teachers and other school personnel (usually motivational in origin), (3) inaccuracies in collecting, reading, analyzing, collating, and reporting of data, and (4) errors in research design and statistical methodology. In such situations, the wisdom and seasoned judgment of the trained evaluator are particularly helpful and necessary if meaningful, honest, and realistic conclusions are to be derived from the data obtained in the evaluation process.

## APPENDIX

### Multiple Criterion Measures for Evaluation of School Programs

1. Indicators of Status or Change in Cognitive and Affective Behaviors of Students in Terms of Standardized Measures and Scales
   Standardized achievement and ability tests, the scores on which allow inferences to be made regarding the extent to which cognitive objectives concerned with knowledge, comprehension, understanding, skills, and applications have been attained.
   Standardized self-inventories designed to yield measures of adjustment, appreciations, attitudes, interests, and temperament from which inferences can be formulated concerning the possession of psychological traits (such as defensiveness, rigidity, aggressiveness, cooperativeness, hostility, and anxiety).
   Standardized rating scales and check lists for judging the quality of products in visual arts, crafts, shop activities, penmanship, creative writing, exhibits for competitive events, cooking, typing, letter writing, fashion design, and other activities.
   Standardized tests of psychomotor skills and physical fitness.
2. Indicators of Status or Change in Cognitive and Affective Behaviors of Students by Informal or Semiformal Teacher-made Instruments or Devices
   Incomplete sentence technique: categorization of types of responses, enumeration of their frequencies, or rating of their psychological appropriateness relative to specific criteria.
   Interviews: frequencies and measurable levels of responses to formal and informal questions raised in a face-to-face interrogation.

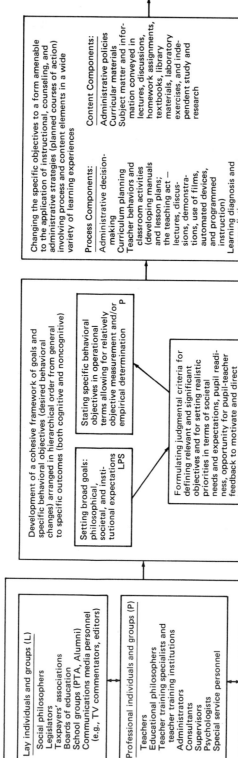

(1) Direct and Indirect Involvement of the Total School Community as Facilitators of Program Evaluation

Lay individuals and groups (L)
Social philosophers
Legislators
Taxpayers' associations
Boards of education
School groups (PTA, Alumni)
Communications media personnel (e.g., TV commentators, editors)

Professional individuals and groups (P)
Teachers
Educational philosophers
Teacher training specialists and teacher training institutions
Administrators
Consultants
Supervisors
Psychologists
Special service personnel

Students and student groups (S)

LPS

(2) Formation of a Cohesive Model of Broad Goals and Specific Objectives

Development of a cohesive framework of goals and specific behavioral objectives (desired behavioral changes) arranged in hierarchical order from general to specific outcomes (both cognitive and noncognitive)

Setting broad goals: philosophical, societal, and institutional expectations
LPS

Stating specific behavioral objectives in operational terms allowing for relatively objective measurement and/or empirical determination
P

Formulating judgmental criteria for defining relevant and significant objectives and for setting realistic needs and expectations, pupil readiness, opportunity for pupil-teacher feedback to motivate and direct learning, and availability of staff and material resources
P

P(S)(L)

(3) Translation of Specific Objectives into a Communicable Form Applicable to Facilitating Learning in the School Environment

Changing the specific objectives to a form amenable to the application of instructional, counseling, and administrative strategies (planned courses of action) involving process and content elements in a wide variety of learning experiences

Process Components:
Administrative decision-making
Curriculum planning
Teacher behaviors and classroom activities (developing manuals and lesson plans; the teaching act — lectures, discussions, demonstrations, use of films, automated devices, and programmed instruction)
Learning diagnosis and remediation
Counselors' participation in helping students to plan programs and to solve learning and personal problems

Content Components:
Administrative policies
Curricular materials
Subject matter and information conveyed in lectures, discussions, homework assignments, textbooks, library materials, laboratory exercises, and independent study and research

Counselors' information on course requirements, on college preparatory programs, on career planning, employment opportunities, avocational activities, study methods, and students' personal capabilities and talents
P(S)

Figure 1
**Paradigm Showing Eight Major Phases in Evaluating School Programs, in Approximate Temporal Sequence.** The facilitating role of lay individuals (L), professional personnel (P), and students (S) is indicated in lower right-hand corner of boxes. The parentheses around L, P, and S indicate a secondary or indirect role and the absence of parentheses a primary role.

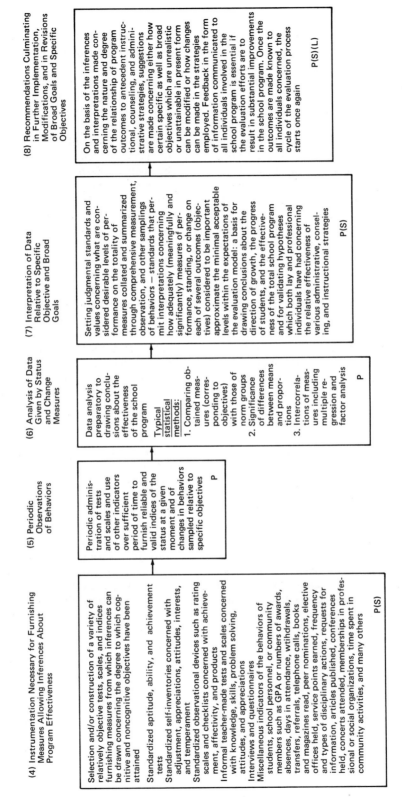

**(4) Instrumentation Necessary for Furnishing Measures Allowing Inferences About Program Effectiveness**

Selection and/or construction of a variety of relatively objective tests, scales, and indices furnishing measures from which inferences can be drawn concerning the degree to which cognitive and noncognitive objectives have been attained

Standardized aptitude, ability, and achievement tests

Standardized self-inventories concerned with adjustment, appreciations, attitudes, interests, and temperament

Standardized observational devices such as rating scales and checklists concerned with achievement, affectivity, and products

Informal teacher-made tests and scales concerned with knowledge, skills, problem solving, attitudes, and appreciations

Interviews and questionnaires

Miscellaneous indicators of the behaviors of students, school personnel, or community members such as GPA or numbers of awards, absences, days in attendance, withdrawals, transfers, referrals, telephone calls, books and magazines read, peer nominations, elective offices held, service points earned, frequency and types of disciplinary actions, requests for information, articles published, conferences held, concerts attended, memberships in professional or social organizations, time spent in community activities, and many others

P(S)

**(5) Periodic Observations of Behaviors**

Periodic administration of tests and scales and use of other indicators over sufficient period of time to furnish reliable and valid indices of the status at a given moment and of changes in behaviors sampled relative to specific objectives

P

**(6) Analysis of Data Given by Status and Change Measures**

Data analysis preparatory to drawing conclusions about the effectiveness of the school program

Typical statistical methods:

1. Comparing obtained measures (corresponding to objectives) with those of norm groups
2. Significance of differences between means and proportions
3. Intercorrelations of measures including multiple regression and factor analysis

P

**(7) Interpretation of Data Relative to Specific Objective and Broad Goals**

Setting judgmental standards and values concerning what are considered desirable levels of performance on the totality of measures collated and summarized through comprehensive measurement, observation, and other samplings of behaviors – standards that permit interpretations concerning how adequately (meaningfully and significantly) measures of performance, standing, or change on each of several outcomes (objectives) considered to be important approximate the minimal acceptable levels within the expectations of the evaluation model: a basis for drawing conclusions about the direction of growth, the progress of students, and the effectiveness of the total school program and for validating hypotheses which both lay and professional individuals have had concerning the relative effectiveness of various administrative, counseling, and instructional strategies

P(S)

**(8) Recommendations Culminating in Further Implementation, Modifications, and in Revisions of Broad Goals and Specific Objectives**

On the basis of the inferences and interpretations made concerning the nature and degree of the relationship of program outcomes to antecedent instructional, counseling, and administrative strategies, suggestions are made concerning either how certain specific as well as broad objectives which are unrealistic or unattainable in present form can be modified or how changes can be made in the strategies employed. Feedback in the form of information communicated to all individuals involved in the school program is essential if the evaluation efforts are to result in substantial improvements in the school program. Once the outcomes are made known to all individuals concerned, the cycle of the evaluation process starts once again

P(S)(L)

Peer nominations: frequencies of selection or of assignment to leadership roles for which the sociogram technique may be particularly suitable.

Questionnaires: frequencies of responses to items in an objective format and numbers of responses to categorized dimensions developed from the content analysis of responses to open-ended questions.

Self-concept perceptions: measures of current status and indices of congruence between real self and ideal self—often determined from use of the semantic differential or Q-sort techniques.

Self-evaluation measures: student's own reports on his perceived or desired level of achievement, on his perceptions of his personal and social adjustment, and on his future academic and vocational plans.

Teacher-devised projective devices such as casting characters in the class play, role playing, and picture interpretation based on an informal scoring model that usually embodies the determination of frequencies of the occurrence of specific behaviors, or ratings of their intensity or quality.

Teacher-made achievement tests (objective and essay), the scores on which allow inferences regarding the extent to which specific instructional objectives have been attained.

Teacher-made rating scales and check lists for observation of classroom behaviors: performance levels of speech, music, and art; manifestation of creative endeavors, personal and social adjustment, physical well being.

Teacher-modified forms (preferably with consultant aid) of the semantic differential scale.

3. Indicators of Status or Change in Student Behavior Other than Those Measured by Tests, Inventories, and Observation Scales in Relation to the Task of Evaluating Objectives of School Programs

Absences: full-day, half-day, part-day and other selective indices pertaining to frequency and duration of lack of attendance.

Anecdotal records: critical incidents noted including frequencies of behaviors judged to be highly undesirable or highly deserving of commendation.

Appointments: frequencies with which they are kept or broken.

Articles and stories: numbers and types published in school newspapers, magazines, journals, or proceedings of student organizations.

Assignments: numbers and types completed with some sort of quality rating or mark attached.

Attendance: frequency and duration when attendance is required or considered optional (as in club meetings, special events, or off-campus activities).

Autobiographical data: behaviors reported that could be classified and subsequently assigned judgmental values concerning their appropriateness relative to specific objectives concerned with human development.

Awards, citations, honors, and related indicators of distinctive or creative performance: frequency of occurrence or judgments of merit in terms of scaled values.

Books: numbers checked out of library, numbers renewed, numbers reported read when reading is required or when voluntary.

Case histories: critical incidents and other passages reflecting quantifiable categories of behavior.

Changes in program or in teacher as requested by student: frequency of occurrence.

Choices expressed or carried out: vocational, avocational, and educational (especially in relation to their judged appropriateness to known physical, intellectual, emotional, social, aesthetic, interest, and other factors).

Citations: commendatory in both formal and informal media of communication such as in the newspaper, television, school assembly, classroom, bulletin board, or elsewhere (see Awards).

"Contacts": frequency or duration of direct or indirect communications between persons observed and one or more significant others with specific reference to increase or decrease in frequency or to duration relative to selected time intervals.

Disciplinary actions taken: frequency and type.

Dropouts: numbers of students leaving school before completion of program of studies.

Elected positions: numbers and types held in class, student body, or out-of-school social groups.

Extracurricular activities: frequency or duration of participation in observable behaviors amendable to classification such as taking part in athletic events, charity drives, cultural activities, and numerous service-related avocational endeavors.

Grade placement: the success or lack of success in being promoted or retained; number of times accelerated or skipped.

Grade point average: including numbers of recommended units of course work in academic as well as in non-college preparatory programs.

Grouping: frequency and/or duration of moves from one instructional group to another within a given class grade.

Homework assignments: punctuality of completion, quantifiable judgments of quality such as class marks.

Leisure activities: numbers and types

of; times spent in; awards and prizes received in participation.

Library card: possessed or not possessed; renewed or not renewed.

Load: numbers of units or courses carried by students.

Peer group participation: frequency and duration of activity in what are judged to be socially acceptable and socially undesirable behaviors.

Performance: awards, citations received; extra credit assignments and associated points earned; numbers of books or other learning materials taken out of the library; products exhibited at competitive events.

Recommendations: numbers of and judged levels of favorableness.

Recidivism by students: incidents (presence or absence or frequency of occurrence) of a given student's returning to a probationary status, to a detention facility, or to observable behavior patterns judged to be socially undesirable (intoxicated state, dope addiction, hostile acts including arrests, sexual deviation).

Referrals: by teacher to counselor, psychologist, or administrator for disciplinary action, for special aid in overcoming learning difficulties, for behavior disorders, for health defects, or for part-time employment activities.

Referrals: by student himself (presence, absence, or frequency).

Service points: numbers earned.

Skills: demonstration of new or increased competencies such as those found in physical education, crafts, homemaking, and the arts that are not measured in a highly valid fashion by available tests and scales.

Social mobility: numbers of times student has moved from one neighborhood to another and/or frequency with which parents have changed jobs.

Tape recordings: critical incidents contained and other analyzable events amenable to classification and enumeration.

Tardiness: frequency of.

Transiency: incidents of.

Transfers: numbers of students entering school from another school (horizontal move).

Withdrawal: numbers of students withdrawing from school or from a special program (see Dropouts).

4. Indicators of Status or Change in Cognitive and Affective Behaviors of Teachers and Other School Personnel in Relation to the Evaluation of School Programs

Articles: frequency and types of articles and written documents prepared by teacher for publication or distribution.

Attendance: frequency of, at professional meetings or at in-service training programs, institutes, summer schools, colleges and universities (for advanced training) from which inferences can be drawn regarding the professional person's desire to improve his competence.

Elective offices: numbers and types of appointments held in professional and social organizations.

Grade point average: earned in postgraduate courses.

Load carried by teacher: teacher-pupil or counselor-pupil ratio.

Mail: frequency of positive and negative statements in written correspondence about teachers, counselors, administrators, and other personnel.

Memberships including elective positions held in professional and community organizations: frequency and duration of association.

Model congruence index: determination of how well the actions of professional personnel in a program approximate certain operationally-stated judgmental criteria concerning the qualities of a meritorious program.

Moonlighting: frequency of outside jobs and time spent in these activities by teachers or other school personnel.

Nominations by peers, students, administrators, or parents for outstanding service and/or professional competencies: frequency of.

Rating scales and check lists (e.g., graphic rating scales or the semantic differential) of operationally-stated dimensions of teachers' behaviors in the classroom or of administrators' behaviors in the school setting from which observers may formulate inferences regarding changes of behavior that reflect what are judged to be desirable gains in professional competence, skills, attitudes, adjustment, interests, and work efficiency; the perceptions of various members of the total school community (parents, teachers, administrators, counselors, students, and classified employees) of the behaviors of other members may also be obtained and compared.

Records and reporting procedures practiced by administrators, counselors, and teachers: judgments of adequacy by outside consultants.

Termination: frequency of voluntary or involuntary resignation or dismissals of school personnel.

Transfers: frequency of requests of teachers to move from one school to another.

5. Indicators of Community Behaviors in Relation to the Evaluation of School Programs

Alumni participation: numbers of visitations, extent of involvement in PTA activities, amount of support of a tangible (financial) or a service nature to a continuing school program or activity.

Attendance at special school events, at meetings of the board of education, or at other group activities by parents: frequency of.

Conferences of parent-teacher, parent-counselor, parent-administrator sought by parents: frequency of request.

Conferences of the same type sought and initiated by school personnel: frequency of requests and record of appointments kept by parents.

Interview responses amenable to classification and quantification.

Letters (mail): frequency of requests for information, materials, and servicing.

Letters: frequency of praiseworthy or critical comments about school programs and services and about personnel participating in them.

Participant analysis of alumni: determination of locale of graduates, occupation, affiliation with particular institutions, or outside agencies.

Parental response to letters and report cards upon written or oral request by school personnel: frequency of compliance by parents.

Telephone calls from parents, alumni, and from personnel in communications media (e.g., newspaper reporters): frequency, duration, and quantifiable judgments about statements monitored from telephone conversations.

Transportation requests: frequency of.

## 19. In Support of the Comparative Field Experiment
### RICHARD C. ANDERSON

Many experts, among them Cronbach (1963), have suggested that evaluative research, which pits one version of a course, program, or curriculum against another, is not the most profitable approach to evaluation. It is argued, probably justifiably, that at the level of mean differences, intra- and interclass variability would confound the evaluation. There are, however, many positive aspects to the comparative study.

With a primary view to summative evaluation, and working from the assumption that basic research and accumulated theories of instruction do not allow us to predict effectiveness, Richard C. Anderson here builds a reasonable case for the comparative field experiment. The use of tightly controlled analytical studies, using relative rather than absolute standards, could provide the consumer with invaluable information for decision making. It would also seem that the federally-sponsored system of regional educational laboratories, which are presently in operation, could be used to implement some of Anderson's suggestions.

A time-honored, but not otherwise honored, form of educational research is the experiment comparing different methods of instruction. Throughout the years there have been numerous comparisons of televised lectures with live lectures, discovery teaching with expository teaching, learner-centered instruction with teacher-centered instruction, programmed instruction with textbook instruction, and so on. The lessons employed in these experiments were of little interest for their own sake. They were merely the vehicles for evaluating a method of instruction it was *assumed* would apply broadly to many lessons. Today I dare say there is general agreement that this was a poor assumption. Nonetheless, I shall argue that the comparative

Reprinted and abridged with permission of the publisher and Richard C. Anderson from an article entitled "The Comparative Field Experiment: An Illustration from High School Biology," which appeared in the *Proceedings of the 1968 Invitational Conference on Testing Problems* Princeton, N.J.: Educational Testing Service, 1969), pp. 3-30. Copyright 1969 by Educational Testing Service. All rights reserved.

experiment, recast for a different purpose, deserves a share of the time and energy of the educational research community.

The argument begins like this: We have little power to predict the kind of instruction that will work best with learners. There are no methods of instruction that have proved consistently better than, or even consistently different from, other methods. There are no procedural features of lessons that are invariably associated with greater student achievement. Neither small steps, nor active responding, nor immediate feedback, nor a warm classroom climate, nor a sequence from concrete to abstract, nor the provision for self-direction and self-pacing, nor multimedia stimulus bombardment—singly or in the aggregate—guarantee successful instruction.

This is a bleak picture, but I think not overdrawn. To be sure, we do know some things. However, there are more things about which we are uncertain. There are many anomalies. It is, in my judgment, a fair appraisal to say that right now, today, we cannot confidently predict the effectiveness of a lesson, given a description of its philosophy, [and] the style, the methods, and the procedures of instruction.

If this is a fair appraisal, then consider the following question: How should the money of funding agencies and the time and energy of the educational research community be allocated to maximize the effectiveness of instruction today and in the future? One answer is to invest in basic educational and behavioral science research. I am very sympathetic with this view. We should, however, be realistic about the impact basic research can have on instructional practice.

There is currently a high "degree of empiricism" in the behavioral sciences. This is doubly true of the applied sciences that look to behavioral science for inspiration. Basic educational research should gradually increase our capacity to specify in advance of tryout the procedures and arrangements of instructional material which are quite certain to facilitate student learning. Gradual progress can be counted on. But it would be unrealistic to expect that we shall ever be able to predict effective configurations of instruction with any more than modest confidence. I have no doubt that instructional development will always be based in part on rules of thumb. And I have no doubt that a considerable amount of trial and error will always be necessary to guarantee successful instruction.

Thus far I have argued that we have little power to predict the features of instruction that will maximize student learning, and that basic research can be expected to add only modest increments to our capacity to predict. There is one thing we can do right now. We can distinguish in tryouts or field tests units of instruction which teach well and units of instruction which teach poorly. The rational thing to do is to make use of this capability to improve instruction. The contention is that lessons should be evaluated in terms of the results they produce with students

and that every step in the development of instructional materials should be guided by student performance. It is not possible on the basis of existing knowledge to warrant methods of instruction, but it is possible to warrant particular lessons, units, or curricula.

Satisfactory lessons can be developed using systematic trial and error. The process consists of the designation of objectives, preparation of instructional materials that hopefully meet these objectives, and then tryouts of the materials with people of the type for whom the instruction is intended. On the basis of successive tryouts, revisions are made in the materials. The process of tryout and revision continues until objectives are being reached or the decision is made that it is impossible to reach the objectives within the limits of available time and resources.

## THE ROLE OF THE FIELD TEST

When the pilot test data indicate students are reaching objectives, it is time for a field test of the instructional materials. Better to say that a total instructional package is to be field tested. An "instructional package" includes not only materials put directly into the hands of students and scripts or guides to the teacher indicating how to conduct discussions, laboratories, problem-solving episodes and so on, but it also may include teacher manuals, provision for teacher workshops, and the supervision of instruction. One purpose of the field test is to determine whether the instructional package will perform successfully under various conditions of use. The pilot test may or may not have involved the full range of students who will use the materials. The pilot tests were presumably completed or supervised by someone who was enthusiastic about the project and knowledgeable about the use of the materials. What will happen if the materials are placed in the hands of teachers who are indifferent or even hostile? Must the materials be used in a certain way or will they be reasonably successful under a variety of conditions? If the curriculum must be used in a certain way, is there provision for teacher manuals or workshops? And are the manuals or workshops successful in getting teachers to behave in the intended way? These are some of the questions which can be answered in a field test.

To use the terms introduced by Scriven (1967), the purpose of pilot tests is formative evaluation, to locate weaknesses in student understanding or performance so that editors, writers, or teachers can revise and presumably improve instruction materials and procedures.

Providing feedback to the developers of the instruction is only a secondary purpose of the field test. The chief purpose is summative evaluation. Data are gathered in order to help potential consumers— education agencies, administrators, teachers, students—make the decision to use or not to use the instructional package.

Some people who argue for empirical validation of instructional materials seem to take the position that effectiveness in modifying student behavior is the sole criterion for judging instruction. Let me emphasize that this is not my position. Lessons, units, and curricula should be judged in terms of the extent to which they reach their goals, but this cannot be the only criterion. Other criteria include the cost of the instructional sequence in terms of student and teacher time, the acceptability of the sequence to students and teachers, and any side effects (Stake, 1967a). The accuracy, up-to-dateness, and elegance of the subject matter has been the important criterion for the prominent curriculum reform projects. A most important criterion is the worthiness of the goals the instruction aims to reach. As Scriven (1967) has noted, "it is obvious that if the goals aren't worth achieving then it is uninteresting how well they were achieved." A complimentary assertion is also true: No matter how worthy the goals, a lesson cannot be valued highly if it is ineffective in reaching these

goals. Effectiveness should be neither overrated nor underrated as a criterion for judging instruction.

Sometimes the field test of an instructional package should be a comparative experiment. This conclusion is inescapable if the function of the field test is to guide consumer decisions. There are several alternative sets of instructional materials for most areas taught in school. To the extent that the objectives and the coverage of different sets of materials overlap, it is entirely reasonable for the practical decision maker to ask which is most effective.

Cronbach (1963) and Scriven (1967) have taken opposing sides as to the value of comparative experiments. With one qualification, I agree with Scriven: Comparative experiments do have a valuable function. But Scriven seems to envision massive Consumer Union-type comparisons of the curricula within every subject-matter area. To this plan, Cronbach has rightly objected that most comparisons probably would show no differences of statistical or practical significance.

Comparative experiments are expensive. They cannot be run indiscriminately. One criterion for deciding whether a comparative experiment should be run is this: There must be considerable confidence that one of the instructional packages is in fact more effective than the other. The playing of hunches has its place in basic research. But this strategy cannot be encouraged in comparative educational research. From the point of view of the person undertaking a comparative experiment, it should simply be a demonstration that one of the instructional packages is superior.

In a comparative experiment, the no-difference result has very low social utility. If you firmly reject the notion that a comparative experiment can show the general worth of a method of instruction and accept the concept that the main justification for the comparative experiment must be to determine which of two or more particular lessons (instructional packages) is the most effective, then obviously it doesn't make any sense to compare lessons on the mere chance that one of them might be better; unless, perhaps, you believe there are many great lessons, unrecognized, lying around waiting to be discovered. Perhaps there is some value to finding that a widely touted curricular innovation is no more effective than other instruction. In general, though, inconclusive comparative experiments cannot facilitate consumer decisions. Consequently, there has been error in judgment when a comparative experiment shows no difference. Time and money, which should have been invested in instructional development and formative evaluation, have been wasted on a premature comparison.

It may be argued that research cannot be justified merely to demonstrate what is confidently believed to be true. The counter-argument is based on the thesis developed earlier in this paper. There are no a priori tests that reliably predict lesson effectiveness and no experts whose acumen in judging lesson effectiveness has been established. In short, there are no acceptable grounds for claims about effectiveness of a lesson except for data which actually demonstrate effectiveness.

## THE NEED FOR RELATIVE STANDARDS

The position that lessons should be evaluated in terms of absolute standards of effectiveness is widely voiced. Indeed, this is the position I take with respect to pilot tests of lessons. When it comes to field tests of lessons, there are reasons to be cautious about relying entirely upon absolute standards. First of all, unlike other practical fields ranging from agriculture to the automobile industry, education has no consensual standards of performance.

Suppose that educators could agree on some general standard, let us say the famous 90–90 standard propounded by the Air Force Training Command under the leadership of Colonel Gabriel Ofiesh. What would it mean if students averaged 90 percent on a criterion measure? Obviously it would not mean that the students had mastered 90 percent of all there is to know about a topic. What it would mean is that they had learned 90 percent of what someone chose to teach and measure. Herein lies the problem. Despite recent advances in clarifying educational objectives, there can still be considerable variance in the intended or implicit level of sophistication with which a concept is developed, given ostensibly the same goals. A further problem is that the level of performance is a function of measurement technique, including such factors as, for instance, the attractiveness of distractors in multiple-choice items. Finally, the fact that an instructional package meets a certain standard of effectiveness does not preclude the possibility that a competing package will exceed the standard in less time at lower cost. The conclusion is that relative standards, and therefore comparative experiments, are necessary to gauge the effectiveness of instructional materials.

Do not mistake me. I believe that the notion of absolute standards of effectiveness is sound in principle. I hope that it will be possible to augment the logic and the techniques for formulating absolute standards. For the indefinite future, in consideration of our fallibility in defining absolute standards and measuring performance with respect to them, absolute standards should be supplemented with relative ones. At the present time, the only dependable way to determine which of two lessons is most effective is to directly compare them.

There is a clear role for the comparative experiment when several lessons (units, curricula) have substantially the same goals. When this is the case, the best lesson is the most effective lesson (assuming other factors such as cost are comparable). The consumer can concentrate mainly on the data from a comparative experiment when choosing among instructional packages. Moreover—and

this is one of the reasons I am advocating comparative experiments—the competition to produce better lessons will itself promote more effective instruction.

## 20. Science Curriculum Evaluation: Observations on the Behavioral Approach

### HENRY H. WALBESSER

A spokesman for the "behavioral school of objectives" articulates, in this article, the way in which curriculum development and evaluation can interrelate to produce a superior hybrid. Again, as is so often the case, it is the formative or feedback nature of the design that allows for the development of an effective curriculum. It is important to note how the nature of the objectives sets the tone and the requirements not only for the development of materials, but also for the evaluation design.

Two of the fundamental positions concerning the purposes, conduct, and expected outcomes of evaluation which are currently assumed in the assessment of experimental curriculum materials are: the content position and the behavior position. It is the intention of this paper to point out the differences between these two conceptions of curriculum assessment and to describe the model, based upon the behavior position, which is being used by the AAAS Commission on Science Education in its curriculum project.

### CONTENT

It would doubtless be valuable to explore the content position in depth, but that will not be done here. Our chief concern is with the behavior position. We need say only enough about the content position to help distinguish those aspects

which are specific to it and those peculiar to the behavior position. In brief— as "content" suggests—those who adopt this view build a curriculum or develop instructional materials as a content-organizing enterprise. They use instructional materials which appeal to a logical, or rational, or historical presentation of a particular discipline or combination of disciplines. Choice of materials is considered in terms of the nature of the items which should be sampled from the content domains and relates to such questions as:

What big ideas from this discipline should be chosen?

What particular topics are fundamental to an understanding of the discipline?

How can certain concepts be best presented?

What particular facts must an individual know if he is to appreciate the significance of this discipline?

Naturally, in the assessment of the instructional materials developed from such a curriculum orientation, the units of

Reprinted with permission of the publisher and Henry H. Walbesser from an article entitled "Science Curriculum Evaluation: Observations on a Position," which appeared in The Science Teacher 33 (February 1966), pp. 34–39.

achievement are taken to be content items.

The primary measurement is most often a sequence of content items or content situations, and the measurement is made almost exclusively in terms of paper and pencil performances. Among those who adopt this content position there are some who use subjective "expert" evaluation, particularly among those who contend that the measurement field has not yet achieved the necessary technology so as to be able to provide useful or constructive information about the effects of the curriculum. However, assessment of instruction materials by means of a rigorous research design *is* possible within the content-directed framework.

## BEHAVIOR POSITION

The second group of curriculum designers reflect what might be termed the behavior position. The AAAS Commission on Science Education subscribes to this position. The "behavioral" group focuses upon the creation of instructional sequences of material which supposedly assist the learner in the acquisition of a particular collection of behaviors rather than a particular collection of content. Unlike those who favor evaluation of content, the curriculum organization which appeals to a behavioral interpretation approaches the development of instructional materials by asking one question: *What do we want the learner to be able to do after instruction that he was unable to do before instruction?*

Then the curriculum designer proceeds to develop materials related to the answers given to this question.

The existence of each curriculum project is dependent upon being able to demonstrate that it accomplishes something. Whether this accomplishment is content assimilation or performance acquisition is of no real consequence. What is important, however, is the recognition and acceptance of the principle that every curriculum project has the honest and inescapable obligation to supply *objective evidence of accomplishment.* Furthermore, the evidence presented by the project must be able to satisfy the criterion that it was obtained by defensible research procedures and that these procedures can be replicated if someone should desire to do so.

For the behavior-oriented group of curriculum designers, reliably observable performance plays the same role as a content item does for the content-oriented group. As a consequence of the behavior-oriented point of view, the evaluation of a collection of instructional materials becomes the assessment of the presence or absence of specific behaviors or specific sets of behaviors. The accomplishment of these objectives of the instructional materials for the behavior-oriented group is determined by observing the learner performing his specified task and thereby exhibiting the desired behavior. Such an assessment obviously demands that the behaviors under observation be clearly stated, the criterion for their presence be explicitly stated, and that the conditions under which the evidence of presence or absence is collected be described in such a way that the procedure used to obtain the evidence can be replicated by others. This investigator has adopted the position that the behavioral view of curriculum development possesses advantages sufficiently unique and productive to the design, development, and evaluation of instructional materials so as to make behavioral description of the objectives of instructional materials an unavoidable partner of content selection. The remainder of this paper is an explanation of this position.

## PRACTICES FOR EVALUATION

What is the purpose of any collection of instructional materials? One response which has a high probability of acceptance by most, if not all, curriculum designers, is that the purpose of a collection of instructional materials is to effect learning. An appeal to this all-encompassing goal of learning leads one quite naturally to ask two questions: What is to be learned? and, Who is to learn it? The question of who is to learn relates, in this instance, to the population of elementary school children. Upon first consideration, one might argue that "what is to be learned" is exclusively within the domain of content selection. However, this view is soon replaced by the more basic behavioral orientation when one considers that the recognition of whether an individual possesses "knowledge of a particular collection of content" is only possible through some observable response on his part.

Does confinement of statements of what is to be learned to statements of observable performance restrict the nature of the content area or the general character of possible objectives of the curriculum? The constraints imposed by behavioral objectives for curriculum description are amazingly few. Consider, for example, the physicist who might set the goal for his curriculum to be that the student will understand Newton's First Law of Motion. How will the physicist distinguish those students who understand from those students who do not understand? Perhaps someone would wish to contend that the physicist is never certain of when the student understands. This position is indefensible for a writer who intends others to adopt an instructional procedure which will teach "an understanding of that concept." Furthermore, how can any author make a selection of instructional procedures, or decide upon an order, or include or exclude instructions from his discussion if he possesses no indicator of when he has succeeded? How can a writer make any decision under these circumstances? It is quite possible, however, that the physicist may not be able to verbalize the class of learner responses with which he is concerned, but the physicist, nevertheless, does possess them. The problem is merely to help the creator of the instructional sequence verbalize a description of the desired behaviors. From this standpoint one may contend that even the comfortable, ambiguous objectives such as understanding, appreciation, and knowing—so commonplace as objectives for contemporary curriculum projects—are potentially able to yield to a behavioral description.

The content selection and organization made by the writing efforts of the past decade are not under question by this discussion, but rather the lack of evidence to support or describe what these programs accomplish is the focus of attention. What is already available by way of instructional materials is not the central issue either, for this material is part of the past development and should remain part of the past. It is not sensible that one propose taking existing materials and attempting to provide a set of behavioral objectives to describe each program. What is important is that curriculum projects learn from these errors so that current activity improves upon past efforts.

Curriculum designers seldom possess professional interest in the problems associated with the clarification and specification of objectives in terms of a behavioral description. It is the obligation of the behavioral researcher to provide the guidelines which will enable the curriculum writer to make the statements of performance.

How will the project proceed after it has adopted the principle that statements of objectives be statements of observable performance? One procedure is to attempt an adaptation of the "Bloom Taxonomy" (1956). However, lack of specification within, as well as between, Bloom's taxonomic classifications and their relationship to test development rather than instructional development make them somewhat unacceptable for the present purpose. Since the behavioral point of view focuses upon the ability of a learner to perform a specific task, the work of Miller (1953, 1954) in the area of task analysis, and that of Gagné (1962, 1965) and Walbesser (1963) in the construction and interpretation of behavioral hierarchies, offer an alternative to the Bloom adaptation. It is this alternative strategy which has been adopted by the Commission on Science Education of the American Association for the Advancement of Science in the description and evaluation of the elementary science curriculum, *Science—A Process Approach*. The model of curriculum evaluation developed in this discussion is illustrated by the evaluation program of *Science—A Process Approach*.

## STATEMENTS OF BEHAVIOR

Can scientists be persuaded to write behavioral objectives? The experiences with the science curriculum effort of the AAAS Commission on Science Education strongly suggests that the physical, biological, and social scientists can be persuaded to adopt this position, without interfering with their creation of instructional materials for science. The first requirement is a firm commitment on the part of the project decision-making body to have behavioral objectives.

Each instructional segment should clearly state the objectives of instruction —what the child will be able to do or say (observable performance) after instruction with the material that he was unable to do or say before instruction. The objectives must be statements of reliably observable behavior, written by the author of the instructional segment, and stated in terms of observable performances which the scientist feels are necessary as well as sufficient indicators of success.

If this procedure is to be effective, each writer will need to be provided with a description of what is desired by way of statements which are acceptable as statements of objectives and those statements which are unacceptable. One example of such a description is contained in the subsequent paragraphs. The description is meant to be illustrative of this one effort and nothing more.

**Criteria to Be Used in the Construction of Statements of Behavioral Objectives**
The statement of objectives should include all of the individual performances one expects the learner to have acquired during the exercise. When conceived as immediately observable performances, these may be thought of as minimal objectives; but as such, none should be omitted from the statement.

Many authors tend to include some goals such as "increasing understanding," "developing appreciation," and so on. A statement of an objective must be considered unacceptable if it includes this kind of statement. The question to be faced is, what specific things is the learner expected to acquire which can be seen when immediate observations of his performance are made?

A major criterion should be clarity, the avoidance of ambiguity. For example, a statement like this is ambiguous: "The child should be able to recognize that some objects can be folded to produce matching parts, that is, are symmetrical." This statement might mean several different things:

A. The child recognizes symmetrical parts when they are folded to produce matching parts.
B. The child can verbally answer the question about what makes the object symmetrical by saying, "A figure is symmetrical if it can be folded to produce matching parts."
C. The child can demonstrate whether or not a figure is symmetrical by pointing out its matching (or nonmatching) parts.

These are not the same things. While the child is unlikely to be able to do C without being able to do A, he could certainly do A without doing C, C without doing B, and B without either A or C.

It is imperative to use words which are as unambiguous as possible. Some examples are:

A. *Identify,* also recognize, distinguish. These mean point to, choose, pick out, or otherwise respond to several stimuli differentially.
B. *Name,* also *state.* These imply that a verbal statement is required. "What color is this ball?" is naming.
C. *Describe.* Means a verbal statement and also that the categories stated are self-generated. "How do you describe this ball?" is describing.
D. *Order,* or *place in sequence.*
E. *Construct, print,* or *draw.*
F. *Demonstrate.* Means that the learner is applying a principle to a specific situation. For example, he may be asked to demonstrate symmetry for a figure by folding or matching halves.

Why the emphasis on performance in words implying behavior? The major reason is to stay away from "mere" verbalization. If one says the child "understands that such and such is true," this might be taken to imply merely that the child can repeat a verbal statement. Much better to have him *identify* something, *construct* something, or *demonstrate* something. Under these circumstances, we know that he "knows."

What does one hope to gain from this procedure? By requesting each author to specify the expected behavioral outcomes for the particular material he has written, we require him to specify what he considers success with this particular piece of instruction. Once this specification is made, any observer—whether he is a scientist, teacher, or interested individual—is able to distinguish those who have successfully achieved the objectives of the exercise from those who have not. Under these circumstances, all that is called for is that individuals making the judgment read the description of the desired performances and then determine whether they are present in the learner being observed.

If a scientist specified the performances one is examining, it can be argued that the scientist should also specify how one goes about the task of determining whether the learner does or does not possess a particular behavior. As an aid to the scientist in the construction of these performance measures, it is helpful to provide him with guidelines which describe the necessary characteristics of such measures.

The guidelines for constructing each of these performance assessments, or competency measures as they are called by the AAAS Commission on Science Education elementary science curriculum project, require that they meet the following criteria:

A. Each objective of the exercise should be represented by at least one task. Hopefully, these tasks should be suggested by the statements of the objectives; but in any case, behaviors proposed as instructional objectives should be measured.
B. The tasks need to be designed to elicit behaviors of the sort described in the objectives. If an objective calls for the construction of something, the task might begin "draw a ———." If the learner is being asked to name something, the task might be "What do we call this?"
C. The description accompanying each task should tell the instructor clearly what to do (not just imply it). For example, an accompanying instruction might be: "Place in front of the child a dittoed sheet containing drawings of an equilateral triangle and a circle." Or, "Give the child the meterstick."
D. The kind of performances that are acceptable should be clearly described so that a correct judgment

can be made concerning the presence or absence of a particular behavior.

The collection of behavioral objectives for the entire instructional program provides a behavioral map (or bank of descriptions of behavior) which may be used to characterize the entire collection of instructional materials. In short, this totality of behaviors represents a measurable description of what this particular instructional program attempts to accomplish. Such a collection of behaviors is at least one means of providing a lower bound on what the curriculum is to accomplish.

A behavioral map such as the one provided by these procedures will in turn yield to analysis by behavioral hierarchies, . . . thereby providing the vehicle through which to obtain an assessment of the instructional program's effect far beyond that identified by this lower bound. Assessment of the long-term behavioral acquisition by the childen exposed to *Science—A Process Approach* is determined by The Science Process Test or The Science Process Instrument which is administered on an annual basis. The Science Process Test is a performance measure administered individually and based upon the behavioral description provided by the behavioral hierarchies which describe each of the simple science processes. The results of this instrument provide an individual profile of the developmental progress of each child within each of the simple processes. The current version of this instrument, The Science Process Test, covers the kindergarten and first, second, and third grades.

## INTEREST MEASUREMENTS

Up to this point, the evaluation has concerned itself with assessment within the cognitive domain. One might reasonably ask, what measures should or can be taken of the affective domain. That is,

most science curriculum projects are interested in the investigation of the student's attitude toward science as well as the teacher's attitude toward science. The following remarks are directed at the question of student interests. Since the investigation of student interest in science has just been initiated by the *Science—A Process Approach* curriculum, it is only possible to describe the nature of the strategies being used.

The first of the three instruments intended to measure the child's interest in science is called the "Extra-School General Information Inventory." The strategy of development calls for the construction of a measure which samples general information from four broad areas: science, fine arts, sports, and literature. The assumption is that the interests of a child will be reflected by his fund of information on topics or in areas to which he is not ordinarily exposed in the formal school environment. Therefore, if the youngster demonstrates that he has a sizable collection of facts, which are miscellaneous from a standpoint of his formal schooling, but all the facts are science related, then one might reasonably infer that this is a reflection of his reading or activity pursued outside of the classroom —that is, a reflection of his interests. The general information categories which were selected as components for the Inventory are intended to reflect divergent interest areas. By appealing to these rather diverse categories, the science interest is not as visible to the child; that is, the child is not able to guess easily that you are interested in his science interests. With such a less visible indirect measure of interest, one works from the assumption that he has improved his probability of sampling the true interests of the child.

The second form of interest measure which is under development is one in which one employs duration of looking time as the measure of interest. Various levels of complexity in pictures depicting several kinds of activities are employed in this procedure. One obtains measures of the length of time which an individual will look at pictures related to four areas: science, fine arts, sports, and literature. The pictures are equated with regard to complexity. The intention is to develop a Looking Time Interest Inventory.

The third interest measure is a Structured Interview of Science Interests in which the interviewer guides the conversation with the child so as to sample the child's recent activities outside of school. It is much too early at this point to decide whether any or all of these interest inventories will be effective with children at this age level. However, they do represent three forms which may be logically supported as possible measures of science interest.

## SUMMARY

By way of summary, then, the evaluation begins with the specification of behavioral objectives for each instructional unit, proceeds to assess the success of each instructional unit in terms of measuring the behaviors acquired by each child as set forth in the objectives, and assesses the annual progress of each child in terms of his acquisition of the behaviors identified in the behavioral hierarchies for each of the processes. Finally, the science interests of children exposed to the instructional program may be included within the evaluation design, but by indirect rather than direct measurement.

The case for the behavioral description of a set of instructional materials is not a case against the content-oriented curriculum efforts. Rather, the behavioral view of curriculum is merely a recognition of the fundamental role which behavior and its specification as observable performance must play in a description of what a content-organized curriculum does accomplish. In this context, a content-oriented view of curriculum represents one plausible extension of the behavioral view. The acceptance of the need for the behavioral description of objectives will enable curriculum projects to carry out comparative studies on a basis which does yield to scientific investigation. Hence the benefits to content-oriented curricula would be clarification of the aims of the instructional materials, the existence of a vehicle for assessing a success or failure of the materials, and a technique for conducting comparative studies of curricula as defensible reasearch investigations. Obviously the same benefits are present for behavior-oriented curricula with one additional possibility. Without stretching the point out of all perspective, one could readily imagine the existence of a curriculum development project which first specifies the tasks all learners successful with the curriculum will be able to accomplish, then describes the behavioral sequence in observable performance language so as to identify the behaviors which are prerequisite to the ability to perform each task, and finally develops the instructional materials which would shape the behaviors identified by each entry in the behavioral sequence. The instructional revolution implicit in such a curriculum development project has the potential of reshaping all educational enterprises, since one would finally direct his attention to the potentials of the learner, rather than the appropriateness of content selections.

The importance of a performance-based evaluation to the adoption of an instructional program by the classroom teacher also yields to a most fascinating behavioral assessment. Imagine the impact teachers could have on the curriculum if they demanded behavioral objectives and supporting evidence of accomplishment in terms of acquired behaviors. Why shouldn't every teacher demand statements of the behaviors their students can be expected to acquire as a result of exposure to every instructional program they are asked to use?

# 21. Cost-Benefit Analysis and the Evaluation of Educational Systems

## J. ALAN THOMAS

Educators are frequently faced with decisions regarding program effectiveness at levels higher and more complex than the classroom or grade. Macroanalysis of entire school systems is periodically required to provide guidelines for allocation of resources. The analytic procedures here described, only recently of concern to evaluators, are very general and could be applied in a number of ways and at a number of levels in the schools. A cost-benefit analysis could, for example, be undertaken between competing curricula of similar content and intent, or between different curricula as a function of ability of student and instruction involved. The reader should note that the general "input-output" format of the methods described in this article follows logically from the general approaches to curriculum evaluation previously described by Stake and by Metfessel and Michael. If it is anticipated that a cost-benefit analysis will be undertaken, this fact needs to be taken into account in the overall design of the evaluative study, particularly in regard to the nature of the data collected. The intent of this article is to expose the reader to this relatively new methodological development as it has been tentatively applied in educational evaluation. There are many technical problems to be overcome, but the basic idea of cost-benefit analysis appears sound.

Psychologists who specialize in testing and evaluation have made major contributions to the development of a scientific base for the improvement of education. Breakthroughs which may be expected in the application of their findings toward the improvement of policy making will, we hope, have a strong impact on the efficiency of educational systems. Psychometrics does not of itself, however, provide a sufficient basis for *school system evaluation*. Consider, for example, the task facing a school survey team charged with the evaluation of a large educational system. The team will wish, as part of its data, to have compilations made of achievement and intelligence test scores in the school system. However, these scores will probably reveal more about the social and economic characteristics of the community than about the effectiveness of the educational system. Nor do differences in test scores among schools within an educational system provide (without the use of additional information) sufficient criteria for school system decisions such as those leading to the manner in which resources shall be allocated.

This paper is based on the assumption that educational organizations must be considered as "open" systems for the purpose of evaluation. Such systems are

Reprinted and abridged with permission of the publisher and J. Alan Thomas from the *Proceedings of the 1968 Invitational Conference on Testing Problems* (Princeton, N.J.: Educational Testing Service, 1969), pp. 89–100. Copyright 1969 by Educational Testing Service. All rights reserved.

considered to be in a constant state of interaction with their environment. They absorb energy (in the form of various inputs—including incoming students) and contribute energy (outputs, including graduates with developed productive capabilities) (Daly, 1968). Educational and other types of systems may therefore be evaluated by comparing their outputs with their inputs. This comparison of contributions with costs constitutes an evaluation of school systems' social productivity.

## EVALUATION BY ECONOMISTS

Some of the most successful attempts to evaluate educational systems have been made by economists. There have been several reasons for their success. In the first place, the professional interests of economists lead them to look upon educational organizations as open systems, which are linked to the total economy through a set of inputs and outputs. In the second place, their concern for costs and benefits provides a context within which evaluation can take place. In the third place, economists have developed analytic procedures which enable them to compare costs and benefits, even though both are incurred over relatively long time periods.

The economist's "evaluation" of an educational system is so different in appearance from the evaluation of measurement experts as to warrant some further explication. Table 1 shows the rates of return calculated for high school graduates, college graduates,. and corporate manufacturing firms in comparable years.

This analysis uses measures of rates of return that are similar in meaning and in derivation in the measurment of the efficiency of both educational and manufacturing systems. These comparative data suggest that high expenditures for education, especially at the high school level, would be desirable from a total societal point of view, since investment in human capital seems to have a higher rate of return than investment in physical capital.

A similar conclusion is reached by Denison (1962), whose research suggested that 23 per cent of the economic growth in the United States, between 1929 and 1957 was due to the effects of education. These results (like other research findings) are affected by the assumptions they incorporate. The assumptions must be examined critically, and the studies need to be replicated as new data are available. These studies, however, suggest that the economist's tools for evaluating educational systems cannot be ignored by educators. Furthermore, the *results* of their research have important implications for social policy.

There will be some immediate objections to permitting economists to share the task of evaluating school systems. It

**TABLE 1**
**Rates of Return from the Sources[a]**

| Sector | Rate of Return | Year |
|--------|:-:|:-:|
| High School Graduates: White Males after Personal Taxes | 28% | 1958 |
| College Graduates: White Males After Personal Taxes | 14.8% | 1958 |
| Corporate Manufacturing Firms: After Profit Taxes but before Personal Taxes | 7.0% | 1947–57 |

[a] SOURCE: Theodore Schultz (1958)

is often thought that economists are interested only in educational benefits that can be expressed in terms of dollars and cents. This is unfair; economists are willing to regard education as consumption as well as investment, and accept both monetary and nonmonetary benefits as being important. However, it is true that their analytic procedures work best when the variables can be expressed in monetary terms, and there may be indeed a bias in favor of studying the material benefits derived from schooling.

Up to this point, their greatest success has been in studying the costs and benefits associated with the national educational system. Although these findings are important, they do not provide the information which is necessary in improving decision making within local school systems, or even in state departments of education. In order that cost-benefit analysis of local school systems may be conducted, some merging of the knowledge, skills, and interests of the economist and the measurement expert in education may be necessary. Before touching upon some aspects of this task, I should like to discuss briefly the techniques of cost-benefit analysis.

## COST-BENEFIT ANALYSIS IN EDUCATION

Economists have made an important contribution to the study of school systems by their development of the human capital concept (Becker, 1964). Human capital (analogous to physical capital) refers to the developed productive capabilities of human beings. Like physical capital, human capital is a produced good, formed as a result of formal and informal schooling—in the home, in school, and in other organizations. The formation of human capital requires the use of resources—whether they constitute the time of a mother who foregoes other activities, the purchased time of teachers, or the efforts of a factory supervisor. The benefits associated with human capital typically constitute a stream of financial and other rewards an individual may receive over the remainder of his lifetime.

Not all benefits and costs associated with education can be expressed in terms of dollars and cents. However, monetary costs and benefits are important. Increased education results (on the average) in additional income. It also results in monetary costs—in the form of out-of-pocket payments and also a loss of earning power during the period while the student attends college or senior high schools.

One of two main procedures is usually used in cost-benefit analysis. One method is to reduce the stream of benefits and the stream of costs to a *present value* at a given year by using the mathematics of compound interest and compound discount. The other is to calculate a rate of return that would equate the stream of costs to the stream of added income. An investment is defined as "worthwhile" if the present value of the benefit stream exceeds the present value of the cost stream (at a selected rate of interest) or if the rate of return exceeds some externally determined figure.

Economists take nonmonetary as well as monetary costs and benefits into consideration in their studies of human capital. In other words, education is considered as *consumption* as well as *investment*. Hence, the stream of benefits will include the many satisfactions that a good education provides, while the stream of costs includes foregone leisure as well as the foregone earnings associated with schooling. These nonmonetary costs and benefits are, of course, more difficult to deal with than those that can be expressed in monetary terms.

Not all costs and benefits are directly attributable to the individual who is the direct recipient of educational services. Some are external—that is to say, they are attributable to people other than those immediately concerned, namely, the students and their families. For example, the entire society benefits from the higher rate of economic growth said to result from education; employers benefit from having a pool of educated potential employees; scholars benefit from living in a society where there is a wide variety of books and magazines; music lovers benefit from a society in which many other people have also been educated to produce and consume music. Similarly, people other than the student help to pay the cost of education. Social costs or benefits are defined as the sum of the private effects and the external effects.

Rigorous cost-benefit studies of local school systems are still far from practical, for the following reasons:

1. Historical information about the postschool income streams of graduates of a given school system are extremely hard to obtain. Furthermore, income streams of past graduates are not completely satisfactory for evaluating decisions made today, under different circumstances.
2. Large-scale migration in and out of our major school systems hampers this type of analysis.
3. This steady-state analysis is partially, but not altogether, irrelevant to the decision-making dynamics of school systems.

Despite these limitations, the cost-benefit model provides a guide in the determination of the kinds of data that should be gathered.

Benefit and cost data should be obtained and should include the following:

1. Information about the post-secondary school academic and occupational careers of students: Percentages of students going on to four-year and two-year colleges, or to post-secondary vocational institutions; proportions who after or before graduation become employed in different categories of occupations; income subsequent to leaving school; unemployment of school leavers—these data are all relevant

in estimating the effectiveness of an educational system. In large school systems, these data should be disaggregated, according to secondary school and to home background (including race, occupation of fathers, economic status of parents). This provides an indication of the school system's effectiveness in dealing with different subgroups of students.
2. Information about costs: The historical cost pattern provides a clue in the determination of productivity trends. If costs have been rising while outputs have fallen or remained constant, productivity also has decreased—unless other factors such as a changed school population have intervened. The costs of educating subpopulations should be calculated as one measure of the allocatory procedures that are at work. For improving decision making, it is also necessary to have detailed information about the unit costs associated with various school programs, changing prices of inputs, and (as one indication of the rationality of the system) the cost of obtaining and processing information. The purpose of cost accounting is not merely to ensure economy. Costs are part of the basic structure of decision making. The cost of providing a given curriculum or if implementing a desired teaching methodology must be gauged in part in terms of the other curriculum or the other methodologies that must be foregone, since total resources, at any given time, are limited.

For some purposes, the cost-benefit terminology is too restrictive since it implies an emphasis on monetary variables with positive and negative signs. The exchange between an open system and its environment can better be expressed in terms of inputs and outputs. Inputs include all the contributions of the environment to the system, including some that cannot be described as costs. Outputs include the products of the system. The following are some kinds of input and output information that are relevant to school system evaluation:

**Outputs**

Post-high school experience of graduates.

Years schooling completed by students (includes a study of dropout and retention rates).

Achievement in the various subjects at the various grade levels. (Ideally, achievement should include measures of affective as well as cognitive learning.)

Rates of promotion and nonpromotion.

These data should be disaggregated by school and by characteristics of the student body, including race and socioeconomic standing.

**Inputs**

*Students:* (Including their home background. Measures of achievement press in the home of the type developed by Dave (1963) and Wolf (1964) would be desirable, as well as the usual social and economic data.)

*Teachers:* Their background, training, experience. Attitudinal measures seem essential, in view of a possible relationship between teacher expectation and student achievement.

*Administrators:* (Similar to teachers).

*Physical inputs:* School buildings, equipment (especially technological books, and so on).

*Management:* (Here we include the seeking and utilization of information in decision making, the utilization of information from outside the system, and the use of the more sophisticated decision-making management procedures now being developed.)

Again, data must be disaggregated. For example, there should be detailed infor-mation about the distribution of teachers among types of schools. This should include attitudinal data, such as differences in attitudes of teachers in all-Negro and in white schools.

A careful analysis of this information can lead to some conclusions about school system productivity. Historical trends are, of course, important. A study of input and output changes within the system may point to hypotheses concerning possible strategies for educational improvement. One superficial conclusion might be that an unequal allocation of funds among the schools of a school system (with, for example, less money being spent on the education of Negro children than of white children) is unproductive, in terms of the total social cost-benefit relationship. A more sophisticated analysis, including a study of the teaching body assigned to the various schools of the city, might suggest that unequal opportunity has deeper roots than the way in which money is allocated.

## THE EVALUATION OF PROPOSED CHANGES

The careful analysis of an organization's inputs and outputs is similar to the development of a detailed profit-and-loss statement of a business firm. However, inputs and outputs of educational systems usually cannot be stated in the same units, and hence the two sides of the equation cannot be compared mathematically. Judgments about efficiency can be made, usually in the form of hypotheses about the effects that might be associated with changes in present procedures.

Alternatively, cross-sectional studies among a number of school systems may provide information about the marginal effects of the various input variables. However, cross-sectional studies do not, as is well known, indicate causation. The logical leap from the marginal relationships implied by multiple-regression analysis to the improvement of efficiency in practice calls for judgments to be made about the effect of proposed changes in a particular situation. Hence, the analysis of changes over time in inputs and outputs in a given school district probably provides the most useful way in which an organization may obtain the data basis needed to improve its productivity.

This type of evaluation is based on the examination of anticipated productivity increases associated with change, and is therefore dynamic rather than static. These changes will include some reallocation of money among the various inputs used by the system, the possible redeployment of inputs, and in some cases the use of new inputs.

This analysis is governed by a well-established rule of economics. This is that productivity will be maximized when money is distributed among the purchase of inputs in such a way that the marginal product of each of the inputs is the same. Thus, efforts should be made to determine whether any possible reallocations among inputs (such as spending more money for books and less for floor wax) will improve productivity.

In order to illustrate this procedure, this paper discusses three proposals made in a recent school survey (Midwest Administration Center, 1968). The purpose of this analysis is not to justify these proposals but to illustrate one use of input-output analysis.

1. One proposal, involving a suggested major allocation of resources, was that increased emphasis be placed on pre-school and early childhood education. Preschool programs for a large section of the preschool population were proposed. These would be associated with a restructuring of kindergarten and primary education. New inputs would be needed, in terms of additional teachers, classrooms, materials, and books for young children. In addition, existing inputs would be improved through extensive in-service education for existing teachers. (The empirical basis for the proposal is Benjamin

Bloom's *Stability and Change in Human Characteristics* (1962).)

From the point of view of the system as a whole, this would mean spending a larger proportion of the total school budget for early childhood education. It would imply emphasizing one type of input (teachers of young children) at the expense of another type of input (teachers of secondary children). Of course, these are marginal changes; it was not proposed that there be fewer secondary school teachers or that their salaries or training levels be changed, merely that there be a new emphasis.

On the benefit side, the hypothesized effect is that this reallocation of resources would lead to an improved total output over a period of time. It is hypothesized that if this program were to lead to the firmer acquisition of basic skills by young children, they would learn more in high school, require less remedial attention, stay in school longer, and earn more and learn more after leaving school.

To be sure, the long-term results of such a change could not be anticipated at the time of its implementation. A careful use of feedback would be needed, in order that gradual year-by-year improvements be noted, and so that the strong aspects of the proposed changes could be emphasized and the weak aspects eliminated.

2. A second proposal, with important cost-benefit implications, was that attention should be given to the restructuring of teachers' roles, with emphasis on greater role specialization. The proposal would include the hiring of teacher aides and other para-professionals. It would also include provisions for creating new roles, such as those of team leader and master teacher. This suggests a major reallocation among inputs, with the possibility of paying higher salaries to the best qualified teachers. It suggests improving efficiency through assigning to individuals

the types of responsibility for which they are most qualified. Clearly, in terms of our previous definition, this attempt to pay teachers more nearly on the basis of their marginal contribution is one potential way to maximize total system productivity. However, changes in salary practice would have to be accompanied by ongoing studies of changes in costs and benefits.

3. A third recommendation was to obtain a different type of input, in the form of staff personnel at the central-office level. School districts tend to be staffed mainly by line personnel, whose task is to give and to carry out orders. Furthermore, line personnel tend to have a common training—usually through their experience as teachers and subsequently as ad-ministrators. Staff people would have as their duties: (a) obtaining and analyzing data, (b) long-term planning, and (c) evaluating. They would be chosen from a pool other than traditional administrators, and might include social scientists or other people with noneducation backgrounds.

One purpose of this recommendation was to reallocate resources in the direction of providing more and better knowledge at the point where decisions are made. To be sure, additional knowledge does not ensure better results; it is probably a necessary but not a sufficient condition for improvement. However, if accompanied by proper monitoring and feedback provisions, better knowledge should result in improved performance.

The major problem in any evaluative effort involves the methods used to capture in symbols, numbers, and/or words the "true" experience of those immersed in the curriculum: students and teachers, as well as administrators, counselors, and other personnel involved in the educational process. Although traditional and experimental methods in the behavioral sciences offer a spectrum of approaches to data-gathering, there still exists a dearth of new developments or adaptations useful to those engaged in evaluative research.

The twelve articles in Part IV provide the prospective evaluator or consumer of evaluation data with a survey of some of the less well-known techniques and highlight for him possible troublesome areas. The material presented here is in no way intended as a substitute for a thorough study of measurement principles and practices. Formal course work, considerable "in-the-field-doing-it" experience, and perusal of reference works in the field (e.g., Thorndike, 1970; Ahmann and Glock, 1971; Ebel, 1965; Payne, 1968; Cronbach, 1970; Buros, 1965; Bloom, et al., 1971; Gronlund, 1959 and 1965; Bonjean et al., 1967; and Payne and McMorris, 1967) will stand the beginning evaluator in good stead.

The best of all possible situations in evaluation is to have the time and money to develop a custom-made measuring device. An example of such a device is described by Robert W. Heath in Article 22. A measure of cognitive preference was developed for research use with the materials of the Physical Science Study Committee. Only when measures are developed in response to the specific data requirements of a particular project can the most relevant evaluations take place.

The next three articles deal with observational techniques. In Article 23, C. Kenneth Murray provides an overall

# Measurement Techniques and Problems Associated With Curriculum Evaluation

part **IV**

picture of the myriad methods, both verbal and nonverbal, that are available. As we observed in the Prologue, the focus of curriculum is being intensively expanded to include groups of individuals, classes, schools, and instructional systems. This shift in emphasis requires the development or adaptation of innovative assessment procedures. Such an adaptation is illustrated in Article 24, in which Louis M. Smith describes the application of a method borrowed from anthropology—the participant observer technique—to the identification of distinctive characteristics and interactions in an urban slum junior high school. The article illustrates how descriptive data can be used to generate theoretical positions and verifiable hypotheses. The participant observer method has the potential advantage over most of the methods described by Murray in the previous article of allowing for a developmental study. Smith shows, for example, how particular patterns of teacher-pupil interactions develop over time. Dorothy Adkins then takes a fundamental look at one kind of performance task, the observational test. Measurement principles and practical guidelines for development are merged in a technically excellent and readable presentation. Adkins' closing comments on the recording of observations through the use of rating scales are particularly useful. Guilford (1954, pp. 263–301) has also provided an excellent discussion of how to develop rating scales.

Two rather unusual measuring techniques are treated in Articles 26 and 27. Steven M. Jung explains how Flanagan's Critical Incident Technique can generate data useful either for direct evaluation or as an information base to be used in constructing instruments. Role-playing under standard stimulus situations in a medical setting is then described by Harold S. Levine and Christine McGuire.

The advent of individually prescribed instruction has introduced a number of measurement problems (Lindvall and Cox, 1969). Paramount among these is the development of tests that will yield scores immediately and directly interpretable and translatable to specific objectives. Such a test is described by Richard C. Cox and Glenn T. Graham in Article 28.

In an article prepared especially for this volume, Donald Chipley next describes several measurement and evaluation problems encountered in attempting to assess curricula in the arts and humanities. Chipley takes the position that the "new humanism" in the schools requires new ways of assessing pupil development and thinking about curriculum.

The importance of affective learning outcomes is underscored in the article by Lewis Mayhew. His survey of techniques should prove to be an extremely valuable reference for both professional evaluators and classroom teachers.

Evaluators, particularly those subscribing to Stake's and Metfessel and Michael's curriculum evaluation models, described in Part 3, are concerned with both inputs and outputs of the educational systems. But these tell only part of the story. The environment—the context within which treatments, learning, or what Stake calls "transactions" take place—also constitutes a significant variable in evaluative research. J. W. Menne describes in Article 31 three methods that can be used to assess educational environments, specifically college climates.

Many evaluation projects require the analysis of change scores. Questions like, "If this is what Marilyn looked like before the treatment, what did she look like afterward?" are being asked increasingly often. There are a number of technical problems associated with use of gain, change, or difference scores. A very lucid presentation of these problems is made by Paul B. Diederich in Article 32.

One of the monumental national educational innovations of the last several decades is Project Head Start. Over a million children since 1966 have participated in the Project. An innovation of this magnitude needs to be thoroughly and intensely evaluated in the light of its intent and considerable cost. Some of the tough-to-live-with practical problems and preliminary evaluation results are reported by Lois-ellin Datta in Article 33.

# 22. Curriculum and Cognitive Style

## ROBERT W. HEATH

Several of the foregoing articles have noted that relevant curriculum evaluation instrumentation often requires new devices. The development and application of such tailor-made instruments is effectively illustrated in this article. The reader's attention is particularly directed to the rationale and specific procedures involved in the development of the Cognitive Preference Test, which raises some interesting issues related to curriculum evaluation. Most new curricula are intended as more efficient and effective ways of nurturing cognitive skills. But surely there are associated outcomes, many related to teacher methodology and personality, that are just as important. Such factors as attitudes, values, and interests need to be examined. These factors may interact with the teacher-learning situation or may emerge as unanticipated effects to color the overall evaluation of a new instructional or training program.

Traditionally, educators have defined the goals of public school education. The objectives set forth for public education have reflected trends in ideology, psychology, and nontechnical philosophy. Based upon postulates from these sources, educators have proposed at various times such objectives as physical and mental health, worthy home life, intelligent use of leisure time, vocational adequacy, citizenship, and ethical character. In contrast, the government-supported science curriculum groups have largely disregarded these broad sociophilosophical goals. Their concern has been directed toward intellectual processes, fundamental principles of the discipline, and a deeper understanding of key concepts. The new courses have emphasized a firm understanding of basic ideas that permeate the discipline rather than technical vocabulary and practical applications.

Educational testing has attempted, with considerable success, to measure the degree to which students achieve certain educational objectives. An efficient technology has developed to assess what facts and applications the student knows. Achievement tests usually call upon the student to demonstrate his knowledge of

Reprinted and abridged with permission of the publisher and Robert W. Heath from an article entitled "Curriculum, Cognition, and Educational Measurement," which appeared in *Educational and Psychological Measurement* **24** (1964), pp. 239–253.

terms and facts, to appropriately apply these elements of information, and to show his comprehension of organizing schemes.

Nearly all of the science curriculum reform groups have faced the problem of evaluating student achievement. Most have turned to professional test development agencies for assistance. As might be expected, traditional achievement testing procedures were adapted to the new courses. To the extent that the goals of the new and the traditional courses correspond, these tests have been of good quality.

In some ways, the objectives of the two types of courses are identical; both courses direct the students to learn facts, terms, applications, and organizing schemes. However, what makes the new courses distinctive is the way in which such knowledge is acquired, evaluated, and retained. The new courses have tried to teach the student how to acquire, evaluate, and retrieve knowledge in a field and have devoted less energy to presenting him with a survey of this knowledge.

The problem of assessing student progress toward the distinctive goals of the new curricula is not a simple one. The body of psychometric skills now available has largely grown out of traditional educational practices. It seems necessary to approach the problem from a frame of reference which is different in its conception of achievement and therefore different in method of measurement.

The interest is not in whether the student can identify correct and incorrect information but rather in what is he likely to do with information intellectually. If a goal of instruction is to change the student's intellectual style within some academic subject, a test of such "achievement" must permit him to demonstrate differing styles. The test items should allow the student to exhibit some preference in cognition. For instance, when told that density is defined as mass per unit volume, one student may notice the utility of the density concept for identifying unknown substances, another may wonder about the effects of temperature on density change, still another student might focus upon the equivalent notational expression, $D = M/V$. These differing modes of attending to the subject matter of a course will be called cognitive preferences.

The cognitive preferences exhibited by students in the conventional and the new science curriculums may be expected to differ significantly. The purpose of this study was to identify four types of cognitive preference in high school physics and to compare them in new and conventional physics courses. The four cognitive preferences chosen were (a) memory of specific facts or terms, (b) practical application, (c) critical questioning of information, and (d) identification of a fundamental principle. With a sample of classes using the Physical Science Study Committee (PSSC) course and a sample of conventionally taught classes, these hypotheses were tested:

(a) that PSSC students demonstrate a stronger preference for fundamental principles and questioning than control group students;

(b) that control group students prefer memory for facts and terms and for practical application to a greater degree than PSSC students;

(c) that preference for fundamental principles and questioning is more positively related to achievement test scores for PSSC students than for the control group students; and

(d) that preference for facts and terms and for practical application is more negatively related to achievement test scores for PSSC students than for control group students.

## PROCEDURE

If, in fact, traditional and new science courses result in different cognitive preferences, it should be possible to structure a test situation in which these differences become apparent. An attempt was made to develop such an instrument. A 20-item device, called The Cognitive Preference Test: High School Physics, was written and administered without pretesting to a sample of conventional physics classes and a sample of . . . PSSC classes. The test was given at the end of the school year. This experimental test was quite short, and subsequent item analyses have identified several nonfunctional items. The instrument has the appearance of a four option, multiple choice test. The items present introductory information in the stem, frequently illustrated with a diagram or graph. Four alternative "answers" follow. Here the similarity ends. Each of the options in each of the test items is correct, and the student is told that all options are correct. The directions read, in part, as follows.

### Directions

In this test you are to indicate which one of four choices you prefer.

Each test item begins with an introductory statement or diagram. This information is followed by four lettered choices.

Each of these choices is correct.

Read the introductory statement and all four choices carefully. Select the choice you prefer most in connection with the introductory information. Then blacken the corresponding space on your answer sheet.

Remember, all the information given is factually correct. You should choose the answer that has most appeal or is most satisfying to you.

You may find that more than one choice for each test item appeals to you. However, select only one choice for each item.

Be sure to answer every question, even though the decisions may be difficult to make.

In each item, each of the four options was designed to demonstrate a different form of cognitive preference in physics. One option was to show preference for memory of specific facts or terms. Another provides a practical application of the information given in the item stem. A third choice reflects some challenging or questioning of the information given. The fourth option is a statement of a fundamental principle (or a conclusion based upon such a principle) of physics underlying the data. For example, this is the seventh item of the test.

The pressure of a gas is directly proportional to its absolute temperature.

(A) The statement, as given above, fails to consider effects of volume changes and change of state.
(B) Charles' or Gay-Lussac's Law.
(C) The statement implies a lower limit to temperature.
(D) This principle is related to the fact that overheated automobile tires may "blow out."

The selection of option (C) contributes to the student's "fundamental principle" score; option (A) would add to his "questioning" score; choosing (D) will add a point to the "practical application" total; and (B) will contribute to his total score on "memory for specific facts and terms." The test yields four scores, the maximum score possible on any one of the four scales being 20. Because the four scores are interdependent, or ipsative, certain statistical treatments of the test are precluded.

At the beginning of the 1961–1962 school year, a list of all known PSSC physics teachers was categorized in a three-variable stratification table. The three stratification variables were (a) region of the country, (b) sex of the teacher, and (c) size of community (over or under 100,000 population). A random sample of these teachers was selected to be invited to participate in the study. All of the 31 PSSC teachers who received invitations agreed to cooperate. These 31 teachers were categorized on the same three stratification variables used for the PSSC population. A chi-square test was performed to test the significance of difference between the distribution of frequencies in the sample and population stratification tables. No statistically significant difference was found.

Next, non-PSSC schools were selected. Invitations were issued to schools in proportion to the PSSC population stratifications on the region and size of community variables. Approximately 90 per cent of the non-PSSC, or control group, teachers who received invitations agreed to participate. In all, 50 control teachers agreed to participate in the study. The distribution of the control sample was tested against the PSSC population; the chi-square was not significant. During the course of the school year, one PSSC teacher and one control teacher were dropped from the study because of improper marking of answer sheets.

In summary, two cluster samples were established. The first was a random sample of clusters of students (each cluster comprising the classes taught by a single teacher) from the PSSC population. This sample of classes was representative of its parent population on the three stratification variables. The second sample is viewed as being representative of a hypothetical population of non-PSSC classes. This control population is parallel to the PSSC population in certain demographic characteristics.

The first step in the treatment of data was an item analysis of the Cognitive Preference Test. Second-stage random samples ($N = 300$ each) were drawn from the cluster samples. Duplicate item analyses were performed on these control and PSSC groups.

As mentioned earlier, these item analyses uncovered several nonfunctional items. Further, since the test was so brief, a rough estimate of the reliability of the four scales when projected to a 60-item test was made. The interpretation of all these statistics is obscured by the ipsative nature of the scales. Each scale is "artificially" negatively correlated with each of the other three. Nevertheless, it was concluded that the four scales were reliable enough for research purposes.

All students in both the PSSC and the control group took the following tests.

1. The School and College Ability Test (SCAT), Parts I and II, Form IA
2. The Cooperative Physics Test, Form Z
3. The PSSC Comprehensive Final Examination
4. The Concealed Figures Test

The SCAT test (survey form) is a 55-item scholastic aptitude test. Part I comprises 30 sentence completion items and Part II contains 25 numerical computation items. This test was administered at the beginning of the school year. The Cooperative Physics Test is a traditionally oriented comprehensive final examination. The publisher's catalog states that the 77 items in the test "are distributed in proportion to the emphasis generally placed on them in high school physics." The PSSC Final Examination is a 60-item, two part, two class-period exam designed to measure achievement in the PSSC course. The Concealed Figures Test is presumed to measure "the ability to change the function or significance of structural elements of an object to use them in a new way." The instrument has shown some promise in earlier research on intellectual styles.

Gardner, Jackson, and Messick (1960) . . . found the test to be a strong contributor to the factor called field-articulation. They describe the factor as follows.

> Individuals differ in their capacity to articulate, or differentiate, complex stimulus fields. When effective performance demands that attention be directed to one of two sets of cues that induce opposing response tendencies persons adept at field-articulation could inhibit response to irrelevant embedded *items* while attending the relevant *surrounds*.

It appears to be only moderately related to the types of ability reflected in SCAT ($r = .41$). All tests, except for SCAT, were given at the end of the academic year.

## RESULTS

The means and standard deviations of all tests, for both groups, were computed. Table 1 shows these statistics which are based upon the first-stage, cluster samples of 30 PSSC teachers (1,027 students) and 49 control teachers (2,110 students). For example, the mean SCAT score of 42.7 and the standard deviation of 3.4 for the PSSC group is the arithmetic average and standard deviation of 30 PSSC cluster means on the test.

Inspection of Table 1 tends to confirm hypotheses (a) and (b). The PSSC group, on the average, demonstrates less preference for memory of specific facts and for practical application options in the Cognitive Preference Test, and a stronger preference for the "questioning of assumption" and "statement of fundamental principle" options than the control group. In three of the four cognitive preference scales, the difference between PSSC and control group means was found to be statistically significant. The group means did not differ significantly on the practical application scale.

The PSSC classes are, on the average, superior in ability as measured by SCAT. The control group performs slightly better on the conventional achievement test but the PSSC group is much superior on the PSSC test. PSSC classes are also considerably higher, on the average, on the Concealed Figures Test. Since the Concealed Figures was administered at the end of the course, the hypothesis is suggested that the ability measured by this test is influenced by instruction.

The possibility that the differences in cognitive preferences can be accounted for by differences in ability (SCAT) was tested and discounted. Correlations of cognitive preference scores with SCAT are so low (see Table 2) that the significance of these differences is not affected by group differences on SCAT.

Training usually has the effect of increasing the variability of test scores. On the memory and application scales, the control group has a larger standard deviation than the PSSC group, while the PSSC group has more variable "questioning" and "fundamental principles" scores.

Table 2 gives the intercorrelations of the mean scores of the eight variables for both PSSC and control group classes.

**TABLE 1**
**Summary Statistics of PSSC and Control Groups**

|  | PSSC Group (N = 30) | | Control Group (N = 49) | |
|---|---|---|---|---|
|  | Mean Score | Standard Deviation | Mean Score | Standard Deviation |
| SCAT | 42.7 | 3.4 | 39.3 | 4.3 |
| Coop. Physics | 39.6 | 7.7 | 41.4 | 6.4 |
| PSSC Final | 29.5 | 5.4 | 18.7 | 4.0 |
| Concealed Figures | 61.8 | 6.0 | 52.4 | 7.7 |
| Cognitive Preference: Memory | 5.6 | .8 | 6.8 | 1.5 |
| Cognitive Preference: Application | 4.5 | .7 | 4.7 | 1.1 |
| Cognitive Preference: Question | 4.5 | .7 | 4.1 | .4 |
| Cognitive Preference: Principle | 5.3 | .6 | 4.3 | .5 |

TABLE 2
Intercorrelations of Class Mean Scores

| | PSSC Group (N = 30) | | | | | | |
| | (1) | (2) | (3) | (4) | (5) | (6) | (7) |
|---|---|---|---|---|---|---|---|
| (1) SCAT | | | | | | | |
| (2) Coop. Physics | .50 | | | | | | |
| (3) PSSC Final | .73 | .78 | | | | | |
| (4) Concealed Figures | .41 | .60 | .55 | | | | |
| (5) Cognitive Preference: Memory | −.08 | −.52 | −.38 | −.19 | | | |
| (6) Cognitive Preference: Application | .21 | −.20 | −.13 | −.17 | −.07 | | |
| (7) Cognitive Preference: Question | −.19 | .24 | .21 | −.01 | −.55 | −.54 | |
| (8) Cognitive Preference: Principle | .05 | .61 | .40 | .42 | −.56 | −.48 | .23 |

| | Control Group (N = 49) | | | | | | |
| | (1) | (2) | (3) | (4) | (5) | (6) | (7) |
|---|---|---|---|---|---|---|---|
| (1) SCAT | | | | | | | |
| (2) Coop. Physics | .77 | | | | | | |
| (3) PSSC Final | .23 | .34 | | | | | |
| (4) Concealed Figures | .42 | .37 | .01 | | | | |
| (5) Cognitive Preference: Memory | .22 | .16 | .03 | .41 | | | |
| (6) Cognitive Preference: Application | −.04 | −.03 | −.07 | −.28 | −.85 | | |
| (7) Cognitive Preference: Question | −.35 | −.30 | −.08 | −.32 | −.73 | .38 | |
| (8) Cognitive Preference: Principle | −.20 | −.08 | .15 | −.32 | −.44 | .01 | .40 |

When one compares PSSC and control group correlations, some rather striking differences become apparent. The Cooperative Physics Test is designed for traditional high school physics courses. In the PSSC group, the classes that demonstrated a preference for memory of specifics tended rather strongly to achieve a lower mean score on the traditional test $(r = -.52)$. The direction of the correlation is reversed in the control group $(r = .16)$. Since the specific facts and terms in the two courses are rather different, it seems clear that the PSSC student who prefers this sort of cognition, despite the emphases of his course, will find himself at a disadvantage on a "foreign" test. The same pattern is present in the correlations of the practical application scale with the traditional exam. Note, however, that this relation is reversed with the other two cognitive preference scales. The PSSC student exhibiting a preference for funda-

mental principles (as his course encourages him to do) is much more likely to score well on the traditional test than a PSSC student with low preference for this style of cognition $(r = .61)$. The fundamental principles of the discipline are apparently recognizable and applicable, regardless of the terminology and factual content of the test items, to the PSSC student who has acquired this cognitive preference. On the other hand, in the control group, preference for fundamental principles shows no relation to scores on the traditional test. However, other cognitive preferences are related to traditional achievement test scores in the control group. The correlation coefficient of .16, Memory with the Cooperative Physics Test, is significantly different from the correlation between Questioning and the Cooperative test $(r = -.30)$.

For PSSC classes, cognitive preference for factual memory and practical application is negatively related to PSSC achievement while preferences for questioning and fundamental principles have positive correlations with achievement on the PSSC test. In the control group, which found the PSSC test extremely difficult, the correlation coefficients are negligible. The only cognitive preference that seems to help them noticeably on the PSSC final is one for fundamental principles.

Next, consideration is given to the relation of cognitive preferences in the two groups to scholastic aptitude as measured by the School and College Ability Test, Parts I and II. In Table 2 it can be seen that aptitude has a positive relation to preference for memory in the control group $(r = .22)$, whereas the relation is negligible, though slightly negative, in the PSSC group $(r = -.08)$. The correlations for the practical application and questioning scales are not consistent with the objectives of the PSSC course. This is particularly puzzling in view of all the patterns previously noted. It may be that a different scholastic aptitude test yielding separate verbal and numerical scores, and a more refined version of a cognitive preference test would throw light on these correlations. In the PSSC group, the correlation between fundamental principles and SCAT is negligible but in the control group higher aptitude classes are less likely to score high on this scale $(r = -.20)$.

The Concealed Figures test demonstrated a correlation with the PSSC Final of .55 in the PSSC group and a correlation of .01 with the same test in the control group. Control group students who score high on Concealed Figures tend to score high on memory for specifics $(r = .41)$; in the PSSC group, students high on Concealed Figures tend to prefer fundamental principles $(r = .42)$. Control group students who do well on Concealed Figures tend to acquire *low* scores on the fundamental principle scale $(r = -.32)$. The same contrasts are apparent in the other two cognitive preference scales though to a lesser degree. The PSSC student

seems to direct his "flexibility of closure" or "field-articulation" to fundamental principles. The control student applies this same cognitive set to specific facts and terms.

Some interesting differences between the PSSC and control groups in the intercorrelations of cognitive preference scores can be noted. Preference for facts and terms has a negligible correlation with practical application in the PSSC group $(r = -.07)$. While in the control group a strong negative relationship $(r = -.85)$ is observed for the same two scores. Similarly, practical application has virtually no correlation with fundamental principle in the control group $(r = .01)$ but the two scores yield a correlation of $-.48$ in the PSSC group. Those differences may signify that practical application has a rather different meaning to students in the two courses.

## DISCUSSION

The Cognitive Preference Test was an untried, brief, and wholly experimental device. Nevertheless, the generally positive results obtained suggest that this type of instrument can identify, in a meaningful context, curriculum-related differences in cognitive style.

The results seem to show that at least one of the new science curriculums (PSSC) produces observably different modes of dealing with the subject matter. One may or may not agree with the objectives of the physicist built course, but the evidence seems to indicate that these objectives are, at least to some degree, achieved by students. PSSC classes demonstrate a clear superiority on their own test with only a moderate loss on a traditional achievement test. Perhaps more importantly, in the long run, the data reported here indicate that PSSC students show a greater inclination to attend to fundamental concepts and to ask questions in pursuit of basic understanding. These differences are consistent with the reported objectives of the PSSC course. For example, note the statement by Finlay (1962).

> But beyond its technological goods and meanings, science as a humanistic study stands on its own terms as a dynamically stable system with its own ends and procedural styles. The student should see physics as an unfinished and continuing activity. The Physical Science Study Committee judged it wise to shift the emphasis in secondary school physics away from technology toward a deeper exploration of the basic ideas of physics and the nature of inquiries that can lead to these ideas.

When such objectives are operationally expressed in a curriculum, it appears that a cognitive preference test can assess curricular effects on the students' styles of cognition in that discipline. The contrasts between groups in Cognitive Preference Test scores and Concealed Figures Test scores are consistent with the notion of different cognitive preferences being formed by differing curriculums. As Bruner (1957) has written:

> In short, an induced set can guide the person to proceed nongenerically and by rote or to proceed as if what was to be learned was a principle or a generic method of coding events. . . . For by virtue of living in a certain kind of profession or social setting, our approach to new experience becomes constrained—we develop, if you will, a professional deformation with respect to ways of coding events.

There are several possibilities for further research. The present preference test could be improved. In addition it would seem worthwhile to attempt the construction of a "discipline-free" cognitive preference test, that is, one in which the stems and options of the items are in a general, nontechnical language. Also, several different forms of directions to students have been suggested. By slightly modifying the nature of the task, it might be possible to bring cognitive preferences into sharper focus.

A cognitive preference test could be applied to a number of currently troublesome problems in education and educational psychology. Evaluation of the effects of training methods (programmed learning, instructional television, classroom films, etc.) has been marked by conflicting, and sometimes confusing, research findings. For example, programmers have claimed "If you will specify what you want to teach, I can prepare a program that will teach it." The phrase "what you want to teach" is usually interpreted to mean "which facts" (spelling words) or "which operations" (factoring, adding fractions). It is difficult to be completely specific about modes of cognition as teaching objectives. Even if the desired cognitive style could be thoroughly explicated, it remains to be seen how effectively programmed instruction can implement varying styles. A cognitive preference test would seem to be a useful tool for studying some of the effects of programmed instruction and other educational innovations. Certainly these uses of such a test would in no way replace traditional achievement testing. Cognitive preference testing can add a dimension to the evaluation of educational attainment when used with existing testing techniques.

Even within a relatively rigorously controlled curriculum (PSSC) the classes of different teachers manifest varying performance on the Cognitive Preference Test. This suggests that teacher effects, as well as curriculum effects, can be identified by cognitive preference testing. This potentiality may provide a new opportunity to deal with an important variable in many educational experiments. This implies new approaches to the study of both instructional methods and the training of teachers. It should be interesting to study what teachers do, and could do, to influence the cognitive processes of their students.

At a more theoretical level, current research on cognition promises a better understanding of the fundamental nature of the phenomenon called cognitive preference. As progress is made toward identifying and measuring the basic elements of cognition, it may be possible to determine the components of differing cognitive preferences.

## SUMMARY

Based on the proposition that the Physical Science Study Committee high school physics course has an objective of encouraging cognitive preferences different from those induced by a traditional physics course, a Cognitive Preference Test was developed. The following hypotheses were tested [and supported by the data]:

(a) that PSSC students demonstrate a stronger preference for fundamental principles and questioning than non-PSSC students;

(b) that non-PSSC students prefer memory for facts and practical applications to a greater degree than PSSC students;

(c) that preference for fundamental principles and questioning is more positively related to achievement test scores for PSSC students than for the control group students; and

(d) that preference for facts and terms and for practical application is more negatively related to achievement test scores for PSSC students than for control group students.

# 23. Kinds of Observational Systems

## C. KENNETH MURRAY

This brief article provides a quick overview of the many observational systems available to the evaluator. These systems differ in (1) the nature of variables measured, (2) the complexity of methodology, and (3) the cost and training required to apply them. There is probably no substitute for the kind of data yielded by these techniques, especially when process outcomes are being assessed.

One might assume from a quick reading of this article that most of the observational systems described are available for use. Nothing could be further from the truth. Most of the systems need further examination of reliability and validity. The requirements of a particular evaluation activity will dictate which method should be considered. Many questions about observational data still need to be asked: for example, does the presence of an observer significantly distort the data? What do the student behaviors imply about teaching and learning? These questions need to be answered before one can unconditionally employ any observational system.

Further information on observational systems can be found in Amidon and Hough (1967), Medley and Mitzel (1963), and Simon and Boyer (1970).

The systematic observation movement provides the in-service or pre-service teacher with a self-analysis technique for identifying, observing, classifying, and/or quantifying specific behaviors in the classroom teaching-learning situation. (Ober, 1968). On the basis of this systematic self-analysis, the neophyte or the established classroom teacher can develop the capacity to modify his instructional behavior in accordance with the variety of requirements necessary to facilitate learning.

## KINDS OF OBSERVATIONAL SYSTEMS

Observational systems for assessing classroom behaviors can be divided into two

Reprinted with permission of the publisher and C. Kenneth Murray from an article entitled "The Systematic Observation Movement," which appeared in the *Journal of Research and Development in Education*, **4** (Fall 1970), pp. 3–9.

kinds: sign and category. A sign system is comprised of a list of classroom behaviors and the task of the observer is to check the behaviors which occur during a specified period of time. Regardless of the number of times the behavior occurs, it is only checked once. The *Florida Taxonomy of Cognitive Behavior* is an example of a sign system.

A category system consists of a discrete set of categories which have been designed to measure or classify classroom behavior. The observer's function is to master the categories of the system and to classify the behaviors exhibited during an observation period into one of the categories assigned to the system. The *Reciprocal Category System* is an example of a category system.

**Early Attempts at Systematically Observing Classroom Behavior** In 1914, Horn (1914) developed an observation system in which he utilized a classroom seating chart. He marked the appropriate student space on the chart with a circle to represent requests for recitation and a square for student recitations. The purpose of his system was to determine the distribution of student participation.

Puckett (1928) utilized Horn's seating chart approach to systematic observation but he developed a much more comprehensive set of 14 symbols. Some of these were:

Pupil raised hand

Pupil raised hand and was called on by teacher

Pupil called on when he did not have hand raised

Pupil called on when he did not have hand raised; made a single word response

Pupil called on when he did not have hand raised; made a fair response

Pupil called on when he did not have hand raised; made a very good response

Pupil asked a question

Another system using the seating chart technique was developed by Wrightstone (1935). He coded a variety of teacher responses and stimulations arising from interaction of the total class or individual students. Some of the responses and stimulations were:

1. Allows pupil to make a voluntary contribution
2. Encourages pupil to make a contribution
3. Proposes a question for pupil or class
4. Discourages or prohibits a pupil contribution
5. Question and answer on assigned textbook subject matter

After using the above technique in a study of schools in New York using "newer practices" with schools not using them, Wrightstone (1934) also developed a series of categories to record pupil responses. The pupil response instrument was scored in three broad categories.

These were: (1) initiative; (2) other items (responsibility, curiosity, and criticism); and (3) memory.

In reacting to early attempts at systematic observation, Medley and Mitzel (1963) suggest that "the quarter-century since these procedures were introduced (Wrightstone's) has seen little improvement in the form of such items. Improvements have been made, however, in procedures for scoring them. A fresh look at classroom behavior with these old items and new methods of analysis might yield interesting results."

From its early beginning, the systematic observation movement has progressed and developed in many different areas of classroom behavior. Some of these areas consist of: (1) verbal interaction; (2) nonverbal interaction; (3) specific subject matter content areas; (4) the general content dimension; and (5) teacher practices. Each area will be explored to indicate some of the trends or movements.

*Verbal Interaction.* The earliest work involving systematic observation of teacher verbal behavior was in the dimension of social climate. During the late 1930's Anderson (1939) assessed the integrative and dominative behavior of teachers as they interacted with students in the classroom. He found that the teacher's behavior pattern influenced the behavior of pupils in various ways. Teacher remarks either required conformity by the child (dominative contacts) or encouraged more participation (integrative contacts). Longitudinal studies by Anderson (1945, 1946a, 1946b) indicated that these two types of behavior could be successfully recorded.

Anderson's work was extended by that of Lippett and White (1943). Using a laboratory approach, they explored the effect of leadership strategies (authoritarian, democratic, laissez-faire) on the behavior of boys participating in club groups. The results of their studies indicated that the strategy of leadership, either adult or peer, significantly altered the social climate of interaction. The amount of aggressive behavior was demonstrated to be related to leadership styles.

Capitalizing upon the earlier exploratory work in social climate, Withall (1949) developed a seven category system which was designed around a learner centered-teacher centered continuum. These seven categories of teacher talk consisted of: (1) learner supportive statements; (2) acceptance and classification statements; (3) problem structuring statements or questions; (4) neutral statements; (5) directive statements; (6) reproving statements; and (7) teacher self-supporting remarks.

Bales (1950) developed a category system designed to record the verbal interaction patterns of small group situations. His categories evidence his interest in the interaction process or group dynamics theory but his major contribution appears to be in the domain of technique. He was the first individual to introduce a timing factor for systematically observing classroom behavior at set intervals.

Flanders (1965) was able to utilize this early research in the formulation of his ten category system which assessed not only teacher talk but also included student talk and silence or confusion. In addition to the student talk and silence or confusion dimensions, he also developed the concept of a matrix which allows the observational data to be more easily counted and sequenced together in instructional patterns. According to Amidon and Simon, who in 1965 reviewed the literature which utilized observational data as a measure of verbal behavior, the best known and most widely used interaction analysis system was the Flanders System.

The *Observational System for Instructional Analysis* is a 16 category system developed by Hough (1964). This system was consciously created to parallel the Flanders System and was designed for testing instructional hypotheses derived from learning theory. The categories for this system have been developed so as to focus on those observable behaviors that are commonly associated with principles of learning. For example, a separate teacher talk category is provided for corrective feedback and separates this dimension from criticism or rejection of student ideas and allows these behaviors to be more clearly studied in the classroom setting.

Ober (1968 and Ober et al., 1968) has created a *Reciprocal Category System* (RCS) which is a modification of the Flanders System. The RCS consists of nine categories which are reciprocal to both teacher talk and student talk and a single category for silence and confusion. . . .

*Non-Verbal Interaction.* Kounin (1970) describes a series of categories for observing management activities in the classroom. Many of the categories are of a non-verbal nature and relate to a teachers "with-it-ness," "overlapping," "smoothness," and "momentum." These categories were created as a result of a five year study. . . .

Galloway (1968) explored the area of non-verbal behavior and developed a non-verbal communication continuum ranging from encouraging to restricting. Within the encouraging-restricting context, six dimensions are assessed. These dimensions are: (1) congruity-incongruity; (2) responsive-unresponsive; (3) positive-negative affectivity; (4) attentive-inattentive; (5) facilitating-unreceptive; and (6) supportive-disapproval. The categories have been systematized for observation activities by using a numerical category approach and also by using an anecdotal descriptive approach to non-verbal behavior.

*Specific Subject Matter Content Areas.* Wright and Proctor (1961) developed a series of categories for classifying verbal behaviors in mathematics classrooms. The behaviors are classified into four broad categories: (1) process: ability to think; (2) content: mathematical structure; (3) attitude: curiosity and initiative; and (4) neutral. Each of the first three categories contains appropriate subcategories; and neutral refers to those teacher and student verbalizations which do not belong in one of the three main categories. The observed behaviors are sampled twice each minute in a rather unique fashion. During the first 15 seconds the observer watches and during the next 15 seconds he records the observed behavior. This technique is continued to provide two categorizations each minute.

The *Michigan Social Issues Cognitive Category System* was devised by Massialas and associates (1969) to explore meaningfully spontaneous classroom discourse focused on social issues. The system consists of nine categories, eight of which are cognitive in nature and one of which is identified as non-cognitive. All categories in this system are classified according to the speaker with no separate categories for teacher talk or student talk. The category system is described as "an attempt to give the teacher an index of his performance drawing some distinction between simple and complex cognitive operations, between value judgments which are justified and those which are not, and between open and closed classroom climates."

In *Teaching Public Issues In High School*, Oliver and Shaver (1966) describe the development and utilization of an observation system created to describe teaching styles as socratic or recitation. The general categories of the system are: (1) affective or socio-emotional; (2) cognitive; and (3) procedural. A central purpose of the system was to study two styles of teaching public issues in terms of the emphasis upon descriptive information or value judgments.

*General Content Dimension.* The *Florida Taxonomy of Cognitive Behavior* (FTCB) was developed by Brown, Ober, and Soar in 1968. The FTCB was an attempt to make operational in a systematic way the concepts developed by Bloom and others (1956) in the *Taxonomy of Educational Objectives: Cognitive Domain*. As indicated earlier, the FTCB is a sign system. . . .

Hill (1969) developed the *Content Analysis System* which was based upon the earlier exploratory work of Duncan and Hough (1966). The theoretical base for the *Content Analysis System* lies in the figure-ground concept of perceptual psychology. The system consists of five main categories consisting of background, naming, defining, examples, and amplification. Five sub-categories of abstract, concrete, personal, vivid, and negative, help to indicate characteristics of the main categories. The procedure for utilizing the system is similar to the verbal interaction systems developed by Flanders and Ober. The concept of a matrix is also utilized in this system.

*Teacher Practices.* The *Teacher Practices Observation Record* (TPOR) was developed by Brown (1968) to systematically observe and record teacher behaviors which are congruent and incongruent with John Dewey's philosophy of education. Brown also has developed a Personal Beliefs Inventory (PBI) and a Teacher Practices Inventory (TPI) which can be used together to assess the consistency between a teacher's beliefs and his actual teaching practices. . . .

## SUMMARY

One of the most profitable areas of exploration in the field of education during the past decade has been the scientific study of the instructional act. Much of the emphasis of this exploration has been placed on the development of objective, reliable means of systematically observing instruction in the classroom setting.

Systematic observation is being used in pre-service and in-service teacher education programs to develop an awareness of the impact of verbal behavior and to analyze teaching behavior. At the same time, systematic observation continues to be used in carefully controlled empirical research designs related to teacher behavior or teacher characteristics.

# 24. The Micro-Ethnography of the Classroom
## LOUIS M. SMITH

Most of the classroom observation methods used to gather data are limited in the scope of interactions described. In addition, the time period involved is usually brief. There are beginning to appear in the literature examples of descriptive studies employing observational methods of considerable depth and breadth. Anthropological, ethnological, and ecological studies can contribute a great deal to our knowledge about the teaching-learning process. Sindell (1969) notes that the anthropological approach is valuable because "The virtue of such broad, holistic studies is their emphasis on the many ways in which teaching and learning in a school are affected by the social and cultural processes occurring in the surrounding milieu, ranging from familial socialization to urbanization and modernization (p. 595)." Some of the flavor of the participant observer approach to description is captured in this article. Aside from the significance of the general overview of the participant observer technique, the reader should find valuable Smith's comments on several methodological issues encountered during the project.

Several years ago we[1] began what we thought was a relatively simple project whose central problem lay in the question, How does a middle class teacher cope with a group of lower class youngsters? The methodology seemed not only simple and naive, but unscientific as well. I proposed to sit in the back of the classroom, observe what the teacher and pupils seemed to be doing and saying, and keep notes of these events. The teacher was to keep a set of notes on his perception of the class and the problems in teaching his group of children. Later we hoped to describe the classroom in considerable detail and to conceptualize the events in more general psychological terms. All of this has come to pass.

Apropos of such classroom investigations as the one we carried out, my friend, Bruce Biddle of the University of Missouri, has written that the participant observer methodology is "the broadest and simplest methodology used in classroom studies" (Biddle, 1966). I once thought this was so; I no longer believe it. As I have engaged in participant observation in several other contexts and especially as I have been involved with graduate students using this "broad and simple" approach and have witnessed their difficulty in developing the written report, some of the latent complexities have been clarified. I would like to raise with you some of these critical method-

Reprinted with permission of the publisher and Louis M. Smith from *Psychology in the Schools,* **4** (1967), pp. 16–221.
Paper read as part of a symposium entitled "Observing in Schools: Studies of Classroom Life" at the American Psychological Association meetings in New York City in September, 1966. The data in this report are based upon Project S-048 supported by the U.S. Office of Education. The paper was written during the author's tenure as a Senior Research Associate of the Central Midwestern Regional Educational Laboratory (CEMREL).

[1] The "we" refers to the classroom teacher, Mr. Geoffrey, who was co-investigator.

ological issues that occurred between the time we started to answer the question and the time the final report was written. First, however, I must describe the general context, the children with whom we were involved, and the day to day procedures of participant observation.

The class was located in a metropolitan slum community; the homes were mostly tenements in need of repair. The Washington School had the reputation of a good school in a difficult neighborhood. Mr. Geoffrey had taught for five years in the building, and had a reputation as a strong teacher and a good teacher. He lived in a suburban middle class neighborhood and commuted by car to the school. The children were not atypical for this community. Of the 34 children assigned to the classroom at the beginning of the year, all but three had tested IQs below 100. One child who entered a few days later had a Kuhlman Anderson IQ of 137. Approximately one fourth had failed seventh grade last year and well over half at some time had failed at least one grade. All but two of the children were white. Many of the children were not born in the city but were migrants from the rural south, and conversations with some of them suggested that their families were originally from lower socio-economic levels of the communities they left. Many of the children spent weekends and holidays "in the country" visiting relatives. After the first month of school, a room in the building was closed due to less than anticipated enrollment, and 20 of the original seventh-grade group were replaced with the 20 sixth-grade pupils. This meant that the teacher taught a split class—approximately 14 seventh-graders and 20 sixth-graders—for the remainder of the semester. In the eyes of the sending teacher this new group was a "difficult group," for they had been giving him trouble since the beginning of the year. "I can't get any work out of them" were his words. He was pleased to have a different bunch of children.

With the pupils, I was introduced as a University teacher who was interested in finding out how children learn, what they find hard, what they find interesting and so forth. In the day to day relationships, as I lived in the class, I never told on them for things they did which the teacher didn't see or for what they did when he was out of the room. I did not pry into their affairs but was always willing to listen and to talk with them. With the other teachers, I was a naive but persistent observer of Mr. Geoffrey's class. I did not go into their classrooms nor observe them teach. As we became friends they told me more and more about what life was like in their school. I tried to listen carefully and to understand the nuances of the latent as well as manifest things they were saying. In general, I tried to stay out of the way of the flow of events. However, I was around as the day to day trials, tribulations, joys and excitement occurred.

In the classroom, I kept copious field notes of the episodes of the day. I bought a portable stenorette and dictated long, daily statements of observations and interpretations, as I drove to and from the school. These daily records grew to a horrifying quantity. The field notes were typed into multiple copies. Ultimately these were the raw data which we processed as we built our models.

## METHODOLOGICAL ISSUES

Methodologically, several interrelated phenomena seem to be critical if one is to find participant observation a productive research approach for classroom analysis. Lying behind the deceptively simple appearance of the method, the several conditions we have found to be important are (a) foreshadowed problems, (b) novelty of the situation, and (c) an attentive ear. In turn these conditions seem to produce two other conditions (d) vivid and concrete data, and (e) interpretive asides. It is to these I wish to direct your attention.

**Foreshadowed Problems** Foreshadowed

problems are those knotty questions, the toughest ones you can find which you keep asking the data to answer. In his monograph, *Argonauts of the Western Pacific*, Malinowski (1922) states his perception of the issue:

> The Ethnographer has not only to spread his nets in the right place, and wait for what will fall into them. He must be an active huntsman, and drive his quarry into them and follow it up to its most inaccessible lairs. And that leads to the more active methods of pursuing ethnographic evidence . . . . The Ethnographer has to be inspired by the knowledge of the most modern results of scientific study, by its principles and aims. I shall not enlarge upon this subject, except by way of one remark, to avoid the possibility of misunderstanding. Good training in theory, and acquaintance with its latest results, is not identical with being burdened with "preconceived ideas." If a man sets out on an expedition, determined to prove certain hypotheses, if he is incapable of changing his views constantly and casting them off ungrudgingly under the pressure of evidence, needless to say his work will be worthless. But the more problems he brings with him into the field, the more he is in the habit of moulding his theories according to facts, and of seeing facts in their bearing upon theory, the better he is equipped for the work. Preconceived ideas are pernicious in any scientific work, but foreshadowed problems are the main endowment of a scientific thinker, and these problems are first revealed to the observer by his theoretical studies (pp. 8–9).

The central thrust of the "foreshadowed problem" is that it selectively guides one's perception and thought while one is in the field. For instance, I was continuously asking myself, How does one teach a group of dull, overage, uninterested children? How does one manage them? How do you get them to listen to you? What's it like to be in the class hour after hour, day after day? What are the satisfactions and the frustrations? As these questions keep turning over and over in one's thoughts one is continually jotting down the concrete overt behavior of the teacher and children. Who said what? Who is where? Who is moving about, talking, playing, reading, and so forth? Such foreshadowed problems, whether cast in lay language or cast in more abstract formulations are different from having preconceived ideas or solutions. The "preconceived ideas," in one instance, were cast as a standing joke between Geoffrey and me. When he was faced with difficult choices he would ask, with a twinkle in his eye, "How does the 'good teacher' handle this?" or "What does Education 101, The Principles of Teaching, say about that?" As an author of a recent educational psychology text, I had some ideas but I was at the Washington School to learn, not to preach.

**The Novel Situation**  A further aspect of the foreshadowed problem thesis lies in observing in a novel situation, a setting where one has not worked or spent a good deal of time. The critical factor here seems to be that by having worked in a situation one already has come to know the "classical solutions to the classical problems" and tends to see these as given rather than as problematic. The teachers at the Washington School were continually puzzled that I could sit in Mr. Geoffrey's classroom, day after day, and not be bored. After all, in their view, Geoffrey was just doing what they were doing and it was part of the same routine. My typical response was "I've never lived in a slum community and I've never taught in a school such as this one. I'm trying to find out what it's like, much like Margaret Mead who went to the South Pacific to study native communities." Nevertheless, whenever I told them how fascinating it was they looked at me with great disbelief. In later studies of "an innovative school" and of an unusual student teaching program, we are finding the same kind of consequence. People living in a well tried situation cannot see what is so fascinating to the newcomer. To them, problems are not foreshadowed, they are resolved issues. This phenomenon was considerably less true in the innovative school for it too was new and novel to the teachers and they were caught in a variety of unanticipated consequences.

**The Attentive Ear**   As one has unanswered questions lying in the novel setting which one is observing, it seems to create a listening set in the observer, an attentive ear. Not only as one observes the processes of interaction but as one talks with the persons involved in the organization, one asks them in a myriad of ways to "tell me what it's really like down here." We have found that the attentive ear is a major reinforcer to participants. It is also a gold mine for "classical solutions" to one's foreshadowed problems. And even more critically, the attentive ear elicits new definitions of those problems as well as many more problems worthy of being foreshadowed but which the field has not begun to analyze. These may be serendipic or latent and unanticipated, to use the "good" words of the field. For instance, an upper-grade teacher, one of the most gracious women I've ever met, told me about the difficulties she had in learning to live in a slum school. She related the disbelief held by her physician that one so gentle and shy as she could handle a group of youngsters with reputations such as those at the Washington School. On one occasion, a time of serious crises in the school, we observed her discipline a big, rough 15 year old who was six inches taller and 50 pounds heavier than she. She verbally went through him like a flame-throwing tank. Now we are developing testable conceptualizations for issues in personality theory which will handle the integration of such divergent components of self, social conceptions to describe the settings when such behavior is "necessary," and the degree to which the latter is a norm or a rationalization within the faculty group. These are issues our "attentive ear" was hearing as we watched and listened in the school.

**The Interpretive Asides**   As we observed we found that aspects of our foreshadowed problems kept arising as insights, guesses, and hunches. We tried to jot these, in parentheses, into the notes. These turned out to be invaluable points of departure, key concepts which later were to carry a heavy burden in the analysis. For instance, we have puzzled for some time over aspects of teacher directiveness and indirectiveness, the Anderson, Withall and Flanders tradition, and we had been asking ourselves, "How does this fit in the Washington School?" Our notes contained an episode surrounding Geoffrey's setting up a recess coffee table for the teachers. I quote from the notes:

> Billy and Edwin bring in a table . . . Geoffrey tells Sandy to move assignment board sometime during the day—to accommodate the coffee table. Looks for a coffee monitor . . . No volunteers. Geoffrey comments: "Don't everyone volunteer at once." Oliver suggests that Mr. Geoffrey volunteer. Geoffrey goes along moving materials. He *does not* push, ask, or plead. (LMS—This seems very significant. Pick up later in the notes as to how it works out. This is part of his aloofness, powerfulness, or autonomy.)

Out of this came the hypothesis, which we now are trying to verify more generally: within a traditional self-contained classroom, teachers who solicit volunteers rather than direct pupils in those situations outside the commonly accepted province of the teachers role qua instructor are held in higher esteem than those who do not. We are trying to pose problems to operationalize the direct versus indirect influence, trying to build measures of teacher esteem, and trying to ascertain situations that qualify as within and without the teacher's instructional role. The interpretive aside in the note helped us in our later conceptualizing the complex phenomenon of teacher-pupil interaction. It cued a series of relevent propositions.

**Vivid and Concrete Data**   One of the most fascinating aspects of the methodology has been the vividness and concreteness of the raw data. As one moves into problems at this level, beneath the glittering abstractions and the prescriptive generalizations so characteristic of education and psychology, we have a strong emotional reaction of being involved with a kind of "bed rock reality." While that may be true or false, the data have a hard quality which we have found most engaging and productive as we have tried to build back to more abstract formulations. The consistent attempt to stay away from prescriptive generalizations and to talk about antecedents and consequences has been aided by the flow of the data, the processes, and by the complexities of the problems as we have looked at the concreteness of this part of the world. For instance, during an early morning reading lesson on word analysis, the observer made the following notes:

Geoffrey offers the general principle: syllabicate to help us read words we know in our speaking. Geoffrey presents "unmanliness." Asks Joe K about the word; he's stuck. Has Harry analyze it into syllables, then has Joe K pronounce it. He comes very close. Then enters into "manly" to get "like a man" and "un" as not. Through most of this Harry is most help. He knows root and prefix as conceptual labels. (LMS—The trick here, in part, is using the able kids to start discussions and to use on rough and difficult points. As the others can respond (easier points, continuity, etc.) you call on them. If the lesson has appropriate difficulty level, you have got to tax the average student and gradually extend him to be differentiated and shaped. The responses of able kids serve as prompts to less able; start the processes and permit reinforcement. This is pertinent to group structure, its development and its use.) (10/21)

In short, grappling with the concrete has seemed most provocative, for it gives the general issues a flint-like response when struck against. One cannot conceptually slip and slide about so easily when one translates into who said what to whom, in a particular sequence, and in a known context.

## CONCLUSION

In this symposium we are raising, mostly, issues of methodology involved in studying classrooms. A colleague[2] who liked what we were doing called our approach the micro-ethnography of the classroom, the study of a small social system. We found this more satisfying than the collection of anecdotal records in the classroom. The approach seems to us to be very fruitful in developing rather than verifying hypotheses. In this regard the "foreshadowed problem" seems an unexplored yet significant issue within the approach. The approach accents problems and problem definition rather than quick solutions; it suggests that one build in— in situ—brief interpretations as they occur; it suggests that one move into relatively novel situations; it provides data which have a vivid and dramatic concrete quality, and it suggests that one maintain continuously an attentive ear for the classic solutions to the classic problems as the actors view the situation. Hopefully it will lead us toward a more general psychology of teaching.

[2] We are indebted to Professor Fred Strodtbeck.

# 25. Principles Underlying Performance Tests

## DOROTHY C. ADKINS

The current emphasis on conceptualizing and stating educational objectives in terms of expected terminal behaviors logically requires that evaluation instruments be judged in behavioral terms. Performance tests, particularly observational methods, provide an excellent opportunity to gather data useful in making curriculum evaluations. Besides the general philosophical and methodological message of Adkins' paper, there are additional reasons to recommend this article. It contains some fine suggestions for developing techniques, and offers a succinct overview of some of the more critical principles of measurement. There is a great deal of common sense here. The article closes with a set of suggestions for improving rating procedures.

One of the common types of observational techniques is the performance test. Not all situations in which performance is under scrutiny are called performance tests, however. Supervisory ratings, based on more or less casual observation of the work of employees and perhaps a few remembered samples, together with an undetermined amount of bias, are appraisals of behavior. Observations of play activity of children also may yield evaluations of behavior. Neither the observations that result in the supervisory rating nor those of the children would commonly be considered a test, however. The test is distinguished from such observations in that elements of the situation likely to be significant are constant for all subjects, so that all respond to the same stimuli. Thus, the factors of inequality in opportunity to reveal behavior are, to a degree, equalized before the observational situation is a test.

A further useful distinction is that between a performance test and a written

Reprinted and abridged with permission of the publisher and Dorothy C. Adkins from an article entitled "Principles Underlying Observational Techniques of Evaluation," which appeared in *Educational and Psychological Measurement*, **2** (1951), pp. 29–51.

test. Although the demarcation is somewhat arbitrary, a performance test calls for the subject to carry out some activity, whereas a written test requires him to answer questions. In a performance test, the subject's behavior or its products are evaluated according to predetermined standards. In addition, the term "performance test" is usually reserved for tests involving physical apparatus or physical movements or products of manual operations.

In the testing of general ability, performance tests were used many years ago where verbal tests were not appropriate, as in testing persons with a severe language handicap. They also occur in scales designed for essentially normal subjects.

Aside from situations where tests depending on verbal ability are misleading, there are functions which printed tests do not adequately measure. Individual apparatus tests are indicated in testing speed or coordination of motor response, and performance tests are essential where accurate timing of single responses is desired (Thorndike, 1949, pp. 41–42). Finally, whenever there must be assurance of the ability to *do* a particular operation rather than to *talk about* or *select* the appropriate response or response sequence, reliance should be placed upon a performance test.

## KINDS OF PERFORMANCE TESTS: APTITUDE VS. ACHIEVEMENT

Two types of performance tests may be distinguished—*aptitude* and *achievement*. Aptitude tests are used to test potentialities. The purpose is to predict either how quickly the subject can develop a particular degree of skill or the level he can reach in a given period of time or with a specified amount of training.

A performance test of achievement, on the other hand, aims at a measure of the subject's skill at the time he is tested. The purpose is to evaluate present performance. Even so, as Cronbach has well stated, "an attempt to predict underlies every use of testing. Whenever a test is given to two people, it tells about some difference between their performances at this moment. But the fact would be of no significance . . . if from it one could not predict that these two people would differ in some future activity" (Cronbach, 1949, p. 9).

Achievement and aptitude tests do not necessarily differ in *form*. The essential contrast lies in the *function* of the test. The distinction is not rigid. The same test sometimes can be used to test aptitude and achievement on different occasions. Then, too, it is almost impossible to construct an achievement test uncontaminated by aptitude or an aptitude test that does not depend on previous experience.

**Work-Sample Tests** A work-sample test requires the subject to do a segment of an operation using tools, materials, and methods characteristic of the total task in which it is desired to appraise performance. Often the test conditions are not exactly the same as the typical working situation. Some writers differentiate work-sample tests and *simulated-conditions* tests, based on the *essential* activities presented in such a manner as to simulate the real situation. The distinction is by no means clear-cut. Drivers' road tests and typing-performance tests are cited as examples of work-sample tests. Yet who would argue that driving an automobile with an officer of the law at his right arm is identical with driving with a more typical passenger? Or that typing in a test situation is the same as in an ordinary working environment? Clearly, the distinction is one of degree, and for a performance-test task to duplicate the *real* situation in every detail would be rare indeed. To observe behavior of persons at work in a natural situation and to quantify such observations is theoretically possible. A test based on this approach might truly be a work-sample test. But when standardization is attempted perhaps the result is almost always a simulated-conditions test.

In any case, in the interests of economy and convenience, a performance test may involve specially constructed apparatus embodying the essential features of that used on the job rather than actual job equipment.

## USES OF OBSERVATIONAL TECHNIQUES OF EVALUATION

**Predictors** Observational techniques of evaluation, including performance tests, can serve the traditional purposes of tests. Thus, they can predict which applicants for a training program will profit most and hence should be selected. They can reveal differences in proficiency at the end of the training. Although often such appraisal is considered to be an end in itself, academic-achievement tests are useful primarily because further predictions arise from them. They can show which applicants are most proficient in a particular kind of work or what even more specific skills are possessed by those selected for hiring.

**Diagnostic Aids** Observational techniques used to *diagnose* deficiencies in performance serve as a teaching aid. A prediction is made of what behavior will result if remedial action is not taken. The emphasis in diagnosis, however, is on differences among characteristics of the same individual. The performance test can diagnose weaknesses if it is so designed that performance on different aspects of the task is separately scorable. The potential contribution of performance tests to educational programs has been too infrequently recognized. They provide motivation by immediately revealing success or failure and show the teacher areas warranting further attention.

**Criterion Measures** Clearly observational techniques can be used in making predictions; they also can provide measures of what one is trying to predict. Criteria consisting of ratings of overall performance on a job (which result from observational techniques, however crude) are familiar. Not so commonplace is the use of a performance test as a measure of what is predicted by another test. Yet such a function of performance tests is frequently desirable.

Performance tests are expensive to construct, administer, and score. If feasible, they should be replaced by another type of measuring instrument, such as a written test. Often the performance test seems to be a more direct measure of the differences in which interest centers. If, however, a less expensive test correlates highly with it, a substitution can be made. This amounts to treating the performance test as a criterion.

*Ultimate vs. Proximate Criteria.* When, then, is an observational technique a predictor and when a criterion? The answer lies in its purpose. The same measure may, in fact, be regarded as both a predictor and a criterion. It is useful to distinguish between the ultimate criterion—the "complete final goal of a particular type of selection or training" (Thorndike, 1949)—and proximate criteria—measures sooner available but not clearly recognizable as the final goal.

The ultimate criterion, especially in directly measurable form, is rarely available in educational or psychological research. In the selection of nursing-school students, it would be the complete post-academic history of each student. Because such a criterion does not lend itself to quantitative expression, resort is had to proximate criteria such as academic grades and ratings of supervisors.

The ultimate criterion must always be determined on rational grounds. Decision as to what constitutes the ultimate aim of any predictive devices, including observational techniques, must be based on judgment. This judgment should be that of qualified persons as to the components of the final goal and their respective weights.

## BASIC REQUIREMENTS FOR MEASURING DEVICES

The essential features of observational techniques are much the same as those of any good measuring devices: validity, reliability, objectivity, and practicality of construction, administration, and scoring.

**Validity** A test does not have validity in a vacuum. It possesses or lacks validity with respect to a particular purpose. If a criterion is available, the degree of validity can be expressed by a quantitative index of relationship.

Observational techniques are not by nature either more or less valid than paper-and-pencil tests. Though a performance test may look more valid, its validity is just as much a matter of careful exploration and research as is that of a written test.

Validity is the most essential characteristic of a test. Experienced test personnel are likely to discard as worthless tests with low validity coefficients. That a test must have some degree of validity above zero is quite correct. But, under certain conditions, a test of low validity is useful in terms of money savings in an employment situation. If the selection ratio (the percentage of applicants hired) is low, a test of quite low validity will be just as useful in terms of effects on production as a test of very high validity when a very high percentage of applicants is hired. Another factor which must be considered in evaluating money savings attributable to the test is the cost of the test.

The validity of observational techniques must be explored whether they are predictors or criteria. The relevance of the criterion depends on the extent to which it requires the same abilities as the ultimate goal. A validity coefficient could be obtained for a more immediate measure by correlating it with one more nearly ultimate. Most often, however, the relevance of a criterion must be determined by a rational approach.

**Reliability** To be reliable, a measure must be relatively little affected by fluctuations in the behavior of the persons measured, in the definition of the task, and in the external conditions. The influence of the former factor can be reduced by extending the observations over a larger and more representative sampling of behavior. Fluctuations in the test situation should be dealt with by more rigorous control of those factors affecting the performance of the subject and the observation of it. Conditions that often can be controlled to some degree relate to equipment, the behavior of other persons, and differences in elements of the task from one subject to another. Factors that affect the observation of the performance include the precision of definition of the behavior, its relative simplicity, the degree to which it is overt, the availability of instruments for precise recording, and the opportunities for observing it. The reliability of observational techniques can be improved by attention to these factors.

If either a predictor or its criterion has no reliability (i.e., a coefficient of zero), the expectation would be that the validity coefficient would be zero. High reliability coefficients have much to commend them.

But some of us have been too prone to discard a predictor or a criterion when its reliability is low. After steps that might be taken to improve reliability have been investigated, a decision on whether to use or reject a measure of low reliability should be made in the light of alternative courses of action. A measure with low reliability may be distinctly better than no measure at all.

**Objectivity as Related to Reliability and Validity** Wherever possible, measuring devices should be free from scoring error, which is a major source of unreliability of observational techniques. Although it is sometimes claimed that subjective, in comparison with objective, methods may yield greater validity attributable to overall clinical insight, the critical factors in such an approach should be objectified. Disagreement among raters clearly must mean that, at best, not all of them could be right, and there may not even be assurance that one of them is.

Mere objectivity does not insure validity. It does not even guarantee reliability. Consider Bellows' experience with a criterion of success in learning precision bombing. The measure in question was definitely objective. A student could complete his training as a bombardier only when his average circular error in 50 consecutive tries at the target was not greater than a specified distance. But the correlation between errors on even-numbered and odd-numbered trials was .00. The accuracy of a shot was determined mainly by factors other than the skill of the bombardier.

Bias in criterion measures may reduce either their validity (relevance) or both their reliability and their validity. Sometimes external sources of bias may be corrected for statistically. Earnings of taxi drivers could be adjusted to take into account the territories to which they are assigned. Records or ratings on nursing performance might need to be adjusted for the particular work assignments involved.

**Practicality of Constructing, Administering, and Scoring** Some observational techniques of evaluation are not very difficult to prepare. Occasionally, behavior automatically results in an objective trace. Certain types of production record, for example, where quality of product is not variable or not important, would fall in this class. Often, however, criteria need adjustment. Even such an apparently ready-to-use criterion as salary needs scrutiny. Thurstone, in studying tests to predict administrative success, corrected salary for age to get a suitable criterion of administrative ability. Young administrators earning a particular salary are probably, on the average, more competent than older persons at the same salary level. An adjustment for age was necessary before individuals could appropriately be classified into upper or lower groups in administrative ability. A somewhat similar result can be achieved by partial correlation.

Many observational techniques are much more difficult and time-consuming to prepare. A typical work-sample test, for example, involves detailed job study, perhaps the construction of special equipment and recording apparatus, the tryout and discard of different combinations of activities, the preparation of rating scales or quality samples, and special instructions and training for raters.

Performance tests used as predictors are notoriously inconvenient and costly to administer. Typically they involve apparatus that is not available in unlimited sets and which may be inconvenient to transport. They are likely to require the close attention of the examiner. Especially if aspects of the performance itself rather than its product must be observed, the test can be administered to only one individual at a time.

Any criterion measure that calls for the accumulation of records not routinely available for special ratings interferes with regular administrative procedures and thus presents a special problem.

Observational techniques generally should be accompanied by special efforts to achieve scoring objectivity, whether in the form of a psychophysical method, special training for raters, or some mechanical method of recording. This necessity adds to the scoring difficulty, inconvenience, and expense. For this reason, observational techniques sometimes are used as criteria for other measures, such as written tests. If the latter prove satisfactory, they can be used in place of the observational techniques.

## THE USE OF ACTIVITY ANALYSIS IN DEVELOPING OBSERVATIONAL TECHNIQUES

In order to be measured, behavior must be analyzed intensively. There is no one orderly way in which activity analyses are uniformly conducted, but some combination of the following techniques usually should be applied.

**Study of Previous Analyses** Only rarely does one find already finished an analysis of activity geared to his particular problem. But analyses for related purposes may provide a starting point. Similarly, previously developed tests or observational techniques may yield hypotheses as to the areas in which measurable individual differences should be sought.

Analyses for job classification, work simplification, training, etc., may also be suggestive, although they will reflect a different point of view and will be too narrow in coverage of needed knowledges, skills, or abilities.

**Survey of Other Written Source Materials** Training manuals, text-books, procedural manuals, reports, and other written material produced as an integral part of an activity may also provide useful clues. These serve as a means of checking ideas arising from other approaches.

**Performing the Activity** The activity analyst who is himself able to perform the activity is at a marked advantage. In some instances an analyst can spend a few days or even weeks in learning an activity. Such expenditure of time provides insight into the abilities required. The value of Viteles' study of Milwaukee motormen was almost certainly enhanced by his actual operation of street cars. Another classic example is Link's assembling guns in order to better select workers for this task.

**Interviews** Both superior and inferior performers should be interviewed in conducting an activity analysis for a measure of performance. Persons engaging in an activity probably constitute the most useful source of information. Those in various stages of learning will also provide helpful clues, either directly or indirectly (Horst, 1941). Additional sources of information are supervisory personnel, teachers, specialists in such fields as job classification, or others recognized as especially competent.

**Observation of the Activity** Critical areas of ability can often be identified by direct observation of the differences between the most and the least efficient persons. Motion pictures may facilitate this process. Careful observation also may reveal the conditions under which the activity is carried out (Horst, 1941). The types of things that can most profitably be observed and the kind of record to be made should be planned in advance.

**Statistical Analysis of Test Validities** Inspection of tests previously found to be valid for a particular activity may add to the analyst's insight. Study of validity data may indicate factors for which better tests are needed. Similar data for related activities may give hints as to types of tests worthy of trial. Such data may serve to check and refine the original analysis but do not provide a basis for extending it to new or unrelated fields.

## JUDGING THE IMPORTANCE OR RELEVANCE OF COMPONENTS OF AN ACTIVITY

In the early stages of assembling a predictor, tentative estimates are made of the relative importance or weight of each component of the activity to be separately appraised. Similarly, in developing proximate criterion measures, decisions often must be reached as to how the components shall be weighted. These conclusions are typically critical, because ordinarily no actual measurement of the ultimate criterion can be made.

The analysis of the activity should provide at least a partial answer. One useful index, which should be tempered by judgment, is the frequency of mention of a component activity by the persons interviewed in the course of the analysis. Another supplementary approach is to obtain ratings on relative importance of components from a panel of experts. This technique again is applicable whether predictors or criteria are sought.

When a criterion is available, these relatively subjective methods may be checked by determining the multiple-regression weights at which the components should be combined linearly to optimally predict (in the least squares sense) the criterion. In the case of the internal weights of components of the criterion itself, the same technique is applicable if a measure of the ultimate criterion is available. Since it rarely is, however, the relevance of criterion components is usually determined by the judgment of experts. Several statistical techniques are aimed at this problem of how best to weight criterion elements. In the last resort, a consensus of qualified judges still is preferable to any available statistical solution.

## SELECTING AND DEFINING THE ACTIVITY TO BE OBSERVED

The elements of an activity to be evaluated should grow out of the activity analysis, which is oriented to the overall purpose of the evaluation. In fact, selecting the particular activity is an integral aspect of the analysis, which has not reached completion until it includes definition of the activity as well. It seems desirable to direct attention to principles applicable to this phase of the analysis.

The results of an activity analysis should be recorded in convenient summary form, so that all aspects of an activity can be considered and decisions reached as to how to set up a measuring device. One type of record, useful for tests involving manual operations that result in some observable product, provides four columns: (1) Qualities directly measurable in product; (2) Qualities subject to judgment; (3) Proper work methods; and (4) Speed. The first column lists the major ways in which quality of operation or degree of skill is directly measurable in the product—objectively measurable factors such as strength and accuracy. The second column lists characteristics of the product that cannot be measured by instruments but which can be rated by inspection—appearance, finish, design, etc. The third column lists ways in which quality of operation is shown in the method of work. The fourth column is for notes regarding the importance of speed in various phases of the operation or perhaps an indication of a reasonable overall time for completing a piece of work.

Just as a written achievement test designed to measure abilities in a certain field consists of a sampling, so observational techniques need not provide for observing an entire activity over an indefinite period of time. Instead, resort is again had to sampling of the operations involved with respect to the time of observation. Following are some principles that serve to yield appropriate sampling.

1. Those elements of the activity should be chosen in which individual differences are likely to be related to success in performance. Crucial operations which are parts of the activity can often be chosen to represent the whole. Nothing is gained by observation of routine steps that everyone can perform. Care should be taken to include operations that are most likely to result in failure.

2. The elements chosen should be capable of clear definition and subject to standardization.

3. Similarly, any apparatus or equipment to be used must be amenable to standardization.

4. Apparatus or equipment should be relatively inexpensive so that multiple copies can be available, and it should not be too bulky for transportation.

5. Each work-piece in the case of a performance test should be used to measure as many of the important activities as possible.

6. The elements for observation should permit accurate records or relatively objective judgment.

7. A number of separately scorable short tasks is preferable from the standpoint of reliability to a single overall rating on a longer task.

8. Observational techniques should be capable of administration in a reasonable period of time. Within that period, the range of activities sampled should be as wide as possible.

9. For some types of observational techniques, particularly where bias is likely if observations are confined to a limited time, principles of time sampling should be applied. If the behavior fluctuates markedly with time, the observations must be made during several periods if reliability is to be achieved.

## WAYS OF EVALUATING BEHAVIOR

Whether or not behavior is susceptible to accurate scoring may be a factor in the selection of the activity for measurement. In any event, consideration must be given to whether only the process, only a product of the activity, or both, are to be observed and scored. Attention must also be directed to the particular features to be observed and how they are to be scored, and to the importance of differences in speed. These steps are followed by development of scoring devices and rating forms so that the final evaluation can be made in quantitative terms wherever possible.

Initial decisions on scoring are based on the activity analysis as interpreted by expert judgment. For a measuring instrument to be used as a predictor, these decisions should be checked by the relationships of the various scores to an independent criterion. When the measuring instrument constitutes the most nearly ultimate criterion available, then expert judgment remains the court of last appeal. Initial judgments, however, may still be modified in the light of how the instrument works.

**Evaluating the Activity in Process vs. the Product of the Activity** In some cases the obvious procedure is to evaluate the activity or performance in process. Thus, for a musical virtuoso, performance in process must be evaluated. Some persons argue that for a truck-driving test there is no product to be judged, which leaves as the only alternative the evaluation of the performance in process. Even in this example, however, previous performance may have left records, perhaps in the form of dented fenders or records of traffic violations. The concept of the activity might be extended to cover driving experience over a period of time and observations be based on products as well as process. Whether or not use of particular methods is considered important, the rate of work or overall speed may be evaluated if it is likely to differentiate good from poor performers.

When the product is all-important, scoring operations may be concentrated on it. This is likely to be true where a spoiled product is very expensive or high quality

essential. In some typing jobs, absolute accuracy might be the primary requirement. Speed or the particular system followed might be almost irrelevant.

In most typing jobs, both speed and accuracy are important, and hence both are ordinarily rated. For employee selection, the work methods used by typist applicants are not observed at all, so that quality of the performance itself apart from its speed is not rated. A typing instructor might well decide, however, that such matters as the typist's position, touch, and evenness of stroke should be observed in order to diagnose difficulties and improve methods of work.

For some types of operations speed is critical and should be weighted heavily. The task itself may be so simple that almost anyone can do it correctly. The difference between good and poor performers would then hinge on the rapidity of errorless performance. If errors are made, penalties can be deducted so that the final score is a speed score corrected for errors, or separate scores may be combined at appropriate weights.

**Objective Records vs. Subjective Scores** The scoring techniques that need to be considered range from the highly objective to the much more subjective. As mentioned earlier, the objective score should be chosen whenever possible, but sometimes steps can be taken to increase the objectivity of what at first appear to be highly subjective ratings.

*A. In Rating Quality of Process.* Quality of an activity in process may, at times, be evaluated by mechanically obtained objective records. More commonly, quality of the process is evaluated by ratings. Evaluations of work methods can be greatly facilitated when the raters have before them an objective record of what the subject does. The ratings are relatively free from subjectivity if they are based on a record of direct observation of clearly limited segments of an activity. One approach is a score sheet that lists all aspects of each operation to be observed and scored as the operation is performed. Such scoring units should be expressed in directly quantitative terms where possible—number, feet, kilograms, etc. A score card in the form of a simple check list may specify the number of points for each operation done correctly, or it may call for finer gradations.

When the sequence of operations is important, a score sheet can list all the component steps in order, and performance can be recorded by check marks showing whether or not each step was performed properly and in correct order.

Sometimes useful are rather crude rating scales, such as a graphically represented continuum for evaluating ability to use a particular tool or machine. If the operation can be subdivided into elements, each accompanied by a description of the approved method, performance on each element can be rated. Verbal descriptions of different quality levels may be used in an effort to make more nearly comparable the standards applied by different raters.

As the operations observed become more complex and the role of the observer looms larger, reliability becomes a problem. Evidence on this feature of the scores should be obtained in each new situation. Ratings of process based on records of an activity at the time it is occurring, however, are likely to be more reliable than such ratings made after the cessation of the activity.

The time required for an activity or for the completion of a product can be scored with a high degree of precision if small differences are important. A stop watch is ordinarily sufficiently accurate. Often it is more satisfactory to count the number of units produced during a given time than to attempt to time each unit.

Some activities do not lend themselves to analysis into components which can be observed and scored separately; for example, the performance of the teacher during a period of practice teaching. Neither the sequence of operations nor the

particular operations that may be called for can be specified. A few major categories can be determined, however, and performance with respect to each be rated. Such ratings may become appreciably unreliable because of dependence on the particular observer. They can be improved somewhat in this respect by the training of raters, attempts to standardize certain aspects of the procedures, establishment of review boards, and so on. They are likely to be better than ratings made after an appreciable lapse of time and based on vague memories and general impressions, contaminated by bias of one sort or another.

*B. In Rating the Product of an Activity.* For measuring the product of an activity, again objective measures are to be desired. For example, in an attempt to approximate accuracy of fire of a flexible gunner in a bombing plane under combat conditions, records of firing on training flights were obtained by a gun camera. It took motion pictures of the point of aim, and later measurement of this point provided an accuracy score. This record, during the course of the activity, is really a record of the yield of the activity.

Evaluation of qualities of the product by mechanical or other objective means should always be explored. Instruments such as vernier micrometers, rules, and drafting tools immediately come to mind. Other types of direct measures are also possible: the strength of a weld or soldered connection can be checked for breaking point; electrical leakage through an electrician's taped splice indicates insulation value. Several approaches can be used when objective measurement is not possible. Patterns and gauges will permit reasonably objective scores for some types of products.

Often more subjective methods must be used. Sometimes, again, rather crude check lists or rating scales are used. Qualities of the product are listed, and the rater evaluates the product with respect to each by perhaps making a mark on a graphically represented continuum, with descriptive labels at several points along it. Such scales are still limited by the uncertain meaning of language, so that the resulting evaluations are likely to be too subjective and hence unreliable.

An approach which escapes some of the semantic difficulties of the typical graphic scale is a "graded-sample quality scale." Samples of products varying from very poor to very good are assembled. To each sample is assigned a scale value based on judgments of experts. A product to be evaluated is then compared with the series of scaled products until the one most nearly like it is found and the product is assigned the corresponding score. Ideally, a psychophysical method such as the method of equal-appearing intervals or the paired comparisons method should be used in scaling the sample products.

## SUMMARY EVALUATIONS

In his discussion of criteria of proficiency, Thorndike under the heading "Summary Evaluations" discusses several points that are pertinent to the broader topic of observational techniques of evaluation, whether they are regarded as criteria or as predictors (Thorndike, 1949, pp. 149–159).

**Summary Evaluations Defined** Summary evaluations differ from measures treated earlier in that they arise from behavior extending over a longer period of time. Measures based on a limited behavior-unit may in some instances be unsatisfactory. They may require special development of the measurement technique and interference with work routine in order to administer them. Observations of limited segments of an activity also may not be sufficiently representative, or they may be based on conditions not typical of the real situation. For these reasons, observations covering longer periods of time and larger samples of behavior are sometimes sought, for example in evaluating training programs or in selecting workers for particular jobs.

Another distinction between summary evaluations and those based on single activity units is that the former are likely to be made with much less rigorous standardization and control. The scope of the summary evaluations and possibly at times the synthesis of judgments, typically made on a clinical basis, may increase their validity. Nevertheless, the lack of experimental control, attended by greater subjectivity and hence unreliability, would operate in the other direction.

Thorndike's analysis shows that various types of summary evaluations differ in the extent to which they are based on specific evaluations, the types of specific evaluations involved, and the manner in which these are combined.

Summary evaluations may be based entirely on specific evaluations, as, for example, average circular error in bombardier training, total volume of sales, and number of cards punched by a key-punch operator. Most periodic service ratings are founded on no direct reference to objective records.

Summary evaluations may be based on combinations of measures of ability—written tests, objectively scored work products, subjectively evaluated work methods, and so on. The components may be combined by statistically determined weights, by weights proportional to their importance as judged by experts, or by a clinical process from which emerges a summary score based on unspecified and unknown weights. The latter procedure is commonly used in general employee evaluations in government and industry. Such ratings, unless they are supported by recorded observations in specific situations, are all too often distorted by biasing factors.

**Types of Summary Evaluations** Let us briefly consider Thorndike's four subheadings under "Summary Evaluations": summary performance records, summary academic grades, summary ratings, and adminstrative actions.

*A. Summary Performance Records.* Summary performance records such as average circular error records for bombardiers, sales records, etc., have the advantage of objectivity and apparent relevance to ultimate criteria. When the observations are not made under experimentally controlled conditions, they may reflect biasing factors to such an extent as to be practically worthless—uncontrolled variation in weather, equipment, other personnel, location, flow of work materials, health, and so on. In some cases, however, summary performance records have enough reliability to use. This characteristic should be investigated.

*B. Summary Academic Grades.* Academic grades may be used both as predictors and as criteria. If training is prerequisite to entrance to a profession, then the selection of students who can successfully complete the training will be of immediate value. Academic marks are easy to predict in comparison with later performance on the job. It is time for concerted effort to be devoted to the relation between academic success and success on the job.

*C. Summary Ratings.* Routinely available service ratings, strongly flavored with the opinion of one rating officer, are only too familiar. Such ratings are prone to be influenced by extraneous factors and probable administrative uses, and the range is too markedly curtailed to reflect individual differences adequately for prediction purposes. Sufficiently reliable summary evaluations for test validation purposes can sometimes be obtained, however, by assuring the raters that the ratings will be kept confidential and will be used *solely* for validation. Such ratings, possibly recorded on a specially devised form or developed by means of the paired comparisons technique, and made by at least two persons, may be expected to yield reasonably satisfactory reliability estimates.

An outstanding weakness of the typical service rating is that conditions permitting any clear-cut estimation of reliability do not exist, so that although there often are fairly cogent reasons for regarding its reliability as suspect—maybe even very close to zero—to demonstrate this conclusively is difficult. Any system of employee evaluation should be overhauled, however, if it consists primarily of ratings each made by a single individual, based on varying periods of acquaintance, often on jobs that differ considerably, with various degrees of biasing factors in the job situation, with little if any systematic observation and recording of specific behavior, and under the influence of factors in the administrative framework that have little to do with job competence.

There are some developments of promise in this area. One of these is "buddy ratings," based on nominations by peers, a technique applied in the armed services and probably growing out of sociometric methods. Basic to this method are the ideas that to identify and rank the individuals who are extremely good or poor in a job is easier than to rank the middle group, and that ratings based on several raters' judgments are more dependable than those based on only one. If a number of persons each nominate the best and poorest four or five members of a group, the difference between the number of "best" and the number of "poorest" nominations for each individual, expressed as a proportion of the number of possible mentions, yields a quantitative index. There is some evidence of merit in the technique, particularly where personality characteristics are significant.

A second technique that escapes some drawbacks of the conventional service rating is the forced-choice technique, which again was initiated in the armed services. Pairs of descriptive statements are presented that have been pre-tested as to generally judged favorableness or unfavorableness and as to the relationship between the behavior described and an external criterion. Both statements in a pair are equally favorable or unfavorable and are equally popular when presented separately. They differ in relation to the independent criterion. One is significantly related to it, the other not. The supervisor who reports on an individual's behavior is "forced" to mark the one member of the pair most descriptive of his behavior.

Secretiveness regarding the scoring key is required. The reporter of the behavior does not know the key; hence, forced to choose between two attractive alternatives, he is encouraged to recall actual instances of observed behavior. The weights of the elements are based on their validities. More complicated extensions of the technique have been made, but these are its essentials.

A third useful approach for improving summary ratings applies to ratings of personal history items, which are most often used as predictors. Data are collected on a large number of personal history items (such as amount of schooling, age, number of dependents, membership in organizations, preferred school subjects, and so on) for a group of persons for whom criterion scores are available or, preferably, will become available. The scoring key for each item is determined so as to maximalize the relation with the criterion. Further, statistical techniques can be applied to select from the items tried out that combination of a smaller number of items that will correlate highest with the criterion. The items selected on the basis of one group are tried out on a new group. This method is a distinct improvement on the typical unanalyzed application blank.

*D. Administrative Actions.* Let us turn finally to Thorndike's fourth subdivision of summary evaluations: administrative actions. These are closely related to summary ratings and may be based largely upon them. Often they are dichotomous decisions—an individual is either hired or not hired, promoted or not promoted, graduated or eliminated. Such actions, while sometimes wrong, are often necessary. They therefore represent a type of summary rating which is of immediate practical consequence. Perhaps their importance causes them to be made with greater care than are most ratings. Still, since they partake of many characteristics of subjective evaluation at its worst, improvements of observational techniques in general should be accompanied by sounder administrative action and thus may be expected to have important bearings on the lives of individuals.

## 26. Application of the Critical Incident Technique in Developing Evaluative Measures

STEVEN M. JUNG

Although considered suspect by some measurement experts (Travers, 1958), the critical incident technique (CIT) provides a rich source of data useful in instrument development. According to the developer of the technique, it ". . . consists of a set of procedures for collecting direct observations of human behavior in such a way as to facilitate their potential usefulness in solving practical problems and developing broad psychological principles. The critical incident technique outlines procedures for collecting observed incidents having special significance and meeting systematically defined criteria" (Flanagan, 1954). Despite problems related to the high degree of subjectivity in gathering and classifying the relatively rare event data, the CIT offers a way of generating an information base, particularly in areas where little systematic literature is available. This article describes not only an application of the technique but also an exciting new individualized instruction program.

Project PLAN (Program for Learning in Accordance with Needs) is a comprehensive system of individualized education which has as its general objective that each student should receive those educational experiences which will best develop his talents in such a way as to achieve maximum satisfactions from the life's activities he chooses to pursue (Flanagan, 1967, 1969). The system provides learning methods and materials in the basic subject matter areas of English, mathematics, social studies, and science for grades 1–12. These methods and materials are designed to enable each student to acquire information, abilities, skills, and behavioral patterns which will enable him to achieve his goals. In addition, PLAN provides a

Reprinted and abridged with permission of the publisher, California Advisory Council on Educational Research, and Steven M. Jung from an article entitled "Evaluative Uses of Unconventional Measurement Techniques in an Educational System" which appeared in the *California Journal of Educational Research*, 1971, **22** (March 1971), pp. 48–57.

guidance program designed to permit students to make use of the best available occupational information and techniques in formulating these goals. A computer-supported testing and information-support system provides the clerical back-up needed to free the teacher from routine classroom activities, allowing her to give attention to students as individuals.

Such individualized education is thought to have a salutory effect on learners which goes beyond the immediate acquisition of facts and skills (Bolvin and Glaser, 1968; Flanagan, 1970a, 1970b). These effects usually are referenced in non-operationalized terms such as self-management, self-responsibility, initiative, resourcefulness, etc. They are generally thought to come about as a result of the individualized system, in which the student is allowed to utilize a certain amount of self-direction acquired perhaps through the nature of the instruction or through peer modeling. The successful experiences generated by these attempts at self-direction are presumed to reinforce and maintain such characteristics.

Project PLAN is not unlike other individualized educational systems in this regard. Three relevant PLAN goals for participating students are as follows:

1. PLAN will assist students to *take responsibility for* their individual development;
2. PLAN will assist students to *plan, manage, and carry out* their individual development; and
3. PLAN will assist students to acquire good patterns of social and civil behavior—*leadership, initiative, integrity, resourcefulness.*

Wright (1970) has presented a complete list of the goals for students in PLAN, stated at roughly the same level of specificity—which is to say that these are not explicitly stated "behavioral" objectives. They are, however, valid educational objectives, not unlike some of those posited by an early attempt to define quality education (QUEPS, 1968).

Such goals are not of vital consequence, however, if (1) there is no possibility of structuring the educational experience so that they might be translated into some form of student behavior, and (2) if there is no way to discover this behavior and make it a matter of public record. PLAN has been designed to require student behaviors that can be classified as interim steps toward such goal attainment. The nature of the teacher training program, the guidance program, the instructional management system, and even the very structure of the teaching learning units (TLUs) themselves are designed to require participation of each student in the educational process.

These factors of educational system design are adequately covered elsewhere (e.g., Shanner, 1968; Dunn, 1970). The thrust of the present problem was to gather evidence that students in PLAN were progressing beyond the interim steps required by the educational system and

were beginning independently to exhibit evidence that they were indeed self-directed. Teachers in PLAN schools were fond of saying that they could tell a PLAN student in the dark, or blindfolded, because the students were so self-directed. Thus, teachers were the first basic source tapped in attempting to verify these claims empirically.

## METHOD

**Critical Incident Study** The critical incident technique (Flanagan 1954) provides a method for collecting specific behaviors which relate most directly to performance in a given enterprise. Persons who are actively engaged in the enterprise are asked to recount specific instances in which they observed people commit particularly effective or ineffective acts. The critical incidents thus collected have proved to possess considerable utility in the development of proficiency measures, training programs, etc., in that the behaviors which are collected tend to reflect the most crucial aspects of success or failure.

In the present study the method of critical incidents was utilized to collect from PLAN teachers observed events having special significance and relating to the areas of self-responsibility, self-management, and resourcefulness. Teachers were asked to think of a recent occasion when they observed a student exhibit an unusual degree of one of the above traits. They were then asked to recount the circumstances surrounding the event and to tell exactly what the student *did* that indicated growth and development with respect to these qualities. Finally, they were asked to indicate why they thought the incident was a result of the student's experience in PLAN.

To collect these data, Critical Incident forms were sent to all PLAN teachers (N = 374) along with stamped return envelopes. In all, 56 incidents were returned. These were analyzed and are summarized by the following six statements:

1. a student started an assigned task promptly without reminder;
2. a student did an unusually thorough job on an assigned task or continued beyond the requirements of an assigned or agreed-upon task;
3. a student used AV media or books more than required by an assigned or agreed-upon task;
4. a student carried out an unassigned learning task without reminder or support from others;
5. a student completed an unassigned civic, social, or playground activity without reminder or support from others; and
6. a student *planned* and *completed* a strategy or a schedule involving several tasks.

In general, the behaviors reported were cases where students carried through on a task or project on their own, with no prodding or reminder. The student was presumably motivated to perform to please his *own* interests, to achieve his own satisfactions, rather than to satisfy the requirements imposed by teacher, parent, or other authority persons.

Next, an attempt was made to obtain hard data on the extent to which PLAN students in general exhibited such behaviors in comparison with students who were enrolled in more conventional educational programs.

**Community Problems Exercise** Within time constraints imposed by the rapidly approaching end of the school year, it was obvious that no massive collection of observations in either a natural or a contrived setting was possible. It was decided that a student self-report type of exercise was the only practical alternative. Such data have proven to have considerable accuracy when the student is asked to respond to questions about public events for which some sort of independent verification is possible (Flanagan and Jung 1970), and they have the advantage of being comparatively easy to

collect. Forms were therefore prepared for grade levels 5, 6, 7, 9, 10 and 11 (the PLAN system for grade levels 8 and 12 was not ready for tryout in the schools until this year).

The forms contained spaces for students to report two types of activities which related to the critical incidents reported previously. These were (1) Independent Learning activities, including those relating to general educational development but not part of the assigned schoolwork; and (2) Community Service activities, including things related to the improvement of the community. Students were asked to report only activities they had performed during the course of the last semester, in order to delimit the reporting period and try to keep it within their memory capacity. They were also asked to indicate their role in the organization and planning of these activities. Each form contained the following basic instructions:

List the activities in which you have participated in the past semester. These should be activities which were undertaken voluntarily by you. For each activity you list, you should indicate your role in the organizing and planning of the activity. Use the back of this page if necessary.

The teacher instructions, part of which were to be read to the class, attempted to: (1) provide enough information to teachers about the purpose of the study to gain their cooperation; and (2) to standardize the conditions of administration such that results would be comparable across classes. As will be noted later, only partial success was achieved in this effort. The instructions indicated that the students should not be given teacher-constructed examples which would influence the responses of the class as a whole, since spontaneous and thoughtful replies were of most interest. However, it was realized that fifth and sixth grade students especially might have difficulty in grasping the concepts involved in "independent learning" and "community service" activities. Therefore, several examples were given which were taken directly from the reported critical incidents. Allowance was then made in the scoring for responses which were obviously just repetitions of these examples.

Materials were sent to the PLAN and control classes via PLAN representatives late in the spring of 1969. Control classes had been selected at the outset of PLAN to serve in comparisons such as the present one. In general, these consisted of non-PLAN classes in the same school or of classes in neighboring schools judged to exhibit a similar student population. Although random assignment of students to classes had been requested, matters of parental consent and local control precluded this in some cases. Exercises were returned from 54 classes, of which 37 were PLAN and 17 were control.

## RESULTS

The number of Independent Learning activities and Community Service activities were tabulated for each respondent (N = 1400) according to a set of criteria which attempted to insure, to as great an extent as possible, that tabulated activities were: (1) learning and community service related; (2) independently undertaken; and (3) not the result of some idea implanted solely as a result of the directions or other instructions by the teacher.

In order to check the adequacy of these criteria for achieving reliability in tabulating activities, two persons independently tabulated a randomly selected sample of six classes. A high level of agreement was achieved.

In order to generate meaningful comparisons in terms of the tabulations of these data, only PLAN data were selected for further analysis for which appropriate control data also existed. This meant that all analyses were made by comparing the data generated by students in PLAN classes with data generated by students in other classes in the same school or in a neighboring school. This resulted in the selection

of 14 classes (7 PLAN, 7 control) at the 5th grade level (PLAN N = 231, control N = 182), 8 classes (4 PLAN, 4 control) at the 6th grade level (PLAN N = 110, control N = 122), 2 classes (one of each) at the 7th grade level (PLAN N = 24, control N = 31), and 4 classes (two of each) at the 9th grade level (PLAN N = 60, control N = 52). The activity categories which formed the basis for generating tabulations and analyzing the data were as follows:

*Independent Learning*
1. Extra non-required reading
2. Research—library, tapes, etc.
3. Knowledge of needing or desiring information.
4. Planned activity (or had major role)
5. Won prize in academic contest
6. Academic clubs
7. Summer school
8. Projects

*Community Service*
1. Organized activities
2. Service activities—own initiative
3. Helped someone
4. Specific responsible position

Frequencies, corrected for differences in sample size (Mann-Whitney $U$ tests), were contrasted for the PLAN and control groups, for grade levels 5, 6, 7, and 9. Comparisons were made for both Independent Learning and Community Service. Statistically significant differences were found at grades 5 and 6 for both Independent Learning and Community Service activities in favor of the PLAN classes.

## DISCUSSION

The weight of the present findings supports the tentative conclusion that PLAN students are indeed making good progress toward the attainment of some of the most important objectives of any educational program. Further, these data were collected in a relatively short period of time with a minimum of expense, pointing out an innovative application of the critical incident technique in evaluating a comprehensive educational program.

The following limitations of the present study are pointed out as a cautionary note against overgeneralizing from the results. First, it is realized that the limited percent of return for the community problems exercises implies a selected sample. The fact that over twice as many PLAN as control teachers returned exercises is also an indication of this selection. The class matching procedures were adopted in an attempt to reduce this source of error. Second, the responses from some classes strongly implied that students had been given instructions which went beyond those which were to have been read. The scoring procedures that were used attempted to reduce this error. In order to correct both of these drawbacks, however, much more control over the testing situation and much more time for following up on nonrespondents would be required than was available in the present study.

To the extent that PLAN and control students were not chosen by random selection procedures, the results of the non-parametric statistical analysis are in question. At present, there is no way to estimate the effects of this deficit.

## 27. Role-Playing as an Evaluative Technique
### HAROLD G. LEVINE and CHRISTINE McGUIRE

Evaluators continually face the problem of judging the relevance of the measuring procedures they use to gather data. Decisions concerning relevance are difficult at best, and always critical when real-life performance criteria (e.g., on-the-job behavior) are involved. Harold G. Levine and Christine McGuire sketch the development and application of a technique potentially useful in the evaluation of many teaching and training situations. Although the results of their efforts were not all that had been hoped, their demonstration of role-playing as a potentially useful methodology constitutes a significant contribution to the measurement literature. Many possible sources of difficulty in construction and application of the role-playing techniques are described in their article. The reader should get a feel for the "formative" dimensions of instrument development.

Although testing specialists concentrate their efforts on paper and pencil instruments, some aspects of performance cannot be sampled by written examinations. Physicians, for example, are required to interact with patients to gather information, to give reassurance, and to provide advice. They must also exchange informa-

Reprinted and abridged with permission of the publisher and Christine McGuire from the *Journal of Educational Measurement*, **5** (1968), pp. 1–8.

tion with colleagues, provide consultative services, solve problems in group settings, and often instruct younger physicians. Those responsible for graduate medical education have recognized the need to evaluate these areas of competence and have relied heavily on oral examinations for this purpose. As these examinations are widely employed, they fall into two general categories: in the first a candidate interviews and examines a patient, after which he presents his findings to, and discusses the problems with, one or more examiners. In the second, a candidate is subjected to an oral quiz on the assumption that his ability to handle such an encounter would provide evidence about how he "thinks on his feet" and thus indirect evidence of his competence in handling interactions with patients and colleagues.

Unfortunately, each of these techniques has serious shortcomings. Each suffers from the lack of reliability characteristic of subjective ratings and each is seriously defective with respect to validity: the first because the scores are usually based on the examinee's discussion of the case, not on an observation of his transactions with the patient; the second because the skills required in responding to an oral quiz differ markedly from those required in interacting with patients or colleagues (McGuire, 1966). While the unreliability arising from disagreements on standards among examiners and from lack of standardized case materials can be remedied by means of examiner training and by preparation of standardized case materials, the validity problem remains.

One possible solution to this problem is to design an examination that combines the face validity of a patient interview with the standardization requisite for obtaining satisfactory reliability: simulated clinical encounters. Such simulations have the additional advantages of assuring that all examinees are confronted with the same clinical problem; of permitting the establishment of performance standards; and of making it possible to sample the examinee's behavior with several cases.

## DEVELOPING SIMULATION EXAMINATIONS EMPLOYING ROLE-PLAYING TECHNIQUES

Since 1964, the Center for the Study of Medical Education at the University of Illinois College of Medicine, together with a major medical specialty board, has been engaged in an investigation of the means by which competence in the specialty

may be determined. In the first stage a critical incident study (Flanagan, 1954) was employed to develop a detailed behavioral description of the critical performance requirements in the specialty. Among those identified was the ability to relate to patients and to colleagues. The considerations noted earlier led to an exploration of simulations as a means of assessing these qualities. For this purpose three standardized role-playing situations were developed:

**The Simulated Diagnostic Interview** In this situation a candidate plays the role of a physician and an examiner is programmed to play the role of a patient. The candidate is required to obtain a history from the simulated "patient," and to obtain any desired information about the physical and laboratory findings. A second examiner observes and rates this process using explicit criteria and a standard rating scale. During the last three minutes of this 15-minute examination the candidate explains and supports his diagnostic impressions to both examiners.

**The Simulated Proposed Treatment Interview** In this technique the candidate is provided with a description of the medical problem presented by a specific patient. His task is to explain to the examiner, playing the role of the patient, the nature of his illness and to gain his cooperation in the proposed plan of treatment. A second examiner observes and rates the 10-minute interview.

**The Simulated Patient Management Conference** This technique, a role-playing variant of the Leaderless Group Discussion (Bass, 1954), is designed to assay minimum acceptable competence rather than leadership. In the 30-minute examination five candidates who have been provided with basic information about two problem cases are required to discuss the management of each patient and reach agreement upon a course of action, in the manner of a typical staff conference. The candidates are observed and rated by two examiners who take no part in the discussion.

## PROCEDURES

**Preparing for the Examination** Each of these techniques requires examiners and candidates to perform functions different from those characteristic of the typical oral examination. To prepare examiners for this task a two-day training program was conducted for examiners, in which they reviewed the basic objectives of the role-playing exercises and the rating methods to be employed. They were given the opportunity to observe and analyze videotaped and live demonstrations of the techniques, and then to practice administering them to resident physicians in training. On the basis of this experience, discussion, and critique, a set of detailed written instructions for administering the examinations as well as revised rating scales were prepared. Finally, a complete set of standardized case materials was developed for each examination.

It was also necessary to provide some orientation for candidates. A brief description of the changes to be introduced in the oral examination format was distributed about a month in advance. The day before the examination each candidate was provided a detailed written statement outlining the procedures to be followed in administering the examination and the criteria to be employed in rating. Finally, the entire candidate group was shown a short sound motion picture film in which each new technique was demonstrated.

After this preparatory work, the three new techniques, together with four conventional oral quizzes, were administered as part of the board certification examination to 383 candidates over a two-day period in January, 1966. Approximately 20% of the simulations were systematically observed by physicians and educators trained to carry out this task. The observers agreed that, with few exceptions, both examiners and candidates adapted to role-playing with remarkable ease. Candidates and examiners were also invited to comment on both the traditional and the new examination procedures. While they did not hesitate to criticize many aspects of the examination, none spontaneously criticized the new techniques. When specifically asked about them, the candidates were primarily concerned with details of the scoring procedure and, like some of the examiners, expressed considerable skepticism about the possibility of accurately rating performance in the *Simulated Patient Management Conference*. Otherwise the response of both candidates and examiners to the role-playing techniques was generally favorable or noncommittal.

## RESULTS

Analysis of basic statistics for all simulations indicated that the difference between mean scores assigned by the role-playing examiner and those assigned by the observing examiner were of little practical significance. Both scores were therefore pooled for an overall rating of the candidate proficiency. Rater reliability as measured by the correlation between two independent ratings is sufficiently high for the *Patient Interviews* to indicate that these techniques should prove to be of value in a battery of tests designed to evaluate individual candidates. Reliability is also sufficiently high to justify the use of each technique independently to evaluate group performance.

While such overall results are encouraging, further analysis points up some of the problems inherent in any evaluative technique that depends on subjective judgments. A one-way analysis of variance of the composite rating for each team of examiners in the *Patient Interviews* clearly indicated that some teams used more stringent standards than others. While such discrepancies may be even more serious in conventional oral examinations, their existence here further underscores the importance of training examiners and of developing clear behavioral criteria for judging competence. This finding also highlights the fact that judgment of individual candidates should be made only on the basis of a sufficiently large number of observations to avoid the effects of examiner bias.

In contrast with the results obtained on the *Simulated Patient Interviews,* rater reliability on the *Simulated Patient Management Conference* proved distressingly low. This was primarily due to the contribution of one team of examiners who had difficulty applying written standards of judgment. In any case, it is clear that revision of rating technique and of examiner training are required.

**Validity** From the point of view of *content validity,* most observers agree that these role-playing exercises sample aspects of behavior that are important in the practice of the specialty and that are not assayed by more conventional techniques. While some observers felt that no candidate behaved in an entirely natural fashion during the examinations, others believed that the situations were sufficiently realistic to justify important inferences about a candidate's habitual behavior in circumstances similar to those sampled in the examination. A more precise answer to this issue awaits detailed study on the *concurrent validity* of the new techniques, but no parallel evaluation of comparable habitual behavior (such as might be derived from supervisors' ratings) is yet available.

With regard to *construct validity,* correlations between scores on the role-playing exercises and on conventional examinations are uniformly low. While this could be a function of the limited reliability of any of the measures, it is also compatible with the hypothesis that the new techniques are measuring components of professional competence not sampled by traditional methods of evaluation. Further, a later study of the performance of 233 residents at various stages of training reveals significant differences among them in the expected direction i.e., fourth year residents scoring higher than third, third higher than second, etc. Additional evidence is available from a check list of specific important inquiries maintained by the examiner observing the *Simulated Diagnostic Interview.*

Detailed analysis of the variations in the information gathering process actually employed by candidates in the *Simulated Diagnostic Interview* may also raise questions about the most efficient and effective procedures to follow in medical diagnosis. For example, on the basis of "conventional wisdom," medical students should be instructed to make a "thorough" history, perform a "complete" physical examination and to use the findings from these to guide laboratory evaluation and therapy. It is possible that such a procedure is more conventional than wise and is based upon medical experience prior to the development of readily available and inexpensive laboratory procedures. However, the investigation of such a hypothesis by direct observation of real life situations is time-consuming and expensive and may prove to be undesirable because of the difficulty of manipulating "real life." Simulated situations such as those used for the *Diagnostic Interview* may offer useful opportunities for testing alternative models of information gathering and processing that may lead to modifications in our conventional wisdom and improvements in our teaching.

# 28. The Development of a Sequentially Scaled Achievement Test

### RICHARD C. COX and GLENN T. GRAHAM

Many of the curricula resulting from the educational reform movement require a heavy dose of individualized instruction. The development of highly individualized instructional programs has created a demand for many different kinds of measurement devices. In addition to criterion-referenced and curriculum-embedded tests, Lindvall and Cox (1969) have called for placement, diagnostic, and continuous assessment devices. This article describes the development of a criterion (content)-referenced test, the total score on which can be immediately interpreted to reveal the kinds of tasks the examinee can perform. Although related here to test items, the idea of "sequencing" can be applied to learning tasks and curriculum development. This has been well illustrated by Gagné (1967).

A program of individualized instruction demands a reexamination of traditional testing procedures (Coulson and Cogswell, 1965). Students must be compared to an absolute standard as opposed to a normative standard, the student's score reflecting the degree of competence in certain behaviors as opposed to the comparison of his performance with that of other individuals. This distinction between norm and criterion-referenced measures has been made by Glaser (1963).

A content-referenced measure provides considerable information for making decisions concerning student advancement. However, unless the test is designed to measure performance on only one behavior, the total test score does not indicate which behaviors the student has or has not mastered. To obtain this information, student performance on each item must be examined.

One solution to this rather laborious task would be a test in which the total score would indicate the response pattern of the individual. Such tests have been employed in the investigation of attitudes, and have been analyzed using the Guttman (1944) "Scalogram Analysis." Essentially, the analysis includes the ranking of scores from highest to lowest, and the ranking of items from most favorable to least favorable. Theoretically, those students with the highest scores (highest being most favorable) would have answered only the most favorable items; those scoring low would have answered only the least favorable items, etc. The analysis yields a coefficient of reproducibility which indicates how well an individual's response pattern can be reproduced knowing his total score. The present study is an attempt to develop such a test.

## PROCEDURE AND RESULTS

In a test designed to be scalable, the objectives must be arranged sequentially. In this study the terminal objective to be tested was the student's ability to add

Reprinted with permission of the publisher and Richard C. Cox from the *Journal of Educational Measurement*, 3 (1966), pp. 147–150.

2 two-digit numerals involving carrying. Using this as a starting point, the question was asked, "What skills must have been mastered previously in order to master this objective?" With this question as a guide, the list of fifteen objectives presented in Table 1 was developed.

With the exception of objective 7b, from 2 to 5 tasks were constructed for each of the objectives. The total number of tasks for the entire test was 50. The tasks pertaining to each objective were combined to form one "item" for each objective. . . . As an example, consider the three tasks:

$$\begin{array}{ccc} 20 & 36 & 54 \\ +11 & +42 & +33 \\ \hline \end{array}$$

These tasks would compose one "item" testing objective 8.

This procedure was followed to construct a 15-item test. The test was administered to a kindergarten, first, and second grade to obtain a wide range of ability levels. Students were ranked according to total score and the response pattern plotted. This pattern indicated that some of the items were not in the correct position to obtain the maximum coefficient of reproducibility, i.e., the postulated sequence of objectives was not empirically verified. The items were rearranged to yield the maximum reproducibility coefficient. The response pattern obtained after the items had been rearranged yielded a reproducibility coefficient of .961. The value of .90 was suggested by Guttman (1944) as an acceptable lower limit.

As a further revision, objectives 3, 7a, and 7b and their corresponding items were omitted—objective 3 because it was dependent on a specific curriculum, and objectives 7a and 7b because of ambiguous directions. The final arrangement of items yielded a reproducibility coefficient of .977.

According to Guttman in Stouffer (1950), the coefficient of reproducibility is a necessary but not a sufficient criterion for scalability. Since the reproducibility coefficient for a given item cannot be less than the proportion of responses occurring in the most frequently chosen category, Guttman suggests that too many extreme items, 80 percent or greater in any one category, can spuriously raise the reproducibility coefficient. Menzel (1953) suggests a procedure, which, when taken in conjunction with the reproducibility coefficient, further contributes evidence of scalability. Menzel's coefficient of scalability reflects the degree to which the individual's performance can be reproduced from knowledge of the marginal totals. The coefficient prevents one from spuriously attributing high scalability from a sample composed of many extreme items and/or individuals. A coefficient of .65 or better is established as a criterion. The scalability coefficient for the revised test was .902.

Although the revised test met the criteria for scalability, it had never been administered in its present form. As a validation study, the final revision was administered to a different kindergarten, first, and second grade. This new response pattern yielded a reproducibility coefficient of .970 and a scalability coefficient of .792.

## DISCUSSION

The results indicate it is indeed possible to develop a sequentially scaled achievement test. However, these results must be tempered by the fact that the test is based upon a restricted area of subject matter. At the present time additional tests are being developed in other areas of mathematics covering a wider range of objectives. These areas include subtraction, addition, time telling, numeration, and money. The reproducibility coefficients obtained range from .85 to .96 on the initial test administration. Further replications with more complex skills and with larger and more heterogeneous samples would be desirable.

**TABLE 1**
**Sample Objectives and Test Items**

| Objective | Sample Test Item |
|---|---|
| The student is able to: | |
| **1.** Recognize numerals from 1 to 10. | **1.** 1    2    3    4<br>"Draw a circle around the 2." |
| **2.** a) Determine which numeral comes before or after another numeral. | **2.** a)    10    8    5    2<br>"Draw a circle around the number that comes just after 7." |
| b) Determine which of two numerals is the largest or smallest. | b)    7    5<br>"Draw a circle around the largest numeral." |
| **3.** Discriminate between $+, -, =$ | **3.** $+$    $-$    $=$<br>"Draw a circle around the sign which means to add." |
| **4.** a) Add two single-digit numerals with sums to 10, vertically.<br>b) Add two single-digit numerals with sums to 10, horizontally. | **4.** a)    $\begin{array}{r} 5 \\ +4 \\ \hline \end{array}$<br><br>b)    $3 + 1 =$ |
| **5.** a) Add two single-digit numerals involving carrying, horizontally.<br>b) Add two single-digit numerals involving carrying, vertically. | **5.** a)    $8 + 3 =$<br><br>b)    $\begin{array}{r} 7 \\ +8 \\ \hline \end{array}$ |
| **6.** a) Add three single-digit numerals involving carrying, vertically.<br><br>b) Add three single-digit numerals involving carrying, horizontally. | **6.** a)    $\begin{array}{r} 1 \\ 8 \\ +4 \\ \hline \end{array}$<br><br>b)    $7 + 3 + 2 =$ |
| **7.** a) Place one and two-digit numerals in a column so they could be added.<br><br>b) Determine which columns of numerals is written so it could be added. | **7.** a)    15    16    2<br>"Place these numerals in a column so they could be added."<br>b)    $\begin{array}{ccc} 15 & 15 & 15 \\ 16 & 16 & 16 \\ \underline{2} & \underline{2} & \underline{2} \end{array}$<br>"Draw a circle around the column which is written so it could be added." |
| **8.** Add 2 two-digit numerals without carrying. | **8.**    $\begin{array}{r} 20 \\ +11 \\ \hline \end{array}$ |
| **9.** Add 2 three-digit numerals without carrying. | **9.**    $\begin{array}{r} 215 \\ +723 \\ \hline \end{array}$ |
| **10.** Add 2 two-digit numerals with carrying. | **10.**    $\begin{array}{r} 58 \\ +36 \\ \hline \end{array}$ |

The results also should be tempered with the realization that the item responses may be a function of prior educational experiences, in school or elsewhere, to which the students have been exposed. This is not to say, however, that it is impossible to have certain skills that are necessarily prerequisite to others, but rather to suggest a possible contaminating factor. It also seems reasonable to hypothesize that by manipulating the content taught in the classroom one could dictate a series of objectives that would yield an empirically scaled test.

One obvious result of the study is that the logical ordering of objectives is not sufficient for the establishment of a scalable test. Empirical evidence must be obtained to verify or refute the postulated order.

## 29. Evaluation in the Arts and Humanities
### DONALD R. CHIPLEY

To what extent are educators in the arts and humanities incorporating recent changes in educational evaluation to build better programs of education? This question forms the basis for Chipley's article. The purpose of the article is twofold. First, Chipley examines existing evaluative efforts in the arts and humanities in order to determine the extent to which they have utilized explicit systems of pupil development specifications to assess desired learning outcomes. Second, he identifies some constructive alternatives that contain concrete points of departure for improving future efforts in evaluating pupil learning in the arts and humanities. The article is important, then, because it supplies us with a detailed account of both what has been done and what needs to be done in a number of areas where evaluation has been viewed as extremely difficult and, hence, often avoided.

The article was prepared especially for this book.

We have recently entered a new age of educational humanism. The new humanism is being forged by educators and others who are questioning the efficacy of formal schooling and calling for the adoption of more humane patterns of educational action. Associated with this humanism are several major queries which challenge local school personnel to demonstrate that a given educational program is producing desired changes in the young as they progress through various levels of schooling.

The new humanists are greatly concerned about the kind of person to be produced through involvement in the process of education, and thus are raising such questions as:

1. What characteristics are to be exhibited by a person who must undergo over a decade of formal education?

2. What experiences and programs of instruction can be utilized at different levels of schooling to aid the young to make continuous progress toward acquiring desired characteristics?

3. What procedures are to be utilized to assess and report on pupil progress both in different areas of develop-

ment and at different levels of schooling?

Questions such as these, then, are used to identify important aspects of pupil development which must be adequately provided for if education is to become a humanistic mode of developmental growth.

School program evaluation has also undergone much change in recent years. The change has not, however, taken place at an equal rate in all areas of the school program. Research and development has proceeded far more rapidly in the academic areas of science, mathematics, language arts, and social studies than in the personal enrichment areas of art, music, and the humanities. Thus, change has taken place in the arts and humanities, but it has not reached the point where one can talk with any substance about the results of schooling in these areas.

Cumulative advancement in any area depends on the extent to which educators in that area are willing and able to adapt new concepts and strategies in pursuing the systematic development of that area. It is clear that evaluative reform is taking place in the arts and humanities. The more germane question at this point is: To what extent are evaluative changes in these areas being formulated in light of the requirements identified in the queries associated with the new humanism? Hence, the purpose of this essay is to examine evaluative reforms in the arts and humanities in terms of the three questions identified above, and to clarify those aspects where further articulation and research are required. With this task in mind, let us turn now to an examination of the questions mentioned above.

*1. What characteristics are to be exhibited by a person who must undergo over a decade of formal education?* Educators in the arts and humanities generally grant that it is important to have some notion of the kind of person to be produced by an educational program. They do not agree as readily, however, to the proposition that this notion must be translated into a detailed system of explicit pupil development specifications. Consequently, the imperative which calls for defining pupil characteristics in terms of behavioral objectives has met with extensive criticism and resistance in the arts and humanities.

In a classic statement of this criticism, Eisner (1967, pp. 253–258) argues that the directive to formulate educational objectives in behavioral terms suffers from four limitations. These limitations can be briefly stated as follows: (1) The process of instruction is dynamic and complex and yields outcomes far too numerous to predict in advance. (2) Certain areas of instruction (e.g., math and science) are highly structured and thus lend themselves to a relatively precise definition of pupil outcomes, whereas other areas such as the arts are loosely structured and more concerned with generating novel outcomes. (3) Behavioral objectives increase educational confusion, since it is rarely clear when they represent a standard for measurement and when they represent merely a criterion for judgment. (4) The specification of behavioral objectives prior to action, although logically consistent in respect to relating ends and means, often produces a situation which ignores the potential of generating more appropriate objectives as psychological processes unfold. Eisner's argument is directed in the main against the behavioral engineer who rejects any educational goal that is not stated in terms of observable and, hence, measurable behavior. Other writers such as Hoetker (Maxwell and Tovatt, 1970, pp. 49–50) also criticize this narrow view of behavioral objectives, but still maintain that higher-level behavioral objectives can be formulated and used to develop improved educational programs in the arts and humanities.

In spite of the widespread objection to behavioral objectives, educators have on several occasions actively sought to establish frameworks of behavioral objectives for programs in the arts and humanities. Kaufman (1971, pp. 105–107) reports that teams of professional artists, teachers, and educational consultants spent six weeks in an effort to evolve a behavioral framework for the CAREL arts and humanities curriculum project (1967–1969). Although the participants agreed that an explicit system of pupil outcomes was needed, they failed to develop an operational framework of objectives. There are other national projects which have been more productive in accomplishing this task, but which are still working toward the completion of their final product. Hook (Maxwell and Tovatt, 1970, pp. 81–84) for example, in a progress report on the Tri-University Behavioral Objectives for English Project describes a perspective and some illustrative literature objectives which were formulated by university project personnel and a wide field of special consultants for incorporation in an English program for youth in grades 9–12.

Finally, there are other projects such as the National Assessment of Educational Progress which have formulated operational frameworks of objectives for several areas of the arts and humanities. This project brought together committees of subject area specialists and staff members of The Educational Testing Service to specify a series of potential achievement objectives appropriate for four age groups —9, 13, 17, and young adults aged 26–35. The proposed objectives were next refined by submitting them to panels of lay citizens for review, and then by comparatively relating them to prior statements of objectives contained in literature produced during the past 25 years. By following this strategy, the National Assessment Project has produced a system of achievement objectives for art, music, and literature, as well as for seven other areas of educational achievement. The established objectives have already been published in a series of monographs that includes the booklets *Literature Objectives* (National Assessment, 1970a), *Music Objectives* (National Assessment, 1970b), and *Art Objectives* (National Assessment, 1971).

Of course, many educators will object to the framework of objectives developed in this latter instance because it is the product of an independent assessment agency. Thus, it is important to indicate some other sources of behavioral objectives which have been developed in detail by educational specialists and which incorporate a sound basis for pupil assessment related to the proposed objectives. In this respect, it is worth noting that there are frameworks of behavioral objectives that have been formulated by individual educational specialists and are available in an operational form. Several frameworks of content-related behavioral objectives are presently available in Part Two of the *Handbook on Formative and Summative Evaluation of Student Learning* (Bloom, Hastings, Madaus, et al., 1971). Moore and Kennedy (pp. 401–445), Purves (pp. 699–766), and Foley (pp. 769–813) each have chapters in the above text which present specifications of pupil learning for writing and literature and identify illustrative testing procedures for assessing achievement in these areas. Wilson (pp. 501–558) also has a chapter in the same text which contains specifications and procedures for evaluating pupil learning in the area of art education.

There are two difficulties, then, which must be resolved in the area of pupil characteristics if evaluative reform is to progress at a faster rate than it has in the past. First, educators in the arts and humanities will have to increase their willingness to accept and apply a modified concept of behavioral objectives as a means for developing improved programs of education in the arts and humanities. Second, they will have to become more proficient in formulating an operational framework of behavioral objectives and further be able to indicate some procedures which can be used to assess various types of behavioral development. Writers such as Hoetker (Maxwell and Tovatt, 1970) have identified an approach toward behavioral objectives which holds some promise as a base for future development.

Similarly there are national project groups and individual specialists working at the university level who have developed operational frameworks of objectives that are presently available for use in building educational programs which can be formatively and summatively assessed. In short, there are some concrete examples of concepts and specifications which identify points of departure for strengthening efforts in relation to defining pupil characteristics in the arts and humanities.

*2. What experiences and programs of instruction can be utilized at different levels of schooling to aid the young to make continuous progress toward acquiring desired characteristics?* The situation in this area of development is very similar to that described above in respect to specifying pupil outcomes. Those educators who object to defining pupil development in terms of behavioral outcomes are generally unwilling to go into specifics about various aspects of instruction. Those who are presently working on the definition of appropriate behavioral objectives have not reached a point of being able to indicate relevant components of instructional specifications to be used to educate pupils in light of the desired objectives. Consequently, there is even less progress in this area than is found in the area of pupil characteristics.

Although development in this area is too limited to analyze it in specific detail, there are certain points which should be noted in order to clarify aspects where change is needed to improve evaluative practices. Research efforts up to now have focused largely on the comparative study of the effectiveness of different teaching methods. The *Handbook of Research on Teaching* (Gage, 1963), for example, has chapters by Meckel (pp. 966–1006) and Hausman (pp. 1101–1117) which summarize a wide range of studies conducted to assess the effectiveness of various teaching methods in the areas of composition and literature and the visual arts. Moreover, this type of research continues to be a rather common type of research despite the fact that as Walberg (1970, p. 562) and others have pointed out, "Research on teaching . . . has consistently concluded that different teaching methods make little or no difference in student learning and attitudes." By way of contrast, there are other, more critical aspects of instructional programs, such as the sequencing of units of instruction, which have been rarely specified and systematically evaluated except in the areas of math and science (Briggs, 1968, p. 118). It is clear, then, that educators in the arts and humanities will have to devote far more attention then they have in the past to differentiating the various aspects of instructional programs and to assessing the impact of these aspects on pupil learning.

There are, once again, some existing sources which can offer educators assistance in working on these tasks. Peak experiences would, according to Maslow (1970, pp. 30–31), provide educators with an explicit concept that can be vitally useful in studying and assessing individual development in music and art, as well as in other areas of education. Peak experiences have value because they can be differentiated in terms of different types and levels, and further because, once identified, they can be used to structure programs of education which can be empirically assessed. Creativity is another area which has been extensively researched and which has models and operational specifications that can be applied to define specific programs of instruction in the arts and humanities. The *Journal of Research and Development in Education's* issue on "Creativity" (Torrance, 1971) includes articles by Williams (pp. 14–22), Cole (pp. 23–28), Davis (pp. 29–34), Torrance (pp. 35–41), Taylor (pp. 42–50), Stevenson (pp. 51–56), Mitchell (pp. 57–62), Parnes and Noller (pp. 62–66), and Witt (pp. 67–73) which describe explicit strategies and procedures designed to foster pupil growth in terms of Guilford's "Structure-of-Intellect" model

(Guilford, 1967) and in other dimensions of affective and productive behavior. There have also been some studies by Burkhart and others (Eisner, 1965, pp. 319–320) which have investigated student creativity in art education, and identified three basic patterns—spontaneous, academic, and divergent—which can be researched in implementing alternative programs of instruction. Finally, there are some special project programs, such as "Man: A Course of Study" (Education Development Center, 1970) which have potential for improving instructional programs in the arts and humanities. Although oriented primarily to the social studies, this program utilizes a strategy and a system of procedures that could easily be extended to design a humanities program that would involve pupils in the study of many different forms of creative expression.

Educators in the arts and humanities will have to devote greater attention to the problems of defining appropriate experiences and programs of instruction before evaluative reform can take place in this area of development. More specifically, it is extremely important that they reduce their efforts to assess the effectiveness of different kinds of teaching methods and explore ways to adapt concepts, procedures, and strategies derived from existing research in such areas as peak experiences, creativity, and developmental courses of study as a means of formulating patterns of instructional specifications that can be formatively and summatively evaluated. It is important, then, that educators do a better job of specifying such aspects as experiences and sequential units of instruction so that, when programs of instruction are evaluated, they will be better able to determine which aspects make a significant difference in relation to gains in pupil learning.

3. *What procedures are to be utilized to assess and report on pupil progress both in different areas of development and at* *different levels of schooling?* Of the areas being considered, evaluation has undergone the most development. Developments in this area have, however, like behavioral objectives, often met with strong criticism, and hence have not gained widespread acceptance among educators in the arts and humanities. Seashore, for example, applied a "theory of specifics" to develop a standarized battery of musical aptitude instruments as early as 1919; but there were many music educators, such as Mursell, who argued that specific attributes did not represent an accurate index of musical ability and maintained that a gestalt approach had to be employed in designing instruments to assess the nature of musicality (Whybrew, 1962, pp. 86–93).

In the 1940s, art educators such as Munro and Rannels objected strongly to the use of component ability tests as a means of measuring aesthetic sensitivity and artistic production. Rannels, in particular, has criticized psychological testing in art on the following counts (Logan, 1955, pp. 236–37): Testmakers generally assume a causal relationship between a specific variable and a particular art response, and in this sense are applying a basic concept of an outworn faculty psychology. Some test aspects have been unconsciously slanted to determine a student's ability in a particular interpretation of art work, such as testing for neatness and precision, which are important to some but not all forms of art expression. Many tests are used without adequate validation, in the sense that they are based on use in a few instances rather than on continuous refinement through numerous replications. Finally, testmakers often have a very shallow interest and background in art, and hence their instruments generally reflect a low-level sensitivity to the aesthetic qualities they are supposedly measuring.

Criticism of measurement concepts and techniques has increased in recent decades; but so have efforts to propose constructive alternatives. Some critics of behavioral objectives have accepted a broader concept of pupil outcomes and gone on to define an operational framework of objectives that can be clearly assessed. Here would be included, as noted in discussing Question 1, the frameworks of objectives formulated by national project groups such as the Tri-University Behavioral Objectives for English Project and the National Assessment Project and those specified by writers such as Moore and Kennedy, Purves, Foley, and Wilson in the *Handbook on Formative and Summative Evaluation of Student Learning*. Another group of specialists has identified some comprehensive strategies for systematizing the evaluation of pupil learning in the arts and humanities. The precedent for this type of effort is found in the Eight-Year Study. In *Appraising and Recording Student Progress* (Smith, Tyler et al., 1942, pp. 245–312). Harris, Bettelheim, and Diederich describe a strategy used to develop instruments for measuring selected aspects of appreciation in literature and art. More recent alternatives have been formulated by other project groups. The CSE School Evaluation Project (Hoepfner, 1970) has established a strategy and a framework of pupil-outcome-based tests for assessing the progress of elementary children in grades 1, 3, 5, and 6, in relation to various aspects of. arts and crafts, creativity, dance, general culture, literature, and music. The "Man: A Course of Study" project (Education Development Center, 1970, pp. 8–15) has identified several research questions and a methodology to be used in studying and assessing the learning development of students involved in a study about global concepts of human nature. Finally, the National Assessment Project has also, as was previously noted, evolved a systematic strategy for both defining achievement objectives and constructing prototype assessment items in art, literature, and music.

Critics of measurement techniques have also formulated alternatives to replace the approaches they have shown to be inadequate. Thomas, for example, states that existing art tests have four major shortcomings:

(1) they have measured only one, or at most a few, of the complex factors that constitute art ability; (2) they seemingly have been based upon the assumption that there is a single, correct criterion of good art; (3) they have failed to distinguish adequately among abilities to judge, to appreciate, and to create art; and (4) they have failed to account adequately for the creativity component in art ability (1965, p. 164).

After examining these shortcomings, he presents a rationale for measuring art aptitude and achievement by the use of three sets of tests, one focusing on art preferences, another on skills of analysis, and the third on art production talent (pp. 170–188). Measurement by means of these tests is considered more adequate because it is grounded in a rationale that includes provisions designed to eliminate the difficulties associated, especially, with the first three shortcomings. Although the rationale advanced by Thomas doesn't resolve the difficulty in the creativity component, there are some other sources that hold promise for improving efforts in this area. The research of Burkhart and his colleagues (Eisner, 1965, pp. 319–320), which was mentioned above, has produced some instruments which can be used to assess different patterns of creativity in relation to student production of art works. At a more general level, the research of investigators in the area of creativity is, according to Khatena (Torrance, 1971, pp. 74–80), contributing to the steady development of instruments for measuring creative behavior which are increasingly less deficient in theoretical rationale, reliability, and validity. Finally, some individual specialists have developed instruments to assess pupil growth in art or music. Eisner has developed an "Art Information Inventory" and an "Art Attitude Inventory," which he has used to assess the knowledge and attitudes of a population of eighth-grade students (Eisner, 1965, pp. 311–314). Colwell has developed a battery of two tests whose content is based on the elementary music program objectives derived from six leading series of music texts, and which are designed to assess pupil skills and understandings in the area of elementary music achievement (Lehman, 1968, pp. 67–68).

Efforts in the area of evaluation are gradually expanding, and new concepts and techniques are being identified and refined. Some educators have adopted a broader concept of behavioral objectives; others have formulated a comprehensive strategy for assessing pupil development; and still others have designed and tested instruments for measuring various aspects of pupil development in the arts and humanities. Hence, efforts to improve evaluation in the arts and humanities have grown, and it is likely that these efforts will continue to grow as more educators become willing to research the impact of their programs on pupil learning.

## SUMMARY STATEMENT: EVALUATION AND THE NEW HUMANISM

The purpose of this paper was to summarize evaluative developments in the arts and humanities in order to determine the extent to which they are consistent with certain requirements associated with the new humanism. Upon investigation, it was found that a few educators in these areas are moving away from the traditional view of education, which is based on a broad liberal arts concept of educational development, and defining their programs in terms of explicit pupil characteristics, learning experiences and programs of instruction, and procedures of evaluation. Evaluative reform is obviously taking place very slowly in these areas, but it is also moving at a snail's pace in many other areas of public education. In this respect, Walberg (1970, pp. 557–570) reviewed the status of research conducted

in connection with the Tyler strategy for curriculum development and concluded that it has not realized its potential as an applied research strategy because of problems encountered by educators in stating objectives, specifying learning experiences, and evaluating pupil learning. Thus, it would be unfair to single out educators in the arts and humanities for criticism in these areas. It is clear, however, that a more sustained effort will be needed in developing specifications for programs of education in these areas if systematic development is to become a reality in the arts and humanities.

Moreover, it is also evident that the effort being expended in relation to evaluative reform in the arts and humanities is uneven in several respects. More attention is being given to specifying pupil objectives and evaluative procedures than to the development of instructional specifications. Educators who are developing explicit frameworks of program specifications are generally doing so as part of some national planning project or in their capacity as university research specialists, and only rarely in cooperation with local school faculties in public school settings, such as was the case in the Eight-Year Study (Smith, Tyler, et al., 1942). Finally, there are also gaps in the sense that systematic development is not generally being carried on in the humanities as a comprehensive area of pupil development, and little work is being done in certain special areas, such as music, drama, and dance. In light of these factors, it seems fair to propose that evaluative reforms must be extended to include all areas in the arts and humanities if cumulative development is to become a vital aspect in revising the entire domain associated with the arts and humanities.

Evaluative reform in terms of the pupil development aspects associated with the new educational humanism is evident in the arts and humanities; but it is taking place both very slowly and at an uneven rate. Moreover, it is apparent that such will continue to be the case until educators in these areas increase their efforts to resolve the conflict that is viewed as existing between science and the arts. A few writers have reexamined this problem and identified some key concepts which can be used to design an educational perspective that would enable the behavioral scientist and the creative artist to unify their educational purposes and patterns of operation. Cornog (1964, pp. 390–392), for example, has argued that science and the arts have in common the search for unity in variety, and that both science and the arts can take as a central point of departure the faith that man can and must remake his world if he is to achieve a better world of things as well as a world of better men. Similarly, Maslow (1970, pp. 29–31) and others have proposed that the new humanistic psychology contains the seeds for generating a more adequate concept of learning, teaching, and education—one which can be used to formulate programs of education that would not only be more relevant but also capable of empirical assessment.

This new concept of education is still more potential than reality. When one turns to the realities of public education, it is found that the public still regards the arts as a trivial part of a child's educational development (Eisner, 1965, p. 324); and many educators both inside and outside the areas that comprise the arts and humanities still support the traditional dichotomy that has been established between science and the arts. Consequently, there is a critical need for a new kind of educator. Such an educator must not only be able to generate a unified vision synthesized from science and the arts; he must also be able to invent strategies for guiding many different kinds of persons, including both educators and laymen, to adapt and implement this vision in terms of their own particular area of concentration. In short, we have many creative artists and creative scientists; but we have all too few creative scholars who can supply us with the insights and actions needed to make the transition from the confusion and conflict of the darkling plain to the humanist world of better men and things.

# 30. Measurement of Noncognitive Objectives

## LEWIS B. MAYHEW

The revitalized interest in affective educational outcomes generates considerable demands on the measurement specialist. For many years this area has lagged far behind others in the development of conceptual schemes and methodologies. A few attempts have been made recently to pull together what we know and to attempt translations of procedures from other disciplines (e.g., Beatty, 1969; Eiss and Harbeck, 1969; Mager, 1968; National Special Media Institutes, 1970; Oppenheim, 1966; and Shaw and Wright, 1967). Lewis B. Mayhew, one of the significant contributors to the field of evaluation, presents in this article an informative and comprehensive overview of available techniques for assessing affective variables. Not only are many techniques identified, but relevant research literature is touched on. Many of the techniques mentioned in this essay are considered in greater detail in other articles in Part IV (e.g., observation in Articles 23 and 25, and role-playing in Article 27).

It is paradoxical that formal education postulates as its most important outcomes such things as attitudes, values, feelings, appreciations and opinions. Yet when it appraises its outcomes it typically seeks evidence of knowledge, the power to manipulate, the ability to think critically and the techniques of analysis and synthesis. In courses in the social studies the objectives of developing citizenship, creating an appreciation of the flow of history, maintaining an open-mindedness about social issues and sensing the relationship between human events and geographical forces are near the top of the list. Courses are justified on the ground that they will continue to have an impact on the lives of students long after the specific knowledge taught has been forgotten. Yet lectures continue to expose facts, discussions to clarify facts and laboratory exercises to uncover new facts. Examinations which really count in the eyes of students are those which require an enormous fund of information which students are expected to arrange in some sort of logical pattern. Even those tests such as entrance examinations to college, which purport to assess transcendent outcomes of schooling seem preoccupied with content and with rational manipulation of information.

There are a number of reasons for this condition. In a democratic society an individual's beliefs are presumed to be his own affair. This faith is even given legal expression in the Federal Constitution and in most state constitutions with respect to religious and political beliefs. In such a society, so long as his overt behavior does not exceed certain gross limits, an individual may like or dislike what he chooses. He may respect or not respect an entire range of activities or beliefs ranging from formal practice of religion, to attitudes toward war, federal aid to education and

Reprinted with permission of the publisher, the National Council for the Social Studies, and Lewis B. Mayhew from an article entitled "Measurement of Noncognitive Objectives in the Social Studies," which appeared in *Evaluation in Social Studies*, ed. H. D. Berg. Thirty–Fifth Yearbook of the NCSS (Washington: NCSS, 1965).

tariff adjustment. He may appreciate great music or the latest forms of jazz. He may believe *Lady Chatterley's Lover* is great literature or pornography. He may believe in equality among the sexes or in a completely male-dominated society. While his parents, teachers or compatriots may not like an individual's choice in such matters, so long as his actual behavior comports with a relatively few standards of conduct the entire gamut of feelings, belief and emotion are exempt from control. This ethos is at the root of the problem of teaching for and evaluating such things as attitudes, values or personal adjustment. Teachers as bearers of the rich American culture are concerned that their students acquire the full culture including the affective components. Yet one essential component is the faith that no one's beliefs should be indoctrinated upon others. Thus teachers claim as objectives those for modifying a wide variety of affections yet they refrain from teaching directly for them and refuse to measure their relative success or failure in accomplishing change.

Unfortunately, even if this ethical dilemma were resolved there are other vexing obstacles to full expression of a concern for noncognitive outcomes of education. In order for broad educational objectives to be effective as conditioners of learning they must be specified as to the exact kind of human behavior they imply. Thus the objective to develop the skills of effective citizenship is virtually useless in aiding a teacher to plan appropriate learning experiences. Similarly the objective to develop skills of critical or rational thinking is unproductive as a conditioner of teaching. Each of these statements must be restated as specific behaviors which can then be the object for modification. Citizenship thus might be defined as knowledge of certain things which can be presented. It can be further defined as ability to assess complicated problems and this again can be taught. Critical thinking can be specified as the ability to define a problem, formulate

hypotheses and make inferences. Each of these is a sufficiently distinct factor that learning materials can be devised and ultimately the success of the learning appraised.

The cognitive outcomes of education can be easily specified. However, the noncognitive or affective outcomes are another matter. First, the very meaning of the terms causes immense difficulty. Does appreciation mean essentially taste and if so whose taste? Or does it mean sensitivity to nuances, but if this is so is a negative sensitivity equal to a positive one? Is dislike as much concern as liking, and if so toward what objects? What are the differences between attitudes, opinions and interests? Do these have a class relationship to each other, and if so which is the higher and which the lower order? Again the term value causes trouble. Are values simply strongly held beliefs, fundamental life principles or basic drives or urges? Virtually every educational discussion finally gets around to the question of values and just as frequently the discussion enters a *cul de sac.*

Even if the terms can eventually be made clear the matter of specifying behaviors remains troublesome. Many of these traits are internalized feelings the existence of which may only be detected by inference. Thus attitudes have sometimes been defined as emotionalized tendencies to act for or against something. Yet the same behavior can with propriety be the basis for inference of conflicting attitudes. A person striking another may be an indication of a positive or a negative attitude. Or an attitude of tolerance for minority groups may be disguised by a need to conform to prevailing social climate. It is difficult further to say precisely what behaviors are reflective of what attitudes because of differences in temperament. Positive attitudes toward a variety of activities may be concealed because of a generally phlegmatic approach to living.

Equally impossible to define as behaviors which can be modified are the other concepts of affection. Appreciation, as commonly used, is so much a part of an individual's own standards of taste that to demand development in another runs the risk of unwarranted indoctrination. One man's art is frequently the pornography of another. Interests may or may not have behavioral concomitants. Further they may be so related to the essential qualities of objects or activities in which interest may be expressed as to preclude modification in the abstract. One demonstrates interest only in connection with something and whether or not the something is significant results from social pressure, temperament, individual taste as well as the historical accidents of time and place.

This difficulty of specifying behavioral meaning to affective traits or factors underlies the extreme difficulty in finding tested learning experiences to develop the traits. Does the teacher cultivate student interest in citizenship by exposing students to the activities of a political ward worker or is this as likely to destroy interest? If contact does foster interest is there optimum intensity of contact? How does one change an attitude so that it really conditions a person's later behavior? There have been, for example, well-recorded instances of changed attitudes toward cheating as measured by verbal statements, yet the same students cheated when given the opportunity (Corey, 1937).

Values prove an especially perplexing matter. Perhaps Freud's greatest contribution to education was to demonstrate the significance which earliest childhood experience has had on value patterns. One can also theorize that the conditions of birth affect an individual's life pattern which involves his values, or that breast feeding might have physiological implications for both mother and child and their subsequent relationships to each other and to the world. If these early years are so important is there any hope that real, lasting changes in values can be made by formal education? The evidence on this matter is spotty. But if the possibility does exist what techniques for change are available? Later reference will be made to the trait of authoritarianism which is found variously in the entire population. If one wishes to change an authoritarian person to a less rigid individual does one place him in contact with structured or unstructured situations? Does one change the authoritarian by making him more or less comfortable?

Since adequate assessment always depends on the adequacy of teaching, this further difficulty does not require extensive elaboration. If one cannot define appreciation, exemplify it as human behavior nor select relevant learning to facilitate its growth how can one tell whether or not the growth has taken place? Even if definition and specification were possible the problem of appropriate evidence and proper inference remains. Assessment invariably demands observing a sample of a particular kind of behavior. The behavior may be a physical action, speaking, writing or something else. After it has been observed as reliably as possible the significance of the behavior must be determined. Both of these tasks pose serious problems which are also involved in the cognitive outcomes of education. An educational objective might be to have students write effectively. Logically one would judge that the best kind of evidence of this ability is student writing. But when one attempts to observe student writing reliably one encounters the first of several difficulties. One finds that one judges the same paper differently on two consecutive readings. Further, several people each judge the same paper differently. A student paper which is worth an A to one reader is worth only an F to another. However, this problem of reliability is not the most severe one to be encountered. The purpose of the writing is to determine if the student has learned to write effectively. It is a sample from which an inference must be drawn. Numerous experiments have shown, however, that a single paper is not an effective index. (Unpublished report prepared by Paul Diederich, Educational Testing Service, Princeton, N.J.) A given student may be a consistently better or worse writer than his single test theme would suggest; thus an inference as to his skill is highly questionable.

The difficulty is compounded when attempts are made to infer achievement of noncognitive outcomes on the basis of observation. An observer may hear much complaining among a student body and infer low morale only to discover that it is normal that, in the few weeks after Christmas, students complain and that actually the student body has a consistently high morale. Or one may judge on the basis of an attitude test that students like the humanities only to discover that they stay away in large numbers from lectures and concerts.

To these general obstacles to adequate assessment should be added several technical ones. Preparing devices which will elicit reliable information about affective traits is a tricky undertaking. Not only must one worry about the normal ambiguities of the language, but deeper psychological meaning as well. One well-respected personality inventory contains the statement "I like tall women." The authors were unable to predict that response to this statement was strongly indicative of a position along a masculinity-femininity continuum (Hathaway and McKinley, 1943). Yet if one is to build proper measuring devices one must anticipate that a response to a particular statement will reveal feeling about the object being considered.

Further, as one attempts to assess outcomes of education, one makes the greatest progress when one has formulated a general theory within which evidence can be interpreted. Unless there is a general theory to account for the various kinds of affective outcomes information gathered does not seem really significant. There are several thousand studies of attitudes and opinions described in the professional literature. Many of these are based on newly developed tests or inventories. Yet with the exception of a relatively few the results from all of these studies do not add up to accepted generalization. These few which do are the ones which involve not only careful instrumentation but a broad theory as well. The California studies resulting in *The Authoritarian Personality* (Adorno et al., 1950) have been widely significant partly because of the theoretical formulations which attached meaning to the results. There have been too few efforts to develop such fertile theory and too many studies attempted without it.

In spite of these problems and difficulties the importance of affective outcomes of education persists and some small progress is being made to assess them. Particularly since the publication of Philip Jacobs' *Changing Values in College* (1957), which was sharply critical of the lack of impact colleges seemed to have on student attitude and values, there have been intensified efforts at assessment. As disquieting news came concerning lack of stern value commitment of American soldiers in Korea the schools have begun to study their efforts more carefully. As criticism of American taste and behavior has emerged from the pens of such people as Vance Packard (1959), who judged us as a nation of status seekers, or Eugene Burdick and William Lederer (1958), who thought the conduct abroad of most of us left much to be desired, renewed attention has been given character building and measurement of its outcomes. . . .

## STAGES IN ATTITUDE MEASUREMENT

To judge the present state of the art of measurement of affective outcomes of education it may be well to review some of the landmarks created over the years. One of the first systematic attempts to study attitude was that of L. L. Thurstone, who, at the University of Chicago, developed a series of tests of attitudes toward various objects (Thurstone and Chave, 1929). The general theory on which he operated is that attitudes are tendencies to act for or against something and that it is possible to create a scale of attitude from being completely for something to being completely against it. Thurstone reasoned that it was possible to create a series of statements about an object each of which would represent a discrete position along a single continuum. He created this series by first accumulating every statement he could which reflected feeling about the object being studied. After he had obtained several hundred he would ask professional judges to sort the statements into piles ranging from the most to the least favorable about the object. When a number of persons had done the sorting, the degree of agreement among them as to the position of each statement was computed. The eleven or twenty-one statements seeming to represent equal distances along the continuum would be selected and these became the instrument with which to measure attitudes. Students were asked simply to mark those statements with which they agreed. Since the ranking of the statements resulted in a numerical value for each statement ranging from 1 to 11 it was possible to compute an attitude score for each student taking the test. For example, a student might have checked as agreeing with statements 1, 4, 7, 9, and 11 which had the values $1 = 6$, $4 = 8.5$, $7 = 9$, $9 = 2.5$, and $11 = 5$. The student's score would be 6.2 or slightly above the median of the attitude scale.

Thurstone created a number of these scales assessing such things as attitudes toward war, evolution, church and God. They had a number of advantages. They were short, easily scored and they resulted in a single score which could be compared with other variables. Further, they seemed reliable in that student's scores were consistent from one administration to the next. They also reflected educational experience relevant to the attitude object. Thus an intense study of genetics resulted in a shift of score of attitude toward evolution. However, they also had serious weaknesses. Each scale was expensive to produce, requiring several hundred hours of sorting just to select the appropriate statements for the scale. Further, each scale assumed that attitudes were uncomplicated feelings along a single continuum. Gradually evidence began to accumulate which made this assumption questionable. Lastly the scales measured verbal adherence to an attitude position which frequently was not related to actual behavior. The classic study revealed a sharp inconsistency between student attitude toward cheating and actual cheating when provided an opportunity to do so (Corey, 1937).

The problems of the Thurstone scales stimulated several other lines of investigation. H. H. Remmers and his students at Purdue University applied the Thurstone technique of creating a scale. However, instead of focusing on a single attitude object they centered their statements on a class of objects. Thus they created attitude scales toward any social institution, any physical activity or any subject. The statements on the scale could apply with equal relevance to any example of the general class. The scale measuring attitudes toward any social institution could be used with respect to the family, church, school or army.

After meeting in part the problem of expense by creating a few scales which could be used in many specific situations, Remmers made important contributions to establishing the validity of his instruments. By creating carefully controlled conditions he established that attitudes change as a result of explicit educational experience and that these changes persist over an extended period. For example, he measured attitude of students toward clean farming before and after study of a Department of Agriculture booklet on soil erosion. His subjects shifted their attitudes and the shifts remained six and nine months later. Also Remmers established validity by showing how different groups would score differently on a relevant attitude scale. His classic experiment involved administration of a scale of attitude toward Sunday church attendance to

Seventh Day Adventists and other Protestant church members. The results were expressed in a completely bimodal curve with no over-lap. No member of the Seventh Day Adventist Church scored above the median point of attitude toward Sunday church attendance and no member of the other Protestant churches scored below that point.

Likert sought to make preparation of attitude scales easier by moving in a different direction (Likert, 1932). He developed a key which could be used in connection with any attitude statement. The parts of the key were: strongly approve, approve, undecided, disapprove and strongly disapprove. He would then use this key with a number of attitude statements and establish a total attitude score by weighting the response to each statement from 5 for strongly approve to 1 for strongly disapprove. With a total score as a criterion he could then determine which statements from his entire list correlated most highly with the total score. This was done by examining which statements were agreed to by high total scoring students and which by low scorers. Presumably statements agreed to more by low scorers than by high scorers were invalid statements and were discarded. Through this process of statement-or item-analysis he refined an attitude test which would discriminate between those favorable and opposed to the object being studied.

One of the most widely used tests is the Allport-Vernon *Study of Values* (Allport, Vernon, and Lindzey, 1959). This is of special interest not only because of the enormous amount of research which has been done on it but also because of the technique of forcing responses. Allport and Vernon started with a theory that there were six types of men who could be distinguished by the kinds of beliefs they held. A series of statements were prepared, each presumed to be reflective of one of these types. Students given the scale were asked to select between statements indicative of different types of men. By forcing students to select between some-

times apparent equally desirable values, a score in favor of one or several resulted. Since this test made use of a principle of forced responses it was impossible for students to score high in all categories. Enhanced emphasis on one resulted in decreased expressed concern on others. The test has been criticized on this score and yet it would appear to be highly realistic since value choices only become important to human beings when conflict between choices exists.

A major milestone in the measurement of attitudes and values came during World War II when the Office of Strategic Services became interested in assessment of personality and the Office of Strategic Services became concerned about problems of troop morale (Office of Strategic Services, 1948). Out of the search for men who could operate behind the enemy lines came methods for creating situations, judging the reactions of men to these conditions and finally making inferences regarding the traits these reactions revealed. For example individuals were placed in a series of stressful or tranquilizing conditions and their reactions observed and recorded. Later as experience accumulated these situations were simply described in writing and subjects were asked what their reaction would be. While results were not completely satisfying they did suggest the possibility of refining descriptions of situations and alternative reactions so that reasonable inferences were supportable.

The major studies of the American soldier in World War II provide a wealth of technical experience for the measurement of affective traits and behaviors. The sampling techniques which utilized serial numbers, the validation of opinion surveys by later morale studies once decisions were made and newer methods for establishing attitudes scales are illustrative.

Assessment of affective matters was advanced considerably by the work of Adorno and others (1950) in a study of the authoritarian personality. This group of California investigators started to study the dimensions of anti-Semitism. They early discovered that anti-Semitism was only one facet of a personality which was inclined to be highly suspicious of all out-group members. The individual who was anti-Semitic was also likely to be against labor, foreigners, modern art and liberal causes. A scale was then developed called the F-scale which solicited opinions about a number of statements. These were carefully worded so as to appear as plausible beliefs but which actually elicited response from deeply embedded psychological forces. For example items such as "Obedience and respect for authority are the most important virtues children should learn" or "If people would talk less and work more, everybody would be better off" were judged to reveal conventionalism. Statements such as "A person who has bad manners, habits, and breeding can hardly expect to get along with decent people" or "Homosexuals are hardly better than criminals and ought to be severely punished" reveal authoritarian aggression.

An important part of this study was the validation of the F-scale through intensive clinical studies of individuals who scored at either extreme of the postulated continuum of authoritarianism. It was found that these people could be described rather precisely in psychiatric terms and with considerable consistency; hence the presumption that what the scale measured had an existence in reality.

The theory of the authoritarian personality and the theory underlying situational tests were employed in studying the affective outcomes of general education in the Cooperative Study of Evaluation in General Education (Dressel and Mayhew, 1954). Two instruments were created, on The Inventory of Beliefs and Problems in Human Relations. The Inventory of Beliefs purported to do two things. By presenting students with 120 statements of belief before and after an educational experience it obtained a measure of the simple change in belief patterns. By constructing the statements to contain

psychological dimensions the Inventory obtained information about personality structure having relevance for education. It was found for example that students high in authoritarianism were uncomfortable in discussions, in studying abstract subjects and in independent study. They liked power- or status-centered vocations and were inclined to be rigid in their thought processes. The disquieting element about the use of the Inventory of Beliefs was that it appeared to measure traits which did not change appreciably during several years of college.

The second instrument was somewhat less successful and less widely used. The Problems in Human Relations presented students with a series of conflict situations. For each the student was asked to pick a response from five, scaled from that reflecting the most to the least regard for human personality. An attempt was made to validate the test by asking such people as residence hall counselors to judge students' regard for others. These judgments were compared to scores on the test. While the results were not clear-cut the relationships were sufficiently positive to suggest further efforts to develop appropriate situations.

Two of the people who worked on the Inventory of Beliefs extended the theory and combined it with another strain of thought to create another development in assessment (Pace and Stern, 1958). Pace and Stern noted that authoritarian students seemed quite uncomfortable in some institutions but quite content and successful in others. Apparently institutions had characteristics which were similar to personality characteristics in people. The school environment thus was seen to have a press or an effect on students which intensified or modified forces within the personality. To assess this they created an instrument consisting of many statements which one could make about a particular school or college. For example "Students here would never get hoarse from excitement at an athletic contest," or "The general atmosphere of this place is relaxed and unhurried." Students were asked to indicate which of these statements were like and unlike their school. Administration of the test revealed wide differences among colleges which were consistent with differences detected by sophisticated observers. At the same time Pace and Stern developed a personality measure to try to discover what kinds of students were most successful at what kinds of institutions. The advances represented by this effort have given researchers a potent new tool in the study of education. It is being used widely in an effort to study institutional differences at the Center for the Study of Higher Education at the University of California.

Another outgrowth of the authoritarian personality studies were the studies conducted at the Mellon Institute of the students at Vassar. Under the direction of Nevitt Sanford, who had been involved with *The Authoritarian Personality,* a group of researchers studied girls as they proceeded through four years of college (Sanford et al., 1956). They found that through an elaborate design involving paper-and-pencil tests, biographical data, interviews and use of participant observers a remarkably consistent profile of student attitudes and beliefs could be obtained. Further and more significantly they obtained evidence that fundamental personality structures did *change* during the college years and that these changes were reflected in different attitudes, values and opinions. If an institution wishes to use a sufficiently broad battery of instruments and to probe affective concerns deeply enough it can discover significant changes taking place. The Vassar studies also suggested the heavy expense to an institution which wanted to study affective outcomes of education.

It is quite clear from the discussion thus far that assessment of noncognitive outcomes of education has moved from assumptions of the unidimensionality to assumption of the high complexity of attitudes, values, and opinions. More recent refinements have sought to explore some of these complexities or have sought to overcome problems of method upon which earlier studies failed.

One important source of information is the opinion poll. After the fiasco of the Literary Digest poll of the presidential election of 1932 polling of opinions fell into disrepute. However, gradually better methods of sampling and better techniques of interviewing were created until polls became if anything too well-regarded. The presidential election of 1948 again raised questions about the validity of polling when the major agencies inaccurately predicted the election of Thomas Dewey. More careful analysis of those results, however, suggests that the opinion poll, as with any other psychometric device, is effective only for the tasks for which it was designed. It is when an instrument is misused in inappropriate situations that stark failure results. As a measure of the existing belief about something the poll can have considerable value. As a predictive device of how people will believe at some point in the future it begins to show weakness (Stouffer, 1953).

Another relatively recent development in detecting attitudes or values is sociometry. Although J. L. Moreno (1941) first advanced the idea prior to World War I the method has been most utilized since the second world war. The method, overly simplified, consists of measuring the degree of attraction or rejection among members of groups of people. This is done by asking which of each member of a group the individual would most, and least, like to have in a specified kind of relationship. It has had application in schoolrooms and other groups to chart the interrelationships within the group. It has been used to determine attitudes toward racial or ethnic groups by asking respondents how they would relate to members of various minority groups. It has also been used administratively to select authorized leaders from among natural leaders of a group.

A major methodological development in the assessment of affective outcomes are the projective techniques first used clinically but which have gradually been adapted for classroom use. Since individuals frequently hold attitudes, interests or fundamental values which are so deeply embedded in their personalities that they cannot be elicited by direct inquiry other means have been established. Especially is this so since some of the most covert of feelings may well be the most powerful motives in an individual's life. With respect to these, projective devices (1) reveal suppressed or repressed attitudes, (2) provide information on the genesis of attitudes and (3) aid in modifying attitudes. In order to achieve these purposes several assumptions are necessary.

1. All behavior manifestations are expressive of an individual's personality.
2. Ambiguous material in a projective device enables the subject to give information about himself otherwise withheld.
3. Each response is caused and is never chance.
4. Individuals organize their responses in terms of their own motivation, perceptions, attitudes, ideas and emotions.

While there are many examples of projective devices, to be effective any one must set a plausible task in which (1) the student will seek to do well, (2) there are sufficient ambiguities to allow individual differences to be demonstrated and (3) there is opportunity to load the situation with the attitude content in which the teacher is interested.

These principles are all illustrated by a number of well-known devices. The Thematic Apperception Test consists of a series of pictures vaguely reflecting human beings in varying situations. The subject is asked to create a story interpreting the scene in the picture. Presumably his interpretations will be projections of his own basic feelings. The sentence completion test presents students with fragments of sentences with instructions to complete the statements. It is theorized that how people finish such fragments as (1) If children ———, (2) Slow learners in our schools are ———, (3) Most Negroes ———, (4) The mentally ill are ———, will tell considerably about their own basic attitudes. While this device is relatively easy to construct it is tremendously difficult to interpret. Interpretation is made doubly difficult since the manifest content of responses to sentence-completion exercises varies radically from one administration to the next. Even the basic attitudes responses seem to reveal inconsistencies.

Related to the sentence completion tests are the various association tests. These may employ words, color, tactile or sound material. The words are presented to students with instructions to respond with the first word to come to mind. Presumably the speed prevents censorship and the responses are seen evolving into a meaningful pattern.

It would be possible to enumerate other studies and devices which have been used in research concerning attitudes, values and personal adjustment. There are available check lists, inventories, biographical data sheets, personality tests, tests of judgment or taste and intricate clinical devices. Generally however they will reflect one of the major approaches which have been described. It now becomes important to determine whether or not the classroom teacher, limited though his time be, can use either available instruments or else can create his own.

## AFFECTIVE TERMS AND CONCEPTS

Before any meaningful study can or should be attempted the definition of traits needs some clarification. While at present there is no general agreement among researchers as to precise meanings for the more frequently used terms, there is probably some uniformity in judging the relative complexity of affective traits.

At the lowest level of complexity and emotional intensity would be opinions or beliefs. These are statements of how an individual perceives a given segment of reality. One can ask how a person believes an election will turn out, whether or not he believes disarmament is feasible or whether or not he feels incest is contrary to natural law. Although the forces which give rise to opinion may be deep and powerful the inventorying of opinion is not extremely difficult. Since opinion is how a person perceives reality it is the most closely related to the familiar functions of teachers in dealing with cognitive matters. A student's opinion may be that acquired characteristics are inherited, or that the church has proven hurtful to civilization, or that Russia has no intention of observing the terms of international agreements. Each of these may be examined cognitively and presumably if enough evidence is presented the opinion will change. Since opinions are so close to the most generally accepted function of the teacher, assessment of opinion will be the most widely used evaluative technique of affective outcomes of education.

Possibly the next most simple trait is an attitude. This has been defined as an emotionalized tendency, organized through experience to act for or against something. At once the problem is more complicated because of the elements of direction for or against and because of the varying intensities of emotional force which are possible. The study of attitudes is also complicated by the fact that it is a tendency which can be studied only through inference of observed behavior. Attitude may exist intensively within an individual yet never be noticed because other facets of personality deny expression which would reveal the tendency.

Interests may also be defined as latent predispositions. However, for purposes of this analysis they are considered as the expressed tendencies of an individual when he is free to make choices. So long as an individual has choices open to him interest is that force or tendency which leads him in one direction rather than another. The features which distinguish interest from attitude are the element of action and the absence of the element of liking. Attitudes can be assessed without reference to more than one object. The question is solely, Do you or do you not like, or favor or approve of this? Interest requires comparison. Given the choice between watching television or reading a book, which will you do? Further attitudes demand feeling or emotion while interests can be decided on the basis of rational factors alone.

Now obviously this is far from a mutually exclusive taxonomy. The line between attitudes and interests is far from clear. The attempt is made and should be made if we are serious in wanting to know what affective effects schooling has on students.

Once the matter of interests are left the meaning of terms becomes even more vague. Appreciations can be defined as simply a particular manifestation of attitudes—that is, a predilection in favor or against something. This meaning certainly underlies popular usage of the term, "I don't know anything about art but I know what I like." However, it would seem that a more productive way would be to assign additional significance to the term. Appreciation might require at least three elements: (1) direction—or for-ness or against-ness; (2) intensity—degree of emotion; and (3) sensitivity—knowledge and understanding. Such an analysis makes the task of studying appreciations more taxing but it may also make the study more rewarding.

Another affective trait which appears to be growing in significance not only in popular speech but in professional literature as well is the trait of empathy. This can be defined as a feeling of identity with something or someone. The matter of feeling for or against has no particular relevance here; hence the trait is distinguishable from an attitude. One may very well identify with someone and be highly resentful of the person. Or one may feel identity with all humanity and have a completely ambivalent attitude toward people. This is not to imply any low educational significance to empathy. Indeed some of the most central learnings take place through identification with some model. The infant begins to be aware of his own characteristics through identification with the mother. This sex role is first formed through feeling with one parent or the other.

The last trait is the most difficult of all to comprehend and to assess. This is the matter of values. Values certainly involve all of the other factors thus far discussed but apparently have or should have a unique entity as well. Perhaps the best way of describing values is to call them feelings for objects of personal significance for the individual. As such they are of greater complexity than simple attitude, although attitude may be involved. A value is an attachment of some of the regard which one holds for himself in his most unique existence to something outside himself. Thus the scientist holds the value of truth in the same high regard he has for his own unique personality. The religious value implies a similar equating of God and self. In this connection it should be indicated that this regard may be equated to some idealized self as frequently as to one's actual self. Thus an individual who really feels himself to be utterly base may still value things highly because they are equated with the self he would like to be or believes he should be.

## MEASUREMENT DEVICES

Definition of traits is one essential step in evaluation of affective outcomes of education. Such distinctions can among other things suggest which traits are and which are not available to modification and study by the school. . . . For this article then it is enough to reiterate that before teachers can attempt to evaluate they must understand what specific behaviors are involved. Only those can be observed and only those can serve as bases for adequate inference. Once behaviors are made explicit there are a number of devices which teachers can use to accumulate examples of student demonstration of them. This is the problem of instrumentation.

Teachers in the social studies will most frequently be concerned with student opinion. Teachers wish to know what their students believe about the United Nations, the possibilities of slum clearance, the two-party system, inflation and a number of other similar subjects. There will obviously be no available instruments for such a variety of topics nor could any but the most affluent schools afford to purchase them if there were. Teachers can, however, construct relatively simple devices, administer and score them, interpret the results to students and move on to the next topic. In preparing the device several cautions should be kept in mind.

1. Understand clearly the object or its attribute about which opinions are to be solicited. Ambiguities first creep into questions when the writer is unclear himself as to the dimensions of the topic. In this connection the more specific attributes of an object or topic are susceptible to more precise opinion measurement. Thus the General Assembly rather than the United Nations and the United Nations rather than international government should be the objects of questions.
2. Be careful in the words used. Many of the words popularly used to determine opinion are too obscure to elicit exact responses. Words selected should point directly to the attribute concerning which response is desired. Thus avoid a question, "What is your opinion about the United Nations?" Rather use a form which allows students to respond "yes," "no" or "don't know" to statements such as "The United Nations has prevented or limited war," "The United

States does not use its veto power," "UNESCO is filled with Communist sympathizers."

3. Do not prepare more questions than can reasonably be used and the responses interpreted. A tendency of people who begin to design a check on opinions is to become overly complicated. Opinions are important and should be checked but the assessment should not be more complicated than the specific opinion warrants. In a unit on the American political party system there are not many opinions which can reasonably be affected by the teacher. These and these only are the ones to study.

4. After preparing questions let them sit for a few days; then revise them. Normally ambiguities creep into the initial writing which remain undetected if revision is attempted at once. A few days later they appear quite clearly. After revision it always helps to try the questions out on others. A few students, colleagues or one's family can spot weaknesses which are invisible to the writer.

5. After administering a set of questions to students, tabulate the responses, discuss the results in class and leave the matter. Much of the assessment of opinion has high teaching or learning potential. It should be exploited.

Developing questionnaires concerning the more complicated affective qualities requires more time and effort. Probably for most classroom exercises the Likert method is most convenient (Corey, 1943; Likert, 1932). Prepare a list of statements believed to reflect attitude, refine them and administer to some students. Then score each paper with five being assigned to the most favorable response down to one for the least. Then tabulate the responses on each question for the upper half of the papers and for the lower half. The questions on which there is favorable response by most of the total high scorers and few of the low scorers are the ones to be included in the final form of the inventory.

There are, however, other techniques. If one wishes to obtain a precise ranking of attitude toward a relatively few objects, the paired comparison technique is appropriate. This involves pairing each object with every other object and in each event asking the student to select the one he favors. For example, pair a picture of a Ford, Plymouth and Chevrolet with each other. A stable ranking will result. A more gross ranking can be obtained by asking students to number the rank order of their preferences from a list of objects. An even more gross ranking can be obtained by asking students to select the three, four or five preferred objects from a larger list. Tabulation of the results reveals the pattern of preferences if such exists.

A more complicated device which can be used is the technique of forced responses. Present students with sets of three statements and require that they select the one they like best and the one they like least. Rather extreme statements can be included in this method which still will yield useful information. Thus one might present a series of sets comparable to (1) Communism, (2) Fascism, (3) Anarchy. No one is satisfactory and without the element of force would not receive many takers. Forcing allows the questions to elicit underlying motivations.

An important source of information about affective factors is the interview, either group or individual. The interview is a tool which is ineffective for predictive purposes, but can be highly useful to obtain information. It can be structured, in which the questions are well worked out in advance, or unstructured, in which the dynamics of the interview situation determine the flow of question and answer. Each has potentiality, but the more structured will result in more reliable information.

The big problem of interviewing is in recording the information once it is obtained. If a mechanical recording device is used, the expense of transcription is high. If the interviewer records in writing while the interview is taking place he may miss nuances of meaning, and if he waits to record until afterwards he may forget important elements.

A frequently overlooked value of interviews is their virtue as a source for ideas for later questionnaires. Some research workers now routinely conduct unstructured interviews before beginning the more precise task of formulating written questions. The importance of this device lies in exposing an issue in the terms and language of the people for whom the questionnaire is intended. There is a gap in how an adult teacher thinks about a problem and how a student thinks about it.

Even more difficult than the interview but sometimes more productive is observation. If the teacher can observe a group of students working on a topic rich in attitude material, and if these observations can be recorded, some fruitful inferences are possible. If social science teachers make use of small-group projects, field exercises and the like, observing student reaction can tell much about modification of feeling. It should be warned, however, that teachers should not be too convinced that they can tell what is in a student's mind by noting his external behavior. The evidence from classrooms is clear that teachers cannot tell which students are and which are not engaging in problem-solving actively. However, if teachers will observe carefully, record completely and then form inferences as hypotheses which need other verification, some insight can be gained.

Observation by a member of a group who can still somehow objectify himself from the group has proven of value. One of the major studies of character development in colleges and universities of the past several years made considerable use of the participant observer. Two recent college graduates spent varying lengths of time on college campuses, meeting with students, attending class and living in the residence halls. At night they would record their impressions and observations. After a number of such visits their notes became the data upon which the interpretation of changes in values were based.

Another device which can make the observation a more effective technique is the daily log. A teacher who is interested in changes in affective outcomes should observe closely during each class period. Immediately after the class he should write down everything he saw or *felt* which was relevant to the trait. These notes are then put away until the full study has been completed. The reason for this last is that one's previous notes can contaminate the next day's impressions. It should be stressed that regularity is essential for the log to be successful. Only the accumulation of many observations can truly provide data for inference.

If teachers require written work from students a potent tool is available for the study of attitudes, values and the like. Theme topics of controversial nature can be assigned. When read with a view to detecting attitude rather than substance they can reveal a great deal about how students feel. Again caution is in order. The teacher is not here concerned with the beliefs of any one student. Indeed, widely inaccurate judgments could be made if this were attempted. But the papers of an entire class will reveal in broad terms the central tendency of opinion or attitude.

The questionnaire, interview, study of documents and observation are in reality the only ways teachers have of learning about student belief. There are, however, devices which can refine the information obtained or allow deeper material to be elicited. Frequently individuals who have deep-seated feelings about something will disguise these or conceal them in all conventional situations. If one were to ask such a person a relevant question one would obtain a conventionally approved answer which might or might not be true. Approaching the same individual through some sort of disguised query can come closer to revealing what actual feelings are. Several methods of disguise have been successfully employed.

Writing questions for an inventory which are ostensibly factual but which in reality are attitudinal is one way. This is illustrated by asking small children to draw a picture of a half-dollar. Children from marginal economic backgrounds will tend to magnify the size of the dollar while children better off draw the coin to smaller scale. Students who come from laboring families will judge the salaries of management higher and the wages of workers lower than they actually are. Careful search in social science content can yield hundreds of such kinds of information which will yield attitude information.

For more refined effort, statistical analysis of the functioning of some items can produce a list of questions which do discriminate between those who do and do not favor a certain thing but which have no face validity. A classic example is a teacher rating scale developed at Purdue University which is highly discriminating but on which even the most astute students cannot tell *a priori* how they rated an instructor. The essential in making such an analysis is to have a stable criterion and a large enough number of questions so that a suitable number of questions can be found which have high discriminating power but low face validity.

Role-playing and the psycho-drama are two refinements for observation. They each consist of asking students to act out someone, usually in a conflict situation, without knowing what lines should be spoken. Students quickly throw themselves into the spirit of the drama and as they imagine what lines their roles require they project much of their own feelings. Teachers can place white students in the roles of Negroes, Gentiles in the roles of Jews and children of management in the roles of workers. Since these are projective devices which uncover deeply held feelings teachers should use care in how

they employ the devices. It is possible to do considerable harm by bringing to the surface beliefs which students are unready to face.

A variation of projective device which can be used in a written form is a self-ideal self-checklist. This presents students with a number of descriptions of a person. He is asked on one day to indicate those traits descriptive of him. Another time he is asked to indicate how others see him and on still another time how he would like to be. The same device can be used about other things. A number of adjectives descriptive of a school can be presented and students asked to pick out those most like the school. At another time they are to select how the faculty might see the school and at still another how parents might view it. The object of this exercise is of course to detect variation in how students believe various types of people perceive reality.

Psychoanalysis has proven the importance of early memories in shaping the attitude of people. Classroom teachers can apply some of the same theory for evaluation purposes. A teacher might ask all students to think back and describe themselves when they were much younger. Or the teacher might ask for an autobiography written as though it were twenty years in the future. In either event students reveal much about their affective selves as they select from the immense range of material available the data with which to construct an earlier or later image of themselves.

One last device will be mentioned which has had considerable use in the study of a variety of behaviors. This is the critical incident technique which was devised originally to select fighter pilots in World War II, but which has been used in judging teaching, speaking and student values. It consists of asking a number of people to tell something they had seen recently which was an effective incident of the behavior being considered and something which was an ineffective example. If a large number of such incidents are collected they will reveal the dimensions of a particular problem. It has been used successfully in studying student values. Students were asked to relate something they had seen recently which was a good act and something they had seen which was a bad act. This study was done of students in elementary school, high school and college and revealed significantly different standards of values at each level of schooling.

Such then are some of the techniques available for the study of the affective outcomes of education. There still remain some of the issues which were raised in the first section of this article. These can best be answered by presenting a general stance toward these concerns.

It is not likely that schools will forsake their concern for values. Indeed the fact of schools existing is an affirmation of a value, as is the act of teaching. The belief in knowledge is attitudinal, as is the faith in a particular form of government. No one can teach in a value-free situation. The selection of some materials over others involves values, as do the responses given individual students. Education would not be significant if it did not concern itself with attitudes, values and beliefs.

Saying this does not imply that the problems involved in this concern are lightly overcome. They will persist and will only yield to intensive effort by teachers and research workers. They can be gradually solved and information can be discovered which will prove useful. Some ten years ago the first *Taxonomy of Educational Objectives* was developed for cognitive outcomes (Bloom *et al.*, 1956). A second *Taxonomy*, this time for affective outcomes, has recently been published (Krathwohl, 1964). The time lag between the two was caused by the sheer difficulty in understanding these traits.

Belief in educational concern for attitudes and values can be held consistently with a democratic faith only if the concern is freed from sanctions. It is possible to be vitally interested in the attitudinal outcomes of education and to study these with a view to modifying practice. However, evaluation of affective traits must be separated from grades, which are the academic sanctions available to teachers. To make this separation teachers must realize that grades are only an indication of a small portion of a student's growth in school. They are important because among its other functions the school is a certifying agency of society. But they are not all-important. The school can rightfully hope and expect its students to modify values, change attitudes and develop new appreciations. It should study to determine whether or not it is successful. However, it cannot reward nor punish students who do not do so any more than a physician should reward or punish parents for following or disregarding his advice.

One last caution should be advanced. There are many things which schools can claim to affect. Its resources will never allow it to succeed in all of these. It can be argued that the school would become a more effective agency if it would be more parsimonious in its claims. If it did reduce the number of stated objectives it could at the same time study its achievement of those it retains. Teachers frequently claim they couldn't possibly assess all of the outcomes the school attempts. They commonly follow this by refraining from assessing any. If the number of outcomes with which they explicitly concern themselves were reduced the perfect excuse would be gone. As all teachers seek to understand what traits they are affecting and to what degree they do so the total educational process can be improved.

## 31. Techniques for Evaluating the College Environment

### JOHN W. MENNE

The teaching-learning process takes place in a physical-social-psychological environment. Any attempt to assess the effectiveness of a curriculum must take into account the context of the learner, teacher, and learning. Such a task requires the application of some fairly sophisticated multi-variate methodologies. Three general approaches to college environmental assessment are described in this article. The three approaches involve evaluating (1) institutional characteristics, such as number of students, budgets, number of books in the library, (2) student perceptions of such factors as quality of social activities, rules and regulations, and characteristics of the faculty, and (3) actual student behavior, such as number of hours spent in class or library. In addition to describing these methods, Menne also comments on (1) their applicability, and (2) criteria useful in their development. Another significant contribution to the environmental assessment literature has recently been made by Stern (1970).

Three basic approaches have been used in studying the college environment.

**Objective Institutional Characteristics** The first approach is concerned with objective, readily-measured institutional characteristics—number of students, percentage of males, tuition, operating budget per student, number of library books, etc. Astin and Holland (1961) appear to be the first to use this approach, and its development has been reported in a series of studies by Astin, (e.g., 1962, 1963, 1965b). Richards et al. (1966) have reported a thorough study of the junior colleges using this "objective" method.

In this procedure a large number of readily-measured "objective" variables (33 for Astin, 36 for Richards) are reduced by factor analysis to a smaller number of

Reprinted and abridged with permission of the publisher and John W. Menne from the *Journal of Educational Measurement*, **4** (1967), pp. 219–225.

relatively independent scales or factors which are labeled in a way which, hopefully, communicates the overall meaning of the variables influencing the particular scale or factor. Institutional scores are scaled for a large number (representative sample) of institutions. Astin's procedure has been called the Environmental Assessment Technique (EAT).

**Subjective Student Perceptions** The second approach is concerned with student perceptions of the institutional environment. Pace and Stern (1958) appear to have originated this approach with the development of the College Characteristics Index (CCI) from which Pace (1963) developed his College and University Environment Scales (CUES). Using a similar approach Hutchins (Hutchins, 1962; Hutchins & Nonneman, 1966) has developed and used an instrument (the Medical School Environment Inventory, MSEI) specifically designed for the study of medical schools, and Fanslow (1966) has developed the College Environment Inventory for Women (CEIW).

In this approach students are asked to respond whether an item does or does not pertain to their institution. The items relate to various aspects of the college environment—e.g., social activities, classroom and extra-classroom performance and procedures, school rules, cultural activities, faculty characteristics. The items then are reduced to a small number of scales, usually by factor analysis. The scales are labeled in such a way as to communicate the overall meaning of the item responses which influenced the particular scale. Again institutional scale scores are derived for a representative sample of U.S. institutions. The scale scores can be profiled.

**Observable Behaviors** The third approach is less developed than the first two. It measures specific observable student behaviors such as time spent in study, number of social activities per week, or attendance at a concert. Astin (1965a) has indicated he is working along this line with his instrument entitled the Inventory of College Activities (ICA), and has reported a study focused on classroom behaviors (Astin, 1965c). A similiar study at the University of Massachusetts was reported by Schumer and Stanfield (1966). In this study an inventory of 192 questions pertaining to observable student behaviors was factor analyzed into eight relatively independent factors thought to describe the institutional environment.

Astin (1965a) believes that all three approaches are needed to describe completely the institutional environment. But the only studies so far reported in the literature have investigated the correlations between the scales or factors of various assessment devices and also the relationship of such scores to measures of student personality (McFee, 1961).

## EVALUATION OF THE THREE APPROACHES

In any evaluation it is necessary to define the purpose. If it is to *compare* institutions, these intentions would be achieved when there is a relatively stable and accurate set of scale scores available for the majority of our college institutions. The interested person can then look up the rankings of the institutions he wishes to compare. Astin (1965b) has made this type of information available. However this approach may not be sufficiently sensitive to environment changes which do occur. For example Hutchins and Nonneman (1966) have shown that the rankings of the medical institutions on various objective variables tend to remain quite stable, and recent rankings are very similar to rankings going back as far as 1910. New buildings, new budgets, increased faculty or students may change ranking temporarily, but will there be a permanent change in any comparison to other institutions?

On the other hand, an environmental change such as an addition to the library, change in dormitory rules, or a new cultural center can have an immediate effect on the student image or perception of the institution (Pace, 1963). It seems reasonable to suppose that the library addition, rule change, or cultural center will also immediately influence student behaviors. Since almost every institution is expanding, the new changes may not change significantly the inter-institution rankings but may change the campus atmosphere —the perceptions and behaviors of the student.

The institutional assessment may also be intended to provide better information to guidance counselors. This would seem to follow as a practical application of the objective comparison purpose discussed above and Astin (1965b) made explicit this combination of purposes. Thus the "objective" approach seems designed to provide a basis for an objective comparison of institutions, and one application of this comparative data is in guiding students to the appropriate institution.

However, just why should the results of this "objective" approach benefit the counselor? Does he have information about a student which can be used to predict a successful outcome in an institution with such and such ratings on the scales of the "objective" measurement? Further, in using data in guidance the important fact may not be that school A has 8000 students whereas school B has 15,000, but that students at school B perceive their institution as having a friendly and congenial atmosphere whereas the students at school A perceive the atmosphere as impersonal, without group loyalty or involvement. Thus the subjective approaches—the students' image or perception of the environment and the students' behaviors in the environment—must complement the objective approach when the purpose of the study is to provide comparative data for the use of administrators and guidance counselors.

The validity of applying any one of these three methods will depend upon the ultimate purpose in gathering the data. The majority of applications will revolve around the assessment of the effect of some change in the environment. A frequently used paradigm of pre-test—treatment—post-test is employed when environmental manipulations are to be made. The most useful technique to use in the pre and post assessment is probably that derived from Subjective Student Perceptions.

Following are five general criteria which should prove useful in developing perception instruments.

## CRITERIA FOR DEVELOPING SUBJECTIVE STUDENT PERCEPTION TECHNIQUES

1. The object studied is the environment, not the students or faculty. The data gathered are furnished by the people in the environment; it is their perceptions of the environment. Yet the perceptions are only the means to get at the object of the study —the environment. A sample of students from various environments would not get at the objectives of the study; but a sample of students from the same environment will yield a measure related to the characteristics of their common environment.

2. The instrument should have a low within-institution variance and high between-institution variance. Students in the same environment should see their common environment in much the same way. If there is a wide variation in the perception of the common environment, it would be questionable whether the instrument was measuring the environment or something else, perhaps a personality factor of the individual student. Also, this criterion requires that the instrument be developed with data from a number of institutions. If the instrument yielded the same scores for dissimilar institutions, it would be questioned just what is being measured—for it is quite unlikely that dissimilar institutions have the same environment. The instrument should also yield approximately the same score when used at one time on various random samples of similarly experienced students in a common environment.

3. The scores should not correlate highly with personality characteristics of the raters. The instrument that is picking up personality characteristics is not measuring environments—at least not only environments. Likewise we would not expect the instrument that is picking up personality characteristics to yield the desired low within-institution variance unless students having a personality aspect in common have been attracted to the same institution.

4. The instrument should have scales that are relatively few in number, not highly intercorrelated, and understandable. This criterion is concerned with the practical usefulness of the instrument. Obviously

any thorough measure of an environment will be multi-dimensional. But if the resulting measures are to provide information for experimental changes—for example, manipulation on the part of administrators—the measures or scales must be readily understandable and verbally communicable, there must not be too many of them, and they should be relatively independent (thus not highly correlated) measures.

Factor analysis often yields factors that are not amenable to verbal explanation and communication. Likewise the factor analyst may reduce dimensionality only to the point where highly independent factors appear. The individual factors resulting may be good measures but the dimensionality remaining (the number of factors) is still much too great to give the administrator the practical information he needs in relatively simple form. Therefore, a compromise is required between the need for a small number of understandable factors and for independent factors. It may be necessary to sacrifice some factor independence in favor of a low number of understandable factors. Thus the factor analytic technique, the reduction in dimensionality, and the rotation must be guided by this criterion.

5. Should the scores correlate with the "objective" measures like school size, budget, and faculty-student ratio? The answer to this reduces to the answer to the question: What is the purpose of these studies? If it is believed that the subjective instrument which correlates highly with certain objective aspects of the environment is a better instrument, then evidence of a high correlation is essential. Yet we previously used an example of school A with 8,000 students wherein the environment is perceived as impersonal, without group loyalty or involvement, and of school B with 15,000 students where the environment is perceived as friendly and congenial. School C may be the same size as school A but the students' perceptions of the environment may be more like that of B rather than A. Thus it would not seem that high correlations with objective measures is essential for the preception-type instrument.

On the other hand, correlational studies between various objective variables and scores on a perception-type instrument can be most useful. If the administrator wants to manipulate the environment in a certain way, how does he know just what to manipulate? Moderate correlations between objective variables and perception scale scores would seem to predict that if the objective variable was manipulated, the perception might change. Thus these correlational studies can be most useful in the environmental manipulation paradigm; they could provide information for the administrator as to what aspect of the environment should be manipulated in order to effectively change the environment.

# 32. Pitfalls in the Measurement of Gains in Achievement

**PAUL B. DIEDERICH**

A frequently used technique to secure data for purposes of evaluating teaching effectiveness and learning is the test-retest method. Intuitively it seems that a measure of growth should provide a more equitable base for grading than final class standing. Consideration of the three major difficulties encountered in using growth scores, pointed out in the following non-technical discussion, should lead the reader to a clearer perspective of a very complex topic. For a more comprehensive and technical treatment of the topic, the reader is referred to a volume edited by Harris (1963).

When a teacher gives a published test of almost any skill that develops more or less continuously, such as reading, writing, or arithmetic, at the beginning of the school year and a parallel form of the same test at the end, the average score is practically certain to rise. In addition to the fact that teachers are better at their jobs than most people realize, all the forces of growth are on their side, just as all the recuperative powers of the body are on the side of the physician. If we ever need evidence to confound our critics, we can find it in the difference between initial and final averages on standardized tests.

If it should occur to the critic, however, or even to a friendly inquirer to find out how much the lowest fifth on the initial test had gained, then the middle fifth, and then the highest fifth, he could upset our apple cart. In most cases it would turn out that the students who made the lowest initial scores had gained by far the most, those in the middle had gained less, and those at the top had gained little or nothing. Some of the latter

Reprinted and abridged with permission of the publisher, The University of Chicago Press, and Paul B. Diederich from the *School Review*, **64** (1956), pp. 59–63.

would even appear to have lost ground. The obvious conclusion would be that instruction had been pitched at the level of the least able, the brighter students had not been stimulated and had loafed on the job, and almost all of the average gain to which we pointed with such pride could be attributed to the fact that the bottom of the distribution had been hauled up to about the level of the initial average.

## COOPERATIVE STUDY DATA

That this is not a fanciful or unusual situation is shown by the 1954 Final Report of the Cooperative Study of Evaluation in General Education (Dressel & Mayhew, 1954). The data presented in Table 1 reflect average gains from the beginning to the end of the freshman year for an average of 1,400 students in nine colleges, from the lowest fifth on the pretest up to the highest fifth, on all instruments developed during the Cooperative Study.

Whatever tests or inventories were used, and wherever they were used, students with the lowest initial scores appeared to gain the most; students with the highest initial scores appeared either to have gained least or to have lost ground. This

**TABLE 1**
**Average Gains of Students on Post-Tests, Classified According to Pretest Standing[a]**

| Test | Low Group | Low Middle Group | Middle Group | High Middle Group | High Group |
|---|---|---|---|---|---|
| Critical Thinking in Social Science | 6.89 | 5.48 | 3.68 | 4.20 | 2.26 |
| Science Reasoning and Understanding | 6.26 | 5.16 | 2.93 | 2.04 | 0.31 |
| Humanities Participation Inventory | 18.00 | 5.05 | 4.94 | 1.39 | −2.07 |
| Analysis of Reading and Writing | 5.33 | 2.89 | 1.81 | 1.22 | 0.25 |
| Critical Thinking | 6.68 | 4.65 | 3.47 | 2.60 | 1.59 |
| Inventory of Beliefs | 9.09 | 5.31 | 4.65 | 3.32 | 1.01 |
| Problems in Human Relations | 3.19 | 1.67 | 1.31 | 1.51 | −0.36 |

[a] Adapted from Paul L. Dressel and Lewis B. Mayhew, 1954.

was true not only of cognitive tests but of instruments attempting to measure appreciations, attitudes, and insight into human relations.

So many students in so many different colleges were tested that the consistent downward trend in the data on gains, from initially lowest to initially highest, cannot be attributed to the population tested. The fact that the same trend is shown by all instruments developed in the study suggests that it cannot be attributed to poor test construction. The colleges participating in the study were selected for the excellence of their general-education programs; they could not all have done a poor job of teaching. It is contrary to all teaching experience to suppose that the initially weak students were, in every case, more highly motivated than the initially strong. The data seem unassailable; yet we cannot accept the conclusion that "poor" students regularly learn more than "good" students. Something in the nature of present test construction or of the test-retest situation gives initial low scorers an advantage. What is it?

**Prophecies Discredited** Unless we can find answers to this question and do something about them, two of our most hopeful prophecies connected with testing are likely to be discredited. The first may be stated in the form of an incomplete sentence: "When testing turns from the mea-

surement of status to the measurement of growth . . ." What will happen is not very clear, but we assume that it is bound to be good. The data just cited suggest that it is bound to be bad. By some quirk in the test-retest situation, poor students will uniformly appear to have grown more than have the good students, no matter who teaches them or what is tested.

The second prophecy is that, when marks are based on growth rather than on final status, the inequities of the present marking system will disappear. So they will, it seems, but only to be replaced by a greater inequity: the guaranteed superiority of the least able. The only way in which good students will be able to get good marks will be to select the most obviously absurd answers to all the items on their pretests.

These prospects, we trust, will not come to pass; the good sense of the profession will reject such outrageous conclusions. But at the same time teachers and administrators are likely to reject testing. They cannot put their faith in instruments that lead to absurd conclusions.

The true conclusion emerging from these considerations, I suggest, is that we do not know very much about the measurement of growth. Testing ad retesting will have to be put on some different basis before we can find out and truly evaluate how much students have learned. I do not know how this will be done, but

I can review three of the most obvious difficulties that will have to be surmounted.

**Ceiling Effect** The first difficulty is that the pretests may have been too easy for the high-scoring students and their initial scores were so near the maximum possible scores as to leave little room for improvement. We usually discard this hypothesis far too hastily when we find that the highest final score was 90 per cent correct and the average went up only from 50 to 60 per cent correct. What we overlook is that the maximum attainable score may be a good deal lower than 100 per cent correct.

Good tests of such complex skills as reading and writing go beyond matters on which everyone can agree into questions calling for insight, judgment, and taste—the very qualities in which we hope our best students will show their greatest improvement. On such questions, however, it is impossible to secure 100 per cent agreement among qualified critics of the test. On the test of Critical Analysis of Reading and Writing used in the Cooperative Study, for example, no item was admitted to the final form of the test on which fewer than eleven out of the thirteen critics agreed. Restricting the test to items on which everyone agreed would have resulted in a very dull test, unlikely to challenge the brighter students. While the standard of agreement seemed strict enough, there were a good many items that only 84 per cent of competent English teachers answered correctly. In such a case we should regard 84 per cent correct as the maximum attainable score. Many of the students in the highest fifth came perilously close to this figure in the pretest.

Even so, the highest fifth should have been able to show more than the average gain of a quarter of a point that was reported in the study, for the lowest members of this group got only half the items right on the pretest. Some other explanation is needed.

**Regression** The most likely explanation of the apparently unfavorable difference in gains is the phenomenon known as "regression." Scores on all objective tests are determined partly by ability and partly by luck. The items presented to the students are only a sample drawn from an almost infinite number of similar questions that might have been asked. The particular sample that happens to be chosen is bound to favor some students more than others. They have had more experience with these kinds of questions or have given more thought to them. But when a different sample is drawn, luck is not likely to favor the same students to the same degree.

Moreover, students are rarely certain in their choice of answers. On a five-choice item they may eliminate one as absurd and two others as common errors of which they have learned to beware. The remaining two appear equally plausible, and they decide by a mental "flip of a coin." The initial high scorers were lucky in their guesses; the initial low scorers were not. On a second test, the proportion of chance success may be reversed.

The phenomenon of regression has been studied by the statisticians, and they have provided an easy-to-use formula to predict what final score is to be expected on the basis of any given initial score—to the extent that chance is involved in both. I can explain how the principle works with a minimum of numbers if we imagine the following situation.

A class has been given a test of reading and writing on their first day in school and a parallel form of the same test on the second day. It is parallel in all respects: covers the same type of content with the same types of items, and the mean, standard deviation, and reliability of the second test are all equal to those of the first. The students have had sufficient practice in taking machine-scored objective tests so that marking the answer spaces is not a problem in either test. They are not told their scores on the first test, nor which answers are correct. They learn nothing about reading and writing in the interim. Let us imagine that the average score on the first test is 16; the average of the lowest fifth is 8; of the highest fifth, 24; and the reliability of the tests, as indicated by the correlation between them, is .70. What average scores of the lowest and the highest fifths may be expected on the second test when chance alone is involved?

In such a situation, final scores may be predicted by multiplying initial differences from the average by the reliability of the tests.[1] Take the difference of the lowest fifth from the average of the total group: it is +8. Multiply this by the reliability (.70), and you get +5.6. Take 5.6 from the initial average (16), and the predicted score of the lowest fifth on the second test will be 10.4. Since their initial average was 8, they will appear to have gained 2.4 points.

Similarly, take the difference of the highest fifth from the initial average (+8), multiply by the reliability (.70), and you get 5.6. Add this to the initial average (16), and the predicted score of the highest fifth on the second test will be 21.6. Since their initial average was 24, they will appear to have lost 2.4 points.

While the situation we have imagined is artificial, the same chance factors will operate to the same extent when the tests are given at the beginning and end of the school year—provided that the two tests are strictly parallel. In the ordinary course of events, of course, they are not strictly parallel, and then chance differences will be even greater. We usually do not realize the magnitude of the differences in test-retest scores that may be attributed to chance alone. The figures I have cited were very close to the actual figures for the tests of Critical Analysis of Reading and Writing used in the Cooperative Study, rounded for the sake of simplicity. We regarded with some horror the find-

ing that the lowest fifth gained 5.33 points while the highest fifth gained only 0.25 points. But when we consider what might be expected to happen on the basis of chance alone, the lowest group should have gained 2.4 points; it actually gained 5.33; therefore it exceeded a chance gain by 2.93 points. The highest group would be expected to lose 2.4 points; it actually gained 0.25 points; therefore the best approximation of the actual gain is 2.65 points.

We can now view the gains of both groups in better perspective. When set against what would have happened by chance, if no learning whatever had taken place, the lowest fifth gained 2.93 points; the highest fifth gained 2.65 points. Such a finding comes closer, although not close enough, to our intuitive judgment of what these two groups probably learned.

Teachers regard such manipulations uneasily. The raw scores seem to be real; the converted scores, hypothetical. But there is nothing fanciful about the phenomenon of regression. It was originally deduced from observations that children of extremely tall parents tend to be shorter and children of extremely short parents tend to be taller than their parents. The formula expressing this principle can be proved as rigorously as any proposition in geometry, and study after study has shown that this principle must be taken into account if the results are to seem reasonable.

Teachers may wonder why fortune uniformly smiles upon the weakest students and frowns upon the strongest in the test-retest situation. It does nothing of the sort. Both groups will "regress" toward the average to precisely the same extent: their distance from the average multiplied by the reliability of the test. The direction of this regression quite naturally has to be upward for low-scoring students and downward for high-scoring students.

My only quarrel with the use of the regression formula is that, if we stop there, we have not gone far enough. We have wiped out the spurious gains and

[1] The actual prediction formula is a bit more complicated, but this simplification is valid for the situation described and illustrates the basic principle that is involved.

losses that may be attributed to chance, but the usual result is that the weakest and the strongest groups appear to have gained about the same amount. We have good reason to believe that this is not true. What else keeps the initially high students from showing how much more they have learned than the initially low?

**Unequal Units of Measurements** A further explanation of the discrepancy in gains may lie in the way in which objective tests are constructed. In a four-choice test we tend to put in one best answer, one that is likely to deceive all but the elect, one common error that students make, and one absurd answer that I shall refer to as a "booby trap." These four types of answers may not appear in every item, but let us suppose that there are equal numbers of each in the total test. Consider the case of the boy who, in the beginning, can rule out only half the booby traps and has to choose among the remaining answers by chance. The part of his score that may be attributed to knowledge or skill is one-eighth. But merely by staying awake in class he may learn to rule out all the booby traps and to avoid the most common types of errors that students make, for these will be emphasized most heavily in class. Hence in the final test he will be able to rule out two out of every four responses on the average and will have to choose, by chance, only between the right and the nearly right. The part of his score that may be attributed to knowledge is now 50 per cent. He has gone from one-eighth correct to one-half correct—a gain of 38 percentage points—on the basis of minimum ability and minimum effort.

Now consider the student who can do this well in the beginning. He can already rule out booby traps and common errors; the only way he can improve his score is by learning to distinguish best answers from those that are equally plausible and almost as good. These are hard choices. While the poor student can gain 38 points in a test of 100 items by learning to make easy choices, the good student may have a harder time gaining 10 points, for he has much harder problems to cope with.

Unfortunately there is not yet any precise way to translate responses to test items into equal units of growth. Standard scores based on the normal curve are an improvement on percentiles in estimating growth, but they do not solve the problem because they rest on the assumption that equal gains of raw-score points represent equal increments in ability, and the whole purpose of this section has been to demonstrate that this is not the case. It is harder to get from the mean up to plus one standard deviation than it is to get from minus one standard deviation up to the mean. All the data presented from the Cooperative Study attest that this is not a fanciful or theoretical argument but a fact, for many students were able to do the latter but relatively few were able to do the former.

The only ultimate answer to this question that I can now foresee is to get norms for gains as well as for status, starting from any given initial score. Until such norms are provided, the best we can do as teachers is to become as familiar with records on our tests as our students are with records in sports. It may be that a gain from 30 to 60 per cent correct, while creditable, is nothing to get excited about, for almost everyone who starts at 30 per cent correct can make it. But a gain from 80 to 85 per cent correct on a difficult test may be breath-taking, for no one has ever made it before.

This plan will not settle the metaphysical argument as to whether a gain from stupidity to mediocrity is better than a gain from competence to brilliance, but at least it will not automatically stack the cards in favor of the former.

# 33. Measuring Changes in Head Start Children
## LOIS-ELLIN DATTA

This article, completed by the former National Coordinator of Head Start Evaluation, points out the many practical problems encountered when attempting to evaluate a nationwide educational intervention program. The considerable problems posed by the program's size and location were confounded by variations in local projects even though the Head Start Centers shared the same general objectives. The task of finding measuring instruments relevant to the objectives of the program and yet appropriate to the backgrounds of the tremendous variety of children involved is an awesome one. The reader should compare the description of Datta's problem in securing adequate control groups with Forehand's comments in Article 15 on the same topic.

All Head Start programs have shared a framework of means and of ends. Head Start's primary objective is to disrupt the poverty cycle of children who are ill-prepared for school, often malnourished, and often ill, who fall progressively farther behind in the acquisition of skills and information and who, as young adults, burdened with desires and responsibilities they may have few resources to fulfill, find little hope for themselves, or, starting the cycle again, for their children.

### THE OBJECTIVES OF HEAD START PROGRAMS

In 1965 a panel of authorities on child development prepared for the Office of Economic Opportunity a report including a list of objectives for a comprehensive Head Start program. These seven specific objectives which have guided the national program are:

1. Improving the child's health and physical abilities

Reprinted and abridged with permission of Lois–ellin Datta from a paper presented to the Society for Research in Child Development, 1969.

2. Helping the emotional and social development of the child by encouraging self-confidence, spontaneity, curiosity, and self-discipline
3. Improving the child's mental processes and skills with particular attention to conceptual and verbal skills
4. Establishing patterns and expectations of success for the child which will create a climate of confidence for his future learning efforts
5. Increasing the child's capacity to relate positively to family members and others while at the same time strengthening the family's ability to relate positively to the child
6. Developing in the child and his family a responsible attitude toward society and fostering constructive opportunities for society to work together with the poor in solving their problems
7. Increasing the sense of dignity and self-worth within the child and his family.

Head Start, as the guidelines define the program, has multiple objectives and offers a comprehensive way of reaching these objectives. In addition, the guidelines offer much opportunity for variations in emphases and organizational structures.

This heterogeneity of objectives and approaches has far-reaching consequences for both the demonstration of change in children in a community who have attended Head Start in contrast to others who have not and for efforts to attribute the change to participation in the program. These consequences generally are that measurement is less complete, that the attribution of change to program elements is less unequivocal, and, as our attempts to measure input, process, and output variables get more ambitious, that the delay is greater in analyzing, interpreting, and reporting the findings than one would wish.

## THE ROLE OF RESEARCH

At least part of the initial support for Project Head Start came from research studies demonstrating the importance of the child's early years, and the impact of deprivation on physical and psychological growth during this period. The role of research is evident in the statement of Head Start objectives and policy. Research has been regarded by Head Start not only as the impetus to the program as it now is but also as the essential growing edge for the future. This commitment has been demonstrated by a proportionately high share for Evaluation and Research (E & R) activities in the total Head Start budget, by the personal interest and support given E & R by the Planning Committee and the Director, and by the fact that research and evaluation studies have been funded literally as long as there has been a Head Start since summer 1965. About 80% of the total E & R budget has been used to fund research projects, about 19% for evaluative research, and about 1% for descriptive studies.

## PROGRESS AND EVALUATION RESULTS

Given such attention, it is reasonable to expect that over the past four years, the state of the art of measuring changes in Head Start children would have advanced considerably. It is also reasonable to expect advances in our knowledge of the extent of the immediate impact of preschool programs, what experiences may most enhance development, and something of the extent of, and optimal conditions for at least intermediate range impact. I think the state of the art of measurement has advanced, although perhaps not as far as might have been hoped. I think that our knowledge of the role of intervention programs such as Head Start in reaching immediate and intermediate range goals has advanced. The results to date seem to be encouraging for those who have expected an immediate impact in some domains. The results to date are less encouraging for those who might have expected a longer-range impact from a relatively brief program. However, both the programmatic efforts and the research efforts are in their early childhood, if not in their infancy, and strong conclusions are probably premature indeed.

There have been five large national-scale studies of Head Start programs. The summer 1965 and full year 1965–66 efforts were post-only studies of children. The criterion measures were the *Preschool Inventory, Peabody Picture Vocabulary Test* (PPVT), and the *Head Start Behavior Inventory*. Little information was available regarding the programs and the families.

The four subsequent studies have had a before and after design. In each of these studies at least some information in most of the areas relevant to Head Start objectives and policies has been collected for the children, their families, and the programs. The first of the four studies involved administration of the *Stanford-Binet*, the *Preschool Inventory,* and the *Behavior Inventory* to children in a random sample of summer 1966 classes. The tests were administered in the second and seventh weeks. 1966–67 was the first year of operation for the regional Head Start Evaluation and Research Center network and the first large-scale operation of full year Head Start programs. For this study, E & R Center Directors tried to select a sample representing programmatic or subgroup variation for their region. There were initial and final *Stanford-Binet*, *Preschool Inventory*, and *Behavior Inventory* data collected on the child, a family interview, and classroom observations using the Observer Rating Form developed at the University of Texas. The 1967–68 study followed a similar design, supplemented by additional in-depth measurements in the social-emotional, perceptual and cognitive areas for subsamples of children, and by extensive classroom observations. The 1968–69 national evaluation study was designed around a series of manipulated intervention studies, with coordinated and extensive measures on the children, their families, and the programs.

**Description of Results** What we have learned in a methodological sense and what were some of the considerations that shaped the designs can be summarized in about 15 points.

1. The children range in age from 3 to 8 years of age. The behaviors to be considered and the measures of these behaviors thus have to be age-relevant for a period of rapid development in both cognitive and affective domains.

2. The ethnic backgrounds include Oriental, Polynesian, American Indian from several tribes, Mexican American and Puerto Rican as well as black and white. The behaviors to be considered in the children, and the family background variables thus have to be relevant for a wide variety of subgroups. Individual measures have to be appropriate for children from diverse backgrounds both linguistically and in terms of the basis for interpreting responses across ethnic subgroups. The distribution also affects design, since random samples would yield too few subjects in relevant subgroups.

3. Almost all of the Oriental children come from English-speaking homes. About 30% of the American Indian, Mexican American and Puerto Rican children come from homes where English is not spoken at all or where some degree of bilingualism exists. This confronts us with a bitter choice: whether to exclude children from important subgroups because we do not have measures of known equivalence in their language or to include data of questionable reliability and validity.

4. Although our most widely used and best standardized tests are cognitive tests, the majority of program directors and of teachers have as their stated primary objective for the children social-emotional rather than cognitive development.

5. Some programs operate in the morning. Some programs operate in the afternoon. Some operate in the morning and the afternoon. This affects time available for observations based on free play, for when the children can be observed relative to their daily activities and the content of the programs.

6. Almost all programs operate miles and hours from where the researcher lives. Some have bus transportation, others have no transportation. Returning to pick up absent children or for repeated measures absorbs hours and hours and hours of time. The impact of distance on study feasibility, costs, and meaning is profound. Even administration of so apparently straightforward a measure as the Picture Play Board Sociometric which requires polaroid photographs of each child in the class can be delayed for weeks while all photographs are obtained. Observations of peer/adult interactions scheduled for certain sample periods are thrown askew due to absences of the target child *and* his friends. The average attendance may be stabilized at 13 out of 15 children— but if two children are absent, very unpredictable hours of observer time may be required to complete even apparently "simple" measures. What is the appropriate choice group if the same two children are typically absent—or if the group is shifting over the six data collection weeks —is another source of difficult-to-resolve variance.

7. Programs follow almost every pattern

imaginable. Some programs have free play almost all day. Some programs have no free play. Measures involving observations during free play may be obtainable only under duress from programs which are anti-free play, and then the data may be of questionable value if free play is atypical for the children.

8. Some programs have a great deal of joint activity among several classes in a Center. Some programs have only one class on a site. Measures involving free play—or sociometric choice—therefore may be atypical for children if only the sample class is considered in data collection while including all children within the Center as a joint class may mean that one Center comprises the entire sample for a geographic region.

9. Some classes have one teacher and one aide. Some classes have two co-teachers and no aide. Some classes have one teacher and several part-time aides and a score of volunteers. Measures based on teacher/child interactions or teacher/aide interactions or child/adult interactions may require the wisdom of Solomon to unscramble in ways that are comparable and meaningful.

10. Most situations do not have meaningful control groups available. All eligible children may be enrolled in the program, leaving the unreachable or the relatively well-to-do as controls. Many Centers where there are more eligible children than space select the most deprived, and would resist a lottery system. In almost all areas, the vertical and horizontal diffusion from Head Start plus the other Community Action Programs operating in the community contribute to the difficulty of obtaining meaningful control groups. One thing that seems crystal clear is that "an eligible child who has not attended Head Start" is likely to be a snare and a delusion in *post hoc* studies and as rare as a unicorn for *a priori* studies. Careful examination of the characteristics of so-called *post hoc* "control" groups usually reveals substantial differences in family pattern and economic indicators. In one

follow-up study, for example, the "control" children came from families with a higher proportion of mothers who graduated from high school, of fathers who were employed, and with fewer children. In another follow-up study, the "control" children came from smaller families with higher overall incomes, so that the per capita income differences were great enough to raise the question of whether the controls would have been eligible for Head Start under Head Start's per capita income requirements. In this study, although the Head Start and so-called control children differed in a number of characteristics, the covariant control was the Hollingshead-Redlich index of head-of-household education and occupation (where the groups differed little) rather than per capita income (where the groups differed a lot). What is an appropriate measure of socio-economic status is a complex and difficult question, made no easier by the dearth of information on relationships within low-income samples of the different possible predictors to various criteria. In one study, for example, we found that the regression of maternal education on IQ was significant for one ethnic group, but non-significant for another. The problems of selecting relevant control groups, and of appropriate corrections for the apparently inevitable failure to achieve adequate matching is an area that deserves further study; it is so basic to the logic of evaluation for decision-making that from some points of view, until a better resolution that is currently available is reached, the question of whether a little information be it ever so qualified and faulty is better than nothing might well be answered by, "A little information is a dangerous thing—."

11. The diversity of the program itself precludes comprehensive measurement. This means that the efforts to relate changes in child measures to process measures are likely to have considerable "error" variance. The efforts to measure classroom input, as complex and sophisticated as they are, are still far from satis-

factory. Consider the metrical complexities of trying to use multivariate models for estimating the relative contribution to change of parental involvement, classroom activities, teacher attitudes, the feeding program, medical/dental intervention, the input directly by volunteers and indirectly through community contacts with parents or teachers, and social work services provided by the community workers.

12. Development of test forms, recording devices, training and monitoring procedures, and manuals for the relatively untrained personnel who are likely to be collecting data is another issue, and one that directly affects the sensitivity of the measures. The measurements are typically designed by a researcher who develops the manuals and approaches with the cooperation of his Ph.D. or Master's level research assistant. The individual administering the measures or collecting data may have a B.A. degree and receive about two weeks' training, a period which often includes training in several measures at once and an orientation to filling out travel vouchers. It is likely that if we are to do research and evaluation at all in some communities, we will be in the business of training paraprofessionals, which might be necessary anyhow, if the data are to represent performance in comparable situations for low-income and middle-class individuals. This will require not only longer training periods than might be expected, but also rethinking approaches to training, to format of data collection devices and to provision of in-service supervision. Several of the E & R Centers have used paraprofessionals extensively. In a major study being conducted by Educational Testing Service, all the data will be collected by paraprofessionals. Their experience may be helpful to other researchers, if these groups can disseminate what they have learned.

13. Data collection will take longer than you expect. On the one hand, collection of a few measures seems unsatisfactory given the complexity of the evaluation tasks; on the other hand, the reliability and validity of measures are typically established by one-time testing of relatively eager subjects. The value of the data when the measure is embedded in one or two hours of testing for a three- to eight-year-old child is questionable; yet, in many instances the entire test battery is administered for the first time under field conditions when the data to be used in the analyses are collected, with no information available on the basic psychometric characteristics of data collected under these conditions. Applications to these data of such criteria of "substantial" as the "difference should be greater than $1/2$ of the norm group standard deviation" or of standard error formulae based on normative data may be mathematically possible—the computer is not critical—but psychologically misleading.

14. Change in some areas may be rapid. What is the appropriate baseline may require careful identification of what component of variance one is most interested in: for low-income children it is likely that affective elements are associated with response to tests that may be more strictly cognitive for middle-income children while cognitive development may determine comprehension and thus performance on measures one hopes are affective. There is some suggestion that affective response to adults may change relatively insensitive to what could be considered a valid component of program impact unless the children are observed as early as possible in the experience.

15. Interpretation of data may be extraordinarily difficult. An individually administered language test, for example, may reflect primarily differences in response to the adult examiner while a group administered test of self-concept may reflect differences in comprehension, attention, or understanding of the format. The conclusion that some children tend to show greater cognitive development and differ but little from others in affective development could, in terms of the processes most intimately involved, more

accurately be that the children show differences in affective development but no differences in some cognitive skills.

## CONCLUSIONS

These factors and others sum to this: we can measure changes in Head Start children but the changes are often going to be from instruments that do not reliably measure what we most want to measure. We can attempt to relate these changes to Head Start or some components within the program, but the relationships are likely to be weak, and often with the least satisfactory measurement of process on component factors where we would most want reliable and meaningful information. We need to be cautious in designing studies, in analyzing results, in interpreting the data and extrapolating to recommendations, lest the data gather authority beyond that justified by the nature of the evidence.

I have been much concerned with the role of evaluative research in social action programs. On the one hand, research studies are often the impetus to the establishment of large-scale programs; to doubt the validity of national data evaluating these social action programs while welcoming their initiation from smaller-scale and possibly more limited studies may seem like convenience criticism. I think that important differences in the purpose and design of research and evaluation efforts make such a distinction less contemptible. The well-designed, carefully conducted small-scale studies often are just grounds for extrapolation; evaluation of a diverse national program may simply be beyond the state of the art in measurement, design, and analysis. One can compute an average from a skewed distribution, but denotation and connotation would diverge misleadingly. There is perhaps an analogy to the application of techniques appropriate to certain experimental situations to evaluating programs such as Head Start; I doubt if analysis of covariance or multiple regression or multivariate statistics of other sorts are likely to be Philosophers' Stones in situations that are fundamentally different from those where such techniques were originally designed to succor. I sometimes think researchers may not realize the power of their data and interpretations to shape social policy, with scholarly qualifications providing a sort of escape hatch for responsibility when quoted "out of context." The researcher and evaluator have a grave responsibility and therefore need to reassess our models for evaluative research in the knowledge acquired over these past few years of both Agora and Academe.

Part V is intended to serve as an overview of how curriculum evaluation is currently practiced in "the real world." The articles exemplify some of the conceptual, theoretical, and methodological suggestions presented in the previous four parts, and were selected to represent a variety of subject areas and approaches. Of necessity, then, the articles as a group are quite diverse, with respect both to content and to quality. No attempt was made to select only exemplary programs, or those yielding only "positive" results. Some are sound methodologically, others are not. They are simply representative cross-sections of the art and science of contemporary curriculum evaluation.

The first article, by Edward J. Furst, is a narrative of the evaluation tasks associated with developing an experimental secondary-level economics course. The close relationship among the tenets of the discipline, the intent of the curriculum materials, and evaluation is one of the strengths of this paper.

Robert L. Ebel, the next author, serves as a consultant to a social studies curriculum improvement project. Employing a rather unusual format for a journal article, he takes a set of project objectives and spells out some alternative approaches to their evaluation. His extended comments about evaluating social attitudes, feelings, and interests are particularly relevant in today's schools, with their increasing emphasis on "humanism."

High school science (Ausubel), middle school English (Burton), elementary level mathematics (Hungerman), and concept-oriented school health materials designed for use at the elementary, junior high, and secondary levels (Creswell, Hastings, and Hoffman) are the subjects of the next series of articles. These areas, from the point of view of the evaluator, have both common and unique characteristics. All begin with objectives. The BSCS sci-

# Illustrative Curriculum Evaluation Projects

part

ence curriculum, however, goes in three different instructional directions from the same initial set of objectives. An attempt is made by William H. Creswell and his associates to articulate concept materials over a number of grade levels. Their sampling unit is the school, but again the same general set of objectives is involved. The intent of the inquiry by Dwight L. Burton was to find out whether or not different objectives and curriculum materials do in fact make a difference. Ann D. Hungerman was asking, among other things, if given a standard set of criterion measures, "traditional" and "new" math programs would show differential effects. Basically, the design of all four investigations was comparative (see Article 19 by Anderson for a discussion of this type of design). In comparative studies there is always the problem of defining the nature of the control group. In Burton's project, for example, one could consider all three competing curricula experimental, or all controls, or some combination. The control groups in the *School Health Education Study* come closest to approaching what a traditional experimenter would call true control groups.

Article 40 is a cleverly designed nonstatistical correlation study. By examining the frequency and sequence of occurrence of selected content topics in mathematics and science, Ralph W. Cain and Eugene C. Lee were able to describe meaningful relationships. More such studies should be undertaken, particularly prior to heavily statistically-oriented research.

Langdon E. Longstreth, Fred J. Stanley, and Roger E. Rice next describe in detail the curriculum and disappointing evaluation results of their work-study program for potential high-school delinquents and dropouts. The value of evaluation data as a basis for program revision is emphasized.

A model for possible national implementation of the "accountability concept" (see Article 5) is described by Jack C. Merwin and Frank B. Womer. This article contains an informative overview of the development of this multimillion dollar project and a readout of some illustrative results. The potential payoff for education of more rational decision making as a result of National Assessment data is considerable, particularly in relation to national legislative action regarding the allocation of federal monies. Whether or not rationality will prevail is yet to be seen.

Several years ago the United States Office of Education sponsored an extensive national tryout of a variety of first-grade reading programs. Article 43 is a succinct evaluative research summary of the effects of the second year of this program in one research center area. William D. Sheldon, Nancy J. Nichols, and Donald R. Lashinger describe extensive statistical analyses using a number of traditional standardized measures.

In the final article, John C. Flanagan provides a brief overview of two different educational program evaluation projects. The methodology of the now famous Project TALENT is first described, together with some examples of initial results. Flanagan then illustrates how a local school system can be surveyed using a variety of paper-and-pencil and interview techniques. One unique methodological feature is the follow-up phase of the evaluation of graduates. (See Cronbach's comments in Article 16, on the advantages and disadvantages of follow-up studies.)

A final word of caution should be added. Data are out-of-date as soon as they appear in print. This is also true of the conclusions derived from them. The conclusions suggested by these articles, therefore, must be considered tentative, not definitive.

## 34. Tasks of Evaluation in an Experimental Economics Course

### EDWARD J. FURST

> It was suggested in the Prologue that one characteristic differentiating "research" from "evaluation" is that the latter is generally not concerned with formal hypothesis testing. This article, however, shows how—at least at an informal level—the focusing and guiding character of hypotheses can be used to direct evaluation efforts, specifying the design as well as the nature of the data to be gathered. The evaluation under discussion focused not only on curriculum materials and learning outcomes, but also on the basic assumptions of the content framework of the project. One should note, finally, the similarity of the ideas expressed in this article regarding the "value" of outcomes and their relationship to antecedent conditions to those expressed by Stake (1967a—see Article 17—and 1970).

This paper will discuss four aspects of an economics curriculum development project. Under each, I propose to consider what needs to be evaluated and the manner in which evaluation in the usual sense can contribute, if it can contribute at all.

### ECONOMICS AS A DISCIPLINE

One set of ideas to be tested consists of assumptions about the nature of economics as a discipline. The basic assumption is that economics has a logic of its own, an inner structure, the major components of which are *scarcity* (including economic decisions); *flows* (of goods and services and of income); and *coordination* of economic activity (that is, of decisions and flows). These three major divisions of the subject, together with two analytical themes that run through the subject—(a) marginal analysis and (b) the use of institutions—comprise the structure of economics (Lovenstein, 1960).

Reprinted and abridged with permission of the publisher and Edward J. Furst from the *Journal of Educational Measurement*, **3** (1966), pp. 213–218.

It seems clear that the validation of assumptions such as these concerning the logic of a discipline is properly left to the philosophers and economists; they are the ones who bear primary responsibility for the types of analysis and logical evaluation required. The contribution of evaluation, in the sense of the data-gathering phase of curriculum development, would be incidental here.

### PREPARATION OF CURRICULAR MATERIALS

A major aspect of our curricular project is the preparation of materials to be used for instruction. Clearly, whatever materials are produced should bear a close relationship to the conception of economics as a subject with an underlying logic of its own. One of the theoretical assumptions would be that the materials provide an orderly sequence of development, and another, that the problems in economics as seen by the experts can also be meaningful problems to students.

Preliminary evaluation of such materials is made by certain of our staff, but especially by a small group of outside economics instructors who will serve as consultants. The evaluator himself can insist that parts of these materials, at the least, be tried out with individual students or small groups, in somewhat the manner in which programmed materials are developed. So, even at this stage, there can be some evidence-gathering.

## EDUCATION OF TEACHERS
## FOR THE TRYOUT

As usual, the key persons in the tryout of new materials will be the teachers. It is almost certain that in this project they will need very careful orientation and education. They will need to be well grounded in the subject of economics as outlined for our purposes. These teachers, like their students-to-be, must also grasp and appreciate the inner structure of economics. To help them attain these ends, and to help them see how this structure can be used for more effective communication of economic concepts and reasoning, a Teacher's Manual is provided. This is an important device in their preparation.

Before being allowed to go in the classroom to teach for us, these teachers should be pre-tested. An important part of the evaluation work in this project should be to ascertain that the teacher is prepared to carry out the course of instruction as conceived. It is not enough to place in the hands of teachers well-prepared materials of instruction; it must be assured that they will understand these materials, and that they will be able to use them properly. This is a phase of our curriculum project, and of any such project, that cannot be left to presumption.

## TRYOUT: INSTRUCTION AND
## LEARNING

This is where evaluation comes in to its own. Here, at last, comprehensive evidence is gathered.

In what way does evaluation enter and

what can it yield? To answer these questions, let us consider the major hypotheses underlying the teaching of these economics materials.

The first major hypothesis is this:

Through a process of "progressive inquiry," ninth-grade "students can reason their way into a comprehension of economics as a whole; the subject can be seen and remembered and used in full compass" (Lovenstein, 1960, p. 165). It is at once obvious that this is a rather complex hypothesis, one that contains statements of method as well as outcome.

Now, to this point, what is the task of evaluation? Since these statements refer to overt and covert activities in the classroom, it is clear that we will need to assure ourselves that these types of activity *do* take place. Do students actually engage in progressive inquiry? Do all, or at least most students actually discover the underlying ideas rather than only a few students who then declare these to the others? Do they actually think as an economist does? The appropriate evaluational procedures must surely include direct observation of classroom interaction, sound recording of teacher and student utterances, interviews with students, and the method of stimulated recall, as well as subsequent logical and psychological analysis of the information so gathered. In short, evaluation must determine the degree to which the instructional activities faithfully follow through on the theory for the course.

The other components of this first major hypothesis refer to desired outcomes: to see economics as a unified and usable system of thought; to remember the orientation, that is, "to keep alive and functional the systematic nature of economic analysis" (Lovenstein, 1960, p. 165); and to use the subject in its full compass. Here the tasks of evaluation are well recognized: to assist in clarifying these desired outcomes, to develop further the specifications for tests and the like, to help construct tests, and so on. It is worth noting that the last two of the outcomes imply some attention to effects that persist beyond the course itself. The measurement of retention may be done, in part, at points throughout the course; for example, to see whether students remember earlier ideas that now come up for further consideration. So, too, with measurement of transfer to later situations in the course. But each of these types of outcome should be rechecked some months or years beyond the end of the course. Indeed, without any prompting from a psychologist who is familiar with such matters, our staff expressed a concern for such follow-up studies. Evidently there is here an implicit hope that this economics course will produce learnings that will carry over nicely into further work in the social studies, so that students, for instance, will "see" the economics in topics brought into American History.

The second major hypothesis underlying the theory of curriculum and instruction for this course seems to me to fall primarily in the affective domain. I would state it as follows:

Inquiry into economic concepts, like scarcity, is itself "the problem" in the Dewey sense and will prove to be highly motivating. It is hypothesized, in other words, that this kind of activity will generate motivation. It is also implied that students will accept abstraction rather than be intimidated by it.

Once more, therefore, evaluation will be called upon to delve into the *meaning* of the students' experiences. Will ninth-grade students be highly motivated by such a course? Will they accept abstraction and show an interest in economics as a "discipline"? I leave it to the reader to speculate about the techniques that might be used to probe such private phenomena.

As though all of this were not enough for evaluation to do, we are then confronted with occasional subtle questions posed by the curriculum developers—in this case, our own staff economist and the social studies specialist. All of you, I think, at some time have encountered examples of the mathematical representations used so frequently in economics teaching materials—supply and demand curves, for example, or cost curves. Our economist asks whether this mathematics is an essential part of economics. Could the subject be taught without all this statistical implementation? We don't really know. Questions such as these indicate gaps in our psychological knowledge. While they set a challenge for specialists in learning, they also tend to implicate the evaluator as well.

Some may be curious as to whether we plan to compare our experimental course with more conventional courses, perhaps to the point of sponsoring a conventional course at the ninth-grade level. The answer is no! The reason is partly a matter of practicality: we have our hands full with this one.

Some of the assumptions previously stated do imply the need for comparative data. Economics is expected to be better understood; easier to teach; easier to learn; easier to apply. It would seem that we would ultimately have to compare our course with the conventional, at least to convince the skeptics. I am not sure that this will be necessary. I keep telling my associates that our job is to accept the theory of the course as given, and to see how far ninth-graders can move toward the objectives. That in itself would be a worthwhile contribution to educational research.

If you look more closely at the effects to be compared, you may appreciate that these effects are not so readily comparable. We say that "it"—economics—will be better retained. But what is the "it"? Surely not the same economics in our experimental course as in a conventional one. The ideas will surely differ somewhat, and the cognitive frameworks in which they are embedded surely every bit as much and probably much more. It would seem that we are trying to compare outcomes that are somewhat incomparable. The economics that will be retained will depend so much upon the economics that was taught. Perhaps what we have in the end is a choice between different kinds of outcomes. If experimental course X can be shown to produce certain degrees of outcomes A, B, C, with a defined group, and course Y can be shown to produce certain degrees of outcomes L, M, N, also with a similar group, then the real choice is between the values of these outcomes—a "values" question in its own right.

In summary, I would underscore the fact that evaluation will be called upon to check the project in more ways and at more points than has been usual in the past. Our concern with the testing of assumptions on teaching and learning activities indicates that we are expecting evaluation to do more than describe outcomes. We are also expecting it to relate these outcomes to antecedent conditions. We are, in other words, expecting evaluation to explain the outcomes on the basis of the conditions that produce them. In this respect, then, we are functioning as educational scientists.

## 35. A Consultant Talks About Evaluating A Social Studies Curriculum Improvement Project
### ROBERT L. EBEL

Assume for the moment that you are the director of a statewide curriculum improvement project experimenting with various curricular organizations and instructional techniques. After specifying your objectives, you have called in an evaluation consultant. His reactions to your objectives and requirements for measuring instruments, in both the cognitive and affective areas, together with a set of recommendations, are presented in the following article. Your attention is directed particularly to the comment on attitudes, values, and feelings in the report.

Your approaches to the teaching problem, and to the evaluation problem, are basically sound. Both the maintenance of good educational programs and the improvement of educational procedures require good evaluation. Good evaluation, in turn, can only be made in relation to the goals of instruction. Too often when teachers make tests they forget their goals and remember only the subject matter they used in trying to achieve those goals.

I should warn you, however, that my

Reprinted with permission of the National Council for the Social Studies and Robert L. Ebel from an article entitled "The Problem of Evaluation in the Social Studies," which appeared in *Social Education,* **24** (January 1960), pp. 6–10.

answers to your question are going to be more complex and less satisfying than either you or I would wish them to be. The plain fact is that we do not have many evaluation instruments which will do the job you want done. What is even worse, our disappointing experience in trying to measure some of these outcomes is beginning to convince us that part of the job simply *cannot* be done. I even suspect that part of it *should* not be done. On the brighter side, there is much more we can do, and do better, than we are typically doing in evaluating student progress in the social studies.

Three broad categories of educational achievement are reflected in various degrees by the listed objectives:

1. Objectives primarily concerned with knowledge and understanding
   A. Transmit our cultural heritage
   B. Teach important historical facts and generalizations
   C. Teach time and space relationships
   D. Acquaint students with basic historical references
   E. Provide instruction and practice in locating information
2. Objectives primarily concerned with attitudes, values, and feelings
   F. Promote moral and spiritual values
   G. Promote the attitude that history is interesting and useful
   H. Promote good mental health
   I. Promote aesthetic sensitivities
   J. Develop democratic citizenship
3. Objectives primarily concerned with instruction and practice in intellectual skills
   K. Writing notes from lectures and references
   L. Writing essay examinations
   M. Judging the validity of evidence
   N. Drawing sound conclusions from data
   O. Working in a group
   P. Facility in oral expression

The overlap among these three categories is substantial. Most of us have attitudes, feelings, or values attached to much of the knowledge we possess. Conversely, most of our attitudes, feelings, and values have some basis in knowledge and understanding. Intellectual skills are heavily loaded with knowledge, and also have values attached to them. Thus some of the differences among the three categories are differences in the relative contributions of knowledge, feeling, and practice to the attainment of the specific goals.

You may have noticed that my grouping omits entirely the second objective in your list, "Provide intellectual exercise for the discipline of the mind." The notion of mental discipline has been the target of considerable psychological crit-

icism. Its most naive form, which assumes that the mind is analogous to a muscle that can be strengthened by exercise in learning anything, especially something difficult to learn, has been generally discredited. Even the notions of general mental *functions* such as memory, reasoning, and will, which were supposed to be separate faculties independent of mental content, have been generally discarded. Modern studies of human and animal learning, and of brain function, suggest that the mind guides behavior by serving as a semi-automatic ready-reference storehouse of ideas derived from experience and reflection. The effectiveness of a mind seems to depend on how many of these ideas are stored in it, how accurately they represent the world outside the mind, and how easily they can be made available for recall and recombination when the occasion demands.

If by intellectual exercise is meant increasing the store of ideas, and if by discipline of the mind is meant improved accuracy and increased integration of these ideas, then this is indeed an important objective—so important, in fact, that it encompasses most of the others. If this is not what is meant, some further clarification may be required. In any case, I cannot suggest any tests which might be used to make a separate evaluation of it.

## KNOWLEDGE AND UNDERSTANDING

For the measurement of knowledge and understanding in the social studies a number of excellent tests are available. The Cooperative Test Division of the Educational Testing Service offers social studies tests in its series of Sequential Tests of Educational Progress, and in its end-of-course achievement tests. The World Book Company offers tests in world history and in American history as parts of its Evaluation and Adjustment series. Science Research Associates distributes the test of Understanding of Basic Social Concepts from the Iowa Tests of Educational Development. Oscar Buros' *Fifth Mental*

*Measurement Yearbook* (Buros, 1959) lists 60 tests in the social studies, with critical reviews of 23 of them. Not all of the tests listed are of high quality. The reviewers are rather critical of some. While the reader must occasionally discount the idiosyncrasies of particular reviewers, their comments are usually unbiased and always informative. This is the best available guide to educational tests of all kinds. It should be consulted by anyone who seeks better tests for specific goals.

You may have hoped for a more specific recommendation of a few tests exactly suited to measure achievement of the goals you listed. Unfortunately, this is not possible. In only a few cases have these particular goals been made the focus of specific test construction efforts. Even if tests of each goal were available, it is unlikely that the test author would conceive of these goals precisely as you do. So many facts and ideas are involved in our cultural heritage, and there are so many different value judgments that can be made of them that tests from different sources are almost certain to differ widely. Hence, even in this easiest area of educational measurement, you are not likely to find ready-made tests to meet your needs.

What, then, is to be done? One solution is to make tests of your own, based on a very specific definition of each goal in the area of knowledge and understanding. This is a difficult task. In the absence of substantial expert assistance (and liberal finances) it is not likely to be done very successfully.

Another solution is to get along with the published tests that come closest to covering the goals as you have defined them. This will be cheaper, and cost less effort, but may not be any more satisfactory in the end. What is really needed, it seems to me, is some nationwide effort by social studies teachers and other educators to agree on a definition of basic goals in this and other areas of common educational concern. Then the effort to build really good tests of the agreed upon goals would be justified, and we would

have a means for making sound evaluations of the achievement of our common goals. Unless a teacher foolishly devoted his whole teaching to the attainment of these common goals, completely suppressing his own special interests and disregarding local conditions and individual pupil needs, this would place no straitjacket on the curriculum. But if we are committed to the defense of the freedom of states, schools, teachers, or even pupils, to define all their own goals in whatever way they think best, then the task of getting meaningful measures of the degree of achievement of these diverse goals becomes almost impossible. The price we pay for what may be an excess of freedom seems rather high.

## ATTITUDES, VALUES, AND FEELINGS

Adequate measurement of achievement toward goals in the realm of attitudes, values, and feelings present other, and still more difficult, problems. There is the problem of getting agreement on a clear definition of just what is meant by "democratic citizenship" or "aesthetic sensitivities." There is the problem of obtaining valid indications of the students' true attitudes, values, and feelings. Direct questions in a test situation indicate mainly how the student thinks he *ought* to feel. Indirect, disguised tests are often low in relevance and reliability. The instability of pupil behavior from time to time and from situation to situation makes any single observation quite limited in significance. Finally, it is very difficult to create a test situation which is realistic enough to give valid indication of a student's probable behavior in a natural non-test situation.

For these reasons, good tests in the area of attitudes, values, and feelings are quite rare. I know of none in the realm of moral and spiritual values. Remmers' multi-purpose instrument, *A Scale for Measuring Attitude Toward Any School Subject*, might be used to reflect general attitudes toward history, but probably would not indicate specifically the students' attitudes of interest in history and appreciation of its usefulness, and possibly not the students' genuine attitudes. Good mental health is a complex, poorly-defined concept. Clinical diagnosis is the best basis for estimating mental health, and even that leaves much to be desired. There are tests of specific kinds of aesthetic sensitivity in art, music, and literature. I wonder if these kinds of aesthetic sensitivity are commonly regarded as goals for a course in the social studies? If not, the concept of aesthetic sensitivity may require further definition. Even when so defined, I doubt that we could do more than measure knowledge of aesthetic principles. There are some tests of civic knowledge. There have been some attempts to predict good civic behavior, but there again the problems of trait definition and test validity have been so troublesome that no existing test can be recommended.

This lack of good, ready-made instruments is bad enough. What is even more discouraging is the lack of any promising techniques for the measurement of attitudes, feelings, and values. It is gradually becoming apparent that the difficulties of measuring these traits with paper-and-pencil tests are inherent in the nature of the traits, and in the limitations of formal, written tests. Techniques of testing which are reasonably effective in measuring knowledge and understanding may never be even passably effective in measuring an individual person's attitudes, values, and feelings simply because these are specific to situations which cannot be realistically reproduced by any test. Further, deficiencies in these traits can easily be hidden from the prying questions of the tester, behind a mask of conventionally correct responses.

Does this mean that teachers should abandon the pursuit of goals in this area? To some extent, yes. Many widely approved goals with respect to attitudes, values, and feelings are generally acceptable only when they are left undefined. What consensus could we get in defining

the activities of a good citizen, or the nature of ideal spiritual values? People in different localities, and of different political, religious, or philosophical persuasions would define them quite differently. Is tolerance a virtue or a fault? No teacher can avoid influencing pupils to adopt his own particular attitudes and values, but I doubt that these should become formal goals of teaching, or objects for testing, unless they are the predominant view of the culture, or unless they can be supported as rational consequences of valid knowledge about the world and man.

This suggests that some of our attitudes, values, and feelings are determined by the knowledge we possess. I am persuaded that this cognitive basis for feelings is very influential, and that it constitutes a proper and productive focus for teaching and for testing. Consider the goal of good mental health. How can a teacher promote good mental health? One way is to understand mental hygiene and the causes of mental illness well enough so that most of his acts in dealing with students tend to improve rather than impair the student's (and the teacher's) mental health. Another is to teach a knowledge and an understanding of mental health to the students themselves. Good tests of this kind of knowledge can be built. But no paper-and-pencil test is likely to do an adequate job of assessing mental health or diagnosing mental illness. That is a task for the specialist who knows how to use complex clinical procedures.

Similarly, one could build good tests of knowledge about good citizenship, about aesthetics, about moral and spiritual values and about the uses of history. Imparting of relevant knowledge does not guarantee development of desired attitudes, values, and feelings, but it surely must contribute substantially to their development.

The chief alternative to the development of desirable attitudes, values, and feelings via knowledge is to develop them by indoctrination or conditioning. Many of our most cherished feelings were developed in this way. As children we learned acceptable social behavior largely through a complex system of rewards and punishments, and only secondarily on the basis of rational understanding of the *why* of the correct form (if indeed it was rational!). Indoctrination is almost the only way of teaching very young children, but it becomes progressively less necessary and less desirable as their minds develop. It is a more appropriate technique in the home than in the school. I seriously doubt that teachers, especially teachers of the social studies at the high school level and beyond, should intentionally have much to do with indoctrination or conditioning. Their attempts to develop desirable attitudes, values, and feelings should have mainly a cognitive, rational base, depending on knowledge and understanding.

This emphasis on knowledge, rather than on attitudes, values, and feelings, troubles some teachers greatly. Knowledge alone is not enough, they say. It is what a person does with his knowledge that counts. Arthur Guiterman (1935, p. 74) said it this way:

Theology, literature, languages, law
    Are peacock feathers to deck the daw
If the lads that come from your splendid schools
    Are well-trained sharpers or flippant fools.

He is right, of course, and so are the teachers. But they err, I think, if they assume that instances of misbehavior are caused mainly by deficiencies in attitudes, values, and feelings which the school could correct if it only would try hard enough. Character traits are important determinants of behavior, but so are environmental circumstances. Teachers err if they assume that character is largely independent of knowledge, or that the same techniques of teaching and testing that have served for knowledge will serve also for attitudes, values, and feelings. There is little in the experience of teach-

ers or testers to support such assumptions. To evaluate individual achievement in these non-cognitive areas we may have to settle for measurement of relevant knowledge of how one ought to feel. We do not yet have good tests to do even this job, but we know how to make them.

For the rest of our evaluation of typical behavior, as influenced by attitudes, values, and feelings, we may have to rely on systematic but informal observation of pupil behavior in real, non-test situations. This does not relieve us of defining clearly the traits we wish to observe. It does not promise to yield reliable measurements with little effort. But techniques for observing and recording typical behavior seem to offer more promise than any test-like instrument designed to probe a student's attitudes, values, and feelings.

Truman L. Kelley, writing on "Objective Measurement of the Outcomes of the Social Studies," stressed the importance of attitudes (Kelley, 1930). His emphasis on developing the basic determinants of behavior, rather than its superficial manifestations, seems eminently reasonable, and he said many true and wise things in supporting his thesis. Social studies teachers could profit much from re-reading his words today. He recognized the difficulties of measuring attitudes but was confident that these *could be* overcome, if only because they *had to be* overcome.

Today many of us are less sanguine. The experience of 30 years of generally unproductive efforts is beginning to convince us that we have set ourselves an impossible task, like squaring the circle or building a perpetual motion machine. Kelley himself later reported the unsuccessful outcome of an "Experimental Study of Three Character Traits Needed in a Democratic Social Order" (Kelley, 1942). He commented, "This study emphasized the universal difficulty which has been experienced by those who have endeavored to obtain objective character measures of school children." But he did not lose faith in eventual success, ". . . for it still seemed practically axiomatic that traits of character and attitudes and interests are essential determiners of human conduct, independent of intellectual, sensory, and motor abilities and attainments."

Since 1942 an enormous amount of work has been done on personality testing. A great many tests have been developed. Some interesting findings have been reported, and some interesting theories proposed. But much of what goes on in the name of personality assessment is not much better than horoscope casting or tea leaf reading. We still have no personality test of demonstrated value that is practically useful in measuring the effectiveness of learning or teaching in the classroom. We may never have. It may be that our search for the "structure" of personality, and our attempts to "measure" its dimensions will be as fruitless as previous attempts to find the fountain of youth, or the philosopher's stone. Perhaps the problem needs to be reformulated. It may be that the really basic, stable determinants of behavior, so far as behavior is internally determined, are not attitudes, values, and feelings, but ideas—rational, cognitive, teachable, testable.

## INTELLECTUAL SKILLS

The third category of goals was concerned mainly with intellectual skills. Here again there are no good, ready-made tests that can be recommended. To the extent that these skills rest on knowledge—and this is a considerable extent—they can be tested by conventional paper-and-pencil tests. To the extent that they rest on facility gained through practice, performance tests judged with the help of rating scales offer the most promise. The best solution may be a combination of knowledge and performance tests as a basis for evaluating skills in note taking, essay examination writing, effective group participation, and oral expression.

There are two objectives in this area—judging the validity of evidence and drawing conclusions from data—that may be so greatly conditioned by a student's background knowledge that the influence of generalized skill on his behavior may be relatively unimportant. I wonder if there are broadly applicable rules for judging the validity of evidence, principles which do not depend on the particular nature of the evidence under consideration. I wonder if the interpretation of data is an abstract procedure, like the diagramming of a sentence, that can be applied with reasonable uniformity to all kinds of data. If so, knowledge about these rules and procedures can be taught and tested as abstract principles. But I am persuaded that attempts to test these skills by asking a student to judge specific evidence or interpret specific data will reveal mainly how much he already knows about the source of the evidence or data, its meaning, and the problem to which it applies. In short, I wonder if these are important enough as abstract skills to deserve the status of goals of instruction.

## RECOMMENDATIONS

What, then, would I recommend for the evaluation of student progress toward the goals of teaching in the social studies?

First, that goals be defined specifically enough so that one can judge how satisfactory a given test will be.

Second, that goals which cannot be defined specifically and with general acceptability, or which hypothesize traits of dubious independence from other more obvious and easily measurable traits, be eliminated or de-emphasized.

Third, that goals which have statewide or nationwide, not just local, validity be emphasized.

Fourth, that command over essential knowledge be emphasized as a primary goal of instruction, even in the areas of attitudes, values, feelings and intellectual skills.

Fifth, that social studies teachers continue to search for, or to construct, evaluation instruments of acceptable validity in terms of specifically defined goals.

Sixth, that the *Fifth Mental Measure-*

ment *Yearbook* be consulted for guidance in judging the usefulness of available tests.

Seventh, that social studies teachers recognize and accept the necessity of building some new tests, whose quality will depend on how much effort and money they are prepared to spend on them, and on how much expert help they get and accept in creating them.

That I have completed this discussion without clearly recommending a single specific test for you to use is something I regret very much. It reflects the complex-ity of some problems of educational measurement. Even more, it reflects our failure to be realistic in setting our goals, and to be objective and precise in defining them. I am persuaded that the main reason why educational measurement sometimes seems inadequate is that we persist in setting impossible tasks for it to do. But I am also persuaded that if we concentrate on the right problems, and work on them energetically and intelligently, we can improve educational measurement substantially.

# 36. Crucial Psychological Issues in the Objectives, Organization, and Evaluation of Curriculum Reform Movements: An Illustration from the Biological Sciences Curriculum Study
## DAVID C. AUSUBEL

Qualitative approaches are certainly not incompatible with the general intents of curriculum evaluation, a point well illustrated in this article by David C. Ausubel, who uses the three versions of "biology, knowledge, and skill" as conceived by the Biological Sciences Curriculum Study. Along the way he comments on the nature and methods of stating educational objectives. It should be noted, incidentally, that some of the shortcomings of the *Taxonomy of Educational Objectives* he mentions have been partially remedied by Metfessel, Michael, and Kirsner in Article 10. From the standpoint of methodology, perhaps Ausubel's chief contribution is his description and suggested applications of "transfer retention" tests as measures of curriculum effectiveness. (For a more detailed content analysis of BSCS materials, see Ausubel, 1966.)

The Biological Sciences Curriculum Study may be taken as typical in approach and objectives to many of the flourishing curriculum reform movements that have arisen in the past fifteen years, particularly those in the natural sciences. Its principal objective is to re-establish the close

Reprinted with permission of the publisher and David C. Ausubel from *Psychology in the Schools*, 4 (1967), pp. 111–112.

contact and congruence of high-school biology with current conceptual and methodological developments in biological science, while still maintaining, and even increasing, its congruence with current psychological and pedagogic ideas about the learning-teaching process as they apply to tenth-grade students (Schwab, 1963). According to Schwab, the content of high-school biology, during the heyday of Progressive Education, "was no longer mainly determined by the state of knowledge in the scientific field," because of its excessive preoccupation with such matters as intellectual readiness, the learnability of material, and individual differences among learners. The BSCS approach, however, has veered precisely toward the opposite extreme in trying to correct this unsatisfactory state of affairs: its three texts[1] are reasonably congruent with the content and methods of modern biology, but, except for the Green Version, are psychologically and pedagogically unsound for the majority of tenth-graders.

Actually, of course, there is no *inherent* incompatibility between subject-matter soundness, on the one hand, and pedagogic effectiveness, on the other. It is no more necessary to produce pedagogically inappropriate instructional materials in an attempt to make them reflective of the current state of knowledge in a given discipline, than it is necessary to present discredited concepts or inaccurate facts in order to make the subject matter more learnable. In practice, however, as the Yellow and Blue BSCS versions demonstrate, preoccupation with the recency of subject-matter content, and with the completeness of conceptual, methodological, and historical coverage, can easily lead to the neglect of such basic pedagogic considerations as the educational appropriateness of course approach and objectives, the adequacy of the pupils' existing academic background for learning the content of the course, and the psychological tenability of the chosen ways of presenting, organizing, and sequencing materials. The inevitable outcome, under these circumstances, is the production of instructional materials that are admirably thorough, accurate, and up-to-date, but so ineffectively presented and organized, and

so impossibly sophisticated for their intended audience, as to be intrinsically unlearnable on a long-term basis.

Although the BSCS does not state explicitly its specific dissatisfactions with conventional high-school biology textbooks, these dissatisfactions can be readily inferred from the content of its numerous publications: (a) Conventional texts abound in outmoded ideas and incorrect information, and ignore important contemporary developments in the biological sciences. (b) They are written at a largely descriptive level, and contain relatively few explanatory concepts; too much stress is placed on structural detail, useless terminological distinctions, and classification, thereby placing a premium on rote memory. (c) Their approach is too naturalistic, and insufficiently experimental, quantitative, and analytical. (d) They tend to focus excessively on the organ and tissue levels of biological organization, whereas recent biological progress has been greatest at the molecular (biophysical and biochemical), cellular, population, and community levels. (e) They are written at too low a level of sophistication and contain a profusion of elementary and self-evident generalizations. (f) Insufficient emphasis is placed on biology as a form of inquiry, as an experimental science, and as an ever-changing, open-ended discipline. (g) The biological ideas they contain are not presented in terms of their historical development, and are not related to the social and technological contexts from which they arise. (h) They lack organizing and unifying themes, present a mass of disconnected facts, and fail to integrate related concepts and different levels of biological organization. (i) They place excessive emphasis on the application of biology to such areas as medicine, public health, agriculture, and conservation, and insufficient emphasis on basic biological principles as ends in themselves.

## Specification of Objectives in Behavioral Terms

For many years now, evaluation specialists have been exhorting curriculum

[1] The three BSCS texts referred to in this paper are the Yellow Version (*Biological Science: An Inquiry Into Life.* New York: Harcourt, Brace, and World, 1963); the Blue Version (*Biological Science: Molecules to Man.* Boston: Houghton Mifflin, 1963); and the Green Version (*High School Biology.* Chicago: Rand McNally, 1963).

workers, "State your objectives in behavioral terms, so that their realization can be subjected more easily to objective evaluation." As Atkin (1963) points out, however, such exhortation often does more harm than good. In the first place, relatively trivial but readily definable goals may be accorded more attention by both psychologists and subject-matter specialists than goals that are intrinsically more important but resistive to precise behavioral definition. Second, few curriculum specialists are trained to define goals in behavioral language. Most important, however, is the fact that behavioral terminology more often obscures than clarifies educational goals. The taxonomy of educational objectives (Bloom, 1956; Krathwohl, Bloom, & Masia, 1964), for example, categorizes educational goals in great behavioral detail. But since such terms as "memory," "application," "understanding," "transfer," "meaning," "cognitive," and "affective" have very different meanings for psychologists and educators of different theoretical persuasion, classification of curriculum objectives along such lines merely results in considerable pseudo-agreement among psychologists and curriculum workers, without ever defining what the actual objectives in question are. Everyone is happy because of the fine degree of "scientific" precision achieved in defining goals, even down to two decimal places; but nobody seems to care whether this achievement is psychologically or educationally meaningful.

**"Basic" versus "Applied" Science Approach** The strong emphasis in the Yellow and Blue BSCS versions on "basic science" principles, and their relative lack of concern with applications to familiar or practical problems, is in accord with current fashionable trends in science education. Current curriculum projects have tended to overemphasize the "basic sciences" (because of their great generalizing power and relative timelessness), and unwarrantedly to denigrate the role and importance of applied science in general

education. If the aim of the science curriculum is to acquaint the student with the goals and limitations of the scientific enterprise, to help him understand, as an end in itself, the conceptual meaning of the current phenomenological world that confronts him, it cannot afford to overlook the applied sciences. They constitute a significant aspect of modern man's phenomenological and intellectual environment, and hence an important component of general education. Knowledge about such subjects as medicine, agronomy, and engineering should be taught not to make professional physicians, agronomists and engineers out of all students, or to help them solve everyday problems in these areas, but to make them more literate and intellectually sophisticated about the current world in which they live.

The time-bound and particular properties of knowledge in the applied sciences has also been exaggerated. Such knowledge involves more than technological applications of basic science generalizations to current practical problems. Although less generalizable than the basic sciences, they are also disciplines in their own right, with distinctive and relatively enduring bodies of theory and methodology that cannot simply be derived or extrapolated from the basic sciences to which they are related. It is simply not true that only basic science knowledge can be related to and organized around general principles. Each of the applied biological sciences (e.g., medicine, agronomy) possesses an independent body of general principles underlying the detailed knowledge in its field, in addition to being related in a still more general way to basic principles in biology.

Applied sciences also present us with many strategic advantages in teaching and curriculum development. We can capitalize on the student's existing interest in and familiarity with applied problems in science to provide an intellectual and motivational bridge for learning the content of the basic sciences. Previously acquired knowledge in the applied sciences, both incidental and systematic, can serve as the basis for rendering basic science concepts and propositions both potentially meaningful to the learner and less threatening to him. There is also good reason for believing that applied sciences are intrinsically more learnable than basic sciences to the elementary-school child, because of the particularized and intuitive nature of his cognitive processes and their dependence on the "here and now" properties of concrete-empirical experience. For example, before the tenth-grader ever enters the biology class, he has a vast fund of information about immunization, chemotherapy, the symptoms of infection, heredity, etc. Finally, knowledge in the applied sciences probably is retained longer than knowledge in the basic sciences because of the greater frequency of their subsequent use (by virtue of more frequent applicability to intellectual experience in adult life).

**Overemphasis of Analytical, Quantitative and Experimental Aspects of Science** One of the characteristic features of the curriculum reform movement is an overcorrection of the unnecessarily low level of sophistication at which many high-school subjects have been and still are taught. In the sciences this tendency is marked by a virtual repudiation of the descriptive, naturalistic, and applied approach and an overemphasis of the analytical, experimental, and quantitative aspects of science. In introductory high-school biology, for example, much of the new content consists of highly sophisticated biochemical content that presupposes advanced knowledge of chemistry on the part of students who have no background whatsoever in this subject. The implied rationale of this policy is Bruner's untenable assertion that any concept can be taught to any person irrespective of his cognitive maturity or level of subject-matter sophistication.

By any reasonable pedagogic criterion, introductory high-school biology should continue to remain predominantly naturalistic and descriptive in approach rather than analytical and experimental. This does not imply emphasis on descriptive information or on disconnected facts unrelated to theory, but on *explanatory* concepts that are stated in relatively gross and descriptive language, instead of in the more technical, quantitative, and sophisticated terminology of biochemistry and biophysics. In short, high-school biology should concentrate on those broad biological ideas that constitute part of a *general* education—physiology, evolution, development, inheritance, uniformities and diversity in life, ecology, and man's place in nature—rather than on a detailed and technical analysis of the physical and chemical basis of biological phenomena or of the morphology and function of intracellular microstructures. This is particularly true for the substantial number of students who will receive no further instruction in biology. As a matter of fact, there is still much significant but as yet unexploited *conceptual* content in introductory biology than can be treated in much more sophisticated terms at a descriptive level, without having to resort to the depth of biochemical and cellular detail given in the Yellow and Blue BSCS versions.

Contrary to the strong and explicitly stated bias of the Blue and Yellow versions, there is still much room in introductory biology for the naturalistic approach. It is much more important for the *beginning* student in science to learn how to observe events in nature systematically and precisely, and how to formulate and test hypotheses on the basis of independent sets of naturally occurring antecedents and consequences, than to learn how to manipulate an experimental variable and control other relevant variables, by design, in a laboratory situation. The former approach not only takes precedence in the student's intellectual development, and is more consonant with his experiential background, but also has more transfer value for problem solving in future "real-life" contexts. To dogmatically equate scientific method with the experimental-analytical approach also excludes, rather summarily from the domain of science, such fields in biology as ecology, paleontology, and evolution, and such other disciplines as geology, astronomy, anthropology, and sociology.

Retention of the naturalistic and descriptive emphasis, and of some applied content, in introductory high school biology is thus consistent with the fact that tenth-grade biology is the terminal course in science for many students. It is also more consistent than is the analytical-experimental approach with the tenth-grader's existing background of experience, his interests, his intellectual readiness, and his relative degree of sophistication in science. This proposed emphasis is also in no way inappropriate for those students who will subsequently take high-school physics and chemistry, as well as more advanced biology courses. These latter students would be much better prepared, after taking such an introductory course, for a second course in biology, in the twelfth grade or in college, that takes a more quantitative and experimental-analytical approach, introduces more esoteric topics, and considers the biochemical and biophysical aspects of biological knowledge. By this time, they would also have the necessary mathematical sophistication and greater experience with experimental methodology.

## LEVEL OF SOPHISTICATION

In the Yellow and Blue BSCS versions, it appears as if little was made to discriminate between basic and highly sophisticated content—between what is appropriate and essential for an introductory high-school course and what could be more profitably reserved for more advanced courses. These versions include topics, detail, and level of sophistication that vary in appropriateness from the tenth grade to graduate school. Only the Green Version gives the impression of being at an appropriate level of sophis-

tication for a beginning course. And since the unsophisticated student cannot be expected to distinguish between more and less important material, he either throws up his hands in despair, learns nothing thoroughly in the effort to learn everything, or relies on rote memorization and "cramming" to get through examinations.

The Blue Version, especially, appears sufficiently sophisticated and challenging to constitute an introductory college course for students who *already* had an introductory biology course in high school as well as courses in chemistry and physics. It is true, of course, that subjects once thought too difficult for high-school students (e.g., analytical geometry, and calculus) *can* be taught successfully to *bright* high-school students with good quantitative ability. But in the latter instances, students are adequately prepared for these advanced subjects by virtue of taking the necessary preliminary, and sequentially antecedent courses in mathematics. The Blue Version, on the other hand, presents biological material of college-level difficulty and sophistication to students who do not have the necessary background in chemistry, physics, and elementary biology for learning it meaningfully. It should also be remembered that college-level mathematics is not considered appropriate for *all* high-school students, but only for those brighter students with better-than-average aptitude in mathematics, who are college bound and intend to major in such fields as mathematics, science, engineering, and architecture.

An introductory high-school course in any discipline should concentrate more on establishing a general ideational framework than in putting a great deal of flesh on the skeleton. Generally speaking, only the framework is retained anyway after a considerable retention interval; and if more time is spent on overlearning the framework, plus a minimum of detail, than in superficially learning a large mass of oversophisticated and poorly understood material, both more of the important ideas are retained in the case of students taking the subject terminally, and a better foundation is laid for students who intend to take more advanced courses later.

Oversophisticated detail is not only unnecessary and inappropriate for a beginning course, but also hinders learning and generates unfavorable attitudes toward the subject. The student "can't see the forest for the trees." The main conceptual themes get lost or become unidentifiable in a welter of detail. Both the average student, and the student not particularly interested in science, would tend to feel overwhelmed by the vast quantity and complexity of detail, terminology, methodology, and historical material in the Blue and Yellow versions. And a student who feels overwhelmed by a subject tends to develop an aversion toward it, and to resort to rote memorization for examination purposes.

It is not necessary for a beginning student to be given so much sequential historical detail about the development of biological ideas, related experimental evidence from original sources, and pedantic information about *all* of the various misconceptions and twistings and turnings taken by these ideas before they evolve into their currently accepted form. As a result, the ideas themselves—which are really the important things to be learned—tend to be obscured and rendered less salient. This practice also places an unnecessary and unwarranted burden on learning and memory effort—effort that could be more profitably expended on learning the ideas themselves and the more significant aspects of their historical development.

To give students the flavor of biology as an evolving empirical science with a complex and often circuitous history, it would suffice to cite several *examples*. It is unnecessary to give the detailed ideational and experimental history of *every* biological concept and controversy. Unsophisticated students also tend to be confused by raw experimental data, and by the actual chronological and experi-

mental history underlying the emergence of a biological law or theory—especially when long quotations are given from original sources that use archaic language, refer to obscure controversies, and report findings and inferences in an unfamiliar and discursive manner. It is sufficient (as the Green Version does) to review the historical background of biological concepts in a schematic, telescoped, simplified, and reconstructed fashion, deleting most of the detail, and disregarding the actual chronological order of the antecedent ideas and their related experiments.

In an introductory course, simplification of content—*without* teaching wrong ideas that have to be unlearned later—is always justifiable and indicated. This can be accomplished by simply presenting more general and less complete versions of much of the same material that can be presented subsequently in greater depth and at high levels of sophistication. Although the Green Version probably lacks sufficient detail, it is less damaging, in my opinion, to present inadequate historical detail and experimental evidence than to obscure the major concepts by providing excessive historical and experimental data. This book unquestionably stimulates the student to delve deeper on his own. In any case, the missing detail can always be furnished by the teacher or from other sources.

It is possible to present ideas relatively simply—yet correctly—by deleting a great deal of the dispensable terminological, methodological, and historical detail, as well as many of the intermediate steps in argumentation; by telescoping or condensing material; by eliminating tangential "asides" and less important qualifications; by limiting the scope of coverage; by omitting formulas, equations, and structural diagrams of complex molecules that are actually meaningless to unsophisticated students; by keeping the level of discourse general and simple; by writing lucidly, using terms precisely and consistently, and giving concise and familiar examples: by using schematically simplified models and diagrams; and by bearing in mind that a satiation point exists for any student. An atypically high level of sophistication may sometimes be employed simply to *illustrate* the complexity of a given topic; but in these instances students should be explicitly instructed not to master the details.

## COLLABORATION OF SUBJECT MATTER, LEARNING THEORY, AND MEASUREMENT SPECIALISTS

A basic premise of all curriculum reform projects is that only a person with subject-matter competence in a given discipline should prepare curriculum materials in that discipline. Only such a person is sufficiently sophisticated (a) to identify unifying and integrative concepts with broad generalizability and explanatory power in the field; (b) to perceive the interrelationships between different ideas and topics so as to organize, sequence, and integrate them optimally; (c) to comprehend the process of inquiry and the relationship of theory to data in the discipline, in order to select appropriate laboratory exercises and to integrate process and content aspects of the curriculum program; and (d) to understand the subject-matter content well enough either to prepare textual materials lucidly himself, or to judge whether others have done so.

To be pedagogically effective, such curriculum materials also have to conform to established principles in the psychology of classroom learning, and must include evaluative devices that conform to established principles of evaluation and measurement. Obviously, it is difficult for any one person to possess all three competencies. But a *pure* educational psychologist or measurement specialist cannot collaborate with a subject-matter specialist in producing curriculum materials and measuring instruments—apart from communicating to him *general* principles of learning theory and measurement.

This type of help, however, is inade-quate for the *actual* collaborative task that needs to be done. In the actual operation of producing curriculum and evaluative materials that are sound on both subject-matter and learning theory-measurement grounds, the educational psychologist and measurement specialist can collaborate effectively with their colleagues in subject-matter fields, *only* if they themselves are sufficiently sophisticated in the subject matter to participate actively in the production of the curriculum materials from the *very start*. Only in this way can they ensure that the *detailed* content and structure of the material conform to established principles of learning and measurement theory. One possible solution to this problem of producing sound instructional materials is to train a new type of curriculum worker: either a subject-matter specialist who is sophisticated (but not expert) in learning theory or measurement to collaborate with learning theory and measurement specialists; or a learning theory or measurement specialist who is sophisticated (but not expert) in some subject-matter field to collaborate with subject-matter specialists.

## SINGLE-UNIT VERSUS INTEGRATED CURRICULUM APPROACH

Generally speaking, it is not pedagogically tenable to produce science curriculum materials apart from an integrated plan encompassing each of the separate scientific disciplines at successively higher levels of difficulty from elementary school through college. A collection of supplementary grade-appropriate units in various scientific disciplines, even when used in conjunction with existing curriculum materials, presents many difficulties: (a) It does not further the construction of a sequentially organized curriculum in any particular discipline at any grade level that is logically coherent and systematic in its component topics. (b) Students fail to develop a conception of each scientific discipline as a sequentially organized, logically integrated, and coherently interrelated body of knowledge. (c) For a given discipline to be organized for optimal learning on a longitudinal basis, one must plan in advance for the articulation of the various levels of difficulty so that some topics are considered at progressively higher levels of sophistication, whereas other topics are introduced *de novo* when specified levels of sophistication are reached.

This kind of large-scale, integrated curriculum planning requires no greater "certainty in the minds of the specialists on exactly how science materials should be scheduled to guarantee learnings" than does the production of small unintegrated units of material. The *same* principles are involved but on a much more massive scale. One starts with the same tentative outline based on logical interrelationships between the component aspects of a discipline, as modified by pertinent developmental and learning theory considerations; prepares tentative units; and revises these units on the basis of try-out experience or alters their grade-placement level. If this is done by a team, say twenty times larger than the one ordinarily envisaged, it can prepare an integrated science curriculum in the same length of time that it takes an average-sized team to prepare an unintegrated series of units. Admittedly, this involves many more administrative problems; but if one adheres to the principle of immediate try-out of component units, there should not necessarily be any problem of "rigidity." The deficiencies in the existing large-scale, integrated projects stem more from (a) untenable theoretical ideas about teaching and learning (e.g., overemphasis on the importance of discovery in learning; overemphasis on the "basic science," experimental-analytic approach); (b) uncoordinated team effort, resulting in the production of textbooks consisting of unintegrated units, and no pervasive organizing ideas that are organically related to the textual material (e.g., Blue and Yellow BSCS versions); (c) failure to try out the materials empirically until the *entire* series is completed; and (d) lack of active collaboration, on a day-to-day basis, of learning-theory and measurement specialists (who are also sophisticated in the subject matter) in the actual preparation of curriculum and measurement materials.

## EARLY TRY-OUT OF MATERIALS

An essential aspect of the preparation of instructional materials that is, unfortunately, ignored much too frequently by many curriculum reform projects is the matter of early and continuous try-out, both with individual pupils and in classrooms. Only in this way is it possible to ascertain their appropriateness and effectiveness, and to modify the original logically-developed outline in terms of empirically relevant information regarding learnability, lucidity, difficulty level, sequence, organization, practicality, and attitudes of pupils, teachers, and administrators. All too often huge sums of money are invested in preparing an integrated series of curriculum materials without making any provision for try-out and evaluation until the finished product is published.

## DIFFICULTIES IN EVALUATING THE NEW CURRICULA

As Brownell (1965) points out, curriculum evaluation is more difficult than it often appears on the surface. This, in large part, is a function of the fact that standardized achievement tests both cover various traditional subject-matter units deliberately ignored by the new curricula, as well as fail to measure knowledge of the more modern concepts which the latter emphasize. Further, many curriculum projects either make no provisions whatsoever for evaluation, or fail to provide for an adequate control group and to eliminate the Hawthorne effect. The weight of the evidence indicates that on the basis of achievement test results the new curriculums in mathematics and science are approximately as effective as existing curriculums. If this were our ultimate criterion of effectiveness, these findings would be quite disappointing. Much more important, however, are results on delayed tests of retention and performance in more advanced, sequentially related courses. Unfortunately, however, such data are not available.

**Evaluation of Learnability and Measurement of Achievement** The principal shortcoming of scores on conventional achievement tests, in my opinion, is that they measure *immediate* retention of understanding and ability to apply knowledge (e.g., quarterly and final tests), instead of (a) delayed retention, and (b) performance in sequentially related, more advanced courses. Ability to make satisfactory scores on immediate retention tests of understanding and application is not proof that the material is adequately learnable, lucid, properly programmed, etc., because any reasonably bright pupil can do enough cramming before an announced test to make a satisfactory score on a test of immediate retention, even if the materials are generally unsound by *any* criterion; in fact, this *has* been the case for the last 2500 years of formal education.

When the learnability of curriculum materials is assessed by conventional tests of achievement, these latter tests often give spurious and misleading impressions of genuine learnability. This is apparently the case when the Yellow and Blue BSCS versions are evaluated by means of the conventional achievement tests. Achievement test data show that the three BSCS versions are approximately as "learnable" as conventional textbooks. It was demonstrated, for example, that students using the BSCS texts score somewhat higher than students using conventional texts, on a final *Comprehensive BSCS Test,* and somewhat lower on a final *Cooperative Biology Test* (Wallace, 1963). In the first place, it is questionable how well such final tests *really* measure the learnability of subject-matter content. Most adequately motivated students can "learn," for examination purposes, large quantities of overly sophisticated and poorly presented materials that they do not really understand; unfortunately, however, in such circumstances, little evidence of retention is present even a few days later. Second, one of the main objectives of any new, elaborately prepared curriculum program is presumably to exceed by far, rather than merely to approximate the level of academic achievement attained in conventionally taught courses.

The didactic use of substantive and programmatic devices to strengthen cognitive structure (and thus to increase the functional retention of background knowledge available for future learning and problem solving) focuses attention on the need to develop more valid measures of the organizational strength and availability of such knowledge. The "transfer retention" test (Ausubel & Fitzgerald, 1962) constitutes a new approach to the problem of measuring functional retention. It attempts to do this by measuring the extent to which retained knowledge of subject matter is sufficiently stable and well organized to be available as a foundation for learning new, sequentially related material that could not be efficiently learned in the absence of such availability. At the same time, of course, it also provides a measure of knowledge available for problem solving, because if retained knowledge is available for new sequential learning, it is reasonable to assume that it is also available for problem solving.

Conventional retention measures, covering previously studied material at the end of a given course of instruction, are not truly reflective of the later availability of this material for new learning and problem solving purposes. Because a short retention interval cannot adequately test the organizational strength and viability of newly acquired knowledge, and because of the contaminating influence of rote memory in poorly constructed retention tests, such conventional measures of retention are often misleading. They fail to distinguish adequately between the individual who merely understands and retains material well enough to answer rote and meaningful questions restricted to the substance of this material, and the individual whose understanding and retention are sufficient to serve as a springboard for learning new, sequentially related material. Both individuals may frequently make identical scores on immediate tests of retention.

Problem solving items, on the other hand, are less influenced by rote memory, and also directly test ability to use and apply retained knowledge. But since successful problem solving also depends on many traits (e.g., venturesomeness, flexibility, perseverance, problem sensitivity) that are unrelated to the functional availability of knowledge, success or failure on such items is as much a reflection of the influence of these latter traits as of the availability of usable knowledge. Hence,

it can be reasonably argued that the most valid way of testing the organizational strength and viability of knowledge is not to test retention per se or to use problem solving items, but to test retention in the context of sequential learning, i.e., in situations where ability to learn new material presupposes the availability of the old.

The transfer retention test may be administered in addition to or independently of the conventional retention test. When used for routine course examinations, the test procedure requires that students study an unfamiliar new learning passage that is sequentially related to and presupposes knowledge of the previously studied material on which they are being examined. Their scores on a test of this *new* material are "transfer retention scores" and measure the functional availability of the previously learned material for new learning.

## 37. Evaluating Three English Curricula in the Middle School Years

### DWIGHT L. BURTON

There are two major reasons for including this article. First, it illustrates a nontechnical presentation of evaluation data. We could perhaps use more easily digested reports like this and fewer huge helpings of analysis variance tables, coefficients, and chi-squares—assuming, of course, that the more digestable report is based on an accurate and qualified data interpretation. In addition, Burton toward the end of his article "breaks away" from the evaluation results to describe some observations that came about simply as a result of having experienced the project. It is frequently these kinds of subjective reports that prove to be of greatest value in the process of curriculum innovation.

My title represents weasel wording. I began with "Junior High School" as the last three words because our Curriculum Study Center at Florida State University, which completed its work in 1968, took the junior high school as its province. While our work was in progress, though, the middle school movement gained momentum, so I decided that I should substitute "Middle School" for "Junior High School." My conscience, at that point, got the better of me as I was forced to admit that I am not sure yet (is anyone?) what the middle school is. I compromised, then, with "the Middle Years." I make no apology for the first part of my title, for whether middle school or junior high school, the middle years of the curriculum have been a kind of educational no man's land.

Developments in English in recent years fall into three general movements which are related but which actually have been carried on quite independently. The first

Reprinted and abridged with permission of the publisher and Dwight L. Burton from an article entitled "English In No Man's Land: Some Suggestions for the Middle Years," which appeared in the English Journal, **60** (1971), pp. 23–30. Copyright 1971 by the National Council of Teachers of English.

of these might be called the curriculum content movement, featuring the attempts to define English as subject, to identify sequences, and to produce instructional materials. Foremost in this movement, of course, were (most of them have completed their projects) the curriculum study centers and demonstration centers funded by the U. S. Office of Education and independent curriculum work such as that of James Moffett and Geoffrey Summerfield. This movement centered mostly on subject matter and its arrangement and was geared in large part to traditional systems of school organization, to both the traditional grade hierarchy and the allocation of the school day.

But at the same time, the rebellion against what has been termed the "cells and bells" system of education gained full stride and much publicity. The thrust of this second movement has been toward finding more viable and effective ways of bringing students and teachers together for teaching and learning in English. Other subjects, of course, were involved in this movement, which was spearheaded generally by people who were not specialists in academic subjects and who relied on traditional content, just as the leaders in the curriculum content movement relied on traditional patterns of school organization. The mission of our Curriculum Study Center was to develop programs for the junior high school, Grades 7–9, and to establish some guidelines for English in the junior high school. As I suggested at the outset, we were well into the project when we became aware that in a number of places the junior high school was being phased out in favor of the organization involving the middle school.

Team teaching; large group-small group instruction; modular scheduling; ungraded programs; short-term electives; individualized instruction; independent study—all these are now familiar in the vocabulary of the profession. But so far, substantive programs have not been devised to fit most of these innovations in student-teacher relationships. The student materials published to date by the Curriculum Study Centers in cooperation with commercial publishers look, in the main, much like those of old, with juxtaposition of materials rather than innovation their chief characteristic.

Yet the third major movement of the past few years is that of packaging materials for use in English programs. If not already gone, the day when the English curriculum depends on one hardbound book for literature and one for language composition is in its twilight. The packaging movement was pioneered some years ago by such publishing ventures as the Scholastic Literature Units which feature use of a variety of paperbound books and plans for total class, small-group, and individual activities within a thematic framework. The preoccupation recently with the culturally disadvantaged student has brought new materials such as the Holt *Impact* program, Macmillan's *Gateway English*, *The Way It Is* of Xerox, and *What's the Name of the Game?* of New Dimensions in Education, in which multimedia materials are furnished—paperbound books, records, transparencies, slides.

A major problem of the profession now, and one of which we became keenly aware toward the end of our work in the Curriculum Center, is to put together the best fruits of the three movements I have just identified, just as a football team, on a given Saturday, must put together in the most effective way its running game, its passing game, and its kicking game if it is to be successful. A new era in our work thus suggests itself.

Since the purpose of our Curriculum Study Center was to establish some guide lines for the English program in the middle, or junior high school, years, we were interested not only in preparation of new teaching materials but with tryout of existing materials in three different curriculum sequences, representing what we thought were major rationales underlying what was already being done or being advocated.

The first curriculum, which we titled "tri-component," consisted of a series of units, more or less discrete, in literature, composition, and language. The outline of the program was as follows:

*Seventh Grade*
  Literature:
    1. Myth, legend, and folklore
    2. Introduction to modern imaginative forms of literature
  Languages:
    1. Semantics I
    2. Lexicography
    3. Morphology and syntax I
  Composition:
    1. Micro-rhetoric I
*Eighth Grade*
  Literature:
    1. The novel—symbolism in fiction
    2. The short story—plot development
    3. Narrative poetry
    4. One-act play
  Language:
    1. Morphology and syntax II
  Composition:
    1. Micro-rhetoric II
    2. Modern forms of oral communication

Ninth Grade
Literature:
1. Satire
2. Drama
   a. Comedy
   b. Classical tragedy
Language:
1. Grammar of transformed sentences
2. Semantics II
Composition:
1. Rhetoric and composition—invention, ordering, strategy (voice, tone, and attitude)
2. Oral persuasion

The second curriculum, titled "Literature-Centered," was based on six "thematic categories," with one unit in each category presented in each grade. Written composition and oral composition were related exclusively to the literature language study partially related. This program is outlined in Table 1.

The third curriculum, based on our interpretation of some of the work of Jerome Bruner and Jean Piaget, was organized around certain cognitive processes; in the seventh and eighth grades, recognition of form and perception of meaning; in the ninth grade, perception of relationships—linear, inverse, analogical, and correlative. The content of literature, language, and composition was considered in terms of these processes.

Six junior high schools in various areas of Florida participated in the program. During each year, two classes in each school followed each of the programs. About 60 per cent of the students who began in each program completed the full three years. For purposes of comparison, a control group was made up of students who had been in each of the schools for three years but had not participated in any of the experimental programs. Fifty-four teachers and approximately 3,000 students were involved in the experimental programs.

A rather elaborate program of evaluation was carried out. Throughout the three years of the project, participating teachers and members of the Center staff kept anecdotal records, and the participating teachers gathered various samples of student work. The final, terminal evaluation was carried out during the last weeks of the ninth grade. The various instruments used in the evaluation were these:

*Objective Devices*
1. *Sentence Relationships Test* (designed by Professor Roy O'Donnell). A fifty-item multiple-response test designed to measure the student's ability to recognize structural relationships of words in sentences without use of grammatical terminology.
2. *Sentence Combining Test* (also con-

**TABLE 1**
**Outline of Literature-Centered Middle School English Curriculum**

| Category | Seventh Grade | Eighth Grade | Ninth Grade |
| --- | --- | --- | --- |
| Decisions: | Courage | Responsibility | Justice |
| Teamwork: | Team Leaders | The Family | The Team and the Individual |
| Man in Action: | Man and Nature | Man Among Enemies | Man Alone |
| Relationships: | Adolescents We Learn About | Close Adolescent Relationships | Mirrors (relations with self) |
| The Unknown: | Qualities of Folk Heroes | Deeds and Qualities of Men and Myth | Concern for the Unexplained |
| Frontiers and Horizons: | Far Away Places | The Village | Frontiers in Space |

structed by O'Donnell). This device was designed to furnish a measure of the student's maturity in syntax. Students were given a passage consisting solely of simple declarative sentences and were asked to rewrite the passage, combining sentences as they saw fit. The rewritten versions were then analyzed according to techniques developed by Kellogg Hunt and Roy O'Donnell.

3. *Language Concepts Test.* A twenty-item, multiple-response test designed to gauge the student's understanding of broad language concepts.

4. *Poetry Reading Test.* A forty-item, multiple-response test based on a sequence of ten short poems.

5. *Short Story Reading Test.* A twenty-six item, multiple-response test based on the story "Trial at Arms" by Walter Van Tillburg Clark.

*Nonobjective Devices*

1. *Analysis of Writing Samples.* Two writing samples were gathered, two and a half months apart. In each instance, the situation was controlled as carefully as possible. The first time, the students were asked to develop a brief paper in which they voiced and supported a specific kind of "protest." The second time, after some explanation and preparation, the students were asked to develop a paper answering these questions: "What does *Mod* do or not do for you? What does it say about your generation?" The samples then were analyzed by two raters according to a technique explained by Paul Diederich, of the Educational Testing Service, in the *English Journal* (April 1966).

2. *Free Response to a Short Story.* Students were given one class period in which to respond in writing, in any way they saw fit, to John O'Hara's "Do You Like It Here?" The responses were analyzed by a method based on the one reported by James Squire in *The Responses of Adolescents While Reading Four Short Stories* (NCTE, 1964).

3. *Free Response to a Poem.* In the same way, the students wrote unstructured reactions to Fred Lape's "From This the Strength." The responses were analyzed by a technique similar to that used in the analysis of the responses to the short story.

4. *Semantic Differential.* This instrument was developed by Professor Peter Dunn-Rankin, now of the University of Hawaii. Composed of a series of bipolar adjectives, the device is a way of indirectly measuring student attitude in three major categories—evaluation of the curriculum, unusuality of the curriculum, and complexity of the curriculum.

Given this barrage of evaluation and the welter of statistical analysis one would encounter in our final report to the Office of Education, one might well be disappointed with the meagerness of specific, major findings which we can now report. Certainly more questions were unanswered than answered at the end of the project.

Ignoring for my purposes here the many bits and pieces of information yielded by the various statistical analyses and by the anecdotal records, I content myself with a few general, what I hope are pertinent, findings concerning student achievement and attitude.

Statistically, there was no overall superiority of one of the experimental programs over the others, though there were occasional significant differences in favor of one or the other of the programs in individual analyses. There was a clear statistical superiority, though, of all of the three experimental groups over the control group. Probably the reason for this is obvious: we developed the programs and we developed the tests! But at least we were convinced that at the end of their junior high school years, the students in the experimental programs excelled the control students in some matters we think significant in the English program.

There are a few more specific findings we think may aid our quest for guidelines for English programs in the middle years. For one, traditional critical assessment and formal analysis of literature seem of small use in the junior high school. We were largely unsuccessful in getting students involved in analysis except in connection with plot in fiction. There was plentiful evidence to support Frank Whitehead's statement "Until well on into adolescence these reactions [to what is read] are intuitive, impermanent, and intensely personal." Student response to literature, when asked for formally in controlled situations, tends to parallel quite closely the kind of teaching the students have been exposed to. Students in the tri-component program, in which there were formal units on the genres and modes of literature, did somewhat better than the others on the short story and poetry tests and made more purely literary judgments on the free responses to the short story and poem. Students in the cognitive processes program tended to be the most "far out" in their responses.

Students in the literature-centered program tended to rate higher than the others rather consistently on the writing samples, though there was less formal teaching of composition in their curriculum than in the other two. Perhaps the thematic unit, with literature at the center, provides built-in motivation and invention in writing.

Students in the tri-component curriculum, which featured more formal and elaborate study of syntax than the other programs, did better than the others on the Sentence Relationships Test and the Sentence Combining Test, but not on the writing samples. The implication here is not new: grammar teaches grammar, not writing.

Comparative achievement, of course, was not our only interest. We were interested at least equally in student response to the curriculum models. We were left bleak because we did not gain greater insight than we did, but we were grateful for small gleanings. Again, it was obvious that students gave more favorable evaluations to the experimental programs than the control students gave to traditional English. It is pretty apparent that English can be an exciting subject to junior high school students if it means something more than spelling, punctuation, looking up words, diagramming sentences, and answering questions about literature.

It came as no surprise certainly that literature was the most popular strand of the curriculum, no matter how it was packaged, and that junior novels—*Third Man on the Mountain, Shane, Call It Courage, Swiftwater*—ranked high in the memories of students. Attempts to provide for group study of individual works proved frustrating: almost every selection chosen for group study rated both the lowest and the highest possible esteem in the eyes of students!

The literature-centered curriculum evoked, in general, the greatest enthusiasm from students, and yet was rated as the most "complex" according to analysis of responses on the semantic differential device. Perhaps this somewhat contradictory finding is explained, first, by the general popularity of literature over language and composition, and, second, by the problems that many junior high school students have in keeping in mind the relevance in a thematic context of activities that extend over five or six weeks.

There is little doubt, judging from student reactions and anecdotal records, of three things: oral language activities —especially dramatization and oral reading—were enjoyed; grammar, no matter of what vintage, was not enjoyed; and work with broad matters of language such as elementary semantics and varieties of language were found highly relevant by a majority of the students.

One other finding was of interest to us—and I hesitate to mention it in the present climate. We found little difference in the general interests and responses of our culturally disadvantaged students, represented by a black school in Miami, from those of students more favored in cultural milieu, though the achievement of the culturally deprived students was consistently lower. Culturally disadvantaged students in Miami may well be different from those in the ghettos of Harlem or Chicago, but we are tempted to search for guidelines for English programs for human beings of similar age levels, though of different race or economic status, rather than to concern ourselves with unique programs for the disadvantaged.

I want to follow this brief report on some of our findings with some recommendations, representing purely my own thought as I view in retrospect our project and some modest follow-up experimentation in several schools in Florida and Texas, and which, at points, may well "go beyond the data," that ominous phrase that haunts our doctoral students as they write their dissertations.

First, a few recommendations concerning the English curriculum generally in the middle years.

1. Greater attention needs to be given to individualization in literature (Where have you heard that before?) A few book reports to supplement the study of the anthology will not do. A majority of the time given to literature should be spent in individualized, rather than group, study, with the aim of helping the student to find himself in literature, to find some handles he wants to grasp and can feel satisfaction with. Systematic planning of individual reading programs and designs should be a major activity of the English teacher in the junior high school.
2. More attention, obviously, needs to

be given to oral language activities in the English classroom. The primitive attempts at oral composition in the programs developed in our Center fell far short of what is needed. We may not be completely sure, at this point, what directions oral language activities should take, but scholars such as Whitehead, Moffett, Summerfield, and Hoetker suggest some possibilities particularly in the area of dramatic activities. Since the close of the Curriculum Center, we have gathered some tentative evidence of the value of dramatic improvisation as readiness for the reading of selections of literature.

3. Grammar—whether transformational or otherwise—be damned in the middle years! The attempt to dump a heavy load of "new" grammar on junior high school students is the major boondoggle of the curriculum study centers, ours included. Rather, language study for the middle years should take a broad focus, stressing the nature and functions of language and varieties and dialects of English.
4. The thematic unit, despite its scoffers of recent years, is far from dead as a way of organizing the English program to make clear the relevance of literature to life concerns and to provide motivation for written and oral composition. Having writing and oral language activity merely "growing out of" study of literature is not enough, though. We need to look for the reciprocal relationships, to structure those activities in oral and written language that naturally grow out of literature study but which also reinforce understandings in literature.

Now, a few recommendations concerning the preparation of English teachers for the middle years:

1. Systematic training is needed in myth, legend, folklore, and junior literature or literature for adolescents.

At present, few prospective teachers are required to take, or even give the opportunity to take, work in myth and legendry. Some colleges and universities long have required a course in literature for adolescents, but for the majority of future teachers, such a course is not available.

2. Prospective teachers should have a good knowledge of the language development and language learning of children and adolescents. A number of colleges and universities, of course, now require some course work in linguistics of prospective English teachers, but the program usually does not include the kind of psycholinguistics this recommendation suggests. (A large number of institutions, particularly the small liberal arts colleges, still require no work at all in linguistics of prospective teachers of English.)

3. Prospective teachers need to learn as much as possible about how to *teach* composition. This may seem an over-obvious suggestion. Most prospective teachers have work in methods of teaching English in which there supposedly is concern with how to teach writing, but often there really isn't treatment of how to *teach* writing, but only talk of how to make writing assignments, how to evaluate student papers, etc. Even many experienced teachers don't know what to do about the matter except to motivate students as best they can, then criticize the works the students produce, and hope for the best the next time. Parenthetically here, group work in composition proved a saving factor for teachers of low-ability classes in our Center project, lending support to James McCrimmon's contention that "whether the assignment is difficult or easy depends more on the teaching procedure than on the subject matter. If students are required to work independently on this assignment [an assignment described by McCrimmon], many of them will have difficulty and some of them will be frustrated. But if they are allowed to work as a group, sharing each other's insights and doubts, they will tend as a group to profit from individual contributions and to correct false leads" (McCrimmon, 1966). Quite probably some adaptations to middle grades can be made of Robert Zoellner's (1969) "behavioral pedagogy."

4. Prospective English teachers need to learn how to plan systematically for individual reading, how to work out reading designs with individual students. A helpful reference on the subject is the article by Stephen Dunning several years ago. ("Sequence and Literature: Some Teaching Facts," *High School Journal*, October 1963.)

5. More training obviously is needed in oral language. Very few colleges require anything of prospective English teachers beyond the course in fundamentals of speech. Recently, we have added a required six-quarter-hour bloc in oral interpretation and dramatics to our undergraduate curriculum in English education at Florida State University.

There has been concerted national attention to improving teacher preparation in English in recent years. Most recommendations, though, are in the form (like those of mine above) of the kinds of courses or content which should be offered to prospective teachers. We think that another matter needs to be given importance—teaching styles, not just methods of doing this or that. In this connection, I quote from the final report to the Office of Education on our Curriculum Center:

. . . efforts to devise and test elaborate structural models for organizing and teaching junior and senior high school English should be augmented by research programs which might include:

1. attempts to determine what actually is meant by *style of teaching* (as opposed to description of what is to be taught and how content might be best structured).

2. attempts to discover correlations between teaching style and various learning styles. In other words, which students learn best from which teachers?

3. attempts to discover what determines given styles of teaching in English. This suggests courses focussed on a study of styles of teaching in addition to those on the organization of the material to be taught. Some universities, including the Florida State University, have initiated such courses, or units of courses, which depend heavily on the videotaping of microteaching sessions and of actual classroom instruction, with subsequent analysis of the tapes by the students themselves.

Acknowledging its dubious relevance here, I add a postscript. One of our major failings in our Curriculum Center work was our attempt to do too much too soon, a failing shared, I think, by a number of other curriculum experimenters. In this time of rigor and drive and earnestness in education, with students spiralling (or not spiralling) through sequences, we don't give students sufficient time for reflection, for considered decision-making. Contemplation of the navel, exposed or otherwise, is still essential both for the individual and society.

## 38. Achievement and Attitude of Sixth-Grade Pupils in Conventional and Contemporary Mathematics Programs

### ANN D. HUNGERMAN

This article, based on the author's doctoral dissertation (Hungerman, 1965), describes an elaborate attempt to investigate a set of four questions uppermost in the minds of mathematics educators. "New math" programs, for example, have been accused of being strong on theory but weak on skill development, particularly computational skills. How valid is such a contention? In addition, questions relating to the influence of such variables as attitude and socioeconomic class are also investigated. Extensive data are presented in support of the somewhat unexpected—at least for this reader—conclusions. As a student of curriculum evaluation, the reader is urged to examine critically the relationship of (1) the four research questions, (2) the tabular data, and (3) the conclusions. Did the evaluation design follow logically from the questions? Were the data responsive to the questions? Did the conclusions follow logically from the data presented?

When contemporary mathematics programs were introduced at the elementary level, the question raised most often was "What will happen to computational skills?"

The purpose of this study was to provide a factual basis for answering this question and three others that reflect some of the major issues in the current controversy over the value of the newer elementary mathematics programs.

1. Will pupils studying contemporary mathematics maintain achievement in conventional arithmetic, particularly computational skills, comparable to that of pupils studying conventional arithmetic?
2. Are the newer mathematical ideas, symbols, and vocabulary equally suitable for pupils of all intelligence levels and all socioeconomic backgrounds?
3. What effect are contemporary mathematics programs having on attitude toward mathematics?
4. Are conventional arithmetic achievement, contemporary mathematics achievement, and attitude toward mathematics related in any way?

A comparative study was designed, measuring variables of intelligence, socioeconomic background, conventional arithmetic achievement, contemporary mathematics achievement, and attitude toward mathematics for a group of pupils who had studied contemporary mathematics, against similar data for a control group of pupils who had not had any such experience. The School Mathematics Study Group program (SMSG) was chosen as the experimental course of study. This nationally piloted program was one of the most influential and one of the earli-

Reprinted with permission of the publisher, the National Council of Teachers of Mathematics, and Ann D. Hungerman from *The Arithmetic Teacher,* **14** (January 1967), pp. 30–39. Copyright 1967 by NCTM.

est, permitting selection of an experimental group with three years of contemporary mathematics experience.

## PROCEDURE

The sample group included pupils of average intelligence, from two metropolitan Detroit area school systems of similar size (fifteen to twenty elementary schools), and of average to somewhat-above-average socioeconomic level. The experimental group consisted of ten classes ($N = 305$) of sixth-grade pupils who had studied the School Mathematics Study Group program during Grades 4, 5, and 6. The control group consisted of ten classes ($N = 260$) of sixth-grade pupils who had studied a conventional arithmetic program during Grades 4, 5, and 6.

The *California Test of Mental Maturity* and the *California Arithmetic Test* were administered in March 1965. The *California Contemporary Mathematics Test* and the *Aiken-Dreger Mathematics Attitude Scale*, revised for use at the elementary level, were administered in April 1965. Warner's socioeconomic scale, based on the occupation of the family's main wage earner, was employed to collect socioeconomic data. The *California Test of Mental Maturity* was selected in order to obtain verbal and nonverbal subscores as well as a measure of total intelligence.

The *California Arithmetic Test*, a "good instrument for surveying performance in fundamental operations . . . easily administered and scored," had the advantages of involving a minimum of reading, and having individual tests which facilitated analysis of results by separate subscores for the various operational skills. Ten scores were collected:

| Classification | Number of items | |
|---|---|---|
| Part I   Reasoning | | |
| Test 1   Meanings | 15 | |
| Test 2   Signs and symbols | 15 | |
| Test 3   Problems | 15 | |
| Total reasoning items | | 45 |

| Classification | Number of items | |
|---|---|---|
| Part II   Fundamentals | | |
| Test 4   Addition | 20 | |
| Test 5   Subtraction | 20 | |
| Test 6   Multiplication | 20 | |
| Test 7   Division | 20 | |
| Total fundamentals | | 80 |
| Total *California Arithmetic Test* | | 125 |

The search for a contemporary-mathematics achievement test not oriented to any specific program of contemporary mathematics revealed two in the process of being published. The California Test Bureau agreed to release the research form of their contemporary mathematics test for use in this study. To permit a more meaningful interpretation of the results, the forty-two items were classified according to the basic mathematical idea involved and the type of symbolism and vocabulary used. The basic mathematical ideas were numeration, base 10; numeration, base $x$; geometry, nonmetric; number systems and properties; measurement; graphs; other (logic and modulo). The symbolism and vocabulary were designated as contemporary if understanding of the new symbol or vocabularly term(s) was a necessary condition for the correct solution of the problem. The remainder of the items were classified as having conventional symbolism and vocabulary. Thus ten scores were collected:

| Classification | Number of items | |
|---|---|---|
| Numeration, base 10 | 3 | |
| Numeration, base $x$ | 3 | |
| Geometry, nonmetric | 5 | |
| Number systems and properties | 23 | |
| Measurement | 3 | |
| Graphs | 3 | |
| Other (logic and modulo) | 2 | |
| Contemporary (new) symbolism or vocabulary | | 24 |
| Conventional symbolism and vocabulary | | 18 |
| Total *California Contemporary Mathematics Test* | 42 | |

A Likert-type mathematics attitude scale, in which one indicates agreement or disagreement with every statement, appeared simpler to administer and easier for elementary pupils to take than the Thurstone type. The *Aiken-Dreger Attitude Scale* was used as a model, but revised for use at the elementary level. Simpler, more complete directions were written, and practice examples of both positive and negative items were provided. The vocabulary was adjusted by means of interviews with sixth-grade pupils of varying reading ability. Pretests of this revised instrument produced a reliability coefficient of .89. No problems of reading difficulty arose in the pretest or the final study. The Mathematics Attitude Scale consisted of twenty items—ten positive, ten negative—concerning arithmetic. Reacting to each statement with agreement or disagreement on a five-point scale resulted in scores from a possible minimum of twenty to a maximum of one hundred. Significant chi-squares proved discrimination power of all twenty items to be satisfactory.

Warner's socioeconomic scale has an eight-point range from professional to unemployed.

## DESCRIPTIVE DATA

Preliminary analysis of descriptive data (reported in Table 1) revealed an advantage favoring the control group in intelligence and socioeconomic level. Results were therefore analyzed using a covariance program which adjusted for the differences in these two variables. The *California Test of Mental Maturity* results indicated no substantial incidence of pupils having a higher nonlanguage I.Q. than language or total I.Q. Furthermore, the total I.Q. was found to correlate more highly with achievement than either intelligence subscore and was subsequently used as the intelligence covariant in final analyses.

Intercorrelations were computed for all variables; and data were also analyzed by subgroups of sex, intelligence, and socioeconomic level.

**TABLE 1**
**Analysis of Descriptive Data, by Treatment Groups**

| Group | Analysis of variance ($df = 564$) | | | | | |
| --- | --- | --- | --- | --- | --- | --- |
| | N | Mean | Effect | S.D. | F | p |
| Socioeconomic level | | | | | | |
| Experimental | 305 | 4.23 | 0.40 | 1.77 | 29.70 | .01 |
| Control | 260 | 3.37 | −0.46 | 1.98 | | |
| Language I.Q. | | | | | | |
| ($df = 606$) | | | | | | |
| Experimental | 334 | 103.24 | −1.91 | 14.49 | 13.00 | .01 |
| Control | 273 | 107.48 | 2.33 | 14.32 | | |
| Nonlanguage I.Q. | | | | | | |
| ($df = 606$) | | | | | | |
| Experimental | 334 | 100.90 | −1.65 | 15.61 | 8.45 | .01 |
| Control | 273 | 104.56 | 2.02 | 15.25 | | |
| Total I.Q. | | | | | | |
| Experimental | 305 | 102.76 | −1.82 | 14.74 | 10.10 | .01 |
| Control | 260 | 106.71 | 2.13 | 14.66 | | |
| Age (C.A. in months) | | | | | | |
| Experimental | 305 | 142.93 | 0.27 | 5.39 | 1.61 | NS |
| Control | 260 | 142.35 | −0.31 | 5.39 | | |

## FINDINGS

1. *California Arithmetic Test.* The control group, with data controlled for intelligence, achieved significantly higher than the experimental group on five of the ten conventional arithmetic test scores: *California Arithmetic Test* total; Part I—Reasoning; Part II—Fundamentals (computation); Test 2—Signs and Symbols; and Test 5—Subtraction. For individual tests of addition, multiplication, division, problems, and meanings, the differences were not significant (Tables 2 and 3).

Item analysis of unadjusted data revealed a difficulty rank order which was quite similar for both treatment groups. Generally the whole-number problems were easiest, the rational numbers more difficult, and decimals and denominate numbers least successful, but not equally so for both groups. The discrimination rank order scale data indicated that—

(a) The control group was favored on most items of the four computational tests, but the trend was reversed, favoring the experimental group, on eighteen of the eighty items. The number of such items was greatest in division, six, and multiplication, five; fewer in addition, four; and least in subtraction, three.

(b) Of the twenty items (five from each test) which gave the control group their greatest advantage over the experimental group, eleven were whole-number problems, including money and denominate number problems; eight were rational number problems (three addition, three subtraction, and two multiplication); and one was a decimal-fraction division problem.

(c) Of the eighteen items favoring the

**TABLE 2**
**Analysis of the California Arithmetic Test—Total Score; Part I (Reasoning); and Tests 1, 2, and 3—by Treatment Groups**

| Group | Mean | I.Q. correlation | Adjusted mean | S.D. | F | p |
|---|---|---|---|---|---|---|
| CAT, total score | | | | | | |
| Experimental | 75.06 | .741 | 76.66 | 18.76 | 9.10 | .01 |
| Control | 81.62 | | 79.74 | 16.20 | | |
| CAT, Part I (reasoning) | | | | | | |
| Experimental | 30.93 | .734 | 31.47 | 6.22 | 17.06 | .01 |
| Control | 33.55 | | 32.91 | 5.70 | | |
| CAT, Test I (meanings) | | | | | | |
| Experimental | 9.96 | .611 | 10.15 | 2.76 | 2.31 | NS |
| Control | 10.64 | | 10.41 | 2.31 | | |
| CAT, Test 2 (signs and symbols) | | | | | | |
| Experimental | 12.27 | .525 | 12.39 | 1.79 | 41.60 | .01 |
| Control | 13.37 | | 13.23 | 1.79 | | |
| CAT, Test 3 (problems) | | | | | | |
| Experimental | 8.68 | .677 | 8.92 | 2.86 | 2.94 | NS |
| Control | 9.50 | | 9.22 | 2.76 | | |

Experimental $N = 305$  Variance $df = 564$
Control $N = 260$  Covariance $df = 563$

**TABLE 3**
**Analysis of the California Arithmetic Test—Part II (Fundamentals);**
**and Tests 4, 5, 6, and 7—by Treatment Groups**

| Group | Mean | I.Q. correlation | Adjusted mean | S.D. | F | p |
|---|---|---|---|---|---|---|
| CAT, Part II (fundamentals) | | | | | | |
| Experimental | 44.13 | .693 | 45.19 | 13.50 | 4.84 | .05 |
| Control | 48.15 | | 46.90 | 11.24 | | |
| CAT, Test 4 (addition) | | | | | | |
| Experimental | 12.75 | .634 | 13.03 | 3.80 | 1.94 | NS |
| Control | 13.70 | | 13.37 | 3.43 | | |
| CAT, Test 5 (subtraction) | | | | | | |
| Experimental | 11.91 | .653 | 12.21 | 4.10 | 6.07 | .05 |
| Control | 13.18 | | 12.82 | 3.41 | | |
| CAT, Test 6 (multiplication) | | | | | | |
| Experimental | 10.05 | .535 | 10.29 | 4.03 | 1.88 | NS |
| Control | 10.95 | | 10.67 | 3.41 | | |
| CAT, Test 7 (division) | | | | | | |
| Experimental | 9.41 | .562 | 9.64 | 3.51 | 2.88 | NS |
| Control | 10.31 | | 10.04 | 3.11 | | |

Experimental $N = 305$      Variance $df = 564$
Control $N = 260$      Covariance $df = 563$

experimental group by any margin (these item analysis data were unadjusted for the control advantage in intelligence), two were whole number problems, seven were rational-number problems( two multiplication and five division), and nine were decimal-fraction problems (three addition, three subtraction, two multiplication, and one division).

Examination of the textbook studied indicated that these performances were closely related to the scope and emphases of the program each treatment group had followed.

When the *California Arithmetic Test* data were analyzed by sex, intelligence, and socioeconomic subgroups, their performance followed a rank order pattern of ability, rather than of background or sex. Thus, the girls in each treatment group achieved higher than the boys in most scores but also had a higher mean I.Q. In two tests, a departure from the ordinary pattern was evident. Subtraction significantly discriminated the Experimental Boys, the sex subgroup with the lowest I.Q., from the other three subgroups. Division significantly discriminated the Control Girls, the sex subgroup with the highest I.Q., from the other three subgroups.

2. *California Contemporary Mathematics Test.* The experimental group, with data controlled for intelligence, achieved significantly higher than the control group on seven or ten contemporary mathematics test scores: California Contemporary Mathematics Test total, numeration using base 10, nonmetric geometry, number systems and properties, other

(logic, modulo), new symbolism and vocabulary items, and conventional symbolism and vocabulary items. Differences were not significant for three scores: numeration using base $x$, measurement, and graphs (Tables 4 and 5).

Item analysis of unadjusted data produced a difficulty rank order that was less similar for the treatment groups than in the *California Arithmetic Test*. Graphs appeared the easiest content area for both groups and base $x$, the most difficult. Other content areas ranged dissimilarly for the two groups. The experimental group had no more difficulty with new symbolism and vocabulary than with the conventional. For this group, the ratio for contemporary items to conventional items was 12:9 for both the more and the less difficult halves of their difficulty rank order scale. The control group understandably demonstrated difficulty with new symbols

and vocabulary, their ratio for contemporary items to conventional items being 7:14 for the less difficult half of their scale and 17:4, or more than 4:1, in the more difficult half of their scale.

The discrimination rank order scale indicated that most items favored the experimental group, although the trend was reversed on nine of the forty-two items.

(a) The majority of the ten items favoring the experimental group by the largest differences contained distinctly contemporary material such as value and use of negative integers, factorization, nonmetric geometry, intersection of sets, expanded notation.

(b) The nine items favoring the control group included more conventional areas such as graphs, percent problems, value of the denominator, area of a rectangle.

When *California Contemporary Mathe-*

**TABLE 4**
**Analysis of the California Contemporary Mathematics Test—Total Score and Four Content Subscores—by Treatment Groups**

| Group | Mean | I.Q. correlation | Adjusted mean | S.D. | F | p |
|---|---|---|---|---|---|---|
| CCMT, total score | | | | | | |
| Experimental | 15.42 | .475 | 15.76 | 5.47 | 174.24 | .01 |
| Control | 11.63 | | 11.23 | 4.05 | | |
| CCMT, numeration, base 10 | | | | | | |
| Experimental | 1.49 | .368 | 1.54 | 0.96 | 51.60 | .01 |
| Control | 1.08 | | 1.02 | 0.89 | | |
| CCMT, numeration, base x | | | | | | |
| Experimental | 0.42 | −.004 | 0.42 | 0.61 | 0.06 | NS |
| Control | 0.40 | | 0.40 | 0.59 | | |
| CCMT, geometry | | | | | | |
| Experimental | 2.09 | .230 | 2.12 | 1.19 | 54.14 | .01 |
| Control | 1.48 | | 1.44 | 1.08 | | |
| CCMT, number systems and properties | | | | | | |
| Experimental | 7.85 | .384 | 8.02 | 3.35 | 181.85 | .01 |
| Control | 5.21 | | 5.00 | 2.53 | | |

Experimental $N = 305$    Variance $df = 564$
Control $N = 260$    Covariance $df = 563$

**TABLE 5**
**Analysis of the California Contemporary Mathematics Test—Three Content Subscores and Two Terminology Subscores—by Treatment Groups**

| Group | Mean | I.Q. correlation | Adjusted mean | S.D. | F | p |
|---|---|---|---|---|---|---|
| CCMT, measurement | | | | | | |
| Experimental | 1.00 | .233 | 1.02 | 0.80 | 2.34 | NS |
| Control | 0.95 | | 0.92 | 0.81 | | |
| CCMT, graphs | | | | | | |
| Experimental | 2.11 | .452 | 2.15 | 0.83 | 0.15 | NS |
| Control | 2.18 | | 2.13 | 0.75 | | |
| CCMT, other (logic and modulo) | | | | | | |
| Experimental | 0.48 | .078 | 0.49 | 0.56 | 11.76 | .01 |
| Control | 0.33 | | 0.33 | 0.55 | | |
| CCMT, new symbolism and vocabulary | | | | | | |
| Experimental | 7.82 | .317 | 7.97 | 3.33 | 174.01 | .01 |
| Control | 5.04 | | 4.86 | 2.64 | | |
| CCMT, conventional symbolism and vocabulary | | | | | | |
| Experimental | 7.59 | .531 | 7.77 | 2.87 | 56.18 | .01 |
| Control | 6.60 | | 6.38 | 2.36 | | |

| | |
|---|---|
| Experimental $N = 305$ | Variance $df = 564$ |
| Control $N = 260$ | Covariance $df = 563$ |

*matics Test* data were analyzed by subgroups, there was no consistent pattern to support the superiority of any intelligence, socioeconomic, or sex subgroup. The most frequent pattern of differences favored both sexes, experimental, over both sexes, control. It is interesting to note that in contrast to *California Arithmetic Test* results, the boys achieved higher than the girls in both treatment groups, although their I.Q. was lower. These differences were not significant but occurred in sixteen of thirty scores, favoring Experimental Boys over Experimental Girls, when both had studied the material, and in twenty-two of thirty scores, favoring Control Boys over Control Girls when neither had studied the material. This was a test of contemporary mathe-

matics material not studied by the control group.

3. *Mathematics Attitude Scale.* There was no significant difference between treatment groups in attitude toward mathematics. There was a significant difference within the experimental group favoring the high intelligence subgroup over the low intelligence subgroup (Table 6).

A comparison of the ranges of attitude scores for experimental and control classes revealed that the mean high score for the ten experimental classes (95.8) was higher than that for the ten control classes (94.9). The mean low score for the ten experimental classes (33.3) was lower than that for the ten control classes (35.4). This indicated a wider range of attitude

**TABLE 6**
**Analysis of the Mathematics Attitude Scale Total Score, by Treatment, Sex, Intelligence, and Socioeconomic Groups**

| Group | N | Mean | Adjusted Mean* | S.D. | F | p |
|---|---|---|---|---|---|---|
| Treatment | | | | | | |
|   1. Experimental | 305 | 69.86 | 70.35 | 17.38 | 0.33 | NS |
|   2. Control | 260 | 71.70 | 71.13 | 15.51 | | |
| Sex | | | | | | |
|   1. Experimental boys | 157 | 69.56 | 70.37 | 17.36 | 0.15 | NS |
|   2. Experimental girls | 148 | 70.18 | 70.37 | 17.40 | | |
|   3. Control boys | 135 | 71.64 | 71.45 | 15.37 | | |
|   4. Control girls | 125 | 71.77 | 70.78 | 15.65 | | |
| Intelligence | | | | | | |
|   1. Experimental high | 154 | 72.42 | 72.29 | 16.31 | 1.63 | NS |
|   2. Experimental low | 151 | 67.25 | 68.33 | 18.04 | | |
|   3. Control high | 132 | 72.23 | 71.11 | 15.56 | | |
|   4. Control low | 128 | 71.16 | 71.20 | 15.43 | | |
| Socioeconomic | | | | | | |
|   1. Experimental high | 160 | 71.48 | 71.96 | 16.27 | 1.24 | NS |
|   2. Experimental low | 145 | 68.07 | 68.57 | 18.37 | | |
|   3. Control high | 136 | 72.26 | 71.32 | 15.20 | | |
|   4. Control low | 124 | 71.09 | 70.93 | 15.81 | | |

| | t values | | | | | |
|---|---|---|---|---|---|---|
| Group | Pair 1–2 | Pair 1–3 | Pair 1–4 | Pair 2–3 | Pair 2–4 | Pair 3–4 |
| Sex | 0.31 | −1.07 | −1.10 | −0.75 | −0.79 | −0.06 |
| Intelligence | 2.62† | 0.10 | 0.66 | −2.46 | −1.92 | 0.55 |
| Socioeconomic | 1.71 | −0.42 | 0.20 | −2.07 | −1.43 | 0.61 |

\* The correlation for I.Q. and total attitude score was .244 for the total sample.
† Indicates $p < .01$, the only level of significance accepted for paired comparisons.

for the experimental group, exceeding the control group limits at both extremes of the scale.

4. Correlation data revealed a marked positive relationship between I.Q. and conventional arithmetic achievement for both groups; a marked positive relationship between I.Q. and contemporary mathematics achievement for the experimental group, but a moderate positive one for the control group and total sample for the same variables. Correlation data also revealed a low positive relationship between I.Q. and attitude toward mathematics for experimental, control, and total groups (Table 7).

5. Correlation data revealed a low positive relationship between socioeconomic level and conventional arithmetic achievement. Correlations for socioeconomic level with contemporary mathematics achievement and with attitude toward mathematics were negligible.

6. The relationship of conventional arithmetic achievement with contemporary mathematics achievement was a moderate positive one for the control group and marked positive for the experimental group. Attitude toward mathematics demonstrated only a low positive relationship with either conventional arithmetic, or contemporary mathematics, achievement.

**TABLE 7**
**Intercorrelation of Descriptive and Final Variables by Experimental, Control, and Total Sample Groups***

| Variable | Group | Language I.Q. | Non-language I.Q. | Total I.Q. | Age | CAT Total | CCMT Total | MAS Total |
|---|---|---|---|---|---|---|---|---|
| Socioeconomic level † | Experimental | —.22 | —.26 | —.26 | .18 | —.24 | —.18 | —.09 |
| | Control | —.20 | —.14 | —.19 | .09 | —.23 | —.13 | .00 |
| | Total | | | —.249 | .145 | —.267 | —.060 | —.063 |
| Language I.Q. | Experimental | | .66 | .93 | .31 | .66 | .63 | .20 |
| | Control | | .68 | .93 | —.34 | .72 | .33 | .15 |
| Nonlanguage I.Q. | Experimental | | | .89 | —.21 | .64 | .61 | .30 |
| | Control | | | .89 | —.28 | .69 | .40 | .22 |
| Total I.Q. | Experimental | | | | —.30 | .71 | .68 | .27 |
| | Control | | | | —.34 | .77 | .40 | .20 |
| | Total | | | | —.320 | .741 | .475 | .244 |
| Age | Experimental | | | | | —.28 | —.19 | —.07 |
| | Control | | | | | —.32 | —.08 | —.09 |
| | Total | | | | | —.298 | —.118 | —.082 |
| CAT | Experimental | | | | | | .75 | .37 |
| | Control | | | | | | .42 | .34 |
| CCMT | Experimental | | | | | | | .32 |
| | Control | | | | | | | .24 |

* Significance levels for correlation (from Henry E. Garrett, *Statistics in Psychology and Education* [New York: Longmans, Green & Co., 1960], p. 201):

| | .05 | .01 |
|---|---|---|
| N = 200 (control N = 260) | .138 | .181 |
| N = 300 (experimental N = 305) | .113 | .148 |
| N = 500 (total sample N = 565) | .088 | .115 |

† Interpret negative numerical correlation as positive relationships, since socioeconomic level varies inversely with the numerical value assigned.

## CONCLUSIONS

1. Achievement data significantly favored the control group in the area of conventional arithmetic and the experimental group in the area of contemporary mathematics.

2. Achievement, both conventional and contemporary, demonstrated a marked positive relationship to intelligence and appeared closely related to the scope and emphasis of the textbook studied.

3. Attitude toward mathematics was similarly positive for both treatment groups and appeared to be less a function of achievement or the type of mathematics program studied than might have been expected.

4. Socioeconomic level demonstrated little or no relationship to either achievement or attitude toward mathematics.

## DISCUSSION

In the light of these findings and conclusions, how can the four questions raised at the beginning of this article be answered?

1. Will pupils studying contemporary mathematics maintain achievement in conventional arithmetic, particularly computational skills, comparable to that of

pupils studying conventional arithmetic?

Since the experimental group performance did not equal that of the control group on computational scores of the *California Arithmetic Test*, the answer must be, "No, in this case they did not maintain comparable computational skills, and, presumably, other pupils in the future would not either unless the program were modified."

2. Are the newer mathematical ideas, symbols, and vocabulary equally suitable for pupils of all intelligence levels and all socioeconomic backgrounds?

The value of contemporary mathematics programs for children of varying socioeconomic background and intelligence level is reflected in intercorrelation and other data collected in this study.

The low correlation for socioeconomic level with conventional arithmetic achievement and with intelligence, and the negligible correlation of socioeconomic level with contemporary mathematics achievement and attitude toward mathematics, suggest that socioeconomic level not be a criterion by which curriculum decisions are made concerning contemporary mathematics.

Relevant to ability levels, the experimental group correlation for I.Q. and conventional arithmetic achievement was .71, while their correlation for I.Q. and contemporary mathematics achievement was .68. This indicates performance was related to ability in contemporary mathematics to approximately the same degree that it was in conventional arithmetic. However, examining attitude toward mathematics, the only significant difference occurred between the high and the low I.Q. subgroups within the experimental group.

The answer to this part of the question, then, is that contemporary mathematics is equally suitable for all ability levels if only achievement is measured. If attitude is considered, this program was not as satisfactory for the lower ability pupils as it was for the upper ability pupils.

3. What effect are contemporary mathematics programs having on attitude toward mathematics?

Contemporary mathematics appears not to have had any significant effect on attitude toward mathematics, with the one exception noted above.

Examining attitude data, one might ask why the correlation of attitude and achievement was not higher than .2 or .3, or why the correlation of attitude and intelligence was also at that low level. If this was because some of those with less ability and low achievement like mathematics as well as those with outstanding ability and high achievement, this is a valuable goal to have reached. If, however, it suggests that those with the greatest ability who have demonstrated high achievement may nevertheless lack the motivation to continue studying mathematics at higher levels, this problem must be recognized. The role of attitude and its relationship to future specialization in the field of mathematics needs to be explored further.

4. Are conventional arithmetic achievement, contemporary mathematics achievement, and attitude toward mathematics related in any way?

Yes, there is a relationship, marked for the experimental group and moderate for the control, between conventional and contemporary mathematics achievement. There is also a relationship, albeit not a strong one, between attitude toward mathematics and both types of achievement.

## SUMMARY

Mathematics educators naturally want "the best of both worlds" for the students—a program which retains the timeless, proven values of previous programs, but accomplishes much more. The current debate over newer methods, content, and goals is both generated by, and, to some extent, resolved in, the process of choosing a new elementary mathematics textbook. The importance of this decision can hardly be overestimated, as indicated by the performance of the control group on conventional items of the contemporary mathematics test, the performance of the experimental group in certain areas of the conventional arithmetic test, and the very close relationship between test performance and textbook studied.

Continuous evaluation of elementary school mathematics programs is essential and must include all the goals of school mathematics.

## 39. Results of Experimental Group Testing of the School Health Education Study Materials

**WILLIAM H. CRESWELL, J. THOMAS HASTINGS, and WARREN J. HUFFMAN**

> A good subtitle for this article might have been "The Biography of a Curriculum Project." Not unlike Grobman's monograph (1968), this paper relates the development of school health curriculum materials to formative and summative evaluation. The concept of formative evaluation suggested by Cronbach (1963—see Article 16) and explicated by Scriven (1967) is well illustrated here. In addition to the general "evaluation strategy" employed, the reader should also appreciate the very practical application of item analysis procedures, here aimed at improvement of the instructional materials.

The School Health Education Study had its inception in the long-standing concern within the profession over the lag between the stated objectives of health education and what appeared to be the actual practice in the public schools. Like many other projects, this study is a part of the curriculum reform movement which was triggered into action by the launching of Sputnik I. Efforts toward curriculum reform can be traced to the critics of public school practice, to troubled and discouraged parents, and to scholars concerned about the outmoded curriculum in schools. The School Health Education Study, therefore, is a part of the general trend in all disciplines to re-evaluate their positions in light of the great changes developing in all subject areas at all levels.

The present study has as its central purpose the effecting of a long-range program of improved health instruction in the elementary and secondary schools of the United States. The first phase of the study consisted of a survey of current health instruction programs in the nation's public schools. This was done in order to establish a baseline of data against which future progress could be measured. As far as can be ascertained, no other curriculum study has conducted a scientific survey of current programs before initiating curriculum change. Utilizing the results from this survey, a second phase of the Study was launched. New materials were developed by a group of writers, who were given special assistance by health and medical authorities, health educators, public school teachers, and

Reprinted and abridged with permission of the publisher and William H. Creswell from *The Journal of School Health*, **36** (1966), pp. 154–164.

curriculum specialists. Employing a conceptual scheme, ten major ideas or concepts were identified, which served as guides in formulating a curriculum scope and sequence for health education. Teaching-learning guides relating to two of the ten concepts were developed for use at the elementary, junior, and senior high school level. These new teaching materials were then utilized in four tryout school locations.

How can a new curriculum be evaluated? Do these new materials contribute substantially to the general objective of better health teaching? Recognizing the importance of these questions, the process of evaluation was established as an integral part of the curriculum development and tryout experience. This follows the dictum of Cronbach (1963) that "Evaluation used to improve the course while it is still fluid contributes more to improvement of education than evaluation used to appraise a product already placed on the market."

Insofar as possible, according to Cronbach, evaluation should be used to understand how the course produces its effects and what parameters influence its effectiveness. Therefore, it was assumed that evaluation of the tryout school's experience would result in revision of the new course materials.

The importance of adopting objectives for purposes of evaluating has long been recognized. When such objectives are sharply defined and stated in operational terms, the measurement of the progress or the effectiveness of the program under study is greatly enhanced. Accordingly, evaluation of these materials was planned in light of the objectives of the new health education curriculum. The objectives were:

1. to effect a greater student knowledge gain than that attained by means of the traditional curriculum;
2. to reveal inter-relationships of health knowledge, thereby increasing the student's general health knowledge;
3. to produce increased student interest in the study of health; and
4. to improve teacher effectiveness and interest in health teaching.

Cronbach defines curriculum evaluation as "the collection and use of information to make decisions about an educational program." Such a broad definition draws attention to the full scope of the evaluative function. To meet this criterion, a variety of evaluative approaches were employed in this study. These techniques and procedures included questionnaires, interview schedules, teacher logs, and class observations at all tryout schools. However, for purposes of this paper, only the more formal research procedures which utilized the experimental and control classes tested in the tryout schools will be considered.

## RESEARCH PROCEDURE

In order to assess the effects of the experimental teaching-learning guides, a number of factors incorporated in planning the research design had to be considered. Rarely, if ever, is it possible to assign classes in the actual school setting in such a manner as to satisfy fully the requirements of the classical experiment. The researcher usually has to conduct his experiment within the confines of the established school schedule, utilizing classes they occur therein. Such considerations as teacher assignments, teacher load, and student schedules make it difficult, if not impossible, to accomplish randomization of classes and teachers.

The research procedure set up for the experimental evaluation of the two teaching-learning guides involved a three parallel group design: an experimental, control, and an extended control class.

The design is illustrated in Figure 1.

(The three parallel lines represent three different classes: 1 experimental and 2 traditional or control classes.)

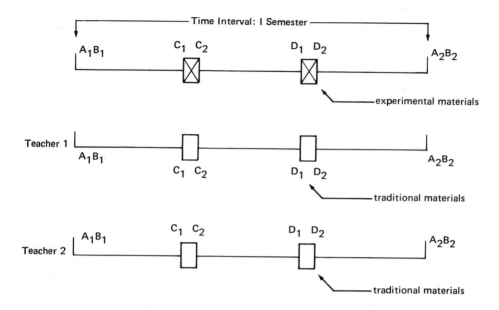

**Figure 1**
**Design for Experimental Evaluation of School Health Education Study Materials**

$A_1A_2$: Pre- and Post-Test Health Behavior Inventory

$B_1B_2$: Pre- and Post-Test Attitude Toward the Health Course
(Scale Form A and B)

$C_1C_2$: Pre- and Post-Test Consumer Health Test

$D_1D_2$: Pre- and Post-Test Family Health Test

Teacher 1: A teacher who participated in development of experimental materials.

Teacher 2: A teacher teaching traditional materials and not associated with development of experimental materials.

As illustrated by the diagram, the experimental and two control classes were taught the same course of study except for the two experimental teaching-learning guides which were included in the curriculum of the experimental class. The control classes were taught the regular or traditional units covering the same subject matter, but without recourse to the new teaching-learning guides. This particular experimental design was adopted in order to assess the effects of the:

1. experimental materials as determined by student gain scores on a general achievement test of health knowledge;
2. experimental materials as determined by student gain scores on the two teaching-learning guide tests;
3. experimental materials as determined by changes in student attitude scores toward the health course; and
4. teacher on the student gain scores.

## RESEARCH HYPOTHESIS

The concept approach serves to identify those major areas or generalizations which facilitate the classification of the content. Once this is done, it can then be organized in relation to the major concepts forming a logical structure for curriculum development.

It is thought that such a concept-oriented curriculum improves the efficiency of both the teaching and learning process. In health education, it is believed that the concept approach will provide

1. a greater depth and breadth in the learner's understanding of factors affecting health;
2. accelerated learning by establishing a logical structure to which new health facts and ideas may be related;
3. greater transfer of learning in the study of health, because of the inter-relationships of ideas revealed in a conceptual structure; and
4. increased student interest in the study of health science by virtue of greater understanding.

## TEST INSTRUMENTS

The *Health Behavior Inventory* (HBI) is a seventy-five item, multiple-choice test, covering ten health topic areas. It has a reported reliability coefficient of .91. For the purposes of this study, it was used as the measure of general health knowledge.

The *Consumer Health Test* (CHT) is an experimental test, developed by the investigators and designed specifically for use with the School Health Education Study. The test contains sixty-seven multiple-choice type items relating to the area of consumer health. It is a knowledge instrument and attempts to measure some of the higher intellectual abilities such as the ability to analyze, interpret, and extrapolate. The test has a reliability coefficient of .79 as calculated by the Kuder-Richardson formula (KR21).

The *Family Health Test* (FHT) was developed by Roscoe J. Dann of Oakland Community College, Auburn Heights, Michigan. Like the *Consumer Health Test,* this is an experimental test developed specifically for use with the School Health Education Study. It, too, is developed as

a knowledge test and attempts to measure certain higher intellectual abilities in the area of family health. The test contains multiple-choice items and has a reliability coefficient of .73 (KR21).

The attitude scale employed was *A Scale to Measure Attitude Toward Any School Subject,* published by Purdue University (1960) and copyrighted by the Purdue Research Foundation. Form A and Form B of the scale each contain seventeen items which are weighted according to scaled values for scoring purposes. The reliability for the original full scale instrument reportedly ranged from .71 to .92 for various population samples.

**Statistical Analysis** Since it could not be assumed that the classes constituted random groups, differences between the experimental and control classes were evaluated by use of the $\pm$ test of significance on each of the four pre-test score measures. When the experimental and control classes revealed a significant difference (.05 level) on the pre-test scores, the analysis of co-variance method was then used to adjust for the class differences in order to achieve greater precision in the measurement of gain score differences. For those classes judged to be comparable on the basis of their pre-test scores, the $\pm$ test of significance was again employed in evaluating gain score differences.

Only one of the tryout school centers was able to establish the two control group experimental design, as illustrated. The second control group or extended control class could not be included. As a consequence, the simple parallel group or experimental and control group design was employed. The loss of the extended control class in these studies limited the interpretation of any gain score differences occurring between the experimental and control classes. Without the extended control class, no differentiation could be made between possible teacher effect or new material effect on the gain score difference.

## REPORT AND DISCUSSION OF SELECTED FINDINGS FROM THE EXPERIMENTAL STUDIES

Four broad experimental studies were conducted at the tryout school locations as a part of the overall evaluation plan. Each experiment was confined to a particular school and grade level, and within each study a number of differentiations were made according to school, sex, and test measure.

Although the experimental groups achieved a greater gain score in a number of instances, statistical analysis revealed that only three of these differences were significant at the .05 level. Two of the significant differences were achieved on the general health knowledge test (HBI) at schools A and B. The third significant difference was shown on the CHT at School A. Data from School A on the HBI and CHT, and from School B on the HBI are presented in Tables 1, 2, and 3. The FHT did not reveal any significant differences.

The data in Table 3 obtained at School B reveal that while the male and female experimental classes did show greater gain scores, the differences were not significant. However, when test scores for the male and female subjects were combined the resulting difference was significant.

These data illustrate the very practical problem of obtaining comparability of experimental and control groups when conducting experiments in schools with fixed classes. As shown in Table 3 there are marked differences between the pretest mean scores of the male experimental and control classes. With mean scores of 51.26 for the experimental and 57.26 for the control class, the mean difference indicates that the male groups at this school do differ significantly. In the same table, however, the pre-test means and standard deviations for the female experimental and control groups show that they are quite similar.

The gain score for the male groups shows a difference (although not statistically significant) in favor of the experimental class.

Because of this difference on the pretest means of these two groups, the decision was made to apply the analysis of covariance method. The rationale for this decision is set forth by Clarke and Phillips (1959) in their discussion of the procedure. "The advantage of the analysis of covariance . . . lies in the increased precision of the error of estimate." This gain in precision is accomplished by equalizing

## TABLE 1
Pre-Test, Post-Test, Mean, Standard Deviation, and Mean Score Differences for School A on the Health Behavior Inventory

|  | | Pre-Test | | Post-Test | | Mean Gains | S.D. Gains |
|---|---|---|---|---|---|---|---|
|  | N | Mean | S.D. | Mean | S.D. | | |
| Female | | | | | | | |
| Experimental | 48 | 50.90 | 8.88 | 58.35 | 6.61 | 7.45 | 6.88 |
| Control | 19 | 54.42 | 7.73 | 54.84 | 7.47 | 0.42 | 6.09 |
| Differences | | −3.52 | | 3.51 | | 7.03* | |
| Female | | | | | | | |
| Experimental | 48 | 50.90 | 8.88 | 58.35 | 6.61 | 7.45 | 6.88 |
| Ex-Control | 47 | 49.98 | 10.78 | 52.94 | 9.96 | 2.96 | 4.18 |
| Differences | | .92 | | 5.41* | | 4.49* | |

* Difference significantly different from zero to $p < .05$.

**TABLE 2**
**Pre-Test, Post-Test, Mean, Standard Deviation, and Mean Score Difference for School A on the Consumer Health Test**

|  |  | Pre-Test |  | Post-Test |  | Mean Gains | S.D. Gains |
| --- | --- | --- | --- | --- | --- | --- | --- |
|  | N | Mean | S.D. | Mean | S.D. |  |  |
| Female |  |  |  |  |  |  |  |
| Experimental | 48 | 37.44 | 6.36 | 43.56 | 5.43 | 6.12 | 5.07 |
| Control | 19 | 35.63 | 5.77 | 39.11 | 6.62 | 3.48 | 4.75 |
| Differences |  | 1.81 |  | 4.45 |  | 2.64* |  |
| Female |  |  |  |  |  |  |  |
| Experimental | 48 | 37.44 | 6.36 | 43.56 | 5.43 | 6.12 | 5.97 |
| Ex-Control | 47 | 34.94 | 8.65 | 38.81 | 9.04 | 3.87 | 5.34 |
| Differences |  | 2.50 |  | 4.75 |  | 2.25* |  |

\* Difference significantly different from zero to p < .05.

**TABLE 3**
**Pre-Test, Post-Test, Mean, Standard Deviation and Mean Score Differences for School B on the Health Behavior Inventory**

|  |  | Pre-Test |  | Post-Test |  | Mean Gains | S.D. Gains |
| --- | --- | --- | --- | --- | --- | --- | --- |
|  | N | Mean | S.D. | Mean | S.D. |  |  |
| Male |  |  |  |  |  |  |  |
| Experimental | 27 | 51.26 | 8.54 | 54.15 | 8.27 | 2.89 | 6.12 |
| Control | 19 | 57.26 | 7.00 | 57.47 | 8.30 | 0.21 | 3.63 |
| Differences |  | −6.00* |  | −3.32 |  | 2.68 |  |
| Female |  |  |  |  |  |  |  |
| Experimental | 31 | 58.23 | 5.52 | 60.53 | 5.78 | 2.30 | 4.60 |
| Control | 19 | 58.21 | 5.54 | 59.26 | 6.89 | 1.05 | 3.85 |
| Differences |  | .02 |  | 1.27 |  | 1.25 |  |
| Combined |  |  |  |  |  |  |  |
| Experimental | 58 | 54.90 | 7.88 | 57.52 | 7.70 | 2.62 | 5.35 |
| Control | 38 | 57.74 | 6.25 | 58.37 | 7.61 | 0.63 | 3.72 |
| Differences |  | −2.84 |  | .85 |  | 1.99* |  |

\* Difference significantly different from zero to p < .05.

the initial differences. To achieve this equality, adjustments are made to the final criterion scores or the post-test scores in this instance. Continuing, Clarke and Phillips (1959) add that "this adjustment of scores introduces a precision which is comparable to that obtained when groups are initially matched."

The important point made here is that by using the analysis of covariance the size of error estimated is reduced. This fact may cause the investigator to reach an altogether different conclusion than the one obtained by employing a less precise statistical technique.

The resulting computations did not,

however, reflect a significant difference in the post-test means after adjusting for the initial differences.

Knowing whether the new course or curriculum materials are superior to the old is of basic importance in any curriculum improvement effort. Before schools adopt changes there should be reasonable assurance that the new approach will produce better results. However, to confine curriculum evaluation to a comparison of performances between groups of students who have been exposed to the new course and those who have not, falls far short of meeting the needs of the curriculum builder. What is also needed is to know *how* the curriculum produces its effects. Are all elements of the new curriculum equally effective? If not, which parts are weak and which are strong? How can the present version be revised for further improvement?

To secure answers to these questions, an item analysis was conducted on the test data from those groups showing significant gain score differences. This microscopic analysis of test results was conducted in order to identify the specific test items responsible for the difference between the experimental and control classes.

Also, an item analysis of the general health knowledge test results (HBI) was undertaken in an attempt to test the transfer of learning effect of the new materials. If the conceptual approach to curriculum development does show idea relationships which help students generalize what they've learned, then, presumably, classes exposed to the new materials will show greater gains on the test of general health knowledge.

As previously noted, the experimental classes at two of the tryout schools did achieve greaer gain scores as anticipated.

However, the data from School A was eliminated from the item analysis after closer examination of the experimental group pre-test results. It was discovered that an excessive number of items had been omitted on both the *Consumer Health* and general health knowledge pre-tests. This fact raises the possibility of a spurious gain score for the experimental group on both of these test measures.

Since there was a significant difference between the experimental and the control groups on the total test, it was assumed that the experimental group should do better than the control group on individual items of the test. Similarly, it was assumed that a greater percentage of students should pass a test after receiving instruction whether being taught by use of the experimental materials or the traditional materials.

It was found that the experimental group made significant changes or improvements on sixteen test items over the course of the semester, while suffering losses on three items. By contrast the control group had significant negative changes or losses on five items and made significant gains on three items during the experiment.

It is of interest to know more about the health content of the sixteen test items on which the experimental group made significant positive changes or gains. Do these items represent several health content areas or are they confined to one or two areas closely related to the content in the experimental teaching-learning guides? Analysis of these items reveals that they relate to eight different content areas. Although the new curriculum materials are concerned with but two content areas, there appears to be a general benefit to the experimental groups as shown by the significant changes on the sixteen items which are related to a number of different content areas.

This finding would seem to support the hypothesis that the concept approach used in developing the new curriculum does reveal relationships between ideas which help the student to make generalizations and broader applications of his health knowledge.

Thus, it would appear that the experimental class made greater progress than did the control class. However, a note of caution should be interjected. Due to the relatively small number of subjects in the control class, certain restrictions are imposed upon the analysis of these data.

In summarizing, a re-examination of the objectives adopted for the evaluation is in order. Do the new teaching materials produce greater student learning in health education? While the data presented here show that experimental groups did make greater gain scores in three instances, a question has been raised about two of these gain score differences because of the number of item omissions on the pretest measure given the experimental groups. With respect to the effect of the materials on student interest and attitudes the difference between the experimental and control groups were not significant.

It is apparent that efforts to conduct experimental studies as a part of the plan to evaluate new curricula is beset with a variety of problems. Coordinating the experimental study evaluation with the developing stages of the new curriculum is a major problem.

It would appear that the use of experimental and control groups in curriculum evaluation would be more effective in the later stages of curriculum development. In this way, some of the troublesome problems relating to curriculum refinement, teaching approaches, teaching time, and test instrument development could be reduced.

Certainly experiences such as this should strengthen future efforts in evaluation, both from the standpoint of methodology and the necessary instrumentation.

## 40. A Content Analysis of the Relationships Between Science and Mathematics at the Secondary-School Level

### RALPH W. CAIN and EUGENE C. LEE

Curriculum researchers are frequently called upon to examine the impact of an innovative subject-matter program on other content areas of the curriculum. Many statistical procedures, some quite sophisticated, are available to help measure such influences. There are a number of less cumbersome and complicated procedures which may yield extremely valuable information. It is frequently worthwhile, for example, for a Curriculum Director to examine, on a content basis, relationships among instructional units of his curriculum. By examining the order of the teaching of eighteen mathematical concepts and processes in both traditional and new math and science programs, the authors of this article were able to recommend changes in the scope and sequence of the material.

During the past few years extensive curriculum development programs have been undertaken in both science and mathematics. These projects range from individual group projects at the local level to operations financed at the national level. Most of the programs at the national level number among their participants secondary school and college teachers in the subject matter field, professional educators, and active research workers. This combination of talents would seem to insure a comprehensive coverage of the subject matter under consideration.

There appears, however, to be little or no effort to coordinate content and sequence among the different programs and to take into account the contribution that one program could or should make to the

Reprinted by permission of *School Science and Mathematics*, the Journal of the School Science and Mathematics Association, and Ralph W. Cain from an article entitled "An Analysis of the Relationships Between Science and Mathematics at the Secondary School Level," which appeared in *School Science and Mathematics*, **63** (1963), pp. 705–713.

development and use of other programs. Many of the programs in the sciences depend on knowledge and understanding of a number of mathematical concepts and processes. For example:

1. Measurement and quantification
2. Determination of relationships by analysis of measurement
3. Language to communicate relationships and results
4. Manipulative operations for problem solving

It would seem profitable, therefore, to analyze the mathematical content of the traditional and new secondary science programs and to explore the matter and extent to which they have been included in the traditional and new secondary math programs.

Although several analyses of the new mathematics programs have been made, one of the outstanding omissions is reference to the relationship of these math programs to the new science programs. A look at the number and extent of proposed changes in high school sciences and mathematics curricula would indicate the difficulty of attempting to analyze all the programs from every point of view. In this study, therefore, an attempt will be made to analyze selected programs in science for their mathematical content and the sequence in which the mathematics is encountered, and to analyze selected mathematics programs for their content and sequence in order to determine the correlation existing between the mathematics programs and the mathematical content of the science programs.

## STATEMENT OF THE PROBLEM

Specifically, the problem to be investigated may be stated as follows: Have the newly developed science and mathematics curricula improved the correlation between the mathematical content and sequence of secondary science courses and the content and sequence of secondary mathematics courses?

In order to answer this question, the answers to two other questions must be determined:

1. What degree of correlation between the two areas has existed in traditional courses?
2. What is the degree of correlation between the two areas of the new programs?

Once the answers to these questions have been obtained, it is possible to determine whether or not improvements have been made.

## DESIGN OF THE STUDY

In this study, three relationships between mathematics and science curricula in secondary school (grades 9, 10, 11, 12) are to be examined:

1. The mathematical concepts and processes which are used in selected secondary school science courses, both traditional and new.

2. The *extent* to which mathematical concepts and processes are used in the science courses.
3. The sequence of utilization of the mathematical concepts and processes in the science courses compared to the sequence in which the same mathematical concepts and processes are taught in secondary school mathematic programs both traditional and new.

In order to examine the above-mentioned relationships, it was necessary to establish a workable framework from which to proceed. To accomplish this, the following steps were taken: (1) representative, traditional, and new secondary science programs were selected; (2) representative, traditional, and new secondary math programs were selected; (3) a list of mathematical concepts and processes considered important to this study were selected; (4) selected courses and programs were examined for the content and sequence of the selected mathematical concepts and processes.

## SELECTION OF MATERIALS

Selection of *traditional* science courses and mathematics programs for examination made on the basis of the following criteria:

1. The courses and programs must have been, insofar as possible, unaffected by the development of the new programs.
2. Individual courses must represent the components of a total program if more than one program (as in mathematics) is involved in a sequential pattern. In all traditional courses the materials examined were the textbooks used in the courses; the traditional mathematical courses selected for examination were those contained in the mathematics course outline for the Austin (Texas) Public Schools, 1955.

Grade 9—First Year Algebra

Grade 10—Plane Geometry

Grade 11—Second Year Algebra

Grade 12—Solid Geometry (second semester)

Plane Geometry (second semester)

The textbooks suggested for the above-named courses were examined for their content and sequence. Textbooks examined for each course were:

Grade 9—Mallory, Virgil S. *First Algebra*. Chicago: Benjamin H. Sanborn & Co., 1960.

Grade 10—Morgan, F. M., and W. E. Breckenridge. *Plane Geometry*. Boston: Houghton Mifflin Co., 1951.

Grade 11—Mallory, Virgil S., and Kenneth C. Skeen. *Second Algebra*. Chicago: Benjamin H. Sanborn & Co., 1952.

Grade 12—(First semester)—Morgan, F. M., and W. E. Breckenridge. *Solid Geometry*. Dallas: Houghton Mifflin Co., 1953.

(Second semester)—Seymour, F. Eugene, and Paul J. Smith. *Plane and Spherical Trigonometry*. New York: The Macmillan Co., 1945.

Similar criteria and method of selection were employed with respect to the traditional science courses. The courses taught in the Austin (Texas) Public Schools during the 1961–62 school year were selected. The selected sequence is as follows:

Grade 10—Biology

Grade 11—Chemistry

Grade 12—Physics

The general science course, grade 9, which would have been included in a complete sequence, is omitted because of the lack of a parallel course in the new science courses.

The materials examined for the traditional science courses were the textbooks listed for use in the Austin schools for the 1961–62 school year. These textbooks were:

Grade 10—Moon, Truman J., Paul B. Mann, and James H. Otto. *Modern Biology*. New York: Henry Holt and Co., 1951.

Grade 11—Dull, Charles E., William O. Brooks, and H. Clark Metcalfe. *Modern Chemistry*. New York: Henry Holt and Co., 1957.

Grade 12—Dull, Charles E., William O. Brooks, and H. Clark Metcalfe. *Modern Physics*. New York: Henry Holt and Co., 1955.

The selection of *new* programs in science and mathematics for examination was made on the basis of the following criteria:

1. The new program was different from traditional courses with respect to content, sequence, and/or approach.
2. The new program must have undergone its major development in the past ten years (1952–1962).

In the new programs the materials examined were the student editions of the textbooks and laboratory manuals, course outlines, or reported list of topics from a secondary source.

The materials examined for the new mathematics programs were:

SMSG—An outline of the content and sequence of the program as reported in Hancock, John D. "The Evolution of the Secondary Mathematics Curriculum: A Critique" (unpublished Ed.D. dissertation, School of Education, Stanford University, 1961), pp. 101–102.

CEEB—College Entrance Examination Board. *Program for College Preparatory Mathematics*. Report of the Commission on Mathematics. New York: College Entrance Examination Board, 1959.

UICSM—An outline of the content and sequence of the program as reported in Kelley, Charles E. "Trends in Secondary School Mathematics, 1955 to 1960" (unpublished Ed.D. dissertation, University of Missouri, 1960), pp. 27–28, 48, 63–64, 75–76.

The materials examined for the new science programs were as follows:

Grade 10—(BSCS)—Biological Sciences Curriculum Study, *High School Biology.* Yellow Version (development and genetics approach). Text and laboratory manuals. For experimental use during the 1960–1961 school year.

Grade 11—(CBA)—Chemical Bond Approach Committee, *Chemistry.* Second edition, Portland, Ore.: The Reed Institute, 1961. Text and laboratory manuals. (CHEM)—Chemical Education Material Study. *Chemistry an Experimental Science.* Second trial edition. The Regents of the University of California 1960, 1961. Text and laboratory manuals.

Grade 12—(PSSC)—Physical Science Study Committee. *Physics.* Boston: D. C. Heath & Co., 1960.

## SELECTION OF CONCEPTS

The selection of the particular editions of materials in some of the new science and mathematics programs was arbitrary. Since most of the programs are still in a state of revision, and will be for some time to come, it was necessary to choose a certain edition of the materials for examination. The only criterion employed was the availability of the materials for examination.

The mathematical *concepts* and *processes* selected and a brief description of what is included in each is as follows:

Linear equations—first degree equations in one unknown; most often used in the solution of problems at the end of a chapter or section.

Quadratic equations—second degree equations in one unknown; usually used in problem solving.

Ratio, proportion, and variation—algebraic and geometric, including similar triangles; used in problem solving and discussion of science principles.

Conversion factors—conversions between the metric and English systems of measurement and conversions within each system; used in problem solving and in showing relationship between units of measure.

Graphs—graphs of linear relationships, regular curvilinear relationships, and irregular relationships derived from experimental data; constructed from data, read for values, or used to illustrate the relationship between two variables.

Probability—simple probability of chance; used in problem solving and discussion of science principles.

Tables—tables of numbers and values; constructed from data and read for values.

Statistics—simple statistical concepts and processes; includes randomness, sampling, chi-square test, etc.

Formulas—algebraic formulas using symbols to represent values; used to express relationships and in problem solving.

Trigonometric functions—limited primarily to sine, cosine, and tangent functions; used in problem solving and in the expression of relationships.

Vectors—graphical vectors; used in problem solving and in the pictorial representation of science principles.

Intuitive plane geometry—informal application of the idea of two-dimensional space; no proofs of formal development; used in pictorial representations.

Intuitive solid geometry—informal application of the idea of three-dimensional space; no proofs or formal development; used in pictorial representations and in discussions of shape and spatial arrangement of objects.

Logarithms—logarithms to base ten; used in problem solving and discussion of relationships.

Powers of ten—the expression of numbers as the product of a number between one and ten and some power of ten; used in the expression of very small and very large numbers and in problem solving.

Nuclear or chemical equations—symbolic representation of quantitative relationships; used in problem solving and to represent phenomena.

Intuitive calculus—informal application of some of the simple concepts and processes of differential and integral calculus, including delta notation, area under curves, and volumes of rotation; used in the discussion of relationships and pictorial representation.

Measurement—the gathering of quantified data; used in laboratory experiences.

## ANALYSIS AND RESULTS

An analysis was made of all the materials selected for inclusion in the study. The factors examined in this analysis were:

1. What mathematical concepts and processes ( as previously outlined) are included in traditional science courses and in what sequence?
2. What mathematical concepts and processes (as previously outlined) are included in *new* science courses and in what sequence?
3. To what extent are the mathematical concepts and processes taught in *traditional* mathematics courses and in what sequence?
4. To what extent are the mathematical concepts and processes taught in the *new* mathematics and in what sequence?
5. A comparison of the utilization of mathematical concepts and processes in science to the sequence in which the same mathematical concepts and processes are taught in mathematics.

The results of this analysis are reported in Table 1.

The symbols and abbreviations used in Table 1 are to be interpreted as follows:

*Column headings*
Trad.—traditional science programs
BSCS-Y—the Yellow Version of the program of the Biological Sciences Curriculum Study
CBA—the program of the Chemical Bond Approach Committee
CHEM—the program of the Chemical Education Material Study
PSSC—the program of the Physical Science Study Committee
T—traditional mathematics program
S—program of the School Mathematics Study Group
U—program of the University of Illinois Committee on School Mathematics
C—program of the Commission on Mathematics of the College Entrance Examination Board

*Symbols in cells*
a—mathematical concept or process is taught in mathematics program same year *after* it is used in science course
b—mathematical concept or process is taught in mathematics program same year *before* it is used in science course
s—mathematical concept or process is taught in mathematics program in the *same* year it is used in science course
x—mathematical concept or process is not used in science course
q—mathematical concept or process is used in science course but is not taught in mathematics program.

Each cell relates the mathematical concept or process to a particular mathematics program and science course from the standpoint of the time the concept or process is taught in the mathematics program and used in the science course.

The symbols "x", "q", and "a" in Table 1 may be considered as representing a negative coordination of the mathematics programs with the science programs in regard to certain selected mathematical concepts and processes. Such an interpretation is justified if *positive* coordination

**TABLE 1**

**The Coordination Between the Utilization of Selected Mathematical Concepts and Processes in Selected Secondary Science Programs and the Teaching of the Concepts and Processes in Selected Secondary Mathematics Programs***

| Mathematical Concepts and Processes | Science Programs | | | | | | | | | | | | | | | | | | | | | | | | | | | |
|---|---|---|---|---|---|---|---|---|---|---|---|---|---|---|---|---|---|---|---|---|---|---|---|---|---|---|---|---|
| | Grade 10—Biology | | | | | | | | Grade 11—Chemistry | | | | | | | | | | | | Grade 12—Physics | | | | | | | |
| | Traditional | | | | BSCS-Y | | | | Traditional | | | | CBA | | | | CHEM | | | | Traditional | | | | PSSC | | | |
| | T | S | U | C | T | S | U | C | T | S | U | C | T | S | U | C | T | S | U | C | T | S | U | C | T | S | U | C |
| | 54 | 56 | 58 | 60 | 65 | 68 | 70 | 72 | 76 | 79 | 81 | 83 | 87 | 90 | 92 | 94 | 98 | 101 | 103 | 105 | 109 | 112 | 114 | 115 | 120 | 123 | 125 | 129 |
| Linear equations | x | x | x | x | b | a | b | b | b | b | b | b | b | b | b | b | b | b | b | b | b | b | b | b | b | b | b | b |
| Quadratic equations | x | x | x | x | a | a | b | b | s | b | b | b | s | b | b | b | s | s | b | b | b | b | b | b | b | b | b | b |
| Ratio, proportion, & variation | b | b | s | b | b | b | s | b | b | s | b | b | s | b | b | b | s | b | b | b | b | b | b | b | b | b | b | b |
| Graphs | x | x | x | x | a | a | s | a | x | x | x | x | b | s | b | s | s | s | b | s | b | b | b | b | b | b | b | b |
| Probability | q | q | q | a | q | q | q | a | x | x | x | q | x | x | x | x | x | x | x | a | x | x | q | q | s | q | q | s |
| Statistics | q | q | q | a | q | q | q | a | x | x | x | x | x | x | x | x | q | q | q | q | q | s | s | q | q | q | q | s |
| Formulas | b | b | b | b | b | b | b | b | b | b | b | b | b | b | b | b | b | b | b | b | b | b | b | b | b | b | b | b |
| Trig. functions | x | x | x | x | x | x | x | x | x | x | x | x | x | x | x | x | x | x | x | s | s | s | s | s | b | s | s | b |
| Vectors | x | x | x | x | x | x | x | x | x | x | x | x | x | x | x | x | x | x | x | x | b | b | b | b | b | b | b | b |
| Intuitive plane geometry | x | x | x | x | x | x | x | x | x | x | x | x | b | b | b | b | b | b | b | b | q | b | b | q | b | b | b | b |
| Logarithms | x | x | x | x | a | a | a | a | x | x | x | x | s | s | s | s | x | x | x | x | b | b | b | b | x | x | x | x |
| Powers of Ten | x | x | x | x | q | q | b | q | q | a | b | q | b | q | b | q | q | b | q | q | q | b | q | q | q | b | q | q |
| Intuitive solid geometry | x | x | x | x | a | s | q | s | a | b | q | b | a | b | q | q | a | b | q | b | b | s | q | b | b | q | q | q |
| Intuitive calculus | x | x | x | x | x | x | x | x | x | x | x | x | q | q | q | q | q | q | q | q | x | x | x | x | q | q | q | q |

* For the meaning of symbols and abbreviations used in this table see text.

is defined to mean that the mathematical concepts and processes are utilized in the science courses and are taught in the mathematical program before or during their utilization in the science courses. From such a definition, it is readily seen that the symbols "b" and "s" represent a positive coordination.

Using the above classification of symbols, one may develop a "coordination ratio" for any combination of the science and mathematics programs. This "coordination ratio" is defined as the ratio of the number of positive coordination symbols in any mathematics-science program combination to the total number of symbols in that combination. For example, in the combination of traditional mathematics and traditional science programs there is a total of forty-two symbols; of these, fifteen are positive coordination symbols, "b" or "s". Thus, the "coordination ratio"

between traditional mathematics and traditional science programs is fifteen divided by forty-two (.36).

Tables 2 and 3 show the "coordination ratios" for various combinations of mathematics and science programs. Table 2 indicates the relationships among the traditional and new programs taken collectively, whereas Table 3 shows the relationships among the individual traditional and new programs. A higher "coordination ratio" is to be interpreted as representing better coordination between two programs than would a lower "coordination ratio." In Table 2 can be seen a trend toward better coordination as changes are made from a combination of traditional programs to a combination of new programs. This trend is also indicated in Table 3, and a further trend of improved coordination from traditional to new programs in the sciences can be seen.

**TABLE 2**

**Comparison of the Coordination Among Traditional and New Science and Mathematics Programs with Regard to Selected Mathematical Concepts and Processes by "Coordination Ratios"**

| Mathematics Programs | Science Programs | |
| --- | --- | --- |
| | Traditional | New |
| Traditional | .36 | .43 |
| New | .41 | .53 |

**TABLE 3**

**Comparison of the Coordination Among Individual Science Courses and Mathematics Programs with Regard to Selected Mathematical Concepts and Processes by "Coordination Ratios"**

| Mathematics Programs | Science Courses | | | | | | |
| --- | --- | --- | --- | --- | --- | --- | --- |
| | Biology | | Chemistry | | | Physics | |
| | Trad. | BSCS-Y | Trad. | CBA | CHEM | Trad. | PSSC |
| Traditional | .14 | .21 | .29 | .50 | .43 | .64 | .57 |
| SMSG | .14 | .29 | .36 | .57 | .50 | .71 | .64 |
| UICSM | .14 | .43 | .36 | .57 | .50 | .71 | .64 |
| CEEB | .14 | .36 | .36 | .57 | .50 | .79 | .79 |

## CONCLUSIONS FROM THE STUDY

The following conclusions were based on the results of this study:

1. There is a marked increase in the use of mathematics in tenth grade biology from the traditional to the new course.
2. The new chemistry and physics courses show only a slight increase in the use of mathematics over the traditional courses.
3. The great increase in the use of mathematics from traditional to new science programs is in the use of graphs.
4. There are numerous mathematical concepts and processes apparently useful in the science courses, both traditional and new, which are not used in these science courses.
5. There are mathematical concepts and processes which are used in the science programs which are not taught in the mathematics programs.
6. Much of the content which has been added to the new mathematics programs is not directly applicable to the science programs.
7. The coordination of traditional mathematics programs with the mathematical content of traditional science courses is quite poor.
8. The coordination of new mathematics programs with the mathematical content of new science courses is higher than for traditional programs.
9. There is some improvement in the coordination of mathematics programs with the mathematical content of science courses from the traditional to the new programs, although the percentage increase, as represented by increase in "coordination ratio," is quite small.

The conclusions presented are interpretations of the findings; this study was not undertaken with the idea that mathematics programs should be built according to the mathematical needs of science courses. Neither has it been the intention to suggest that science courses should be designed to fit the mathematics program. However, since changes are being undertaken in mathematics and science courses at the secondary level, at great cost in time, money, and effort, it would seem that improved coordination between the two areas should be included as one of the objectives. When improved coordination can be developed without weakening either the mathematics or science programs individually, and since improved coordination might improve both the individual programs, it should be considered during the development of the new programs. It is hoped that this study will call the attention of program developers to this important facet of their problem.

## 41. Experimental Evaluation of a High-School Program for Potential Dropouts

LANGDON E. LONGSTRETH, FRED J. STANLEY, and
ROGER E. RICE

Although not as effective as had been hoped, the project reported in this article does offer many contributions. Among other things, it highlights the problems inherent in identifying real-life relevant criteria. It also demonstrates how evaluative data can be used to identify areas of the educational program in need of revision, and suggests four sound reasons for undertaking evaluative research in the first place. Must a project yield positive results in order to be considered worthwhile? Definitely not! An effective evaluation design and effort will allow even negative or inconclusive results to provide valuable leads for improvements and for indications of "what not to do again."

The present paper reports the evaluation of a dropout prevention program. The experiment was carried out over a 3-year period in a Southern California school system. During this time period approximately 75 male potential dropouts were enrolled in a work-study program, and their progress was compared with an equal number of potential dropouts enrolled in the regular school program.

### METHOD

The selection of variables defining the work-study program was guided by current theoretical conceptualization and one important practical consideration: that the selected variables be within the reach of the average school system, without an undue expenditure of money or personnel. Space does not permit a complete description of all the selected variables nor of the theoretical rationale underly-

Reprinted and abridged with permission of the publisher and Langdon E. Longstreth from the *Journal of Educational Psychology*, **55** (1964), pp. 228–236. Copyright 1964 by the American Psychological Association.

ing their selection. As a general orientation, experimental students attended classes from 8:30 to 11:30 each day; attended a gym class after lunch; and then left campus for afternoon jobs, where they worked approximately 3 hours per day. When and if students were not employed, they attended a shop course until 2:30 P.M., and then were allowed to leave school. A short description of the program's four main characteristics, with a brief statement of the underlying assumptions, is provided below.

*Characteristic 1: A Curriculum Designed to Appeal to the Potential Dropout.* The rationale underlying the curriculum was simple: academic success requires effort, and effort requires motivation and interest. Therefore, a major goal of the curriculum was to orient the subject matter of each course toward the existing interests of the students, e.g., considerable emphasis upon the development of appropriate work habits on the job. Three courses were ultimately developed: English, practical mathematics, and social studies. All three courses were geared toward practical implications. A second major goal was to individualize academic assignments in order to account for individual differences and maximize the possibility of successful academic performance.

*Characteristic 2: A Stable Pupil-Teacher Relationship.* There were two experimental classes each year, with about 15 students per class. Not only was the pupil-teacher ratio small, but also all three courses within each class were taught by the same teacher. The rationale was that this small, stable pupil-teacher relationship would facilitate communication and understanding between teachers and students.

*Characteristic 3: A Counselor Who Was Immediately Available.* A counselor was assigned to the experimental program whose main responsibility was to be immediately available for counseling with experimental students. His function was that of a detached, impartial adult to whom the students could communicate their feelings of frustration without fear of reprimands or counteraction.

*Characteristic 4: Afternoon Jobs for Pay and School Credit.* An attempt was made to obtain employment for all experimental students. These jobs usually were for 3 hours each weekday afternoon, although some students also worked weekends and evenings on these jobs, as well as during summer vacation. Students were paid by the hour and obtained school credit for their jobs. Jobs were obtained by school and by Youth Studies Center (University of Southern California) personnel in the local community and consisted of such tasks as grocery box boys, employment in city government (electrical and plumbing shops, street maintenance, park custodian tasks, etc.), grease monkeys in auto agencies, etc. Seventy-seven per cent of the experimental students were employed at one time or another. Some had several consecutive jobs, others lost their jobs

and did not obtain others, and some kept their jobs for more than a year. Of those who held jobs, the average number of hours worked was 320.5, and the median, 326. The range was from 13 hours to 840 hours.

It was assumed that employment would serve several goals. First, it would tend to satisfy the vocational goals assumed to be characteristic of potential dropouts. Second, it would show them that the school could actually do something for them that was practical and provided immediate rewards (money in the pocket). Third, the students were given an opportunity to learn good work habits, which perhaps would increase their job potential after leaving school.

**Subjects** The primary criterion for inclusion in the program was a constellation of factors which might be termed the "dropout syndrome." It consisted of a school record of excessive tardinesses and truancy, retardation in basic academic skills, and poor academic grades. Candidates were classified as either "aggressive" or "passive" in an attempt to form homogeneous groups. Aggressive candidates had long records of school difficulties with rules and authority figures, such as defiance of teachers, fighting, swearing, smoking on school grounds, etc. Passive candidates were characterized by considerably fewer such instances.

All candidates but four had finished the ninth grade of one of two junior high schools (these four were midsemester ninth graders). Following their classification as aggressive (A) or passive (P), they were further subdivided in terms of school last attended (one of two schools). Within these subgroups, students were rank-ordered in terms of age. The first student on each age list was then assigned to either the experimental (E) or control (C) condition, and the second to the other condition, in an alternate fashion, until all students on the list were accounted for. Following assignment to the experimental and control conditions, pairs of experimental and control students were then matched on the basis of IQ, maintaining homogeneity with respect to age, school last attended, and aggressive-passive classification.

Students selected for the experimental condition (work-study program) were contacted and told they could participate in the program if they wished. In case of refusals, the remaining students were contacted until the two experimental classes were filled.

The preceding procedure was carried out for each of the 3 years of the program, except that students who decided to remain in the work-study for more than 1 year were allowed to do so.

*Characteristic of Classroom Organization and Teachers.* The E students were divided into two classes of approximately 15 students each. About one third of the students in each class were A, and two thirds P.

In keeping with the requirement of a practical program, work-study teachers were picked from the regular teaching staff of the city school system. They had not had intensive training for the environment they subsequently entered. The primary criterion for selection was a reputation for being a good teacher in general and an expressed interest and some prior experience in working with deviant students. Of the three work-study teachers (one taught for 1 of the 3 years of the program, another for 2 years, and a third for all 3 years), one had taught mental retardates (IQ from 70 to 90) the previous year, and the other two had a reputation for being unusually successful in working with problem boys at the elementary and secondary school levels.

*Evaluation Procedure.* Evaluation of the work-study program was based upon three main sets of data: dropout proportions of E and C students, before-after interviews, and before-after police records. The priority of these three criteria was judged to be in the same order, with

dropout proportions the most precise and specific measure, and police data least precise and least concerned with school behavior.

## RESULTS

**Dropout Proportions** A dropout (DO) was defined as follows: if a student left school prior to graduation, he was considered a DO unless another school requested his cumulative record. In the latter case he was considered a transfer. The schools of all transfers were contacted by letter or telephone to determine whether the student was actually enrolled or not. If not, he was classified as a DO. If he did enroll, and had not dropped, he was classified as a nondrop (ND). The records of all those classified as DOs were then examined to determine if withdrawal from school had been instigated by the student or the school. If instigated by the student, with no formal action by the school, the student was classified as a voluntary DO. If the school instigated the action, the student was classified as an involuntary DO. It became apparent, almost without exception, that involuntary DOs possessed a record of excessive absences prior to being released by the school, and, indeed, were released because of excessive absences as well as because of disruptive behavior in some instances. The voluntary-involuntary classification was therefore abandoned, and all students were classified simply as DO or ND.

The frequencies of DO and ND for E and C groups, separately for A and P students, are presented in Table 1.

Interpretation of the data in Table 1 leads to the conclusion that almost exactly the same proportion of E students dropped from school (57%) as C students (60%). Thus there is no evidence that the work-study program was more effective than the regular school program as far as holding power is concerned. It is also apparent from Table 1 that a greater proportion of A students in both E and C groups

**TABLE 1**
**Number of DO and ND for E and C Groups, Separately for A and P Students**

|  | E | | | C | | |
|---|---|---|---|---|---|---|
|  | A | P | Total | A | P | Total |
| ND | 8 | 22 | 30 | 9 | 17 | 26 |
| DO | 18 | 21 | 39 | 18 | 21 | 39 |

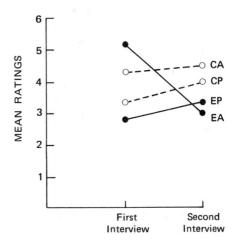

**Figure 1**
**Mean Ratings in Response to Nine Quantitative Questions on First and Last Interviews**

dropped from school (68%) than P students (52%).

**Interview Data** All interviews were private, carried out by personnel from the Youth Studies Center. Students were informed that answers were confidential and would definitely not be given to the school system. The interviews lasted about 20 minutes and consisted of two general types of questions: qualitative questions, with open-end answers which were recorded verbatim; and quantitative questions, requiring the student to respond with a rating on a 10-point scale. Replies to both kinds of questions were essentially similar, and therefore only the results of replies to the nine quantitative questions will be discussed.

The nine questions related to

General enjoyment of school
Teacher enjoyment of classes
Teacher understanding
Teacher interest in students
Teacher ability
How much you learned
How much you studied
Importance of courses
Counselor understanding

It was found when all nine questions were considered together, that the E students showed a significant improvement in attitude while C students deteriorated. Furthermore, E students improved more than C students on the seven of the individual nine questions, and on no questions did C students improve significantly more than E students. These data clearly

suggest that the work-study program had a beneficial effect on school attitudes as measured by these nine questions.

Mean ratings for the nine questions are presented in Figure I. A lower mean indicates a better attitude. These data are interpreted as allowing the conclusion that (a) A students manifested poorer attitudes than P students on the first interview; (b) EA were the only students to improve from the first to the last interviews, improving significantly more than CA; and (c) on the first interview EA manifested significantly poorer attitudes than CA, but significantly better attitudes on the last interview. These data again strongly suggest that the work-study program positively affected the school attitudes of A students, but not the attitudes of P students. The reliability of the better improvement in attitudes of EA students is also indicated by the fact that it was clearly apparent for each of the 3 years of the program considered separately. The fact that A students manifested poorer initial attitudes than P students is consistent with the assumption that A students were more hostile toward the school environment than P students.

## POLICE DATA

Police records were obtained for all E and C students for two time periods: (a) the 14 months preceding enrollment of E students into the work-study program, and (b) the 14 months beginning with enrollment of E students into the work-study program (this was a 12-month period for E and C students in the third year of the program). The second time period began with the last academic year of the program for those students who remained in the work-study program for 2 or 3 years. Proportions of students with at least one recorded police contact within either of these two time periods, and excluding traffic offenses, are presented in Table 2, separately for E and C students, and separately for A and P students.

TABLE 2
**Proportion of E and C Students with Police Contacts during First and Second Time Periods, Separately for A and P Students**

| Student group | N | Time period | |
|---|---|---|---|
| | | First | Second |
| EA | 28 | .29 | .32 |
| EP | 42 | .26 | .33 |
| CA | 27 | .52 | .41 |
| CP | 39 | .13 | .18 |

Table 2 indicates (a) a greater proportion of A than P students had police contacts during the first time period; (b) this difference was in the same direction, but not significant, during the second time period; and (c) there is no evidence that enrollment in the work-study program reduced number of police contacts (i.e., the change from first- to second-period contact proportions is not significantly different for E and C students).

## DISCUSSION

In terms of the main evaluative criterion (dropout rates), the program was not suc-cessful. In terms of the secondary criteria, the program was not successful in reducing police contacts, but was successful in improving school attitudes of A students (not P students). The fact that more A students that P students dropped from school, however, is inconsistent with the interview results and suggests that either interview responses were not valid indexes of attitudes or that attitude changes, though real, were not related to observed behavioral indexes. A third possibility is that the attitudes of A students did not improve enough to effect changes in observed behavior.

Other sources of data suggest the program may have had some beneficial effects. For example, academic grades improved more for E students than for C students. Also, fewer E students were reported to the Dean of Boys for rule violation. However, both of these differences might be accounted for by variations in grading practice and referral practice between experimental and regular school teachers. A number of E students substantially improved their work habits on the job (as measured by employer ratings), but no comparable data for Cs were available because of their full-day attendance in school.

In attempting to explain the results of the present study the program staff has drawn upon data based on observation in the experimental classrooms and on the reported experiences of teachers, counselors, and Center staff. While no definitive explanations can be derived from these data sources, two general considerations appear most relevant.

1. *Program procedures were too limited in scope or were introduced too late.* In considering this possibility, it is to be recalled that a stated objective was to develop a work-study program which would be financially and operationally feasible for the typical school system. This objective necessarily placed limits upon the types of change which could be introduced into the classroom setting. Thus it might be concluded that far more sweep-

ing changes of educational objectives and process in the high school setting would have been necessary to fully achieve the program's stated objectives. On the other hand, the program in its present form might have been successful if it had been introduced at an earlier age.

2. *Program procedures would have been successful had they been fully operationalized.* During the 3 years of program operation, a number of problems were encountered which may have influenced the degree of actualization of defined program characteristics. These problems can be thought about in terms of: (a) School organization—the program was initially seen as a special experiment operating "outside" the regular organizational structure of the school; (b) Procedural definition—for example, group discussion was identified as an important program element which was designed to facilitate the modification of deviant attitudes and behaviors of E students. However, considerable difficulty was experienced in developing a specific form of group discussion which appeared to contribute to this objective; (c) Teacher motivation—teacher morale appears to have been initially affected by the relative "isolation" of the program from regular school process and by the low status assigned their position by other teachers in the high school; (d) Teacher performance —some classroom procedures appeared not to have been fully implemented because they required marked modification of the teachers' behavior and educational philosophy. In retrospect, it is suspected that unrealistic demands may have been made on them in terms of expected changes in "teaching style" which were explicit in the definition of certain classroom procedures.

These two interpretations, inadequate educational change *in principle* and inadequate educational change *in fact* represent the major thinking of the authors. They found themselves unable to choose between them. However, the sharp contrast in the nature of these interpretations suggests the utility of further evaluations of such programs in order to establish with greater clarity their general feasibility.

Summarizing from a slightly different point of view, the present experiment yielded four important kinds of information. First of all, the recorded experiences of program activity for the past 3 years represent a useful body of knowledge regarding program development and problem resolution which will facilitate planning and operations of other programs of this type.

Second, the body of formal and informal data collected as a result of this experiment provides a basis for the development of theory regarding deviant behavior in school and its treatment in that setting.

Third, the present findings indicate in an unequivocal fashion the importance of formal evaluation of such programs. Staff members returned from the yearly interviews to consistently report the favorable verbalizations of experimental students. Sole reliance upon interview results, therefore, would have led to the conclusion that the program was successful, at least for A students. In a related sense, the findings also emphasize the need for an effective system of classroom observation which would provide a basis for determining the extent to which defined program procedures were effectively implemented.

Fourth, and probably most important, the present findings indicate there are no panaceas or easy cures for the dropout problem. The characteristics of the present program are believed to be representative of current conceptualizations concerning the dynamics of the potential dropout and his interactions with the school environment. Developing a prevention program on the basis of these conceptualizations is no guarantee of success. As previously mentioned, both theoretical formulations and their implementations need to be carefully developed in order to maximize the probability of success of such a program.

## 42. Toward National Assessment: History and Results

### JACK C. MERWIN and FRANK B. WOMER

One of the most, if not *the* most, significant large-scale evaluation or—perhaps more accurately—data-gathering efforts to be mounted during the last several decades is National Assessment of Educational Progress (NAEP). Tyler (1966) has described the general philosophy of NAEP as

. . . evaluation which is to assess the educational progress of larger populations in order to provide the public with dependable information to help in the understanding of educational problems and needs and to guide in efforts to develop sound public policy regarding education. This type of assessment is not focused upon individual students, classrooms, schools, or school systems, but furnishes over-all information about educational attainments of large numbers of people. (p. 1)

The potential usefulness of the results of NAEP has been likened to that of the Gross National Product or the Consumer Price Index because of the influence they can have on rational legislative action and allocation of resources.

The controlling organization, which began in 1964 as the Exploratory Committee on Assessing the Progress of Education, eventually dropped the "Exploratory," and is now the National Assessment of Educational Progress—since 1969 a project of the Education Commission of the States.

The first portion of this article describes some of the early developmental work on NAEP's overall design. It is a kind of biography or anatomy of a large-scale measurement project. The section on results, drawn from a report by Frank Womer, describes a typical NA exercise report and several generalizations that seem warranted from an initial readout of the data.

The application of the item-sampling technique (Lord, 1962; Walberg and Welch, 1967) is well illustrated. (Cronbach, in Article 16, also commented on the technique.) Basically, the process involves breaking up a large group of potential examinees into smaller units and administering a subset of the total item pool to each unit, with the option of overlapping some of the units. Rather than administering a 70-item test to 1,000 subjects, it might make more sense and be more economical of student time to administer a set of 10 tests with seven items each to groups of 100 subjects. The validity of the item-sampling technique has been verified by several investigators (Cook and Stufflebeam, 1967; Plumlee, 1964).

The Exploratory Committee on Assessing the Progress of Education started its work by holding conferences with educators, curriculum specialists, administrators, and school board members. From these conferences came a number of recommendations concerning characteristics of a national assessment and procedures that the Committee might use in seeking to carry out its work. These recommendations included: (1) The assessment should be developed in cooperation with teachers and tried out in the schools. (2) Even though all important areas cannot be started at once, the initial effort should include more than the three R's. It was suggested that as time goes on the project should include additional important areas and become more comprehensive. (3) Over the years, as educational objectives change, assessment procedures should change, just as the components of the Gross National Product have changed as our patterns of production have changed. (4) The assessment should be under the direction of a private commission and not be a project of Federal or State Governments. Related to this, it was recommended that financial support of the Committee's initial work come from private sources. The Carnegie Corporation and Ford Foundation provided considerable support; virtually all support now comes from the Federal Government.

## GENERAL DESIGN OF NATIONAL ASSESSMENT

On the basis of consultations with various groups and subsequent deliberations the Committee decided that its efforts might

This article is a composite of two publications which are reprinted and abridged with permission of their authors and the joint copyright holder, the National Council on Measurement in Education: J. C. Merwin, "The Progress of Exploration Toward a National Assessment of Educational Progress," *Journal of Educational Measurement*, **3** (1966), pp. 5-10; and Frank B. Womer, "National Assessment Says," *Measurement In Education*, **2** (1970), pp. 1–8.

best proceed within the following guidelines.

1. Age levels will define the groups to be surveyed and it is practical to consider assessment at four age levels: ages 9, 13, 17, and adult. Age 9 was included because by this age children might be expected to have achieved some of the goals of primary education. By age 13, there should be substantial progress in attaining the goals of elementary education. Seventeen-year-olds are normally high school seniors and the last age group still in school in large numbers. Adults (ages 26–35) were included to provide a look at the residual of elementary and secondary education as well as a means of identifying areas where there may be a general continuation of development.

2. At each age level three descriptions should be sought. There should be an attempt to identify behaviors that 90 per cent, 50 per cent, and 10 per cent of the age group can exhibit.

3. The instruments and procedures should be aimed at descriptions of what large groups can do.

4. The objectives used as a basis for developing exercises should be considered authentic by scholars, be goals the schools are trying to achieve, and be considered by thoughtful laymen as things desirable for American youth to learn.

5. Originally it was expected that every exercise used must sample an objective set forth for the project and be meaningful to thoughtful laymen. Both cognitive and non-cognitive objectives should be considered, and cover the areas of reading and the language arts, mathematics, science, literature and the fine arts, vocational education, citizenship, social studies, and music.

One of the goals of the Committee is to evolve instruments and procedures that will be acceptable to informed, education-interested laymen. It was considered desirable to involve such laymen at this point by having them review and critique the sets of objectives developed. The first step was to contact a number of individuals and associations with an interest in education and request nominations of thoughtful, public spirited citizens who might be asked to assist in this review. Groups contacted included the National School Boards Association, the Chamber of Commerce, the National Congress of Parents and Teachers, the National Education Association, the National Committee for Support of the Public Schools, the National Catholic Education Association, and many others. Using the various lists of nominees, invitations were extended to people to attend one of four regional conferences. An attempt was made to get a balance of people from large cities, suburban areas, and other types of communities. People from various parts of the United States with primary interest in private education, as well as those basically interested in public education, were invited.

Laymen from large cities, suburban areas, and other types of communities comprised working groups, and each group reviewed all . . . sets of objectives under the chairmanship of one of its members.

Reports on the . . . projects were summarized into a . . . booklet containing the objectives and supporting illustrative statements. Panels were asked to judge each objective in terms of the questions: "Is this something important for people to learn today? Is it something I would like to have my children learn?" While each panel was chaired by one of the lay panel members, staff members sat with each panel and had the complete set of contractors' reports available for further elaboration and clarification of the objectives as they were discussed.

Most of the objectives developed by the agencies in their work with scholars and teachers were accepted as desirable

for American youth by these laymen. There were recommendations for reworking and rewording some of the objectives and these were taken back to the contractors for reconsideration by their scholar-teacher consulting groups. It will come as no surprise that the most difficult area to pin down with any success was social studies. Most of the lay groups, the Technical Advisory Group, and the Exploratory Committee itself felt the need for a more extensive consideration of this very complex area. For this reason a special conference on the objectives for social studies was held. Scholars from various disciplines that contribute to the area of social studies, leading social studies teachers, and professors specializing in social studies education were called together to review and discuss the objectives in hand and make recommendations for further development of objectives.

Since a large portion of the objectives developed by the scholars and teachers in each area was generally accepted by the lay panels, the Committee moved on to the initial steps in exercise development. The Committee turned to test development agencies for help in this phase of the project.

Since the assessment is aimed at describing what groups can do, it is the sampling of the behavior of *groups,* rather than of *individuals,* that enters into reliability considerations. Responses can be pooled across individuals in a group and thus some of the practical considerations of testing individuals become less important. The time spent by each individual can be relatively short, and it is not necessary that all exercises be completed by every participant. In fact, each person in the sample will take only a small portion of the exercises and possibly spend as little as 30 minutes or so on them. Since we are not after a reliable sample of the individual's behavior, there are dimensions of freedom both in the selection of exercises to be taken by any one individual and the length of time to be spent on an exercise. If certain exercises are somewhat time consuming, an increase in sample size will be called for to maintain the desired level of reliability. The Committee asked the contractors to concern themselves primarily with creating the best designed exercises they can produce to sample the behaviors set forth in the objectives.

The Committee has made progress in its consideration of methods of reporting the results of a census, though much work remains to be done on this aspect of the project. It was decided that no report is to be made for individual students, teachers, or school systems and that there will be no scores. Rather, descriptions based on the exercises themselves will be used to report the outcomes. Such descriptions are presently contemplated for a number of sub-populations which may change over the years. Originally it seemed desirable to incorporate four age levels, four types of community—large city (above 200,000), middle-size cities (25,000–200,000), urban fringe, and small town-rural (below 25,000)—two socio-economic levels, four geographical regions (Northeast, Southeast, Central and West), and two sexes in defining the sub-populations.

For example, the first census might identify science problems that can be successfully solved by 40 per cent of the 13-year-old girls in the country and by 60 per cent of the boys of this age. An examination of the results for sub-populations, however, might show that 80 per cent of the girls of this age from the higher socio-economic level of large midwestern cities can solve this type of problems while only 40 per cent of the boys from the lower socio-economic level of large midwestern cities have success. In other words, it would indicate that boys in this particular sub-population have operated at a level similar to girls across the nation on this type of exercise while the girls from this other sub-population are more successful, as a group, than boys across the nation.

## PRELIMINARY RESULTS

The projected type of report just described was followed in the initial readout of results in the Summer of 1970. For example, it was found that more young adults between the ages of 26 and 35 (9 out of 10) are aware of the fact that the President does not have the right to do anything affecting the United States that he wants to do than are 17-year-olds (8 out of 10), 13-year-olds (7 out of 10), or 9-year-olds (5 out of 10). The question on which these results are based and the results themselves are presented in Table 1.

It comes from a Citizenship exercise for National Assessment. While most of the young adults in the National Assessment sample could state an acceptable reason for their answer (8 out of 10), the younger age groups did not do as well (only 2 out of 10 of the 9-year-olds). These results suggest that for this specific bit of information there is continuing growth through the school years and even into young adulthood.

Perhaps the most striking feature of National Assessment's first reports is that there are no scores or norms—just individual exercises (questions, items) along with the percent choosing or producing each response (p-values), both correct and incorrect, for each exercise. Those who developed the plan for National Assessment felt that the best way to describe what young people know is to present the questions or tasks that they were asked along with information about how well they performed. This directs attention at actual samples of behavior rather than at some summation of behaviors. It allows the reader of the reports to make his own evaluation of each exercise. He can accept the results as meaningful information useful in teaching and/or curriculum evaluation and/or policy making and/or allocation of educational funds, etc. He can reject a question as meaningless or inappropriate if his judgment leads him to that conclusion. The point is that the reader

**TABLE 1**

A. Does the President have the right to do anything affecting the United States that he wants to do? (Yes, No, I don't know)

B. (If yes) Why? (Part B was not scored; it was asked to insure that respondents understood Part A and to give them a chance to explain their position.)

C. (If no) Why not?

   (If answer to C is vague) Who or what would stop him from doing what he wants?

Acceptable reasons to C (examples): People could stop him; elected officials could stop him; checks and balances system of government; laws stop him; country would be a dictatorship; not the democratic way.

Unacceptable reasons to C (examples): Police or Vice President would stop him; he wouldn't be doing his job; he might do something that could hurt the country; he would be doing what is right; people vote for him not to; he can't do it; everybody, even the President, has some limitations; he just advises us; he can't do everything since he is only one person.

| **Results** | | Age | | |
|---|---|---|---|---|
| | 9 | 13 | 17 | Adult |
| Stated that the President does *not* have the right to do anything affecting the United States that he wants (No to A) | 49% | 73% | 78% | 89% |
| Stated that the President does not have the right and gave an acceptable reason (acceptable reason to C as well as No to A) | 18 | 53 | 68 | 80 |

of a report has all the results before him rather than an average or a summary or a conclusion.

Eventually National Assessment will generate its own standards, although not in the same sense as those established for the usual standardized test. Only half or fewer of the exercises administered by National Assessment in a given year are released that year. The others are retained to be used again three or six years hence. At that time it will be possible to compare the results from a second or third assessment with those obtained previously. Then one can see whether change (progress?) is taking place in the knowledges and skills of young people over time. This is the ultimate goal of National Assessment—to measure changes in knowledges, skills and attitudes over time.

Since the first results of National Assessment are benchmark data, they provide neither instantaneous "indictments" of American education nor instantaneous "whitewashing." This fact has been of considerable disappointment to persons who looked upon the project as one which will provide "answers" to all sorts of educational questions. An information-gathering project is not designed to provide such answers. But it can and should provide decision-makers with information useful in decision-making.

Even though the ultimate goal of National Assessment is to assess change, the first results do point to some generalizations of considerable import, as well as illustrating specific knowledges and skills and attitudes that young people have and have not attained. The generalizations discussed here are based on total national results for Science and on partial national results for Citizenship. Later reports will include comparisons, item by item, for four geographic regions, size and type of community, sex, color (black versus white), and an educational index of the home.

**Learning in Science and Citizenship Progresses Regularly Through the School Years** The evidence for this statement is based on "overlap" exercises, those administered to more than one age level. Consistently on the overlap exercises 17s did better than 13s and 13s did better than 9s. There were 15 overlaps between 9s and 13s for Science and 17 for Citizenship. All of the Science overlaps and 13 of the 17 Citizenship overlaps favor the 13s over 9s. There were 23 overlaps between 13s and 17s for Science and 73 for Citizenship. All of the Science overlaps and 47 of the 73 for Citizenship overlaps favor the 17s over 13s. Note that the generalization does not take a position as to whether the schools, or other social organizations, or the family, or any other causal factor or combination of factors are responsible.

A statement that learning is taking place as young people proceed through the school years is not exactly revolutionary. Observation and common sense have indicated as much. But National Assessment documents this generalization in terms of specific knowledges and skills. Perhaps the greatest utility of this specific type of information from overlap exercises will be as an aid to understand when growth is taking place in specific skill and knowledge areas.

**Variability in Science and Citizenship Achievement Is Characteristic of Young Adults and Seventeen Year Olds** There were 58 Science and 57 Citizenship exercises administered to both 17s and adults. Of these, 38 Science and 10 Citizenship overlaps yielded higher $p$-values for the correct answer for 17s, while 20 Science and 47 Citizenship overlaps yielded higher $p$-values for adults. Because the 17s did better on more Science exercises than the adults one might be tempted to assume general superiority of the 17s. However, that would be a hasty and unsupported generalization. Careful examination of the overlap exercises has led several reviewers to the conclusion that the exercises for which 17s did better tend to be of a different type than the ones for which adults did better.

The generalization that young adults sometimes show greater achievement than 17s in Science and Citizenship may, like the first generalization discussed, seem to many readers to be another bit of "common sense", but documentation of common sense can have its own utility. Documentation can focus attention upon an area of learning in a way that common sense may not. This simple generalization helps to remind us that much learning takes place outside of schools, that "textbook" learning may have limited utility (if textbook implies rote memory primarily), and that if the ultimate goal of education is an enlightened citizenry one needs to examine carefully what knowledge and skills adults truly need to acquire and retain.

**There Are Meaningful Knowledge and Skills and Attitudes in Science and Citizenships at All Difficulty Levels** The impact of this generalization suggests that all young people have acquired meaningful knowledge and skills that relate directly to objectives of instruction in Science and in Citizenship. Most people probably would have paid lip service to this statement prior to any results of National Assessment, but unfortunately too many of us (including us teachers, who should know better) have acted as if we felt that some youngsters were completely devoid of useful skills or knowledges. As National Assessment results are accumulated over the years, it should be possible to develop a picture of what knowledges and skills all 9s, 13s, and 17s have attained. Whether we will be satisfied with that picture is another question, but at least we will know where students stand. This should be of considerable help in planning for group learning experiences, in avoiding knowledge already acquired and in building knowledge not yet acquired.

The results in Table 2 suggest that society has done a fairly good job in getting young people to indicate lack of bias toward people of other races, *in a paper and pencil situation*. The obvious response to this is that what people say they would be willing to do and what they really do may not be the same. Nevertheless, if young people did not indicate tolerance, there would be little chance for further progress in race relations. To the authors the most disturbing aspect of Table 2 is that almost half (44 percent) of the respondents at each age level did indicate an unwillingness to accept a person of another race in at least one of the five categories.

**Item Writers May Not Be Good Enough Judges of Exercise Difficulty in Criterion-Referenced Situations**    When reporting the results for Science, three categories of correct responses were established: rather few (0–33 percent), good many (34–66 percent) and most (67–100 percent). The original writer's and reviewers' estimates have now been plotted against the actual results. Of 498 comparisons made for Science, 339 (68 percent) were the same whereas 159 (32 percent) were different. Thus, the item writers and reviewers judged difficulty correctly two thirds of the time and judged incorrectly one third of the time. This is not outstanding success. This is not to suggest that the particular writers and reviewers for National Assessment were poor judges, since it is not known whether other writers could have done better or whether writers in other subject areas could have done better.

Across the four age groups the percentages of agreement were 70, 65, 70, and 67 for ages 9, 13, 17, and adult. Thus, judgments were quite similar across ages. The writers were correct 80 percent of the time for the easy exercises (the 90s) whereas they were correct only 60 per-

**TABLE 2\***

People feel differently toward people of other races. How willing would you be to have a person of a different race doing these things?

**Results**

| [For each situation below, the choices were: Willing to, prefer not to] | % willing to Age | | |
| --- | --- | --- | --- |
| | 13 | 17 | Adult |
| A. Be your dentist or doctor? | 81% | 74% | 75% |
| B. Live next door to you? | 83 | 77 | 67 |
| C. Represent you in some elected office? | 81 | 82 | 82 |
| D. Sit at a table next to yours in a crowded restaurant? | 80 | 90 | 88 |
| E. Stay in the same hotel or motel as you? | 88 | 92 | 89 |
| Willing to for one or more of the above | | | |
| two or more | 96 | 97 | 93 |
| three or more | 94 | 94 | 90 |
| four or more | 89 | 88 | 86 |
| all five | 56 | 56 | 56 |

\* Not administered to the in-school sample in one large western state, one southeastern county and one southwestern city at the request of state or local authorities.

cent of the time for the others (50s and 10s). The need for making statistical checks is obvious. And in the final analysis it is the students who must tell us what they know and don't know, and what they feel or don't feel.

**Adults Select "I Don't Know" More Frequently On Multiple-Choice Tests Than Students** It may be that school-age youngsters are so geared to guessing on multiple-choice exercises (and rightly so) that many of them never seriously considered the "I don't know" alternative. Adults, who are assessed in their own homes, probably are less concerned about a "score" that they might be achieving than about giving their best response or straightforwardly admitting a lack of knowledge. Whether it is good or bad that 17s seem to be prone to more guessing than adults is a debatable question.

**Initial Results Provided Many Surprises** The fact that trained item writers and reviewers were "surprised" with respect to estimated difficulty fully one third of the time is strong support for this statement. Noneducators probably will be surprised even more. Evidence for this assumption comes from the initial newspaper articles written about National Assessment results. The education writer for the *Washington Post* was unhappily surprised that, while 70 per cent, 91 per cent, and 92 per cent of the 13s, 17s, and adults respectively knew that the Senate was the second of the two houses of Congress, 17 per cent, 5 per cent, and 4 per cent respectively thought that the Supreme Court

was the answer. From a psychometric viewpoint, any *p*-value above 90 per cent might seem to be good, but to a Washington reporter anything less than 100 per cent on such an item is unthinkable. The same reporter was disturbed that only half of the 17s and adults could solve this problem correctly: "A motor boat can travel five miles an hour on a still lake. If this boat travels downstream on a river that is flowing five miles per hour, how long will it take the boat to reach a bridge that is 10 miles downstream?"

One reviewer of the National Assessment Science results finished his comments by listing eight pleasant surprises and 10 unpleasant surprises. He was pleased that 89 per cent of 17s knew that living dinosaurs have never been seen by man ("The Flintstones notwithstanding") and was displeased that only 33 per cent of 17s and 25 per cent of adults knew that doubling the linear dimensions of a cube increases its volume eightfold.

Readers of the National Assessment reports may want to play the same game— estimating what they think students know and can do in specific exercises before looking at the *p*-values. Another potentially fruitful approach for teachers and curriculum specialists is to look at the *p*-values of wrong responses as well as of the correct responses. Such analyses have the potential of shedding considerable light on specific misconceptions that are commonly held. For teachers, broad generalizations that may be abstracted from National Assessment results may be of much less interest than specific, item-by-item analyses. Such analyses probably are best done by subject matter specialists.

## 43. The Effect of First Grade Instruction Using Basal Readers, Modified Linguistic Materials, and Linguistic Readers on Second Grade Pupil Progress

WILLIAM D. SHELDON, NANCY J. NICHOLS, and
DONALD R. LASHINGER

The most commonly used traditional approach to educational program evaluation is the application of standardized achievement tests. Typical of this approach is the following "methods study" in reading. One of many such studies conducted throughout the United States and funded by the Office of Education, it followed the usual pattern of comparing the results of students involved in several presumably different programs. When using a standard instrument, there is always the danger of overlooking highly valid and worthwhile objectives peculiar to a specific program. All relevant program objectives should be measured, not just those covered by the available commercial measuring instruments. The reader is encouraged to refer to Articles 16 and 19 for a discussion of the pros and cons of comparative evaluation.

The pupils who were studied at second grade level during the 1965-66 school year had all participated in the similar study of first grade reading achievement the previous year. All remained in the same instructional treatment group throughout the two-year period.

The methods of instruction studied were a basal reader approach, a modified linguistic (synthetic phonic) approach, and an approach using linguistic materials. The average achievement of pupils who had been instructed by these three methods did not differ significantly at the end of grade one (Sheldon and Lashinger, 1966).

### OBJECTIVES

This study was continued through second grade level (1) to determine if any sig-
nificant differences that were immeasurable at the conclusion of grade one occurred among mean scores on word study skills, word recognition, spelling, and comprehension tests that could be attributed to method of instruction, (2) to determine which method, if any, appeared to be most successful as an instructional tool for either boys or girls of high, average, or below average ability under the conditions of this experiment, (3) to determine any significant differences between test scores resulting from method of instruction when pretest scores of intelligence were held constant, and (4) to determine which method, if any, produced significantly superior results when achievement levels of children as judged by pretest results were held constant.

### PROCEDURE

Twenty-one classrooms of children took part in the study. Each experimental treat-

Reprinted with permission of the publisher, the International Reading Association, and William D. Sheldon from *The Reading Teacher*, **20** (May 1967), pp. 720–725.

ment was used in seven classrooms. Of the 467 children who took part in the first year of the study, 376 were still available for participation in the second year.

The Ginn basic readers were used for basic instruction in seven classrooms. The Ginn second-year program provides for continued sequential development of word recognition and comprehension skills. The skills introduced in first grade are refined and extended. Greater emphasis is placed on phonic and structural analysis of words at this level. The approach to this instruction is essentially an analytic one in which the child uses known words as a basis for developing his auditory perception of sounds, and then learns to associate this auditory image with the correct visual symbol within the structure of a known word. He then learns to extend the utility of these skills through analogy to unknown words. The Ginn basic readers emphasize reading for meaning by systematic training in a wide variety of evaluating, comprehending, and organizing skills.

Seven classrooms continued work in the modified linguistic materials of the Singer Structural Reading Series begun in grade one. The techniques used in this method, of learning the sounds of letters and structural parts of words and then learning skills of combining these elements into words, would indicate its classification as a synthetic phonic approach. The emphasis is on recognizing and combining structural elements within the word. Words are studied in phonetically related groups so that the child can achieve independent recognition of words by insight into these phonetic relationships. This program, like the basal system used in the study, is planned to develop reading comprehension and thinking skills. "Ample opportunity is given to develop related reading skills, such as generalization, summarizing, following directions, developing astuteness of observation, and developing the ability to think logically" (Stern, 1963).

The seven classrooms that formed the remaining treatment group continued to receive instruction in the Bloomfield-Barnhart Let's Read linguistic readers. The vocabulary of these readers is strictly controlled in that words are introduced in linguistically regular patterns. The child is taught a single technique of word recognition. He spells and pronounces words in regular patterns (such as *cat, hat, fat,* and so on) until all the possible regular patterns are mastered. In this process the child is dealing with a minimal contrast auditorally and a minimal contrast visually as he moves from word to word. At all times the child is dealing with the letter symbols in a specific environment and therefore with constant sound-symbol correlations. At no time are phonemes pronounced outside words, nor are letters dealt with in isolation. It is not until the child has established a stable concept of the alphabetic system of writing that he is introduced to the irregularities, which are taught as exceptions to the known patterns.

The linguist's point of view of the basic task for pupils at the beginning stage of reading is expressed by Fries as he defines the goals of what he terms the "transfer" stage of reading. "Learning to read in one's native language is learning to shift, to transfer, from auditory signs for the language signals, which the child has already learned, to visual graphic signs for the same signals" (Fries, 1962). It is the opinion of the authors of the Let's Read materials that any emphasis on comprehension skills at this stage of learning will inhibit development of these high-speed discrimination responses. This cannot be interpreted to mean that comprehension is not the ultimate goal of reading at more mature stages.

## TESTING

Achievement of the three treatment groups was evaluated in the areas of word and paragraph reading, comprehension, reading accuracy, and rate of reading. Skills in the supporting area of word analysis were evaluated. The related skills of spelling and written composition were also studied. Comparison among treatment groups was made on the amount of free reading by pupils and on their attitudes toward reading.

Comparisons on the above skills were made for the total treatment groups. In addition, performance on these skills was compared across treatment groups for subgroups formed on the basis of ability level and sex.

Pretreatment reading readiness and intelligence testing was conducted in September 1964 before first grade instruction was begun. In September 1965 achievement tests were given to determine the presecond grade skills of the population. Posttreatment achievement testing was carried out at the close of 140 days of second grade instruction, in May 1966.

Pretreatment testing included the following tests administered in September 1964: (1) *Murphy-Durrell Diagnostic Reading Readiness Test,* (2) *Metropolitan Readiness Test,* (3) *Thurstone Pattern Copying and Identical Forms Test,* (4) *Pintner-Cunningham Primary Test,* and (5) *Allyn and Bacon Pre-Reading Test.*

Presecond grade achievement of the three groups was evaluated by the *Stanford Achievement Test,* Primary I Battery.

At the close of the second grade instructional period in May 1966 the following achievement measures were used: (1) *Stanford Achievement Test,* Primary II Battery, Form W, (2) *Gilmore Oral Reading Test,* (3) *Fry Phonetically Regular Word List,* (4) *Gates Word Pronunciation Test,* (5) *San Diego Pupil Attitude Inventory,* and (6) a sample of written composition prepared by the pupils in response to a standard stimulus.

The *Stanford Test* was administered to all pupils; other tests were administered to a randomly selected subsample of fifty children from each treatment group.

**Analysis**  Analysis of covariance was used to compare achievement means of the three treatment groups. The *Pintner-*

*Cunningham* mental age, *Metropolitan Readiness* total score, and the Word and Paragraph Meaning subtest scores of the *Stanford Test* scores at pretesting were used as the covariates for this analysis. The comparison was made for means of classroom means, since the treatments had been randomized on the basis of classroom groups.

## RESULTS

1. The treatment groups did not differ significantly in intelligence as measured on a group test at the beginning of first grade.

2. Analysis of eighteen reading readiness subscores revealed no significant differences between treatment groups except for one subscore. A significant difference in Auditory Discrimination-Rhyming Words was found to favor the basal reader group.

3. No significant differences were found in reading or related skills achievement level of the three treatment groups at the beginning of the second grade instructional period.

4. No significant differences between treatment groups were found in prefirst grade school attendance.

Examination of pre-experimental data revealed that no significant differences existed between groups at the beginning of the second grade instructional period.

An analysis of covariance of posttreatment test results revealed the following:

1. Both the linguistic group and the modified linguistic group means were significantly superior to the mean of the basal reader group on the *Stanford* Word Meaning subtest when the factor of presecond grade treatment reading skill was held constant. The means of the linguistic and modified linguistic groups were not significantly different.

2. Differences among the three treatment groups in Paragraph Meaning were not significant.

3. The means of the linguistic and modified linguistic groups were both signifi-

cantly above the mean of the basal reader group in Spelling on the *Stanford Test,* when the factors of presecond grade treatment reading skills, readiness, and intelligence were held constant. The means of the linguistic and modified linguistic groups did not differ significantly.

4. No significant difference in *Stanford Word Study Skills* was found among the three groups.

5. The mean of the linguistic group was significantly superior to the means of the other two groups on Comprehension as measured by the *Gilmore Oral Reading Test,* when the factor of presecond grade treatment reading skill was held constant. The means of the modified linguistic and basal reader groups did not differ significantly from each other on this variable.

6. No significant differences between means of the treatment groups were found, either in Reading Rate or Accuracy as measured by the *Gilmore Oral Reading Test.*

7. There were no significant differences between groups in ability to read the phonetically regular words presented in the Fry list.

8. The groups did not differ significantly in ability to read the *Gates Word Pronunciation Test.*

9. No significant differences were found when analysis was made of the written composition sample in number of words spelled correctly, number of running words, number of different words used, number of polysyllabic words used, or percentage of accuracy.

10. The treatment groups did not differ significantly in attitudes toward reading that could be measured with the *San Diego Pupil Attitude Inventory.*

11. The linguistic group read a significantly greater number of books as independent reading during the sampling period when this count was kept than did either of the other two treatment groups. The modified linguistic and basal groups did not differ significantly from each other on this variable.

12. The three treatments appeared to be equally successful for instructing boys in the high and low ability ranges.

13. All mean grade level scores on the four Stanford Achievement variables of average ability boys who were instructed in the modified linguistic materials were above actual grade placement at the time of final testing. Average ability boys instructed in the basal reader materials achieved a mean score just at grade placement on one variable—Word Meaning. The other three means were below actual grade placement. Average ability boys instructed in the linguistic materials had no mean achievement score at or above actual grade placement on the Stanford Achievement Test variables.

14. The three treatments appeared to be equally effective for instruction of girls at all three levels of ability.

A comparison was made of the relative achievement of boys and girls in subgroups based on ability level to determine whether either of the treatments produced higher achievement scores for a given subgroup than did another. A summary of the findings based on the *Stanford Achievement Test* variables follows:

1. At the high ability level boys and girls showed no differences in achievement when all children of this ability level were considered.

2. Boys and girls at the high ability level scored equally well in each of the treatment groups.

3. All means on the Stanford subtests were above actual grade placement norms at the time of testing for both boys and girls in this high ability group, regardless of treatment.

4. At the middle ability level girls scored higher than boys when all children in the experiment were considered.

5. Average ability girls scored equally well in each of the three treatment groups. All means for girls of this ability were at or above actual grade placement norms at the time of testing.

6. There were no differences in achievement between boys and girls of

average ability who were instructed in the modified linguistic materials. Both boys and girls scored above actual grade placement norms in this group.

7. Average ability boys in the linguistic and basal reader groups did not achieve at as high a level as girls in the same treatment groups. In both treatment groups achievement means for boys on the *Stanford* variables were below actual grade placement at the time of testing.

8. At the low ability level boys and girls scored equally well when all children in the experiment at this ability level were considered.

9. There were no differences in achievement between boys and girls of low ability who were instructed in the basal reader materials.

10. Low ability boys who were instructed in the modified linguistic materials scored slightly above the level of girls in this group on the four *Stanford* variables.

11. Low ability boys who received instruction in the linguistic materials scored slightly below the level of girls in this group.

12. The average *Stanford* means for low ability boys and girls were below the actual grade placement at time of testing.

## CONCLUSIONS

All three of the approaches to primary instruction proved to be effective for reading instruction at second grade level. Although some significant differences were noted in some of the subskills or related skills of the total reading process, as they were measured in this study, none of the approaches was demonstrated to be superior in all aspects of reading.

When average achievement scores are considered, each of the three groups was shown to be reading at an acceptable level at the end of grade two.

Further investigation is indicated in two areas. First, two of the methods of teaching reading that were compared in this study attach great importance to the development of comprehension skills. The third, the linguistic method, avoids emphasis on this area of instruction during the beginning or "transfer" stage of reading. The three groups showed equal achievement in comprehension at the conclusion of grade two. Further study of this problem is indicated to determine what the emphasis on comprehension skills should be in beginning reading programs and what interaction may exist between methods and instruction in comprehension skills.

Second, two of the methods that were compared provide the child with training in a variety of word recognition skills. The third, the linguistic method, provides just one technique of word recognition. All three groups achieved equally well when tested on word study skills and word recognition. Further investigation is needed to determine whether the recognition skills learned in the three approaches will continue to serve the children equally well as they move into more advanced reading in the intermediate grades.

# 44. Assessing Educational Program Effectiveness: Examples of Cross-National and Public School System Surveys

JOHN C. FLANAGAN

After describing four general data requirements for effective educational program evaluation, the author of this article presents two interesting examples. First, Project TALENT and the results of its initial follow-up studies are described. Project TALENT is one of the most fascinating, informative, and important large-scale assessment projects of modern times. A tremendous pool of information and data of great variety has been accumulated. This data bank, when augmented by invaluable longitudinal data, should provide an extremely valuable base upon which to build an understanding of the human resources represented by today's students, and to undertake meaningful research. Clever data-gathering methods and analyses are characteristic of Project TALENT.

Second, a comprenhensive survey of the educational program of a school system, with data-gathering samples taken from grades 4, 6, 9, and 12, is briefly summarized. The usual methods—standardized tests, as well as intense personal interviews and questionnaires—were used.

Valid assessment depends on the availability of four types of information. The *first* of these relates to the student appraisal; a comprehensive inventory of the capabilities and talents of each student is needed. It has been very difficult to interpret the performance of the student on aptitude and achievement tests in relation to his subsequent performance in various occupational and other adult roles. The follow-up studies of Project TALENT will provide very meaningful data to assist in this interpretation. Many additional studies of this type are needed. The *second* type of information needed relates to the better definition and prediction of the educational requirements for preparing each student for his effective functioning in his future roles. The *third* requirement is evaluating educational content and materials with respect to their effectiveness in preparing the individual to function in these roles. The last requirement is for efficient procedures for evaluating the student's progress toward meeting these requirements. A comprehensive program including these four factors should be of great help in enabling teachers and schools to provide the type of education that will enable each student to develop his own unique talents.

A description of how these four types of information were collected in two different situations will now be presented. In the first case a cross-national project will be described, and in the second a local school system survey.

Reprinted and abridged with permission of the publisher and John C. Flanagan from an article entitled "The Evaluation of the Effectiveness of Educational Programs," which appeared in *Bulletin de Psychologie* (University of Paris, Psychological Study Group), 257, XX, 10–15 (1967), pp. 763–769.

## PROJECT TALENT: A STUDY OF THE IDENTIFICATION, DEVELOPMENT, AND UTILIZATION OF TALENTS

In March of 1960 a comprehensive two-day battery of tests of aptitude, ability, and achievement along with a detailed inventory of background, characteristics, and plans was administered to 440,000 students in secondary schools throughout the United States. This study was supported by the United States Office of Education and other government agencies and involved the cooperation of 1353 secondary schools. These students are being followed up one, five, ten, and twenty years after their graduation from high school.

Evidence from these follow-ups suggests that the talents of many of today's young people are not being adequately developed and utilized.

For many purposes of using test scores it is of great importance that the scales on which the scores are reported are comparable. When test results are interpreted by referring them to national norms, substantial errors are sometimes introduced. These so-called national samples on which the various publishers' tests are standardized may be sufficiently different that as much as a full grade's variation can be introduced by simply choosing one form rather than another of published standard achievement tests. In the Project TALENT survey a careful effort was made to obtain a relatively precise national sample of secondary school students. Schools were stratified in terms of states, size of school, and the ratio of the size of the graduating class to the entering class. This provided a very representative sample of secondary school students. It is proposed that publishers gain increased comparability for the various tests in common use by adjusting their norms to the national standard determined by the Project TALENT results.

The basic requirement for using these results to obtain scores comparable to the national standards determined in the study are, first, in equating test scores the content of the test or combination of tests on which the comparable scores are to be obtained should be as similar as possible. The second requirement is that the sample used for equating should be as similar as possible to the national sample on which the norms were obtained in the Project TALENT survey.

These two requirements have a rather interesting relation in that, if either condition is fully met, the other can be ignored. For example, if the test content is similar enough to be practically identical, the equating sample need not be similar to the national norms sample. Or, to consider the other possibility, if the sample is sufficiently comparable to the original national norms sample so that there is virtually no difference in the characteristics of the two groups, the contents of the tests being equated need not be closely similar.

In selecting the sample the relation of performance on the test to such factors as region of the country, rural or urban location, level of education, age, and socio-economic status should be studied. It seems probable that for most types of tests a carefully selected sample of about 1,000 students should provide adequate precision in equating scores for two rather similar tests. It should be emphasized that larger numbers cannot provide a satisfactory substitute for fulfilling the two requirements stated above (Flanagan, 1964).

Three types of findings from the analysis of the 1960 tests illustrate the value of such surveys (Flanagan et al., 1964). The first of these involves the direct interpretation of the test performance. For example, it was learned that 12th grade students can learn the English equivalents for three words in a foreign language per minute of study time. The average 12th grade student is able to spell 92.5 per cent of the 5,000 most commonly used words in the English language based on the Thorndike-Lorge word count. The average 12th grade student, for example, was able to answer about two thirds of the questions probing his understanding of sample paragraphs from the books of Louisa May Alcott and less than 60 per cent of the questions based on paragraphs from the stories of Robert Louis Stevenson. He answered correctly less than half of the questions based on paragraphs from Rudyard Kipling and just about half of the questions referring to the contents of paragraphs from the stories of Jules Verne. These students answered less than 30 per cent of the questions correctly based on paragraphs from the novels of Thomas Mann.

The average 12th grade student was able to do problems involving the addition, subtraction, multiplication, and division of two numbers (usually of two digits each) at the rate of 4.6 problems correct per minute with 0.3 errors per minute. On a test of clerical checking comparing two names in a list of pairs of names, the average 12th grade student correctly identified whether the two names were the same or different at the rate of 13.3 correct comparisons per minute with 1.3 errors per minute.

The second type of finding relates to individual differences. A good example of these is afforded by the proficiency of the best five per cent of the students on the clerical checking task. These students did nearly three times as well as the average of the 12th grade students. Similarly, the best five per cent with respect to reading comprehension correctly answered 85 per cent of the questions based on paragraphs from Jules Verne as compared with 50 per cent for the average.

Another way of looking at individual differences is to compare the performance of 9th grade and 12th grade students. For example, 22 per cent of the 9th grade students score higher on the vocabulary test than does the average 12th grade student. Twenty per cent of the 9th grade students achieve higher scores on the English test than does the average 12th grade student. Twenty-one per cent of 9th grade students score higher than does the average 12th grade student on the reading comprehension test, and 27 per cent of the 9th grade students achieve scores higher than those of the average 12th grade student on the social studies test.

These findings strongly suggest the need for individualizing education to develop the pattern of talents of each of the students in a given grade level.

The third type of finding from this survey relates to the comparative scores of boys and girls in grades 9 and 12 in basic skills such as reading comprehension, arithmetic reasoning, arithmetic computation, and creativity. The difference between the boys and girls in the motile age groups in grade 9 and grade 12 suggest that the increase of the boys as a result of their secondary school training is substantially greater than the comparable increase for the girls. This finding suggests that the content of secondary education being given to most girls in these schools should be examined carefully to determine whether or not gains in certain important educational objectives are being sacrificed for inadequate reasons.

Analysis of the findings also suggests that there is inadequate review of information learned by students and application of this information in other fields. Many students forgot more than they learned in various fields such as science and mathematics if they were not specializing in these fields.

Another point regarding the achievement of students in the Project TALENT survey relates to the fact that in all sections of the country there were high and low schools with respect to the average performance of their students. The number of students in the school and the school's location in an urban rather than a rural area were not found to be substantially related to the educational achievement of the students. It was found that students living in neighborhoods where the socio-economic status of the parents was generally high tended to learn more than students living in neighborhoods where the socio-economic status of the parents was generally low. It appears that much can be done to improve the level of achievement of the students.

The final point to be mentioned with respect to Project TALENT relates to the follow-up survey of this group (Flanagan and Cooley, 1966). Students were asked while in the 9th grade in which of approximately 30 occupations they planned to make their career. Four years later, after they had completed secondary school or dropped out of school, they were again asked in what field they planned to make their career. Only about 17 per cent of the boys were still planning the same career. Even in the 12th grade only 31 per cent of the boys' career choices were the same one year after they completed high school. For only physician and clergyman were there as many as half the students with the same career plans one year later. It is evident that these students are not given adequate information on which to base their plans while in the secondary schools.

## THE EVALUATION OF THE EDUCATIONAL PROGRAM IN THE SCHOOL SYSTEM

In the spring of 1965 the American Institutes for Research was asked to evaluate the educational program of a public school system including about 13,000 students (Flanagan, 1966). The purpose of the survey was to discover ways in which the educational program could be improved. The study was focused on several points. These included: (1) the learning abilities of the students and their achievement in comparison to comparable groups in the state and nation; (2) the appropriateness of the subject matter and instructional methods for individual students; (3) the effectiveness of the staff and teachers in helping students to select and work toward appropriate goals; (4) the extent

to which the students are given an opportunity to develop a sense of responsibility for their own behavior and are stimulated to learn beyond minimum requirements; and (5) the provisions for the education of children with exceptional needs.

One of the first analyses carried out in this school system was to compare the achievement of the students on standardized achievement tests with those of other school systems for which the occupational index for the parents was similar. The occupational scale was a relatively standard one running from professionals, farm owners, proprietors, managers, clerks, through skilled workers, semi-skilled workers, laborers, and servants. The performance of students in various grades was compared with that of the students in a group of schools for which the occupational index of the parents was closely similar. The students in this school system did slightly better than students in comparable systems both in the state and in the nation. Although intelligence or academic aptitude scores were also used to compare this group with other groups, it was felt that such a procedure was circular at least in part since many of the types of items in the intelligence and aptitude tests are quite similar to some of the kinds of items in the educational achievement tests.

To obtain specific information regarding the educational development of individual students, 10 per cent of the students in grades 4, 6, 9, and 12 were selected in such a way as to be representative of the total group of students in these classes in terms of learning ability.

Various types of data were collected. First, the pertinent information in the cumulative record for each of the students was summarized. Next, the students in grades 6, 9, and 12 were asked to complete a questionnaire regarding their school program. On the basis of these two sources, teachers and specialists were consulted regarding these students and some of their problems as indicated from these data. The final step was the interview of each of the students by counselors and other special service personnel of the schools.

To check on the consistency and the completeness of these interviews, 40 students were selected at random from among the 400 interviewed. An additional 40 students were selected after reading the evaluative reports by the interviewers to identify particularly interesting problems for further exploration. In response to the question, "Is instruction suited to the student's ability?" 82 per cent of the interviewers answered with an unqualified "Yes." In 14 per cent of the cases they responded "Yes, with some exception," and in 4 per cent of the cases the answer was "No." Another judgment the interviewers were asked to make was in answer to the question, "What is the quality of student motivation for learning?" For the four classes combined the evaluators rated the motivation for learning as "outstanding or excellent" for 30 per cent, as "fair" or "good" for 60 per cent, and as "poor" or "very poor" for 10 per cent.

A very interesting finding is that there was a very definite downward trend in motivation on the part of the students in the judgment of these interviewers, with 41 percent of 4th grade students having excellent or outstanding motivation and only 12 per cent of the 12th grade students having excellent or outstanding motivation for learning. It seems very likely on the basis of other evidence that similar findings would be obtained in most school systems throughout the country.

The interviewers were asked to give a summary evaluation indicating the overall effectiveness of the schools in meeting the needs of children in education and guidance. The interviewers estimated the schools were meeting the students' needs "nearly perfectly" for 25 per cent of the students, "in most respects" for 49 per cent of the students, "well in some re-

spects and poorly in others" for 22 per cent, and either "fairly unsatisfactorily" or "very poorly" for 4 per cent. The reasons for the unsatisfactory evaluations were such items as the schools' having failed to detect a severe visual handicap, misplacement of a student, failure to provide psychological assistance, lack of remedial instruction in the early grades, and lack of personal counseling.

Although the students are not regarded as authorities on the quality of instruction they receive, it seemed worthwhile to ask them whether instruction in a particular class made them want to learn more or not want to learn more about the subject than was required in the course. In replying to this question, at the 9th grade level the only subject in which close to half the students felt the instruction made them want to learn more was science. The subject making the poorest showing in this respect was English, where less than one in five indicated they were motivated to learn more than was required.

The graduates of the class of 1960 and 1964 in this high school were sent questionnaires in the summer of 1965. The data supplied by these groups was useful in determining the extent to which these students had actually continued the educational and occupational plans for which they were prepared while in high school. One of the items on the questionnaire asked students to complete the sentence, "The best thing provided for me by this high school was _____." In both classes the most frequent responses were "a good, basic education" and "good preparation for college." In both classes another frequent response was "good, competent, interested teachers."

Another item in the questionnaire requested that they complete the sentence, "The main thing I believe I needed which was *not* provided by this high school was _____." Approximately 25 per cent of the students in each class indicated that guidance and counseling was the most important unfilled need in their high school education. The only other comment from the two classes which was made by an appreciable proportion of the students was assistance in learning how to study. The other replies were scattered over a wide variety of needs.

Only about 1 per cent of the males and 2 per cent of the females in each of these classes reported that they were unemployed in 1965. These graduates were asked to provide an overall evaluation of the preparation they received in the schools by answering the following question: "Immediately following graduation from high school, how well do you believe you were prepared to enter into your new role as a paid worker or as a student?" About 30 per cent of each of the classes indicated that they were very well prepared; 45 per cent in each class indicated they were fairly well prepared.

The remaining 25 per cent in the two classes indicated they were generally prepared but lacked some specific or that they were not well prepared.

The detailed studies of the replies reported above and the other evaluations of the extent to which schools were meeting student needs were supplemented by observations and studies of the curriculum by experts in various subject matter fields.

On the basis of the study of all available data it was suggested that the greatest improvement in the school program could be expected from focusing on the two concepts of, first, individualization of instruction and, second, increased student orientation, responsibility, motivation, and maturity in planning and preparing for important life roles.

# EPILOGUE
## Future Directions, Problems, and Needs of Curriculum Evaluation

If one were to judge solely by the number of recent publications—books, articles, and monographs—dealing with curriculum and curriculum evaluation, one could conclude with confidence that a revolution is underway. Observers of the educational scene also note that teachers are focusing intense efforts on affective and humanistic curricula and other instructional innovations. Administrators and the public are voicing concern about educational accountability. Public and private groups are turning to the evaluator for assistance in judging the worth of their efforts. The arsenal of the evaluator is somewhat outdated and depleted when faced with these new demands. Both the theory and the practice of evaluation as applied in assessing new curricula need to be revitalized, revised, refurbished, and realigned with today's information and decision-making requirements.

This epilogue will briefly summarize some of the challenges facing curriculum evaluation and evaluators. Further, suggestions will be made for policy decisions and directions that research and applications might take.

The future of curriculum evaluation looks bright. It has progressed rapidly in the relatively short period since its rebirth at midcentury. But there is a long way to go. Many new techniques have been developed. Educators, as well as the public, have become aware of the value that evaluative data may have in developing and assessing the effectiveness of large-scale educational programs. The "mod world" of curriculum evaluation looks different than its older version. Provus (1969), for example, notes five myths that can be put to rest, the beliefs that:

1. Evaluation interferes with curriculum development.
2. Experimental designs are required for effective evaluation.
3. The interests and desires of evaluators are at odds with those of the program staff.
4. Evaluators must help specify program objectives.
5. Evaluation is only a long-term proposition.

In fact, it can be argued quite effectively that:

1. Evaluation and curriculum are intimately related, with evaluation providing data to build upon.
2. The design of an effective evaluation plan should first be dictated by the needs of the program, the nature of the staff and program, and the outcomes expected

and the decisions to be made. Actual manipulation of variables on subjects may not be required.

3. The aims and interests of the evaluator and the educational program staff are basically the same—to improve the teaching-learning process and product. Curriculum developers are charged with the development of instructional systems that will maximize learning. Evaluators are then expected to gather data that will (1) indicate the extent to which learning has been maximized, and (2) suggest revisions and modifications potentially beneficial for the system. Students benefit from the efforts of both groups.

4. The task of an evaluator may or may not include the specification of program objectives. The evaluator's role with regard to objectives will depend upon the needs of the program. If the context is one of a large curriculum development project and he is an internal evaluator, he would probably be involved in specifying program goals and change objectives from the outset. If the evaluator is external to the project, he may only be required to help assess whether or not the objectives have been met.

5. Evaluation data should continuously be gathered to assist in decision-making. The role of formative or feedback evaluation is an extremely important one. As the project, program, or curriculum is being developed and field-tested, information can be systematically gathered and evaluated with an eye toward improvement of the final product or process.

If the foregoing suggests some changes in the role of the evaluator and of evaluation, and highlights some problem areas, what are the needs and directions that evaluation might take in the future?

Stufflebeam (1966) and Stake and Denny (1969) have examined the needs of curriculum evaluation with regard to methodology, training, and theory. A brief summary of their recommendations follows.

## METHODOLOGY

Several reforms are needed in the general area of evaluation methodology. There is a need for noninterventionist evaluation designs. Ways need to be found of assessing the effects of a new program without influencing the outcomes. Webb et al. (1966) have used the terms "unobtrusive measures" and "non-reactive research" to describe this methodology. Another need in the area of methodology relates to the flexibility of the design. Because of modification of objectives, revision of treatment, or changes in personnel, projects must continually reassess their evaluation criteria. There is a real danger of misevaluation—both under- and overevaluation—of the program. Many new data collection procedures are needed. Observational devices, measures of affective outcomes, creativity tests, ways of assessing the nonreader, systems for the efficient production of criterion-referenced measures, and diagnostic techniques are among the data-collection methods that need to be developed. One final area in need of development involves the methods available to analyze change or gain scores, which so frequently form the basis for evaluating program effectiveness.

## TRAINING

Education lacks trained evaluators—at least the kinds of evaluators needed to assault the new collection–analysis–decision-making activities of the schools. Personnel trained only in the classical methodologies of statistics, research design, and testing are less able to cope with new process and product objectives. It may be that the "new-generation" evaluator must be even more of a generalist than was his predecessor. In addition to being a master of the usual quantitative tasks, he must be a little bit of a sociologist, economist, social psychologist, anthropologist, and philosopher. He must be blessed with a strong self-concept, high tolerance for ambiguity, and the patience of a United Nations arbitrator.

## THEORY

We have theories about almost everything in education—mental tests, learning, intelligence, and personality—except evaluation. We need systematic models (not unlike that of Provus, 1969) that allow objectives, data, and decisions to be integrated. A taxonomy of decision making is required. Decision-making methods need to be straightforward enough so that any school administrator, project director, or teacher can apply them without a high degree of mathematical sophistication or access to a computer. Work like that of Forehand (1970, 1971) should be encouraged and applied.

It seems clear, as Stufflebeam (1966) has noted, that:

1. Effective evaluation is required for the enlightened development of education; and
2. there is a general lack of trained personnel, adequate data collection, and evaluation theory and designs.

But let's close on a more positive note. Fairweather (1967) has suggested that by integrating research, evaluation, and action, behavioral scientists can effectively attack and significantly contribute to the solution of many social problems before they reach crisis proportions. He suggests that multidisciplinary teams of behavioral scientists define and study social problems in naturalistic settings. One of the major contributions that evaluation can make is the mere description of what has happened. If there has been an effect, we need to know what the treatment was.

It is also appropriate to note that the importance of the federal government cannot be overlooked. For it is the government that is creating a demand for the new breed of evaluator, as well as serving as a source of funds for training him.

In the final analysis, Caro's comment—made in 1969—is still pertinent: from practical and methodological standpoints, an imperfect strategy is emerging. Although far from consummate, it is superior to the impressionistic procedures that guide most social action programs today.

# REFERENCES

Adorno, T. W., et al. *The Authoritarian Personality.* New York: Harper & Row, 1950.

Ahmann, J. S., and M. D. Glock. *Evaluating Pupil Growth,* 4th ed. Boston: Allyn & Bacon, 1971.

Alkin, M. "Evaluating Net Cost-Effectiveness of Instructional Programs." In *The Evaluation of Instruction: Issues and Problems,* edited by M. C. Wittrock and D. E. Wiley. New York: Holt, Rinehart & Winston, 1970.

Allport, G. W., P. E. Vernon, and G. Lindzey. *Study of Values—A Scale for Measuring the Dominant Interests in Personality.* Boston: Houghton Mifflin, 1959.

Amidon, E. J. and J. B. Hough (eds.) *Interaction Analysis: Theory, Research and Application.* Reading, Mass.: Addison-Wesley, 1967.

Amidon, E. J., and A. Simon. "Teacher-Pupil Interaction," *Review of Educational Research,* **35** (1965), pp. 130–139.

Anderson, H. H. "The Measurement of Domination and of Socially Integrative Behavior in Teachers' Contacts with Children," *Child Development,* **10** (1939), pp. 73–89.

Anderson, H. H., and H. M. Brewer. "Studies of Teachers' Classroom Personalities. I. Dominative and Socially Integrative Behavior of Kindergarten Teachers." *Applied Psychology Monograph* no. 6 (1945).

Anderson, H. H., and J. E. Brewer. "Studies of Teachers' Classroom Personalities. II. Effects of Teachers' Dominative and Integrative Contacts on Children's Classroom Behavior." *Applied Psychology Monograph* no. 11 (1946a).

Anderson, H. H.; J. E. Brewer; and M. F. Reed. "Studies of Teachers' Classroom Personalities. III. Follow-up Studies of the Effects of Dominative and Integrative Contacts on Children's Behavior." *Applied Psychology Monograph* no. 11 (1946b).

Anderson, R. C. *Stimulus Sequence and Concept Learning (Experiment 1).* Mimeographed. Urbana: University of Illinois, 1964.

Astin, A. W. The Inventory of College Activities (ICA): Assessing the College Environment Through Observable Events. Paper read at Annual Meeting of the American Psychological Association, Chicago, 1965a.

Astin, A. W. *Who Goes Where to College.* Chicago: Science Research Associates, 1965b.

Astin, A. W. "Classroom Environment in Different Fields of Study," *Journal of Educational Psychology,* **56** (1965), pp. 275–282c.

Astin, A. W. "Further Validation of the Environmental Assessment Technique," *Journal of Educational Psychology,* **54** (1963), pp. 217–226.

Astin, A. W. "An Empirical Characterization of Higher Educational Institutions," *Journal of Educational Psychology,* **53** (1962), pp. 224–235.

Astin, A. W. and J. L. Holland. "The Environmental Assessment Technique: A Way to Measure College Environments," *Journal of Educational Psychology,* **52** (1961), pp. 308–316.

Atkin, J. M. "Behavioral Objectives in Curriculum Design: A Cautionary Note," *The Science Teacher,* May 1968, pp. 27–39.

Atkin, J. M. "Some Evaluation Problems in a Course Content Improvement Project," *Journal of Research in Science Teaching,* **1** (1963), pp. 129–132.

Ausubel, D. P. "An Evaluation of the BSCS Approach to High School Biology," *American Biology Teacher,* **28** (1966), pp. 176–186.

Ausubel, D. P., and D. Fitzgerald. "Organizer, General Background, and Antecedent Learning Variables in Sequential Verbal Learning," *Journal of Educational Psychology,* **53** (1962), pp. 243–249.

Bales, R. *Interaction Process Analysis.* Cambridge, Mass.: Addison-Wesley, 1950.

Bass, B. M. "The Leaderless Group Discussion," *Psychological Bulletin,* **51** (1954), pp. 465–491.

Beatty, W. H. (ed.) *Improving Educational Assessment and an Inventory of Measures of Affective Behavior.* Washington: Association for Supervision and Curriculum Development, 1969.

Beberman, M. *Searching for Patterns.* Mimeographed. Urbana: University of Illinois Committee on School Mathematics, 1963.

Becker, G. S. *Human Capital.* New York: Columbia University Press, 1964.

Bernabei, R., and S. Leles. *Behavioral Objectives in Curriculum and Evaluation.* Dubuque, Iowa: Kendall/Hunt, 1970.

Biddle, B. Review of Related Literature: Teacher-Pupil Relationships. Unpublished. Columbia, Mo., 1966.

Blau, P., and O. Duncan. *The American Occupational Structure.* New York: John Wiley, 1968.

Block, J. H. "Criterion-Referenced Measurements: Potential," *School Review,* **79** (1971), pp. 289–297.

Bloom, B. S.; J. T. Hastings; G. F. Madaus, et al. *Handbook on Formative and Summative Evaluation of Student Learning.* New York: McGraw-Hill, 1971.

Bloom, B. S. *Stability and Change in Human Characteristics.* New York: Wiley, 1962.

Bloom, B. S. "Quality Control in Education." In *Tomorrow's Teaching.* Oklahoma City: Frontiers of Science Foundation, 1961, pp. 54–61.

Bloom, B. S.; M. D. Englehart; E. J. Furst; W. H. Hill; and D. R. Krathwohl (eds.). *A Taxonomy of Educational Objectives: Handbook I, the Cognitive Domain.* New York: Longmans, Green, 1956.

Bolvin, J. O., and R. Glaser. "Developmental Aspects of Individually Prescribed Instruction," *Audiovisual Instruction,* **13** (October 1968), pp. 828–831.

Bonjean, C. M.; R. J. Hill; and S. D. McLemore. *Sociological Measurement: An Inventory of Scales and Indices.* San Francisco: Chandler, 1967.

Briggs, L. J. *Sequencing of Instruction in Relation to Hierarchies of Competence.* Pittsburgh: American Institutes for Research, 1968.

Broudy, H. S. "Can Research Escape the Dogma of Behavioral Objectives?" *School Review,* **79** (November 1970), pp. 43–56.

Brown, B. B. *The Experimental Mind in Education.* New York: Harper & Row, 1968.

Brown, B. B.; R. L. Ober; and R. Soar. "Florida Taxonomy of Cognitive Behavior." Unpublished. 1968.

Brownell, W. A. "The Evaluation of Learning under Different Systems of Instruction," *Educational Psychologist,* 3 (1965), pp. 5–7.

Bruner, J. S. *On Knowing.* Cambridge, Mass.: Harvard University Press, 1962.

Bruner, J. S. *The Process of Education.* Cambridge, Mass.: Harvard University Press, 1960.

Bruner, J. S. "Going Beyond the Information Given." In *Contemporary Approaches to Cognition,* edited by J. S. Bruner et al. Cambridge, Mass.: Harvard University Press, 1957.

Burdick, E., and W. J. Lederer. *The Ugly American.* New York: Norton, 1958.

Buros, O. K. *Sixth Mental Measurements Yearbook.* Highland Park, N.J.: Gryphon Press, 1965.

Buros, O. K. *Fifth Mental Measurements Yearbook.* Highland Park, N.J.: Gryphon Press, 1959.

Butler, J. G. "An Analysis and Measurement of Value Orientations as Related to Delinquent Behavior." Ph.D. dissertation, University of Illinois, 1957.

Cahen, L. S. "Comments on Professor Messick's paper." In *The Evaluation of Instruction: Issues and Problems,* edited by M. C. Wittrock and D. E. Wiley. New York: Holt, Rinehart & Winston, 1970, pp. 204–210.

Campbell, D. T., and J. C. Stanley. "Experimental and Quasi-Experimental Designs for Research on Teaching." In *Handbook of Research on Teaching,* edited by N. L. Gage. Chicago: Rand McNally, 1963.

Caro, F. G., (ed.) *Readings in Evaluation Research.* New York: Russell Sage Foundation, 1971.

Caro, F. G. "Approaches to Evaluative Research: a Review," *Human Organization,* 28 (Summer 1969), pp. 87–99.

Case, C. M. "The Application of PERT to Large-Scale Educational Research and Evaluation Studies," *Education Technology,* 9 (1969), pp. 79–83.

Charters, Margaret. "A Study of the Congruence Between Curriculum Intent and Evaluation Objectives Using Two Strategies for Stating Curriculum Objectives." Ph.D. dissertation, Syracuse University, 1970.

Clarke, H. H., and Marjorie Phillips. "Tools for Analyzing and Presenting Data." *Research Methods in Health, Physical Education, and Recreation.* Washington, D.C.: AAHPER, 1959.

Cohen, D. "Politics and Research: Evaluation of Social Action Programs in Education," *Review of Educational Research,* 40 (1970), 213–238.

Coleman, J. S., et al. *Equality of Educational Opportunity.* Washington: U.S. Office of Education, 1966.

Cook, D. L. *Program Evaluation and Review Technique: Applications in Education.* (Cooperative Research Monograph Number 17, U.S. Government Printing Office). Washington: U.S. Department of Health, Education, and Welfare, 1966.

Cook, D. L., and D. L. Stufflebeam. "Estimating Test Norms from Variable Size Item and Examinee Samples, *Educational and Psychological Measurement,* 27 (1967), pp. 601–610.

Corey, S. M. "Measuring Attitudes in the Classroom," *The Elementary School Journal,* (April 1943), pp. 457–461.

Corey, S. M. "Professed Attitudes and Actual Behavior," *Journal of Educational Psychology,* **28** (1937), pp. 271–280.

Cornog, W. H. "Teaching Humanities in the Space Age," *School Review,* **72** (Autumn 1964), pp. 377–393.

Coulson, J. E., and J. F. Cogswell. "Effects of Individualized Instruction on Testing," *Journal of Educational Measurement,* **2** (1965), pp. 59–64.

Crane, P., and C. C. Abt. "A Model for Curriculum Evaluation," *Educational Technology,* **9** (1969), pp. 17–25.

Cronbach, L. J. "Course Improvement through Evaluation," *Teachers College Record,* **64** (1963), pp. 672–683.

Cronbach, L. J. *Essentials of Psychological Testing.* New York: Harper & Brothers, 1949 and 1970.

Daly, H. E. "On Economics as a Life Science," *Journal of Political Economy,* **76** (1968), pp. 392–406.

Dave, R. H. "The Identification and Measurement of Environmental Process Variables that are Related to Educational Achievement." Ph.D. dissertation, University of Chicago, 1963.

Denison, E. F. *The Source of Economic Growth in the United States and the Alternatives Before Us.* New York: Committee for Economic Development, 1962.

Diederich, P. B. "Design for a Comprehensive Evaluation Program," *School Review,* **58** (April 1950), pp. 225–232.

Downey, L. W. *The Task of Public Education.* Chicago: Midwest Administration Center, University of Chicago, 1960.

Dressel, P. L. "Evaluation as Instruction." In *Proceedings of the 1953 Invitational Conference on Testing Problems.* Princeton, N.J.: Educational Testing Service, 1954.

Dressel, P. L. and L. B. Mayhew. *General Education: Explorations in Evaluation.* Washington: American Council on Education, 1954.

Duncan, J. K., and J. B. Hough. "A Content Classification System." Unpublished, 1966.

Dunn, J. A. "The PLAN Approach to Curriculum Definition," *Education,* **90** (1970), pp. 221–226.

Easley, J. A., Jr. *Features of UICSM Mathematics Project of Possible Interest to Psychologists.* Mimeographed. Urbana: University of Illinois, 1964.

Ebel, R. L. "Criterion-Referenced Measurements: Limitations," *School Review,* **79** (1971), pp. 282–288.

Ebel, R. L. *Measuring Educational Achievement.* Englewood Cliffs, N.J.: Prentice-Hall, 1965.

Education Development Center. *Man: A Course of Study—An Evaluation.* Cambridge, Mass.: Education Development Center, 1970.

Eisner, E. W. "Educational Objectives: Help or Hinderance?" *School Review,* **75** (Autumn 1967), pp. 250–260.

Eisner, E. W. "Educational Objectives: Help or Hinderance?" Paper read at 50th annual meeting of the American Educational Research Association, February 1966, in Chicago.

Eisner, E. W. "American Education and the Future of Art Education." In *Art Education,* edited by W. R. Hastie. Sixty-fourth Yearbook of the National Society for the Study of Education. Chicago: University of Chicago Press, 1965, pp. 299–325.

Eiss, A. F., and Mary Blatt Harbeck. *Behavioral Objectives in the Affective Domain.* Washington: National Science Supervisors Association, 1969.

Fairweather, G. *Methods of Experimental Innovation.* New York: Wiley, 1967.

Fanslow, Alyce M. "Environments in College Home Economics Units as Perceived by Students." Ph.D. dissertation, Iowa State University, 1966.

Ferguson, G. A. "On Learning and Human Ability," *Canadian Journal of Psychology,* **8** (1954), pp. 95–112.

Ferris, F. L., Jr. "Testing in the New Curriculums: Numerology, Tyranny, or Common Sense? *School Review,* **70** (1962), pp. 112–131.

Finlay, G. C. "The Physical Science Study Committee," *School Review,* **70** (1962), pp. 63–81.

Finn, J. D. "Institutionalization of Evaluation," *Education Technology,* **9** (December 1969), pp. 14–23.

Flanagan, J. C. "Individualizing Education," *Education,* **90** (1970), pp. 191–205 (a).

Flanagan, J. C. "The Psychologists Role in Youth's Quest for Fulfillment." Paper read at American Psychological Association meeting, September 1970, in Miami Beach (b).

Flanagan, J. C. "Program for Learning in Accordance with Needs," *Psychology in the Schools,* **6** (1969), pp. 133–136.

Flanagan, J. C. "Functional Education for the Seventies," *Phi Delta Kappan,* **49** (September 1967), pp. 27–32.

Flanagan, J. C. *A Survey of the Educational Program of the East Town Public Schools.* Pittsburgh: American Institutes for Research, 1966.

Flanagan, J. C. "Obtaining Useful Comparable Scores for Non-Parallel Tests and Test Batteries," *Journal of Educational Measurement,* **1** (June 1964), pp. 1–4.

Flanagan, J. C. "The Critical Incident Technique," *Psychological Bulletin,* **51** (1954), pp. 327–358.

Flanagan, J. C., and W. W. Cooley. *Project TALENT One Year Follow-Up Studies.* Cooperative Research Project Number 2333. Pittsburgh: University of Pittsburgh, School of Education, 1966.

Flanagan, J. C., and S. M. Jung. "An Illustration: Evaluating a Comprehensive Educational System." In *Evaluative Research: Strategies and Methods.* Pittsburgh: American Institutes for Research, 1970.

Flanagan, J. C.; F. B. David; J. T. Dailey; M. F. Shaycroft; D. B. Orr; I. Goldberg; and C. A. Neyman, Jr. *The American High School Student.* Technical Report to the U.S. Office of Education, Cooperative Research Project No. 635. Pittsburgh: Project TALENT Office, University of Pittsburgh, 1964.

Flanders, N. A. *Teacher Influence, Pupil Attitudes and Achievement.* Cooperative Research Monograph No. 12, OE-25040. Washington: Department of Health, Education, and Welfare, 1965.

Forehand, G. A. "An Evaluation System for Curriculum Innovation," *Teachers College Record,* **72** (May 1971), pp. 577–591.

Forehand, G. A. "Curriculum Evaluation as Decision-Making Process," *Journal of Research and Development in Education,* **3** (1970), pp. 27–37.

Forehand, G. A. "Psychological Measurement and Research in the Teaching of English." In *Needed Research in the Teaching of English,* edited by E. R. Steinberg. Washington: U.S. Office of Education, 1963.

Frederiksen, N. "In-Basket Tests and Factors in Administrative Performance." In *Stimulation in Social Science: Readings,* edited by H. Guetzkow. Englewood Cliffs, N.J.: Prentice-Hall, 1962.

Fries, C. C. *Linguistics and Reading.* New York: Holt, Rinehart & Winston, 1962, p. 188.

Gage, N. L., (ed.) *Handbook of Research on Teaching.* Chicago: Rand McNally, 1963.

Gagné, R. M. "Curriculum Research and the Promotion of Learning." In *Perspectives of Curriculum Evaluation,* edited by R. W. Tyler *et al.* A.E.R.A. Monograph on Curriculum Evaluation Number 1. Chicago: Rand McNally, 1967, pp. 19–38.

Gagné, R. M. *The Conditions of Learning.* New York: Holt, Rinehart & Winston, 1965.

Gagné, R. M. "The Implications of Instructional Objectives for Learning." In *Defining Educational Objectives,* edited by C. M. Lindvall. Pittsburgh: University of Pittsburgh Press, 1964.

Gagné, R. M. "The Analysis of Instructional Objectives." A paper prepared for the National Symposium on Research in Programmed Instruction, Department of Audiovisual Instruction, National Education Association, 1963.

Gagné, R. M. "The Acquisition of Knowledge," *Psychological Review,* **69** (1962), pp. 355–356.

Galloway, C. "Nonverbal Communication," *Theory Into Practice,* **7** (December 1968), pp. 172–175.

Gardner, R. W. "Cognitive Controls in Adaptation: Research and Measurement." In *Measurement in Personality and Cognition,* edited by S. Messick and J. Ross. New York: Wiley, 1962.

Gardner, R. W.; D. N. Jackson; and S. J. Messick. "Personality Organization in Cognitive Controls and Intellectual Abilities," *Psychological Issues,* **2** (1960), pp. 1–149.

Glaser, R. "Instructional Technology and the Measurement of Learning Outcomes: Some Questions," *American Psychologist,* **18** (1963), pp. 519–521.

Glaser, R.; Dora E. Damrin; and F. M. Gardner. "The Tab-Item: A Technique for the Measurement of Proficiency in Diagnostic Problem Solving Tasks," *Educational and Psychological Measurement,* **14** (1954), pp. 283–292.

Grobman, Hulda. *Evaluation Activities of Curriculum Projects.* A.E.R.A. Series on Curriculum Evaluation Monograph No. 2. Chicago: Rand McNally, 1968.

Gronlund, N. E. *Stating Behavioral Objectives for Classroom Instruction.* New York: Macmillan, 1970.

Gronlund, N. E. *Measurement and Evaluation in Teaching.* New York: Macmillan, 1965 and 1971.

Gronlund, N. E. *Sociometry in the Classroom.* New York: Harper & Row, 1959.

Gross, N. "Who controls the Schools? In *Education and Public Policy,* edited by S. E. Harris. Berkeley, Cal.: McCutchan, 1965, pp. 19–29.

Guba, E. G. "The Failure of Educational Evaluation," *Educational Technology,* **9** (1969a), pp. 29–38.

Guba, E. G. "Significant Differences," *Educational Researcher,* **20** (1969b), pp. 4–5.

Guttman, L. "A Basis for Scaling Qualitative Ideas," *American Sociological Review,* **9** (1944), pp. 139–150.

Guetzkow, H. *Simulation in Social Science.* Englewood Cliffs, N.J.: Prentice-Hall, 1962.

Guilford, J. P. *The Nature of Human Intelligence.* New York: McGraw-Hill, 1967.

Guilford, J. P. *Psychometric Methods,* 2nd ed. New York: McGraw-Hill, 1954.

Guiterman, A. "Education." *Death and General Putnam.* New York: E. P. Dutton, 1935.

Hammond, R. "Context Evaluation of Instruction in Local School Districts," *Educational Technology,* **9** (January 1969), pp. 13–18.

Harris, C. W., (ed.). *Problems in Measuring Change.* Madison: University of Wisconsin Press, 1963.

Harrow, Anita J. *A Taxonomy of the Psychomotor Domain.* New York: David McKay, 1972.

Hartley, H. J. *Educational Planning-Programming-Budgeting: A Systems Approach.* Englewood Cliffs, N.J.: Prentice-Hall, 1968.

Hastings, J. "Curriculum Evaluation: The Why of the Outcomes," *Journal of Educational Measurement,* **3** (1966), pp. 27–32.

Hathaway, S. R., and J. C. McKinley. *Minnesota Multiphasic Personality Inventory.* New York: Psychological Corporation, 1943.

Hausdorff, H. "Empirical Determination of the Relative Importance of Educational Objectives," *The Journal of Experimental Education,* **34** (Fall 1965), pp. 97–99.

Hawkridge, D. G., and A. B. Chalupsky. "Evaluating Educational Programs: A Symposium," *Urban Review* **3** (1969), pp. 8–10.

Heath, R. W. "Curriculum Evaluation." In *Encyclopedia of Educational Research,* 4th ed. Edited by R. L. Ebel. New York: Macmillan, 1969, pp. 280–283.

Hemphill, J. K. "The Relationships between Research and Evaluation Studies." In *Educational Evaluation: New Roles, New Means, Part II.* Edited by R. W. Tyler. Sixty-Eighth Yearbook of the National Society for the Study of Education. Chicago: University of Chicago Press, 1969, pp. 189–220.

Hill. J. C. "The Analysis of Content Development in Classroom Communication." Unpublished Paper, 1969.

Hoepfner, R., et al., eds. *CSE Elementary School Test Evaluations.* Los Angeles: UCLA Center for the Study of Evaluation, 1970.

Hoffman, P. J. "The Paramorphic Representation of Clinical Judgment," *Psychological Bulletin,* **57** (1960), pp. 116–31.

Horn, E. "Distribution of Opportunity for Participation Among the Various Pupils in Classroom Recitations." *Teachers College Contributions to Education,* No. 67, 1914.

Horst, P. (ed.) "The Prediction of Personal Adjustment," *Social Science Research Council Bulletin 48* (1941), pp. 1–57.

Hough, J. B. "An Observational System for the Analysis of Classroom Interaction." Mimeographed. Columbus: Ohio State University, 1964.

Hungerman, Ann D. "A Study of Achievement and Attitude of Sixth-Grade Pupils in Conventional and Contemporary Mathematics Programs," Ph.D. dissertation, University of Michigan, 1965.

Hutchins, E. B. "The Evaluation of Environmental Determinants." Paper read at the Annual Meeting of the American Psychological Association, 1962, in St. Louis.

Hutchins, E. B., and A. J. Nonneman. "Construct Validity of an Environmental Assessment Technique for Medical Schools." Paper read at the Annual Meeting of the American Educational Research Association, 1966, in Chicago.

Ikeda, H. "A Factorial Study of the Relationships Between Teacher-Held Objectives and Student Performance in UICSM High School Mathematics. UICSM Report No. 10. Urbana: University of Illinois, 1965.

Jacobs, P. E. *Changing Values in College, An Exploratory Study of the Import of College Teaching.* New York: Harper & Row, 1957.

Jones, J. B. "Handball as Pseudo-Athletic Proficiency Development," *Journal of Athletics,* **4** (1971), pp. 115–118.

Kapfer, Miriam B., (ed.). *Behavioral Objectives in Curriculum Development, Selected Readings and Bibliography.* Englewood Cliffs, N.J.: Educational Technology Publications, 1971.

Kaufman, I. "The Art of Curriculum Making in the Arts." In *Confronting Curriculum Reform,* edited by E. W. Eisner. Boston: Little, Brown, 1971, pp. 91–112.

Kelley, T. L. "Experimental Study of Three Character Traits Needed in a Democratic Social Order," *Harvard Educational Review,* **12** (1942), pp. 294–322.

Kelley, T. L. "Objective Measurement of the Outcomes of the Social Studies," *Historical Outlook,* **21** (1930), pp. 66–72.

Kibler, R. J.; J. Barker; and D. T. Miles. *Behavioral Objectives and Instruction.* Boston: Allyn & Bacon, 1970.

Kliebard, H. M. "The Tyler Rationale," *School Review,* **78** (February 1970), pp. 259–272.

Klein, S.; G. Fenstermacher; and M. C. Alkin. "The Center's Changing Evaluation Model, *Evaluation Comment,* (Center for the Study of Evaluation, UCLA) **2** (January 1971), pp. 9–12.

Kounin, J. S. *Discipline and Group Management in Classrooms.* New York: Holt, Rinehart & Winston, 1970.

Krathwohl, D. R. "Stating Objectives Appropriately for Program, for Curriculum and for Instructional Materials Development," *Journal of Teacher Education,* **16** (1965), pp. 83–92.

Krathwohl, D. R. "The Taxonomy of Educational Objectives—Its Use in Curriculum Building." In *Defining Educational Objectives,* edited by C. M. Lindvall. Pittsburgh: University of Pittsburgh Press, 1964, pp. 19–36.

Krathwohl, D. R.; B. S. Bloom; and B. B. Masia. *A Taxonomy of Educational Objectives: Handbook II, the Affective Domain.* New York: David McKay, 1964.

Krathwohl, D. R., and D. A. Payne. "Defining and Assessing Educational Objectives." In *Educational Measurement,* 2nd ed. Edited by R. L. Thorndike. Washington, D.C.: American Council on Education, 1970.

Kuhn, T. S. *The Structure of Scientific Revolution.* Chicago: University of Chicago Press, 1962.

Lehman, P. R. *Tests and Measurements in Music.* Englewood Cliffs, N.J.: Prentice-Hall, 1968.

Lessinger, L. *Every Kid a Winner: Accountability in Education.* New York: Simon and Schuster, 1970.

Light, R. J., and P. V. Smith. "Choosing a Future: Strategies for Designing and Evaluating New Programs," *Harvard Educational Review,* **40** (Winter 1970), pp. 1–28.

Likert, R. A. "A Technique for the Measurement of Attitudes," *Archives de Psychologie,* **140** (1 June 1932), pp. 1–55.

Lindvall, C. M., and R. C. Cox. "The Role of Evaluation in Programs for Individualized Instruction." In *Educational Evaluation: New Roles, New Means,* edited by R. W. Tyler. Sixty-Eighth Yearbook of the National Society for the Study of Education. Chicago: University of Chicago Press, 1969, pp. 156–188.

Lindvall, C. M.; Stella Nardozza; and Margaret Felton. "The Importance of Specific

Objectives in Curriculum Development." In *Defining Educational Objectives*, edited by C. M. Lindvall. Pittsburgh: University of Pittsburgh Press, 1964, pp. 10–18.

Lippett, R., and R. K. White. "The Social Climate of Children's Groups." In *Child Behavior and Development*, edited by R. G. Barker, J. S. Kounin, and H. F. Wright. New York: McGraw-Hill, 1943.

Logan, F. M. *Growth of Art in American Schools*. New York: Harper & Row, 1955.

Lord, F. M. "Estimating Norms by Item-Sampling," *Educational and Psychological Measurement,* **22** (1962), pp. 259–267.

Lortie, D. C. "Rational Decision-Making: Is It Possible Today?" *The EPIE Forum,* **1** (November 1967), pp. 6–9.

Lovenstein, M. "Economics, Educational Philosophy, and Psychology." In *The Teaching of Elementary Economics*, edited by K. Knopt and J. H. Strauss. New York: Holt, Rinehart & Winston, 1960, pp. 138–166.

Macdonald, J. B., and Bernice J. Walfron. "A Case Against Behavioral Objectives," *The Elementary School Journal,* **71** (1970), pp. 119–128.

Mackie, R. R., and P. R. Christensen. *Translation and Application of Psychological Research*. Goleta, Cal.: Human Factors Research, 1967.

Mager, R. F. *Developing Attitude Toward Learning*. Palo Alto, Cal.: Fearon, 1968.

Mager, R. R. *Preparing Objectives for Programmed Instruction*. San Francisco: Fearon, 1962. (Reprinted as *Preparing Instructional Objectives*.)

Malinowski, B. *The Argonauts of the Western Pacific*. London: Rutledge, 1922.

Mann, J. "Evaluating Educational Programs: A Symposium," *Urban Review,* **3** (1969), pp. 12–13.

Maslow, A. H. "Peak Experiences in Education and Art," *Humanist,* **30** (September/October 1970), pp. 29–31.

Massialas, B. G., et al. "Developing a Cognitive Category System for Analyzing Classroom Discussion on Social Issues." Paper read at the annual meeting of the American Educational Research Association, February 1969, in Los Angeles.

Maxwell, J., and A. Tovatt, (eds.) *On Writing Behavioral Objectives for English*. Champaign, Ill.: National Council of Teachers of English, 1970.

McGuire, Christine. "The Oral Examination as a Measure of Professional Competence," *Journal of Medical Education,* **41** (1966), pp. 267–274.

McGuire, Christine. "A Process Approach to the Construction and Analysis of Medical Examinations." *Journal of Medical Education,* **38** (1963), pp. 556–563.

McAshan, H. H. *Writing Behavioral Objectives: A New Approach*. New York: Harper & Row, 1970.

McCrimmon, J. "A Cumulative Sequence in Composition," *English Journal,* **55** (April 1966), p. 434.

McFee, Anne. "The Relation of Students' Needs to their Perceptions of a College Environment," *Journal of Educational Psychology,* **52** (1961), pp. 25–29.

McKeachie, W. J. "Problems and Perils in Controlled Research in Teaching." In *Needed Research in the Teaching of English*, edited by E. R. Steinberg. Washington, D.C.: U.S. Office of Education, 1963.

Medley, D. M., and H. E. Mitzel. "Measuring Classroom Behavior by Systematic Observation." In *Handbook for Research on Teaching*, edited by N. L. Gage. Chicago: Rand McNally, 1963.

Menzel, H. "A New Coefficient for Scalogram Analysis," *Public Opinion Quarterly,* **17** (1953), pp. 268–280.

Merwin, J. C. "Historical Review of Changing Concepts of Evaluation." In *Educational Evaluation: New Roles, New Means,* edited by R. W. Tyler. Sixty-Eighth Year Book of the National Society for the Study of Education. Chicago: University of Chicago Press, 1969, pp. 6–25.

Merwin, J. C. "The Progress of Exploration Toward a National Assessment in Education," *Journal of Educational Measurement,* **3** (1966), pp. 5–10.

Metfessel, N. S., and W. B. Michael. "A Paradigm Involving Multiple Criterion Measures for the Evaluation of the Effectiveness of School Programs," *Educational and Psychological Measurement,* **27** (1967), pp. 931–943.

Michael, W. B., and N. S. Metfessel. "A Paradigm for Developing Valid Measurable Objectives in the Evaluation of Educational Programs in Colleges and Universities," *Educational and Psychological Measurement,* **27** (1967), pp. 373–383.

Midwest Administration Center. *Cincinnati School Survey,* vol. 1. Chicago: Midwest Administration Center, University of Chicago, 1968.

Miller, R. B. "The Newer Role of the Industrial Psychologist. In *Industrial Psychology,* edited by B. von H. Gelmer. New York: McGraw-Hill, 1961.

Miller, R. B. *Some Working Concepts of Systems Analysis.* Pittsburgh: American Institutes for Research, 1954.

Miller, R. B. *A Method for Man-Machine Task Analysis.* Technical Report 53–137. Wright-Patterson Air Force Base, Ohio: Wright Air Development Center, 1953.

Moreno, J. L. *Foundations of Sociometry.* New York: Beacon House, 1941.

Morris, C. W. *Signification and Significance: A Study of the Relations of Signs and Values.* Cambridge, Mass.: M.I.T. Press, 1964.

National Assessment of Educational Progress. *Art Objectives.* Ann Arbor, Mich.: NAEP, 1971.

National Assessment of Educational Progress. *Literature Objectives.* Ann Arbor, Mich.: NAEP, 1970a.

National Assessment of Educational Progress. *Music Objectives.* Ann Arbor, Mich.: NAEP, 1970b.

National Special Media Institutes. *The Affective Domain—A Resource Book for Media Specialists.* Washington: Communication Service Corporation, 1970.

National Study of Secondary School Evaluation. *Evaluative Criteria,* rev. ed. Washington: NSSSE, 1960.

Newell, A., and H. A. Simon. "Computer Simulation of Human Thinking." *Science,* **134** (1961), pp. 2011–2017.

Niehaus, S. W. "The Anatomy of Evaluation," *The Clearing House,* **42** (February 1968), pp. 332–336.

Nunnally, J. *Tests and Measurements: Assessment and Prediction.* New York: McGraw-Hill, 1959.

Ober, R. L. "Theory into Practice through Systematic Observation," *Research Bulletin of the Florida Educational Research and Development Council,* **4** (Spring 1968).

Ober, R. L., et al. "The Development of a Reciprocal Category System for Assessing Teacher-Student Classroom Verbal Interaction." Paper read at the annual meeting of the American Educational Research Association, February 1968, in Chicago.

Office of Strategic Services. *Assessment of Men*. New York: Holt, Rinehart & Winston, 1948.

Ohnmacht, F. W. "Factor Analysis of Ranked Educational Objectives: An Approach to Value Orientation," *Educational and Psychological Measurement,* **25** (1965), pp. 437–447.

Oliver, D. W., and J. P. Shaver. *Teaching Public Issues in the High School*. Boston: Houghton Mifflin, 1966.

Oppenheim, A. N. *Questionnaire Design and Attitude Measurement*. New York: Basic Books, 1966.

Ottinger, A. G. *Run, Computer, Run*. Cambridge, Mass.: Harvard University Press, 1969.

Owens, T. R. "Suggested Tasks and Roles of Evaluation Specialists in Education," *Educational Technology,* **8** (November 1968), pp. 4–10.

Pace, C. R. *CUES College and University Environment Scales*. Princeton, N.J.: Educational Testing Service, 1963.

Pace, C. R., and G. G. Stern. "An Approach to the Measurement of Psychological Characteristics of College Environments," *Journal of Educational Psychology,* **59** (1958a), pp. 269–277.

Pace, C. R., and G. G. Stern. *A Criterion Study of College Environment*. Syracuse: Syracuse University Press, 1958b.

Packard, V. *The Status Seekers*. New York: David McKay, 1959.

Parsons, T. *The Social System*. Glencoe, Ill.: The Free Press, 1951.

Payne, D. A. *The Specification and Measurement of Learning Outcomes*. Waltham, Mass.: Blaisdell, 1968.

Payne, D. A., and R. F. McMorris. *Educational and Psychological Measurement: Contributions to Theory and Practice*. Waltham, Mass.: Blaisdell, 1967.

Plumlee, Lynnette B. "Estimating Means and Standard Deviations from Partial Data—an Empirical Check on Lord's Item Sampling Technique," *Educational and Psychological Measurement,* **24** (1964), pp. 623–630.

Popham, W. J. "Objectives and Instruction." In *Instructional Objectives,* edited by W. J. Popham et al. Chicago: Rand McNally, 1969.

Popham, W. J., and Eva L. Baker. *Establishing Instructional Goals*. Englewood Cliffs, N.J.: Prentice-Hall, 1970.

Popham, W. J., and T. R. Husek. "Implications of Criterion-Referenced Measurement," *Journal of Educational Measurement,* **6** (1969), pp. 1–9.

Popham, W. J.; W. E. Eisner; H. J. Sullivan; and Louise L. Tyler. *Instructional Objectives*. A.E.R.A. Curriculum Evaluation Monograph No. 3. Chicago: Rand McNally, 1969.

Provus, M. *Discrepancy Evaluation: For Educational Program Improvement and Assessment*. Berkeley, Cal.: McCutchan, 1971.

Provus, M. "Evaluation of Ongoing Programs in the Public School System." In *Educational Evaluation: New Roles, New Means,* edited by R. W. Tyler. Sixty-Eighth Yearbook of the National Society for the Study of Education. Chicago: University of Chicago Press, 1969, pp. 242–283.

Puckett, R. C. "Making Supervision Objective," *School Review,* **36** (1928), pp. 209–212.

QUEPS: *Proceedings of the First Meeting of the State Advisory Committee on the Assessment of Educational Quality*. Harrisburg: Pennsylvania State Department of Public Instruction, February, 1968.

Randall, R. S. "An Operational Application of the CIPP Model for Evaluation," *Educational Technology*, **9** (1969), pp. 40–44.

Richards, J. M.; Lorraine M. Rand; and L. P. Rand. "Description of Junior Colleges," *Journal of Educational Psychology*, **57** (1966), pp. 207–214.

Richards, J. M.; Lorraine M. Rand; and L. P. Rand. *A Description of Junior Colleges*. Iowa City: American College Testing Program, 1965.

Rodwan, A. S., and H. W. Hake. "The Discriminant Function as a Model for Perception," *American Journal of Psychology*, **77** (1964), pp. 380–392.

Rogers, C. R. *Freedom to Learn*. Columbus, Ohio: Charles Merrill, 1969.

Rossi, P. H. "Evaluating Educational Programs: A Symposium," *Urban Review*, **3** (1969), pp. 17–18.

Runkel, P. J. "Cognitive Similarity in Facilitating Communications," *Sociometry*, **19** (1956), pp. 178–191.

Sanford, N., (ed.) et al. "Personality Development During the College Years," *Journal of Social Issues*, **12** (1956), pp. 3–71.

Sawin, E. I. *Evaluation and the Work of the Teacher*. Belmont, Cal.: Wadsworth, 1969.

Sawin, E. I., and M. R. Loree. "Broadening the Base of Evaluation," *School Review*, **67** (1959), pp. 79–92.

Saylor, J. G., and W. M. Alexander. *Curriculum Planning*. New York: Holt, Rinehart & Winston, 1954.

Schultz, T. W. "Resources for Higher Education: An Economist's View," *Journal of Political Economy*, **76** (1968), p. 337.

Schumer, H., and R. Stanfield. "Assessment of Student Role Orientation in College." Proceedings of the 74th Annual Convention of the American Psychological Association, 1966, pp. 285–286.

Schwab, J. J. *Biology Teacher's Handbook*. New York: John Wiley, 1963.

Scriven, M. "The Methodology of Evaluation." In *Perspectives of Curriculum Evaluation*. AERA Monograph Series on Curriculum Evaluation No. 1. Chicago: Rand McNally, 1967.

Shanner, W. M. "A System of Individualized Instruction Utilizing Currently Available Instructional Materials." Paper read at meeting of the American Educational Publishers Institute, May 1968, in Miami.

Shaw, M. F., and J. M. Wright. *Scales for the Measurement of Attitudes*. New York: McGraw-Hill, 1967.

Sheldon, D., and R. Lasinger. *Effect of First Grade Instruction Using Basal Reader, Modified Linguistic Materials, and Linguistic Readers*. Final report of Cooperative Research Project No. 2683. See also *Reading Teacher*, **19** (May 1966), pp. 576–579.

Silberman, C. E. *Crisis in the Classroom*. New York: Random House, 1970.

Simon, Anita, and E. H. Boyer. *Minors for Behavior: An Anthology of Observation Instruments*. Philadelphia: Research for Better Schools, 1970.

Simpson, Elizabeth J. "The Classification of Educational Objectives: Psychomotor Domain," *Illinois Teacher of Home Economics*, **10** (1966), pp. 110–144.

Sindell, P. S. "Anthropological Approaches to the Study of Education," *Review of Educational Research*, **39** (1969), pp. 593–605.

Smith, E. R.; R. W. Tyler; and the evaluation staff. *Appraising and Recording Student*

*Progress.* Adventure in American Education, vol. III. New York: Harper & Row, 1942.

Smith, B. O.; W. O. Stanley; and H. J. Shores. *Fundamentals of Curriculum Development.* New York: World Book, 1957.

Sorenson, G. "A New Role in Education: the Evaluator." *Evaluation Comment* (Center for the Study of Evaluation of Instructional Programs, UCLA). **1** (January 1968), pp. 1–4.

Stake, R. E. "Objectives, Priorities, and Other Judgment data," *Review of Educational Research,* **40** (1970), pp. 181–212.

Stake, R. E. "The Countenance of Educational Evaluation," *Teachers College Record,* **68** (1967), pp. 523–540 (a).

Stake, R. E. "A Research Rationale for EPIE," *The EPIE Forum,* **1** (September 1967), pp. 7–15 (b).

Stake, R. E., and T. Denny. "Needed Concepts and Techniques for Utilizing More Fully the Potential of Evaluation." In *Educational Evaluation: New Roles, New Means,* edited by R. W. Tyler. Sixty-Eighth Yearbook of the National Society for the Study of Education. Chicago: University of Chicago Press, 1969, pp. 370–390.

Stake, R. E., and D. C. Sjogren. "Activity Level and Learning Effectiveness." Title VII Project No. 753. University of Nebraska, 1964.

Stern, Catherine, et al. *Structural Reading Series, Book B. Teacher's Edition.* Syracuse, N.Y.: L. W. Singer, 1963.

Stern, G. G. *People in Context.* New York: John Wiley, 1970.

Stouffer, S. "Trends in Public Opinion Polling Since 1948 and Their Probable Effect on 1952 Election Predictions." *Proceedings of the 1952 Invitational Conference on Testing Problems.* Princeton: Educational Testing Service, 1953.

Stouffer, S., et al. "Studies in Social Psychology in World War II." *Measurement and Prediction,* vol. 4. Edited by S. Stouffer et al. Princeton: Princeton University Press, 1950.

Stufflebeam. D. L. "Toward a Science of Educational Evaluation," *Educational Technology,* **6** (1968), pp. 5–12.

Stufflebeam, D. L. "The Use and Abuse of Evaluation in Title III," *Theory Into Practice,* **3** (June 1967), pp. 126–133.

Stufflebeam, D. L. "A Depth Study of the Evaluation Requirement," *Theory Into Practice,* **5** (1966), pp. 121–133.

Stufflebeam, D. L., et al., *Educational Evaluation and Decision-Making.* Itasca, Ill.: F. E. Peacock, 1970.

Suchman, E. A. *Evaluative Research: Principles and Practice in Public Service and Social Action Programs.* New York: Russell Sage Foundation, 1967.

Taba, Hilda. *Curriculum Development.* New York: Harcourt, Brace & World, 1962.

Taba, Hilda, and E. I. Sawin. "A Proposed Model in Evaluation," *Educational Leadership,* **20** (October 1962), pp. 57–71.

Taylor, P. A. "The Mapping of Concepts." Ph.D. dissertation. Urbana: University of Illinois, 1966.

Taylor, P. A., and Doris M. Cowley (eds.) *Readings in Curriculum Evaluation.* Dubuque, Iowa: William C. Brown, 1972.

Taylor, P. A., and T. O. Maguire. "A Theoretical Evaluation Model," *Manitoba Journal of Educational Research,* **1** (1966), pp. 12–17.

Thomas, R. M. "A Rationale for Measurement in the Visual Arts," *Educational and Psychological Measurement,* **25** (1965), pp. 163–189.

Thorndike, R. L. *Educational Measurement,* 2nd ed. Washington, D.C.: American Council on Education, 1970.

Thorndike, R. L. *Personnel Selection.* New York: John Wiley, Inc., 1949.

Thurstone, L. L., and E. T. Chave. *The Measurement of Attitude.* Chicago: University of Chicago Press, 1929.

Torrance, E. P. (ed.) "Creativity," *Journal of Research and Development in Education,* **4** (Spring 1971), pp. 1–106.

Travers, R. M. W. *An Introduction to Educational Research.* 2d. ed. New York: Macmillan, 1964.

Tyler, R. W. "The Objectives and Plans for a National Assessment of Educational Progress," *Journal of Educational Measurement,* **3** (1966), pp. 1–4.

Tyler, R. W. "Assessing the Progress of Education," *Phi Delta Kappan,* **47** (1965), pp. 13–16.

Tyler, R. W. "Some Persistent Questions on the Defining of Objectives." In *Defining Educational Objectives,* edited by C. M. Lindvall. Pittsburgh: Pittsburgh Press, 1964, pp. 77–83.

Tyler, R. W. "The Functions of Measurement in Improving Instruction." In *Educational Measurement,* edited by E. F. Lindquist. Washington: American Council on Education, 1951, pp. 47–67.

Tyler, R. W. "General Statement on Evaluation," *Journal of Educational Research,* **35** (March 1942), pp. 492–501.

Vollink, Mary Ann, and Marilyn Jones. "The Effect of Rigorous Tennis and Swimming on Appetite and Caloric Intake," *Home Economics Quarterly,* **5** (1970), pp. 286–304.

Walberg, H. J. "Curriculum Evaluation: Problems and Guidelines," *Teachers College Record,* **71** (May 1970), pp. 557–570.

Walberg, H. J., and W. W. Welch. "A New Use of Randomization in Experimental Curriculum Evaluation," *School Review,* **75** (1967), pp. 369–377.

Walbesser, H. H. "Curriculum Evaluation by Means of Behavioral Objectives," *Journal of Research in Science Teaching,* **1** (1963), pp. 296–301.

Walker, D. F. "A Study of Types of Goal Statements and their Uses in a Curriculum Development Project." Paper read at annual meeting of the American Educational Research Association, 8 February 1969, in Los Angeles.

Wallace, W. W. "The BSCS 1961–62 Evaluation Program—a Statistical Report," *BSCS Newsletter,* **19** (1963), pp. 22–24.

Webb, et al., *Unobtrusive Measures: Nonreactive Research in the Social Science.* Chicago: Rand McNally, 1966.

Weiss, J. (ed.). *Curriculum Evaluation: Potentiality and Reality.* Curriculum Theory Network Monograph Supplement. The Ontario Institute for Studies in Education, Department of Curriculum, 1972.

Welch, W. W., and H. J. Walberg. "A Design for Curriculum Evaluation." *Science Education,* **52** (February 1968), pp. 10–16.

Westbury, I. "Curriculum Evaluation," *Review of Educational Research,* **40** (1970), pp. 239–260.

Whybrew, W. E. *Measurement and Evaluation in Music*. Dubuque, Iowa: William C. Brown, 1962.

Wick, J. W., and D. L. Beggs. *Evaluation for Decision-Making in the Schools*. Boston: Houghton Mifflin, 1971.

Withall, J. "Development of a Technique for the Measurement of Socioemotional Climate in Classrooms," *Journal of Experimental Education*, **17** (March 1949), pp. 347–361.

Wittrock, M. C. "The Evaluation of Instruction: Course-and-Effect Relations in Naturalistic Data." In *The Evaluation of Instruction*, edited by M. C. Wittrock and D. E. Wiley. New York: Holt, Rinehart & Winston, 1970.

Wolf, R. M. "The Identification and Measurement of Environmental Process Variables Related to Intelligence." Ph.D. dissertation, University of Chicago, 1964.

Worthington, K. "Criteria Suggested for Evaluators." Mimeographed. Utah State Board of Education, undated.

Wright, C. E. "PLAN Progress Report," *Education*, **90** (1970), pp. 261–270.

Wright, E. M., and V. H. Proctor. *Systematic Observation of Verbal Interaction as a Method of Comparing Mathematics Lessons*. Cooperative Research Project No. 816. Washington: U.S. Office of Education, 1961.

Wrightstone, J. W. *Appraisal of Newer Practices in Selected Public Schools*. New York: Columbia University Teachers College, 1935.

Wrightstone, J. W., "Measuring Teacher Conduct of Class Discussion," *Elementary School Journal*, **34** (1934), pp. 454–460.

Yellen, Sylvia; A. D. Colebank; E. H. LeMaistre; and Marion B. Pollock. *Health Behavior Inventory*. Monterey Park, Cal.: California Test Bureau, 1962.

Yelon, S. L., and R. O. Scott. *A Strategy for Writing Objectives*. Dubuque, Iowa: Kendall/Hunt, 1970.

Zoellner, R. "A Behavior Pedagogy for Composition." *College English*, **30** (January 1969), pp. 267–320.

# INDEX

1 2 3 4 5 6 7 8 9 10